THE
DIM
HYPOTHESIS

THE
DIM
HYPOTHESIS

WHY THE LIGHTS OF THE WEST

ARE GOING OUT

LEONARD PEIKOFF

 NEW AMERICAN LIBRARY

NEW AMERICAN LIBRARY
Published by New American Library, a division of
Penguin Group (USA) Inc., 375 Hudson Street,
New York, New York 10014, USA
Penguin Group (Canada), 90 Eglinton Avenue East, Suite 700, Toronto,
Ontario M4P 2Y3, Canada (a division of Pearson Penguin Canada Inc.)
Penguin Books Ltd., 80 Strand, London WC2R 0RL, England
Penguin Ireland, 25 St. Stephen's Green, Dublin 2,
Ireland (a division of Penguin Books Ltd.)
Penguin Group (Australia), 250 Camberwell Road, Camberwell, Victoria 3124,
Australia (a division of Pearson Australia Group Pty. Ltd.)
Penguin Books India Pvt. Ltd., 11 Community Centre, Panchsheel Park,
New Delhi - 110 017, India
Penguin Group (NZ), 67 Apollo Drive, Rosedale, Auckland 0632,
New Zealand (a division of Pearson New Zealand Ltd.)
Penguin Books (South Africa) (Pty.) Ltd., 24 Sturdee Avenue,
Rosebank, Johannesburg 2196, South Africa

Penguin Books Ltd., Registered Offices:
80 Strand, London WC2R 0RL, England

First published by New American Library,
a division of Penguin Group (USA) Inc.

First Printing, September 2012
10 9 8 7 6 5 4 3 2 1

REGISTERED TRADEMARK—MARCA REGISTRADA

LIBRARY OF CONGRESS CATALOGING-IN-PUBLICATION DATA:

Peikoff, Leonard.
The DIM hypothesis: why the lights of the West are going out/Leonard Peikoff.
p. cm.
Includes bibliographical references and indexes.
ISBN 978-0-451-23481-0 (hardback)
1. Knowledge, Theory of. 2. Civilization, Western—Forecasting. I. Title.
BD161.P425 2012
303.45—dc23   2012005918

Printed in the United States of America

ALWAYS LEARNING   PEARSON

"Integration . . . is the key to man's consciousness, to his conceptual faculty, to his basic premises, to his life."

—Ayn Rand

To Ayn Rand,

who made an integrated life possible

CONTENTS

ACKNOWLEDGMENTS

David Harriman, historian of physics, was my greatest intellectual ally in writing this book. I talked with him often to help me clarify my ideas. He was also my expert in physics, who taught me what I needed to know for this book, and then showed me how my theory applied to the field. Steve Jolivette, a world historian (as I think of him), was another essential mentor, who consented to answer, in detail and with bibliography, the stream of questions I posed to him across the years, ranging from pre-Greece through the present. Without David and Steve, I could not have undertaken this book. Of course, neither of them nor anyone identified below is responsible for the use I have made of their knowledge and help.

Yaron Brook was instrumental to my understanding of America today, particularly in economics and foreign policy. John Allison suggested to me, in regard to a problem I was having with the ending, what my last few pages should say; much of his wording is there. Carl Barney gave me a nice rationalization to desist from further editing. "Even if it's not perfect," he said, "isn't wonderful enough?" Tara Smith at UT Austin asked me early on a question which remained with me as a challenge to be met. "I agree with your theory," she said, frowning, "but why is it so difficult to understand?"

Many others helped, answering questions, recommending readings, e-mailing links, sending in clippings. Of these individuals, the ones of whom I asked the most are Professor Robert Mayhew of Seton Hall U (on

Greece) and Professor John Lewis, now tragically deceased (on Rome). I also learned from Tore Boeckmann (Romantic literature), Eric Daniels (Colonial America), Andrew Lewis (general research), Keith Lockitch (environmentalism), Amy Peikoff (law and political theory), and Lisa Van Damme (education). Further, in the last few years, hundreds of people have attended lecture courses in which I presented the main content of the book. These audiences' wide-ranging questions, well-thought-out objections, and enthusiastic interest were both intellectual help and emotional fuel.

Arnold Dolin went through the manuscript twice, and gave me many helpful suggestions. So did Tracy Bernstein, my easiest-ever editor to work with at NAL. My daughter Kira brainstormed with me to get the subtitle. Richard Ralston was my liaison with the publisher. Tore Boeckmann compiled the index. Jenniffer Woodson researched and typed during the early stages. Dr. Lewis Engel enabled me to endure for so long the struggle that writing always is for me, and to deal with the pain when it came.

Kim Marzullo, my assistant, worked on the book more cheerfully and efficiently than I would have thought possible, given her already overcrowded life. She not only typed the manuscript multiple times and helped with research, but also organized and formatted all the references and checked the quotations for accuracy. Thank you, Kim, especially for staying on with me three extra years, until the book was done.

At the start of the book, I did not know her. But thank you, Jackie, for putting up with me during the years at the end.

PREFACE

The purpose of this book is to gain an understanding of our past and on that basis to predict our future. The method is to identify a specific factor operative in our cultural history, one hitherto unappreciated but nevertheless indispensable if we are to reach the understanding we seek.

Is the world going to hell? I do not approach this question by reference to our current economic crises, our political impotence, or Islamic terrorism. Instead, guided by a hypothesis, I ask: Does our inability to cope with these problems reflect our failure to grasp an overarching factor, one always at work in the two and a half millennia behind us—a factor shaping in each era the minds and distinctive achievements of its cultural creators? If we could identify such a factor, we might make sense of our past and of its sequel. From this perspective, only the study of past cultural heroes—of Homer, Augustine, Newton, Dewey, and many more—can give us the key to tomorrow.

In part one, I explain the nature of the factor and the DIM Hypothesis that it suggests. Parts two and three examine the evidence for my hypothesis through a survey of Western cultures from Greece to the present. Part four draws the lessons and infers what's next.

Because I attempt to interrelate on so broadly inclusive a scale, the book is unavoidably complex. I identify five different modes of thought that, alone or in some combination, have dominated four different cultural areas during six different Western periods. Thus I cover dozens of units that the reader ultimately must hold in mind together. A spread-sheet at the back of the book indicates the range of topics. By intercon-necting all these units, I attempt to gain an overview of the kinds of causal sequences that have been decisive in our history, and thus to justify an extrapolation from them.

To connect so many diverse units, I can discuss each in terms only of essentials. I present a given thinker not in order to capture his unique-ness, but as an expression of a broader movement that has been histori-cally influential. I do not ignore differences within a movement, and I do mention these peripherally, if I regard them as historically relevant. My discussion of each unit, accordingly, is brief, a condensation possible because I do not analyze texts, look for a school's stages, or mention the disputes among scholars as to its real viewpoint. You will not find here a treatise on the *Aeneid*, an introduction to relativity, or a dissertation on egalitarianism. Tens of thousands of books that cover separately one or two of the topics in this book are readily available. Because of their spe-cialized nature, however, none can provide an overview of the total, not even if one conscientiously reads them all. The reason is that no mind can hold and integrate such a mass of data. To gain an overview, one needs not a microscope, but a telescope. The author must, of course, present the factual basis of his theory, but he must offer his material not as an ency-clopedia, but in a single volume, preferably not too long.

An essentialized account is not of course a proof that the account is accurate; to offer such a proof is the province of a specialized study. In the context of my book, I must leave the decision to the reader. If my sum-maries are not consonant with his own understanding, he can study the topic(s) further on his own, or follow my book's development but defer judgment, or cease reading it. I do very often offer quotations from pri-mary sources and from recognized commentators. This is primarily to indicate to the novice or the incredulous that I am not making up the horrors or heroism I recount. But out-of-context quotes can be used to prove virtually anything; they are not put forth here as proof.

The essentialized approach is the opposite of that practiced by today's academic establishment, who reject system-building—that is, broad integration—in favor of the analysis of minutiae. I am as far from today's philosophy departments as an atheist is from the pope or, in more positive terms, as a man who wants to live is from an ascetic writhing in the desert. My explanation of today's philosophers is offered below, in my discussion of the D_2 mentality.

As I say in my dedication and as is generally known, my debt to Ayn Rand cannot be exaggerated. My theory is based on her philosophy, Objectivism, especially but not only on her work on epistemology, *Introduction to Objectivist Epistemology*, a knowledge of which this book presupposes. I have also relied on my own summary of her philosophy, *Objectivism: The Philosophy of Ayn Rand*. Because of the need to condense, I have not repeated material, on any issue, that Ayn Rand or I have covered elsewhere—not even when this material is necessary to a proper understanding. Whenever the overview perspective permits it, however, I have briefly synopsized the relevant background, or at least pointed a newcomer to sources where he can find a full discussion, but these terse inserts are no more than suggestive asides. In addition to Objectivism, I must add, the reader needs to have some knowledge of three epochal philosophers—Plato, Aristotle, and Kant—especially of the distinctive basic principles of each. My summaries in chapter two of the Big Three, as I call them, are the fullest in the book, but they are hardly enough to make the ideas of these thinkers clear to the uninitiated.

The need for such a philosophic background presents an obvious problem for a novice in the field. Another problem is the condensed nature of the writing. The book speeds the reader back and forth through the centuries by identifying relationships that the unprepared may well find unclear and in places ungraspable. The general reader, however, need not flee, because he may well find specific discussions of interest taken by themselves. I recommend that he browse the sections pertaining to modern literature, education, and politics (chapters five, seven, and eight), and above all that he take a look at the book's final three chapters, dealing with America's future.

I started working on *The DIM Hypothesis* in the summer of 2004. Several years earlier, when the idea first occurred to me, I intended to use it as a chapter in a lengthy work that I eventually abandoned. Instead, I went into retirement, but restlessly. My wife at the time, Amy Peikoff, objected to my unemployment and urged me in 2003 to give a lecture course on the subject. It would be relatively easy, she said, since "you know the material, and lecturing, as against writing, comes so easily to you." Without her urging, I doubt that I would have started on this project. So thank you, Amy—I think.

I gave fifteen weekly lectures by telephone to some interested students around the country and was happy with the results. I soon decided that the language of the course could easily be smoothed out and the material published as a book. In other words, I succumbed again to my lifelong delusion that there is, for me, such a thing as a brief editing of a lecture course. It is now seven-plus years later. Far from "smoothing out," in the end I had to throw out all fifteen lectures; not a single page could be used. Thinking the issues over methodically and as (rational) devil's advocate, I came to discover how much the initial material suffered from omissions of the indispensable, inclusions of the unnecessary, outright errors, and a lack of full clarity so pervasive as to be traumatic to me. Only after writing the book from scratch, stumbling through the bloody gauntlet of its ideas and sentences, did I fully understand the nature and implications of my hypothesis, and only then did I become convinced that it was both true and important.

(As an aside here for readers of my first book, *The Ominous Parallels*, one result of my new understanding is that I have a better grasp of the philosophy of Nazism, which I treated at the time primarily as a secular movement, based on a senseless reading of biology. It was not clear to me then that materialists, just as much as idealists, are not secular at all, but rather are supernaturalists and thus essentially akin to religionists. This is an issue I now regard as fundamental to understanding any totalitarian ideology. The omission of it does not affect the truth of what I wrote, but it is an important supplement, which makes possible a deeper insight into the Nazi mind and its popular appeal. My mature analysis of materialism is presented in chapter eight.)

As I look back on my life's work, it seems that my three books represent three stages in my development. *The Ominous Parallels* was my way of refuting—and thus of blasting out of my system—all the negatives crammed into my mind during ten years of graduate school. *Objectivism:*

The Philosophy of Ayn Rand, by contrast, is a direct statement of the positive, of the philosophy I accept, with the negatives touched on only peripherally. *The DIM Hypothesis* connects these stages to each other and to everything else of philosophical importance that I have since learned; it is my final, overall integration.

Without presuming to compare myself to Ayn Rand—no one knows better than I how foolish such a presumption would be—it seems to me that her major novels perhaps suggest a similar sort of development. In *We the Living*, she exposed and blasted Soviet Russia, which (ignoring scale) was in effect her equivalent of my graduate school, the negative that ruled her youth; thereafter she was finished with it as a subject of serious work. In *The Fountainhead*, her purpose was to make real for the first time the positive, her kind of hero, to whom all the other characters are subordinate; as she herself noted, the essential conflicts are clashes among the positives, among Wynand, Dominique, and Roark. *Atlas Shrugged*, of course, is her magnum opus, her all-inclusive integration. (The foregoing is merely a chance observation; it is not an illustration of Hegel's dialectic nor, even if accurate, of any law of psychology known to me.)

Typically, I edit a manuscript about eight times, ending only when I can see no further improvement. In my earlier books, accordingly, the words I used conveyed my meaning as smoothly and simply as my ability permitted. This book has been different. So far I have edited it about a dozen times, but after each time—I'm not sure why—the next pass revealed the need for more improvement, not so much to make the content clearer, but to make the writing smoother. I can foresee no end to this process. In my darker moments, I was tempted to agree with a statement made by the Austrian philosopher Wittgenstein about a work he published in his final years; in free translation, he wrote: "I wanted this to be a good book, but it is too late." I was tempted, but, looking at *The DIM Hypothesis* objectively, I do not believe that his statement applies to it. In my judgment, the book's content and structure, the ideas and the method of their presentation, are good enough not to require an apology for the remaining stylistic infelicities.

Despite my debt to Ayn Rand, I must make clear that she is not responsible for any of the ideas in this book other than those she herself stated. I never discussed the DIM Hypothesis with her, and in fact I developed my approach to cultural analysis many years after she died. Although I base it on her ideas, as I have said, I do not claim that her ideas necessarily imply my hypothesis. In theory, it is possible that Objectivism is true, but that I have misapplied it in my interpretation of history. I do not believe that I have done so, but I do not want Ayn Rand's name or philosophy to pay the penalty for whatever errors I may have made. It is a grave injustice to saddle any creator, after her death, with the theories of her followers, however well-meaning and intelligent they may be.

I often wonder what Ayn Rand herself would think of this book, if she were able to read it. Taking a wild (but not completely blind) stab at it, here are the ranges of my guess. She would agree with the book, extol its virtues, and regard it as of historic importance: 80 to 85 percent probable. She would agree, but regard the ideas as too obvious and/or insignificant to be worth writing about at length: 10 to 15 percent. She would disagree with the hypothesis and reject the book as invalid: 5 percent.

So I pose the question to the reader: Is this a pioneering epic, a recycling of the obvious, or the maunderings of a mind that has lost it?

I know my answer.

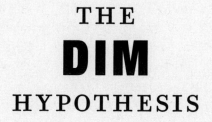

THE
DIM
HYPOTHESIS

PART ONE

EPISTEMOLOGY

CHAPTER ONE

INTEGRATION

THE FALL OF Western civilization—if it does fall—can be traced to its beginning. I do not mean that its beginning led to its end. I mean the opposite: Our rejection of our beginning is what is killing us.

Our beginning was the discovery of the West's distinctive principle, which is implicit in the work of Thales, the father of Western philosophy. The most famous of his four remaining sentences is: "All things are water."

Earlier cultures had perceived a vast array of material objects—rivers, people, pots, cornstalks, stars—and grasped many differences among them. But they did not think nearly as much about similarities. It never occurred to them to ask whether there is a physical connection—a common ingredient or structure or pattern of action—between pots and stars or between rivers and people. They never dreamed of asking whether there might be such connections uniting <u>everything</u>. Hence the door to philosophy and science remained closed.

Thales was the first man in recorded history to face the bewildering diversity of material objects and ask: Do they all have something in common? Is there an underlying similarity that unites into an intelligible whole this riot of differences, and if so, what is it? A century later, Socrates, moving from physics to epistemology,* carried the question to

---

* For those new to philosophy, its two fundamental branches are metaphysics, which studies the nature of existence, and epistemology, which studies man's means of knowledge.

the field of language, the tool of thought. In regard to words central to philosophy—such as justice, knowledge, virtue, beauty—he (and/or Plato) sought clarity by asking: What is the common denominator uniting their various instances? What, for example, is the essence that makes all just acts, despite their many differences, instances of the same concept?

The Greeks soon came to formulate their quest for connections in abstract and immortal terms: What, they asked, is the One in the Many?—a question they soon pursued in a wide variety of areas unknown to Thales or Socrates.*

Like earlier societies, the Greeks observed many different objects, but then proceeded further. They used these observations as a base from which to abstract, and thus to identify essentials and reach generalizations. This new appreciation of thought enabled them to theorize about every aspect of the universe, including its elements, its laws, and even the processes by which man comes to gain this knowledge. The pre-Greeks were the childhood of the human race. The Greeks were man, man the rational animal, starting to grow up.

The fact that Thales' own physics was primitive is irrelevant. His unsurpassed achievement is that he was the first (or the first-known) to conceive a new kind of question, and therefore a new method of cognition. Using the word as I will throughout—that is, in its epistemological, not racial, sense—the method today is called "integration" (less often, "synthesis"). The discovery of this method, along with its philosophic preconditions and implications, was the origin of Western culture—once the greatest of human achievements, now a "fabulous invalid" disintegrating before our eyes.

The goal of the DIM theory is to reach a prognosis. What is the West's disease? How long does the West have? Is there a cure? Fifty years ago, such questions would have been dismissed as outlandish pessimism. Today, however, many Americans (like Europeans) are no longer oblivious to what is happening. They are anxious—in regard not merely to

---

* Following the traditional practice, I capitalize the words "One" and "Many" when I use them in this Greek sense. I also capitalize certain other words, such as "Nature," when used as a philosophic term.

Washington but, more broadly, to obscurely sensed and seemingly ubiquitous factors threatening the welfare and even survival of the country.

The answer to our questions, I hold, requires us to understand the evolution of the Western mind—that is, we must identify its changing approaches to integration. The story and future of the West lie in the rises and falls of the method of thought that once defined it.

Integration as Man's Means of Knowledge

Judging by popular linguistic usage, everyone seems to understand integration and dread its opposite. "What a shattering experience!" we say to a friend. "Try not to fall apart." "No," the friend reassures us, "even though I am broken up, I won't let myself go to pieces. I'm going to pull myself together and become whole again." These and many similar expressions are not insignificant; though they are no longer philosophically understood, they are metaphorical echoes of Thales.

Metaphors, however, cannot give philosophic answers. What we need now is to understand the nature of integration in literal terms. This understanding can be gained only by a process of induction from observable fact. We start then with experience—that is, by observing integration at work in its primary setting: within consciousness.

When I met Ayn Rand, I was seventeen. My first impression was of a figure standing on a mountaintop, seeing relationships I had never imagined. The people in the valley, whence I had come, found it easy to differentiate concretes. Everyone knew that Communism was the opposite of conservatism, that Rachmaninoff's melodies had no relation to Hugo's plots, and that economics had nothing to say about sex. But Ayn Rand put things together; in one evening, while retaining the differences, she could discuss each of these pairs and explain to me by what fundamental similarities their members are connected. I fell in love with integration.

A year or so later, I learned from Ayn Rand that integration is the key to understanding not only the Greek discoveries and the random pairs we had so far discussed, but much more. Integration, she said, was the key to understanding human knowledge as such, all of it, in any field, era, or stage of development.*

Knowledge is the grasp of reality, and reality, according to the Objectivist metaphysics, is that which exists; it is not a supernatural dimension, but this world in which we live. It is and is only the world of natural entities with their attributes and actions. The basic law of reality is that each entity has a definite, limited nature; each is what it is. In other words, each obeys the Law of Identity, A is A, and therefore each exists independent of consciousness. An entity acts not because of the decrees of consciousness—of *any* consciousness, divine or human—but rather in accordance with its nature. Under the same circumstances, therefore, the entity necessarily takes the same action. Hence a corollary of the Law of Identity is the Law of Cause and Effect (or simply the Law of Causality), which is the metaphysical basis of the uniformity of Nature.

In order to discover the attributes of specific entities and the laws governing their action, a man, according to the Objectivist epistemology, must exercise his distinctive faculty of knowledge, <u>reason</u>. This means that he must perceive and then think, checking at each step to ensure that the conclusions his mind draws do not contradict past knowledge or present data. Thus three elements unite to define the Objectivist concept of reason: perception,† conception, and logic. The first requires that all knowledge be derived ultimately from the evidence of the senses. The second requires that such evidence be identified and interrelated through the use of objectively defined language—that is, of objectively formed concepts. The third requires that the use of concepts obey another corollary of the Law of Identity, the Law of Non-Contradiction (nothing can be A and non-A at the same time and in the same respect).

Each of these three elements is a form of integration. Infants do not know entities as such, but merely a flux of sensations of seemingly unrelated qualities; the grasp of an entity, which is perception, results from an

---

* What follows is a brief indication of the metaphysics and epistemology of Objectivism. The preface suggests books that offer a full presentation. Those familiar with this material can skim over to page 9.

† If the context does not demand another reading, "perception" in this book always means "sense perception."

integration of such sensations. Since this process is performed automatically by our brain, there is no choice about doing it and no possibility of error in its regard. Logic pertains to the conceptual level; it teaches the method of integrating conceptual knowledge by defining what conclusions one can draw, without contradiction, from one's premises. In these two respects (perception and logic), the role of integration is generally understood. But what about concepts themselves, the *human* form of cognition, without which logic would be contentless and perception a dead end?

According to Ayn Rand's revolutionary theory, a concept is an <u>integration of percepts</u>. It is an integration of similar percepts that have first been isolated mentally from a background of different percepts. (An example would be integrating one's percepts of tables after isolating them from one's percepts of beds and chairs.) Integrating percepts, in this theory, is the process of blending them into an inseparable whole. Such a whole is a new entity, a mental entity (the concept "table"), which functions in our consciousness thereafter as a single, enduring unit. The formation of this unit is not complete until one chooses a word to denote it. A word is a perceptually graspable symbol, which transforms the vast sum of instances involved into a single, retainable concrete. Such a sum cannot be retained by parading before one's consciousness an endless series of discrete units. But one *can* easily retain the new unit, the word, which denotes all of them.*

Once formed, a concept subsumes an unlimited number of concretes, including countless unobserved ones. It subsumes all instances—for example, all men—belonging to the group, past, present, and future. All these entities can be blended into a whole because, from the perspective of concept-formation, all of them are regarded as the same. Yet they are clearly not the same; in every perceptual respect, from head to toes, men are or can be different from one another. Our blending of them into a single unit, therefore, depends on our ability to abstract, to set aside the seemingly all-pervasive differences, and thereby to grasp similarities not

---

* "Concrete" designates an object as it exists metaphysically—that is, as a particular independent of integration. Thus Tom, Dick, or Harry as against the abstraction "man."

apparent on the perceptual level. How does the mind discover such similarities?

Ayn Rand's seminal observation is that the similar concretes integrated by a concept differ from one another only quantitatively, only in the measurements of their characteristics. When we form a concept, therefore, our mental process consists in retaining the characteristics, but omitting their measurements. Hence her formal definition: "*A concept is a mental integration of two or more units possessing the same distinguishing characteristic(s), with their particular measurements omitted.*"[1]

The cognitive function of concepts, she concludes, is the condensation of mental content. For a consciousness to extend its grasp beyond the animal level, beyond a mere handful of concretes—for it to be able to cope with an enormous totality, like all tables, or all men, or the universe as a whole—a particular cognitive ability is indispensable. It must be able to compress its content—that is, to *economize the units* required to deal with and retain that content. In Ayn Rand's words, the function of concepts is "to reduce a vast amount of information to a minimal number of units. . . ."[2]

Man the rational being is man the conceptual being. Man the conceptual being is man the integrator. The DIM Hypothesis cannot be derived from these two principles; without them, however, it cannot even be conceived.

People use concepts (language) continually; unfortunately, they do not always hold their concepts *as* integrations. In one type of case, a person is unable to identify instances of his concept or its relation to perceived objects. In his mind the word (typically a broad, emotive one like "love," "fairness," "freedom") is a castle in the air, a sound without referent, a "floating abstraction" in Objectivist parlance, a One without a Many. In a second type of case, a person, having been taught a modest level of abstraction, will go no further. Characteristically, he is not alert to discover, or even dismisses as unimportant, broader similarities interrelating his observations, even if these are relevant to his goals; instead, he is predominantly concerned with mere perceptual differences. Ayn Rand describes this type of mentality as "concrete-bound" or "perceptual-level"; in Greek terms, the person is focusing on the Many without a One.

The "floater" misses reality; the concrete-bound person misses understanding. In the proper use of concepts, by contrast, the mind moves easily and regularly between concrete and abstract, between perception and thought. Only this kind of shuttling gives a man the full power to connect and understand the facts he observes. This type of mind seeks to grasp the One *in* the Many.[3]

If integration is the essence of a conceptual consciousness, we would expect every specific form of human cognition to be a form of integration. To check this conclusion, let us travel up the cognitive ladder.

After a man has gained enough of a conceptual vocabulary to identify a range of percepts, the first requirement of expanding his knowledge is <u>induction</u>, which is in essence the process of inferring a generalization from observations. As in concept-formation, so here: The generalizer blends many observed similarities into a new mental One; in this case, the unit is not a single word, but a sentence of the form "All S is P." Most of the instances of a generalization, as of a concept, are outside the range of sense perception. Through measurement-omission applied to what he does perceive, however, a man can condense this kind of totality, too, into a single unit, such as "Opposite magnetic poles attract." He is thus able to grasp and retain an otherwise unknowable mass of data: He can come to conclusions (including predictions) about the actions of an unlimited number of physical objects (such as magnets), objects spread, potentially or actually, across all time and space.

A necessary complement to induction is <u>deduction</u>, the standard example of which is: "All men are mortal. Socrates is a man. Therefore, Socrates is mortal." The role of integration here is obvious: We are expanding our knowledge by applying a generalization to one or more of the concretes subsumed under it yet not so far considered in this context. In essence, we are combining earlier cognitions (the premises) into an "argument," which latter, however complex, we easily retain by condensation into a unit; then we find out whether our conclusion can be integrated without contradiction into a more complex unity, a "proof."

After one learns a body of generalizations, the next major step up the cognitive ladder is the integration of generalizations into <u>principles</u>. A principle is a basic generalization; it unites and thereby explains a wide range of earlier generalizations (and often many isolated facts as well), discoveries previously regarded as unconnected. Thus, when scientists discovered that the atoms of every chemical element have identical masses and electrical properties, they were able, by means of the atomic principles, to make a single mental unit out of many hitherto established but unrelated laws, such as those discovered by Dalton, Avogadro, Faraday, and others. In relation to the new principles, the earlier laws, though still integrations of instances, are themselves seen as instances of one higher-level integration, which typically becomes an instance of a still higher-level one.

After a substantial body of observations and principles has been discovered within several fields of study so far viewed as unrelated, a momentous step up the hierarchy is the grasp of relationships among these fields—that is, the <u>integration of the sciences</u>. This step was all but impossible to the ancients, at the outset of human cognition, but as knowledge has grown it has proved to be indispensable.

Astronomy, for example, was long regarded as unrelated (and even opposed) to physics, since the former was believed to deal with celestial matter and the latter only with the sublunary. Then it was discovered that the proof of Copernicus's new theory of celestial behavior depended in part on Galileo's experiments with the sublunary. The interdependence of these sciences soon became apparent, and the road was open to a universal theory of motion and thus to a new integration: astrophysics. Similarly, for the ancients mathematics and physics were treated largely as unrelated. Now, thanks mainly to Newton, we speak only of mathematical physics. Similarly, until Maxwell, the study of electricity and of magnetism took place in closed fiefdoms. Now we study electromagnetism, a unification that soon subsumed the study of light, and later helped make it possible for Einstein to seek (though not to find) an even more ambitious One, a Unified Field Theory. Knowledge is a hierarchy; it consists of integrations, each level making the next possible and in due course necessary. Thinking, we can say, consists of integrating integrations.

The unification of the sciences is a special case of a broader principle. The need for integration applies to the total of the knowledge available to a thinker at any stage regardless of its content, no matter to what specific sciences or issues the knowledge pertains. The differences among its contents constitute the Many of our knowledge. The conceptual-level mind studies this Many, but—being conceptual-level—it seeks wherever possible to find in the Many a One. The result of this approach is the <u>unity of knowledge</u>.

The unity of knowledge means the unity of a man's conceptual structure. Ayn Rand has compared a mind's stock of concepts to a filing system in which each concept is a folder holding everything known about its referents. If the folders are properly labeled and organized, the material in any folder is accessible to a thinker as needed, no matter what other folders—what other entities or questions—are of primary concern to him. No folder is isolated; all are interrelated parts of a single whole.

When a man inquires into a subject, a fact from *any* field, however remote, is potentially relevant. This does not mean that every fact is relevant to every inquiry, which would make thought impossible. It means that it is possible for a fact discovered tomorrow (or yesterday) in one field to shed important light on the different field being studied today. While pursuing new knowledge, therefore, one must be ready to seize on and use such a discovery. Even if one's study is highly specialized, he must be receptive to the emergence of germane information from any quarter. In other words, he must be ready to integrate in any direction the evidence warrants.[4]

Human knowledge is not a mere collection, but a structure; it is a single body of interrelated cognitions. No item of knowledge is "self-contained"; taken as isolated from all the rest, no item even qualifies as knowledge. On the contrary, such an item, being closed to potentially relevant evidence, is a form of unreason, and as such must be rejected. This rejection does not mean a condemnation of cognitive specialization. What the theory condemns is any specialist who claims a logical right to ignore discoveries in all fields but his own, on the grounds that his exists in a cognitive vacuum and is thus self-validating. Ayn Rand called such individuals "compartmentalizers," and often cited as examples pro-capitalist economists who regard morality as irrelevant to economics.

A long tradition of philosophers has defended the unity of knowledge. Typically, they have held that *all* facts are necessarily interconnected, and that men can reach an ultimate, all-embracing insight through some form of withdrawal from the world. This is the opposite of the Objectivist viewpoint. The unity of knowledge I have discussed does not imply that connections can necessarily be found between every fact and science; perhaps some are simply not connected, and that is all there will ever be to say about the matter. What the principle does require is that we *look* for connections (in this world) wherever there is reason to think they are relevant to an inquiry.

In the above, I have considered integration only as we observe it within consciousness. In due course, we will observe integration as it occurs in man's worldly existence as well—that is, in the actions he takes and the products he creates, such as novels, schools, governments, and more. Since man's consciousness guides his existence, it would be no surprise to discover that the essential process of the one realm is to be found all over the other as well.

Integration: Its Definition

Observing examples of integration is a necessary first step in grasping the meaning of the concept. Now we must identify that meaning explicitly; we must discover the defining factor implicit in the examples. This requires that we relate integration to several other concepts that are distinct from it, yet essential to knowing its full meaning. Five concepts are critical: whole, connection, necessary, system, and unity.

The word "integration" is a form of "integer," which derives from the Latin for "untouched" or "intact" and thus means whole. Integration, according to the *Oxford English Dictionary (OED)*, is "the making up or composition of a whole by adding together or combining the separate parts or elements. . . ." In this definition, "integration" denotes a human activity, although the editors grant that many wholes are not created by man, such as an atom, an organism, or the universe. Since the DIM theory pertains only to man's method of thought and its products, I too limit the word "integration" to the realm of human behavior.

The central term in the *OED*'s definition is "whole," a concept that subsumes a wide diversity of objects, from a single word to the science of physics to the U.S. government. What then is a whole? The *OED* answers that it is "something made of parts in combination or mutual connection. An assemblage of things united so as to constitute one greater thing."

Here, I think, the *OED* is confusing. "Combination" and "connection" cannot be equated in this context. A whole, to be sure, is a combination, it is elements put together, but the combination becomes a whole only when its elements bear a specific type of relationship to one another. They become a whole only when they form a special kind of combination, the nature of which is implicit in the other key term of the definition: "connection."

Connected parts do not merely happen to be together; they *must* be together. If they are truly parts of a whole, their combination is not whimsical, accidental, or coincidental; it is *necessary*. On this point, Hume is clearer than the *OED*; his famous distinction stresses the fact that there are two possibilities in this context: brute "conjunction" and "necessary connection."

The history of philosophy provides many clashing interpretations of the source and nature of necessary connections (including Hume's denial of them). In the Objectivist view, their source is the Law of Identity. A fact is necessary if and only if its non-existence would entail a contradiction. This formulation covers necessity both in metaphysics and in epistemology. Metaphysically, as mentioned earlier, cause *must* lead to effect; the alternative would require that an entity contradict its nature. Epistemologically, a logical conclusion, as we have seen, is one that *must* follow from the premises—because its denial would contradict them. In both fields, the "must" derives from the fact that it is impossible for a contradiction to exist in reality.

In its best formulation, the *OED* defines "whole" in other terms—as "a complex unity or system." Leaving aside "unity" for a moment, let us look at an excerpt from its definition of "system": a "connected group of objects [that are] in orderly arrangement according to some scheme or plan. . . ." Again, connection is essential, but the emphasis here is on its source in human purpose ("plan" and "arrangement"). Before Euclid, for example, there was geometrical knowledge, but no "orderly arrangement." Euclid created the first <u>system</u> of geometry by arranging the relevant ideas, his own and those of others, according to a logical plan, one that showed the necessity connecting all these items. The result was a "system" and a "whole." Had he merely combined the ideas in the order he happened to come upon them, geometry would be neither.

Now consider the other key term in the *OED*'s definition, its description of "whole" as a "complex unity." Just as a whole is a system and vice versa, so a whole is a unity (but not necessarily vice versa). What does "one" add to our understanding of whole, and thereby of integration?

"One," selecting from the *OED*'s lengthy entry, denotes: "The lowest of the cardinal numbers; the number of a single thing without any more, the addition of another to which makes two." And later: "A single thing, or the abstract number denoting a single thing." These characterizations amount to singular versus plural: thing, in contrast to things however many. Since this book is not concerned with the philosophy of mathematics, we can ignore the many complexities involved in the study of numbers; we can say simply that the concept of "one," like all concepts, is derived by abstraction from experience. In particular, it is derived from our perception of a thing from a specific perspective.

"One" denotes a thing—a rock, a person, a cloud—purely in its <u>quantitative</u> relationships, both to things outside itself and, if it has them, to its own parts. Not every "one" has parts. For example, the irreducible particles, pulses, or whatever that comprise matter have no parts, since by definition these are the ultimate parts, the simple "ones" out of which everything else is made. This is why the *OED* defines "whole" as a "*complex* unity"—that is, a unity made of parts that are connected.

Each of the concepts essential to an understanding of integration denotes the same process and result, but each makes explicit a different aspect of it. "System" identifies the fact that it is man who puts the constituents into a definite relationship. "Connection" identifies the specific nature of that relationship. "Necessity" identifies the philosophic base and thus the full meaning of "connection." "Whole" identifies the fact that an entity *is* made of constituents thus related. "One" identifies a whole quantitatively, in contrast to its surroundings and its own constituents.

A unity of systematically connected elements—a triple repetition for emphasis—this is what a whole is, and this is what is created by the process of integration. Verbal repetitions of this kind are often unavoidable if one seeks to highlight different perspectives in a single formulation. I shall try to keep them to a minimum, on the assumption that the reader is bearing in mind throughout the applicability to a given discussion of each of the key concepts even when only one is mentioned.

To denote the opposite of integration, many words could be chosen; the best, I think, is juxtaposition—that is, the mere conjunction of objects in space and/or time. For example, on the simple, physical level, Hiroshima after the atom bomb was no longer a whole because there was no longer a purposeful connection uniting the remains, but only sprawling chunks of glass, random puddles, and scattered flesh; at most one could say that there was a juxtaposition of lesser wholes (doorknobs, bodies, etc.).

Juxtaposition, like integration, is possible at every stage of mental development. At one end, we see what William James called the "blooming, buzzing confusion" of a helpless infant, bombarded by a chaos of unrelated sensations. At the other end, we see prominent philosophers who give us a disconnected jumble of undefined and/or unrelated abstractions, in the form of polysyllabic tomes (European) or hit-and-run articles (Anglo-American). The same mentality is more easily recognized in the politician who calls for deficit reduction and new entitlements, easier money and less inflation, et al. Such a medley of platform planks, like the other cases above, is not an intellectual whole. A series of contradictions adds up to nothing and offers the voter no more than a juxtaposition of slogans. These sloganeers are the congressional equivalent of Heidegger's metaphysics or James's helpless infant.

Another visual image of a non-whole may be helpful. The walls of our galleries are rife with examples, eloquently typified by the artifacts of Jackson Pollock. The only whole in his work is the physical frame and canvas. The painting, by contrast, is a perfect example of non-integration; it is a deliberately unconnected assemblage of smears. Their arbitrary co-existence within the same frame is no more than spatial relationship—that is, juxtaposition.

My obvious disapproval of Pollock and his kin is not meant to imply that integration is always a rational course of action. The purposeful building of a nuclear missile by a belligerent Iran is still a process of integration, however evil, while an act of self-defense by the United States' smashing the missile, however good, would consist of tearing it apart—that is, would be a form of disintegration. Although my examples often reveal my own viewpoint, my purpose is not to evaluate the products of integration or of its opposite, but only to make the distinction clear.

As the above example suggests, even if a man's product is a non-whole, his <u>actions</u> in creating the product may still constitute a whole. In this kind of case, the whole is the connected series of steps necessitated by his goal. A general seeking more stars, a politician seeking election, a painter seeking cocktail invitations, may each be following an integrated course of action (although this is certainly not always the case). Depending on their choices, however, such action can eventuate in mere rubble, random sound bites, or expensive stains.

More commonly, however, a non-whole product stems from a non-whole course of action, one based not on purpose or plan, but on whim. A college student, say, goes to a movie (he's bored), makes a pass at a waitress (aroused), takes a nap in the park (tired), smokes a joint (restless), flies to Buffalo (misses his friends). These episodes, being devoid of connection, do not comprise a whole but merely a temporal succession, a form of juxtaposition. This remains true even if the young man claims to have created a new kind of whole as proved by the fact that all the episodes can be covered by two words, such as "my choices" or "my day." If a man's actions and/or products reflect either his failure to integrate or his successful removal of integration, then what he does or makes, even if nameable by a single word, cannot be described as a "new integration"—just as the absence or destruction of achievement cannot be described as a new form of creativity. A connection among elements does not consist in the absence or removal of connection. Non-connection is not a species of connection.

Valid versus Invalid Integration

Beyond the perceptual level, the process of integration is neither automatic nor automatically right. Since man, in Ayn Rand's words, is a "being of volitional consciousness," he has to choose what cognitive processes he will perform and learn how to perform them validly. The concept of validity is not a primary. Nor is its definition self-evident; rather, it follows from a philosophy's metaphysics and epistemology.

If the object of knowledge, as Objectivism holds, is reality, identified as Nature, then metaphysically, a valid integration is one based on and pertaining to facts, the facts of Nature. And if man's faculty of knowledge is reason in the Objectivist sense, then epistemologically, a valid integration is one reached by the logical conceptualization of percepts. Within the Objectivist system, these two formulations imply each other.

Examples of valid integration so defined are abundant in human life, but they are most striking in the work of scientists. Acceleration in free fall, Galileo tells us, is constant, a claim that subsumes countless unobserved cases. How did he validate it? First, on the basis of experience, he defined certain new concepts, such as speed and acceleration. Then he carried out a series of experiments to "wrench answers from Nature," a series so designed that at the end only one interpretation of the observed data was logically possible; thus did many different experiments lead him to a law, a type of whole. Then he connected his new, unifying law to relevant knowledge that he and others had gained earlier, thereby making his discovery an element of a still greater whole. Galileo's conclusion about free fall, in sum, is an integration of worldly facts reached in conformity with all the requirements of reason. It is, therefore, a model of integrative validity.

By contrast, the conclusions of Nostradamus, a mystic less than a century earlier, are not. What Nostradamus offered was a potpourri of extrapolations to the future reached by consulting such items as actual past experience, popular beliefs, ancient myths, and intuitions from the divine. Together with a long line of non- or anti-scientific thinkers, he did not look for objective proof of his conclusions; he accepted perceptual data when he regarded them as helpful to his viewpoint, but was indifferent to them when they were not. Much of the time, his predictions were so unspecific—on the order of: There will be a great upheaval in the fullness of the seasons—that their truth or falsehood cannot be determined by anyone at any time. Galileo was reason- and fact-oriented; Nostradamus was not.

Now let us consider the issue of validity in regard not to thought, but to its building blocks: concepts themselves. I indicated the Objectivist view of concept-formation earlier. But how, one might ask, can a concept be formed by invalid integration? It would be easy for me to recite as examples all the mystical concepts claimed to transcend Nature and reason, such as god, poltergeist, transubstantiation, and the like. But it is more instructive in this context to analyze a concept not so obviously invalid, indeed one widely accepted even by those who in all sincerity laugh at supernaturalism. I have in mind the term "extremism," which first entered the American vocabulary during the presidential campaign of 1964.

Although rarely given a clear definition, "extremism," in essence, is a term used to condemn those who hold unpopular values intransigently and in action refuse to compromise them; the nature of such action is not delimited by the concept.

On the basis of this definition, the concept blends into a unit—and thus regards as instances of the same evil—two types of people: uncompromising moralists and violent zealots; men of principle (whether good or bad) and crazed activists; exponents of integrity and exponents of insanity. A concept of this kind is not based on observed fact: It is an attack *against* fact by requiring the evasion of profound differences among men. If one observes men's ideas, character, and actions, one can hardly avoid concluding that men condemned in their time for moral intransigence, such as Socrates, Jesus, Gandhi, and Jefferson, are essentially different from Savonarola, Lenin, Hitler, and any Muslim suicide-murderer. The contrast in the meaning of "intransigence" here is so blatant that one can integrate all these men into a unit only on the basis of an emotion in defiance of reason. (In 1964, it was the desire to bring down Goldwater by forcing him to compromise.) Some men of principle, I should add, *are* zealots, and vice versa, but some philosophy professors are alcoholics, and vice versa; neither of these facts is a basis for valid integration.

The concepts of valid and invalid integration are epistemological, not evaluative; the difference between the two lies in the <u>method</u> of the integrator, not in the value of the product he creates. In most cases, to continue our example, Galileo's method does lead to truth, while Nostradamus's does not. But such a correlation is not invariable. A mystic can stumble into what others know to be a truth, and a scientist into an error. The lucky mystic, however, has still integrated invalidly, while the unfortunate scientist, though mistaken, has still integrated validly.

An example of the latter can be found in the work of Kepler. Integrating facts he had observed with empirical knowledge earlier established by Gilbert and Brahe, he came to a false conclusion about the nature of the force exerted by the sun on the planets. His method of thought was rational, though its result was mistaken. His integration, therefore, was valid. Since fallibility is a human attribute, no norm, such as rationality—and no cognitive process, such as integration—can be defined in such a way as to require infallibility. Error as such is not a breach of reason nor of any principle of cognition, unless it is error reached by a rejection of reason or of such principles. Because of his fact-based method, I might add, Kepler's error was short-lived; when more facts became available, the same method was used to correct his theory. Unfortunately, this happy resolution, though common in science, is rare in the humanities.

An important tautology is implicit in all the above: <u>method</u> of integration is method of <u>integration</u>. In other words, an invalid integrating process, just as much as a valid one, <u>is</u> an integrating process. A whole that has been wrongly produced is still a whole, however flawed.

For instance, the notion that history is cyclical—that is, merely an endless repetition of the same course of events probably foretold in ancient myths—is a generalization, just as extremism is a concept. Both result from the blending of unlimited data into a unit through measurement-omission, even though in these cases the blending is unjustified. Both these products are wholes reached by a process of integration. As a result, we can and do know (within limits) the kind of concretes each unit claims to subsume along with the implication that there are a potentially unlimited number of such.

Contrast this with the mentality of concrete-bound (usually primitive) people: people who live in a culture of charismatic mythmakers and of impassioned warriors—but who are concerned only with the striking tale they have just heard or the bloody battle just seen. Such people come to no wider ideas, right or wrong, about the nature of the past or of human character; they perform no conceptual process in regard to these experiences and thus create no new mental product. This non-process, which is not confined to primitives, is neither valid nor invalid integration. It is non-integration.

Though irrationally combined, the elements of invalidly created wholes, like those of valid wholes, are related not by juxtaposition but by necessity. The necessity within the invalid whole derives not from objective facts, but rather from the relationships the integrator can establish based on his non-rational framework. In other words, the source of necessity here is not reality, but the systematic internal consistency of the product—that is, its consistency within its non-rational framework. However unjustified that framework, within it the parts _are_ connected; as with any whole, the parts require one another.

Not every unjustified assemblage is a whole. But those created by integration are—and, as such, do have an inner logic. For example, the medieval Scholastics defended their ideas as elements within a chain of necessary inferences based on self-evident axioms, a chain like Euclid's. In contrast to those of Euclid, however, the Scholastics' axioms rested on faith in the Bible, the Church fathers, and the saints. Their integrating process was detached from reality and thus invalid. But their ideas nevertheless do form a system, because they are connected internally: Given the Scholastics' axioms, the rest follows necessarily. In this way, their Many ideas do form a One. The contrast to a series of random aperçus such as those by Oscar Wilde or in Nietzsche's _Zarathustra_ is obvious.

Now let us sum up the above material in the form of a principle, one that is essential to this inquiry. The principle is that there are *three* distinct alternatives in regard to integration: valid integration (e.g., Galileo), invalid integration (Nostradamus), and non-integration (Pollock). This trinity or trichotomy is the base for which DIM, as I will explain in chapter four, is an acronym. A trichotomy is a trinity each member of which is incompatible with the others.

Here is an example. Three students finishing a lecture course are asked to assess their teacher. One reviews the content and organization of her lessons, her manner of answering questions, her ability to motivate, then, balancing virtues and flaws as impartially as he can, puts it all together, reaching a verdict—say, a favorable one. This is an example of valid integration. A second student considers similar counts, but is steaming because of a career-threatening grade the teacher gave him that he regards as grossly unfair; governed by the steam, he sees flaws everywhere; putting it all together he happily slams the teacher. This is invalid integration. The third student can't recall much of the class material, feels that judging others is subjective, likes the fact that he got a good grade, but dislikes the amount of homework; these factors, he feels, simply can't be lumped together under any simple evaluative word or sentence, so he shrugs. In this case, too, we are being given a distinctive type of response, but the shrug is not a third assessment of the teacher. It is a rejection of the assignment, an example of non-integration—which, taken at face value, seems to be motivated by sincere belief.

The same three alternatives apply to any volitional action: One can do it rationally, non-rationally, or refrain from doing it. In studying any human action, even one as relatively simple as eating, we can often gain valuable knowledge by understanding its three forms—for example, by identifying and trying to explain the fact that some people eat a balanced Western diet, some eat a macrobiotic diet based on the yin-yang principle, and some, such as medieval ascetics or modern anorexics, refrain from eating, insofar as possible.

The fact that integration offers us three possibilities is thus in no way distinctive. There are nevertheless levels of importance in regard to human actions. Perhaps a study of the three integrative alternatives will teach us something new. Perhaps it will shed a unique light on the development of Western culture and history.

Man's method of using his mind, one would think, is more likely to influence his destiny than is his method of feeding his body.

CHAPTER TWO

THE THREE ARCHETYPES

A POLICY IN regard to integration is not a primary, but a consequence, a method of thought that derives from fundamentals. Minds in
every field and eventually the general public learn it from teachers who
specialize in studying the nature of reality and man's means of
knowledge—in other words, men learn it from philosophers. But philosophers have reached different conclusions in regard to fundamental
issues, and have thus upheld different views of integration. In order to
understand the views operative in our culture, therefore, we must first
look at their basic causes in the history of Western philosophy. By common consent, the greatest philosophers of the West—the Big Three, I will
call them—are Plato [427–347 B.C.], Aristotle [384–322 B.C.], and Kant
[1724–1804].

Plato

Drawing on the scattered ideas of his predecessors, Plato was the first
thinker to offer a detailed and connected viewpoint in regard to fundamental issues, thereby creating in the West the first system of philosophy.

Reality, for Plato, is not the physical world of Nature, not the imperfect
sensible world of concrete men and things, with its ceaseless flux of contradictions (the latter because it is a union of "Being and non-Being").

Concretes, including individuals, are merely appearance, the distorted and ultimately unreal shadows of a higher, non-material, truly real dimension, the world of Forms or abstractions, which is motionless, logical, and perfect. The Forms are hierarchical, culminating in the pinnacle of reality, the ineffable Form of the Good (called by later Platonists the One). This Form is what gives unity and meaning to the universe. It is the fundamental fact, from which all the lower Forms (and thus all the shadows) derive and on which they depend. And it is the fundamental value, toward which all things aspire.

Plato's epistemology is a corollary of his metaphysics (and vice versa). Since knowledge is knowledge of what is real, it cannot be based on sensory observation, which has no access to a non-material reality. Sense data, often contradictory to truth, are at best stimuli enabling us to remember ideas gained in an earlier life. Cognition, therefore, entails a break with this world. It requires that we reorient our minds: that we seek out the connections among pure Forms, guided only by pure logic. Stage by stage—each is represented in Plato's image of a divided line—the student rises from his starting point in a shadow-filled cave toward ever-wider abstractions; the culmination of his journey is a mystic experience of the Good. Now, for the first time, he knows why all things are as they are and how human life ought to be lived.

Walter Burkert, a renowned classicist, sums up Plato's metaphysics as: "For the Greeks . . . religion [before Plato] had always meant acceptance of reality. . . . Through Plato reality is made unreal. . . ." In regard to epistemology, Plato himself puts it best: "[I]f we are ever to have pure knowledge of anything, we must get rid of the body and contemplate things by themselves with the soul by itself."[5]

Plato's viewpoint has had a legion of defenders across the centuries. Here are two examples, one ancient and one modern, each with his own variant.

Augustine, the leading philosophic influence from the fifth through the twelfth centuries, offered a Christian version of Platonism. The transcendent unity from which all things flow is not an abstract goodness, but a personal God. Despite His personal nature, however, this God is not a concrete. To the extent that our minds can grasp Him, He is pure abstraction ("infinity," "omniscience," etc.). In stark contrast to His own Unity, God creates the Many, the world of natural, sensible objects, but these Many are merely the actors and stage sets in a divine play, entities devoid of autonomy and independent value. So far from its being true reality, the theater is soon to close.

The foundation of human knowledge, accordingly, is illumination by the One; we "must first believe," Augustine famously tells us, "in order that we may then know." This is the defining formula of Christian epistemology: The knower starts with premises justified by faith apart from sense perception, then deduces their implications.

Since the early nineteenth century, the most influential Platonist has been Hegel. Reality in his system is a spiritual entity that pursues self-knowledge by enacting a process often compared to a career. In this view, reality is a continuous, purposeful, creative movement culminating in the highest creation possible. The movement starts with a single pure abstraction which by its own inner logic generates a self-contradictory triad of such abstractions. This last necessitates a progression of further contradictory triads that eventually creates—evolves into—a material, then organic, then human and cultural world. The process is completed when all its elements are *aufgehoben* in the Absolute—that is, absorbed into a One that is without (though also with) distinctions.

This One is true reality, whereas the material world of the Many is appearance; it is merely an earlier stage of reality's development soon to be transcended. Plato, therefore, is correct: Matter is a semi-real manifestation of abstractions. As to knowledge, Hegel requires that one dispense not only with sense data, but also with Aristotelian logic; the pure thought that moves step by step upward uses Hegelian (dialectic) logic.

Hegel's rejection of Aristotelian logic represents a major change in Platonism; it was made possible by Kant, who had claimed that the laws of logic, like all human knowledge, have no basis in reality. This viewpoint freed Hegel to conceive Plato's world of abstractions as a parade of contradictions, a development that would have been repulsive and unimaginable to the Western tradition before him. Despite this, however, Hegel's new variant of Platonism was highly influential in the West and did not negate the Platonic view of cognition. Like Plato, Hegel conceives of the latter as the interrelating of concepts independent of percepts, and even goes so far as to redefine the term "truth." An idea's truth, he says, consists not in its correspondence to physical reality, but rather in its relationship to (its "coherence" with) other ideas.

Now a word on ethics. As a derivative of metaphysics and epistemology, ethics is not a primary factor shaping men's approach to thought, and as such is only peripheral to our study. But a glance at a philosopher's ethics often helps to bring out more fully certain of the presuppositions or implications of his approach. As in the basic branches, the views of Platonists in ethics differ in detail, but not in essence. All these thinkers ask men to sacrifice themselves to a transcendent entity, such as the One, God, or the state. Since concretes are regarded as shadows, so are human concretes—that is, individuals. The good life, therefore, consists in each man's renunciation of personal, worldly desires in order to serve a higher truth.

Although there are many variants of Plato's system, what makes them the same in regard to integration is their commitment to two fundamental principles. In metaphysics, their principle is supernaturalism. In epistemology, it is rationalism.

"Supernaturalism" is the belief that reality is a non-natural dimension, one that transcends the material world we perceive. As such, the term is very broad, subsuming figures from the earliest Greek Orphics to the latest American televangelists. Western philosophers, however, have almost invariably defined super-Nature in philosophic, and specifically Platonic terms—that is, as a realm of abstractions or concepts. This version of supernaturalism is called <u>idealism</u> (not an ethical term here, but one denoting the view that ideas have primacy over matter). So all idealists are supernaturalists, but the converse is not necessarily true. Since supernaturalism has been endorsed in many different forms, a person's rejection of one of its forms does not necessarily imply that he is a naturalist who rejects all of them. Idealism, for example, is often regarded as the metaphysics of Christianity, but the term can also apply to thinkers who reject Christianity and even religion as such—e.g., the ancient Pythagoreans, who dispensed with the gods, advocating instead a transcendent world of numbers. In the ordinary meaning of the term, these men are atheists, but in their own way they are still idealists.

"Rationalism"—Plato's other cardinal principle—is the theory that conceptualization is the essence of human cognition, but that concepts (or at least the fundamental ones) cannot be derived from the senses. The true base of knowledge, in this view, is the *a priori*—that is, <u>concepts independent of percepts</u>. Like idealism, rationalism is a broad theory, which subsumes many variants. A rationalist may hold that the senses have some lesser, auxiliary role in regard to conceptual knowledge. He may reject Plato's theory of innate ideas in favor of a different version of the *a priori*. He may regard the source of the *a priori* as internal or external, psychological and/or religious, the product of an ordinary human faculty or of an extraordinary one. Whatever their differences, however, all rationalists derogate induction.

The proper means of knowledge, they hold, is not inference from observation. It is deductive logic; so the cognitive model for all subject matters is a geometric system. Some rationalists, such as many Scholastics and most notably Spinoza, have attempted to create just such a philosophy, one with all the rigor of mathematics. Most, however, have followed Plato in this issue. Judging from his dialogues, Plato allows for the frequent emergence in a thought process of new, seemingly independent insights, ones that amplify or advance some deductive progression but are not themselves inferred from any stated axioms. As a rationalist, of course, Plato does not regard such insights as isolated cognitive thunderbolts, a view that would subvert the whole logic of his system. Instead, he holds that these insights are connected to the rest and will be seen eventually to follow from other true premises or in the end directly from one's grasp of the Good.

Because rationalism takes a variety of forms, a thinker's rationalism is sometimes difficult to identify. Religious thinkers, for example, are often described as exponents of faith over reason and thus as non- or anti-rationalist. And Hegel is often described not as a rationalist, but as an irrationalist. In the appropriate context, without any doubt, both these descriptions are valid and even indispensable. This does not, however, affect the fact that Augustine, Spinoza, Hegel, et al, uphold the same basic approach to reality and to knowledge—the one pioneered by Plato.

Rationalists hold that man reaches knowledge of reality through the grasp of *a priori* concepts. Since these exist independent of Nature they can be found only in a realm beyond Nature. Reality, therefore, is in some form a realm of concepts—which is the idealist viewpoint. The converse is also true: A world of concepts, if it existed and was rationally knowable, could be known not by observation, but only by the method of rationalism. Platonism, in short, is not a juxtaposition, but a true system: Idealism and rationalism imply each other.

The system defined by these two principles offers clear-cut advice to each of us qua integrators. Integration, it tells us, pertains not to this world, but to its transcendent source. So do not play the pointless game of the cave dwellers (such as empirical scientists), who look for order in the chaos of shadows. Do not *look*, but think, by turning your attention to the *a priori* ideas comprising reality. Now, with this orientation, you can start to integrate, which means gradually to discover the logical interconnections among ideas. If you keep at it, you will know when to stop, because you will have reached the summit.

Like most of the Greek thinkers, Plato sought to relate the One and the Many. His solution was to write off the Many as unreal, and construe the One as a self-sufficient, all-swallowing entity. Plato is thus the pre-eminent philosophical champion of the One *without* the Many. This is an inevitable consequence of his basic approach. Higher abstractions include lower ones; so if abstraction is reality, in the highest all must merge.

Plato was a master of philosophy and a world-class integrator. He was the first Westerner who identified this process, understood its importance, and consistently practiced it.

"In fact, my friend," he writes, "it's inept to try to separate everything from everything else. It's the sign of a completely uncultured and unphilosophical person. . . . To dissociate each thing from everything else is the complete destruction of all rational discourse. The weaving together of forms is what makes reason [logos] possible for us."[6]

Plato took the first, huge step. Judging by the Objectivist definition of "validity," however, the step was fatally flawed. Plato's method of integration is the archetype of <u>invalid integration</u>. It rejects one element of validity (the senses), and detaches from Nature—supernaturalizes—the other two, logic and concepts.

In regard to cultural interpretation, as we will see, the most obvious indicator of a man's Platonism is usually the last of these. Whenever floating abstractions are essential to the integration of a cultural work, the work to that extent is supernaturalist and rationalist.

Aristotle

Aristotle, "the master of them who know" according to Dante, created a very different system of philosophy. Whereas Plato's metaphysics is supernaturalist, Aristotle's may be called naturalist or secularist. This latter term means the same thing, but from a special perspective: Secularism is naturalism regarded as non-religious. Reality, Aristotle holds, is Nature and nothing more; it is the world in which we live. Nature is not an opaque flux of contradictions or a repository of abstractions, but an intelligible realm of concrete entities ("primary substances"), each with a specific identity consisting of matter shaped by form. There is no matter without form, Aristotle holds, and no form without matter; the two are inseparable. Form is not a transcendent reality, as in Plato, but one of an entity's two worldly elements; it is the structure of an entity's stuff (of its material, as we might say).

In epistemology, Aristotle rejects Plato's theory of innate ideas leading to "pure" concepts, along with any other claim to *a priori* knowledge. The mind, he holds, is at birth a *tabula rasa*, and man must derive all his knowledge from sensory data. To move beyond such data, a man must use his faculty of abstraction: of separating out mentally, from a group of similar concretes, their form, which is the same in all of them. This enables a man to think abstractly while understanding that abstractions cannot exist separately. In modern terms, man forms a vocabulary of <u>concepts</u>, each of which is a "universal" subsuming all the similar concretes. Equipped with concepts, the mind can rise to the level of <u>reason</u>. (There is no recognized term to designate Aristotle's theory of knowledge.)

If concretes are the constituents of reality, then the referents of concepts, that which gives them meaning, are the objects we perceive—that is, our observations, direct or indirect, of entities in Nature. Since we form concepts by grasping the real identities common to these entities, our concepts are objective, not arbitrary or mystical. And since man, unlike animals, is the rational being, he can understand observed facts, but only by conceptualizing his percepts. The learning process, in Aristotle's view, is a series of ever-wider inductions ending with (not starting from) the discovery of basic principles. Plato's turning away from concretes, therefore, is the means not of advancing cognition, but of strangling it.

In contrast to Plato, Aristotle regards man's ability to form concepts not as a puzzle requiring a supernaturalist explanation, but as a natural fact requiring no explanation, at least not by philosophers. "The soul," he writes simply, "is so constituted as to be capable of this process." It is also so constituted as to be able to grasp the laws of logic—at least, after Aristotle had done so. Logical thought, too, he holds, is a worldly process. The Law of Non-Contradiction is not a "pure" tool, unsullied by sense, but a plain description of observed fact. This law, he says, is an absolute, true of this or any world; it is true, in his famous phrase, of "being qua being," which is why compliance with it is a requirement of valid thought.[7]

From the above, Aristotle's advice to the integrator—where to start, how to proceed, when to end—is clear. On every key point, it is the opposite of Plato's.

Like Plato, Aristotle too has had philosophical followers spanning the centuries.

If Augustine's system represents the fusion of Christianity and Platonism, its counterpart and opposite is the system of Thomas Aquinas, which represents the fusion of Christianity and Aristotelianism.

Since Christianity and Platonism agree on idealism and rationalism, Augustine's fusion posed no insuperable problems. Aquinas, however, undertakes to combine such ideas as Aristotle's reason and Saint Paul's faith, sense-perception as the base of knowledge and scripture as the base, Nature as true reality but also super-Nature. As these combinations make clear, Aquinas, unlike Augustine, cannot simply be classified under any one of the Big Three. I treat him as an Aristotelian in the present context, because that is the element of his philosophy, not his conventional

Christianity, which was revolutionary to his thirteenth-century contemporaries. In an era ruled by dogma, Aquinas taught that reason in the Aristotelian definition, reason as a secular, self-sufficient faculty, is valid. Faith, he held, is not the base of reason and may not contradict its conclusions. Nor are the two faculties equal: Reason is the authoritative guide; faith is a supplement, which helps to fill in the blanks when reason is silent.

Similarly, Aquinas taught, the natural world, governed by Aristotelian logic and order, is fully real, not a mere appearance. And to know Nature, one must first observe it, then exercise one's power of thought, setting aside as irrelevant to human cognition any claims to *a priori* knowledge. Even the supreme fact, God, must be proved in this manner. Each of Aquinas's five famous arguments for the existence of God (taken mostly from Aristotle) exemplifies this approach. The Thomistic God, so far from subverting Nature, is an inference from it. As with the subatomic world discovered in the nineteenth century, so here: The discovery cannot have greater reality than the facts that lead us to it.

As against all the above, of course, there are the many anti-Aristotelian views essential to Aquinas the devout Christian, which cannot be ignored in classifying his philosophy. I indicate this side of him in the next chapter.

The culmination of the Aristotelian approach is Ayn Rand's philosophy of Objectivism, which, as she said, builds on Aristotle's naturalism and on his view of reason. She did have several disagreements with him, however. The basic one pertains to his theory of concept-formation— specifically, his idea that the grasp of similarity among objects is the grasp of a common form or structure intrinsic within them. Ayn Rand rejects this "intrinsicist" viewpoint, as she called it, on the grounds that it regards the object of conceptual awareness as a metaphysical ingredient of entities. In her view, such an ingredient could not be grasped either by perception or abstraction therefrom, but would require some form of what is called "intellectual perception" or "intuition." Such a theory, despite Aristotle's intention, would make concept-formation non-rational and thus non-objective; in the end it could be used to support some version of Plato's approach. In Ayn Rand's theory, as I have indicated in chapter one, concepts are neither intrinsic nor subjective, but objective; they are only human devices, and thus nothing apart from man, but devices with a factual, mathematical base. So man does reach unity through abstraction, but he does not find it pre-existing in objects; he creates it by his mind's method of interrelating the measurements of the Many.

Though their ethics are sometimes quite different, all Aristotelians, even Aquinas qua Aristotelian, agree in opposing the Platonists' other-worldliness and demand for sacrifice. Instead, they advise the individual to seek his own personal happiness in this world by the active exercise of his rational faculty.

Plato and Aristotle agree that the cosmos is a unity to be grasped conceptually, by man the thinker. But whereas Plato seeks such unity in the relationships among pure forms, Aristotle seeks it in the relationships among formed matters. Aristotle was thus the first philosopher to interpret the process of integration in wholly secular terms. In the Greek phrase, he sought the One <u>in</u> the Many. From the Objectivist viewpoint, accordingly, Aristotle is the first to define the fundamentals of rational thought. His approach is the first to qualify as <u>valid integration</u>.[8]

Valid integration, I repeat, is only one type of integration. However one evaluates his ideas, Plato no less than Aristotle worked methodically all his life to grasp the connections within reality by conceptual means. As integrators, Plato and Aristotle are the peerless masters of the millennia.

Plato was the greater of the two, because he was the first to discover the existence and the importance of the conceptual level of thought. But from another perspective, Aristotle was the greater, because he was the first to bring thought back to earth. No error of either can diminish these achievements.

Kant

Kant, the last of the Big Three, starts by agreeing with his predecessor Hume. Both hold that logic and causality—principles essential to integration—are baseless; neither can be derived from sense data or validated by reason, whether this last is conceived in Platonic or in Aristotelian fashion. But whereas Hume, stuck at this point, gave up philosophy, Kant undertakes to solve the problem by means of his "Copernican revolution."

The human mind, says Kant, is furnished innately with twelve *a priori* concepts or "categories" (along with other kinds of innate endowments). These concepts are not ideas in the traditional sense; they have no referents to give them meaning, neither on earth nor in heaven. This is because they are not intellectual content, but mental machinery, processing mechanisms that transform the raw data from reality before these data reach our consciousness.

The transformation consists in their imposing on the data a necessary structure (necessary to the human mind), thereby creating the spatio-temporal world, the world of Nature in which men live. Since it is our mental apparatus that makes this world, the world is subjective; Nature is not reality, but merely appearance, merely reality-as-processed-by-man, which Kant calls the "phenomenal world." In the act of creating the latter, our minds have cut themselves off from "things in themselves" or the "noumenal world." True reality, therefore, is in principle unknowable, and more: It is inconceivable.

Kant's revolution rejects out of hand Aristotle's theory that concepts derive from percepts. On the contrary, concepts, or at least the world-shaping ones, come first; percepts are their product. Such concepts, Kant points out, cannot be validated by observation, or by rationalist deduction from so-called "self-evident" insights. Indeed, since reality is unknowable, there is no such thing in this context as validity or truth in the traditional sense. For instance, the Law of Cause and Effect, one of the categories, necessarily rules the phenomena we experience, and thereby creates for us a world of natural law amenable to scientific integration. But no purely human and thus subjective factor, such as causality, can be said to correspond to reality. Science, like all human thought, is a way of organizing our observations of our collectively created nonreality. Logic, some of Kant's followers added, is similarly subjective; since it defines necessary and therefore (to Kantians) *a priori* principles of reasoning, logic too must be an agent of distortion, another barrier between man and reality, trapping him forever in the "logicocentric predicament."[9]

For both Plato and Aristotle, integration is directed to the facts of reality—to the world of forms or of formed matters. Both philosophers, accordingly, extol integration as the means of reaching man's highest form of cognition; it is his means of climbing the ladder to ultimate truth, of growing from animal perception step by step to ever greater understanding of reality. For Kant, these views are delusory; integration does not lead to glowing cognitive achievement; it is no more than the play of Plato's ignoramuses seeking a pattern among the shadows on the wall of their cave.

Kant's philosophy is not a set of affirmations, worldly or otherworldly, but of negations. In metaphysics, Kant denies the reality of this world not in favor of a higher realm, such as God, but in favor of an inconceivable— that is, of a nothing, nothing to human consciousness; he denies for the sake of the denial.

In epistemology, Kant condemns man's consciousness as impotent to grasp real truth, not because our mind is inferior to some higher consciousness, but because, like every kind of consciousness, it requires a _means_ of consciousness. Aristotle identifies the basic means as the senses; Plato, as the faculty of thought; Kant, as the categories. The point is that Kant condemns as subjective knowledge gained by any of these and, by extension, knowledge gained by _any_ means. Any information in any consciousness that has been acquired "somehow," he holds, is thereby disconnected from reality. This is the invalidation not only of man's consciousness but of all consciousness, no matter of what kind, _because_ it is conscious. Again, Kant denies for the sake of the denial.[10]

The implications for integration of these negations are eloquently spelled out in the _Critique's_ most famous section, "The Transcendental Deduction of the Categories." The categories, Kant there explains, are able to achieve their world-creating result because they are processes of a specific kind. In Kant's terminology, they are "synthesizing" mechanisms, whose task is to interrelate an otherwise ungraspable "manifold." In other words, the categories are the mind's fundamental _integrators_, which unite an unintelligible Many into an intelligible One—in the course of which, however, they necessarily blast into unreality all the other concepts reached by men.

In Kant's philosophy, integration is the original sin of cognition; it is the thing that expels man from the Eden of reality. In literal terms, integration, man's method of knowledge, is what makes knowledge impossible. Thus another, derivative negation: Integration is invalid *because* it is integration. This is not merely a rejection of integration. It is a declaration of war against it. It is a call not for non-integration, but for anti-integration.

Kant reaches his conclusions systematically, but he is not a system-builder. On the contrary, he is an *anti*-system-builder and in historical fact the main eradicator of system-building in subsequent Western philosophy. Kant presents an intricate argument—in order to show that argument is ultimately futile. He integrates a complex series of ideas covering all the basic questions—in order to show that integration is invalid. His Critical philosophy is a whole, as earlier defined, a whole with an intricate inner logic—a whole which tells us that wholes are an old-fashioned delusion. A systematic argument claiming to prove that the questions of physics are unanswerable is not a system of physics, but the opposite. The same applies to a systematic negation of philosophy. In the eloquent words of David Harriman, a colleague of mine: "Kant isn't pro-integration just because he punches reason twelve times in combinations of three punches."

Like the other greats, Kant has had many followers, most taking ever-bolder steps along the path he had cleared. These thinkers usually drop Kant's "categories" and "noumena" in favor of their own variants, but most of them (not Hegel) adopt his anti-conceptual essence and as a rule apply it more extensively than he had. A leading exponent of this development is the pragmatist John Dewey, who rejects the very idea of fact independent of man.

Kant's basic theory is correct, in Dewey's view, but what makes the world conform to men is not some immutable inbuilt mental mechanism, but the flux of people's daily choices and acts. In order to achieve their goals, people need a "plan of action," which is Dewey's definition of "idea." An idea's truth, therefore, is its expediency, not its correspondence to an alleged external reality; the standard of validity is the idea's ability to remove, at least for a while, some obstacle to men's action. If an idea succeeds in this endeavor, it is true, which means that the plan works for now; if the idea fails, it is false. For man, said Kant, truth is that which conforms to the requirements of our subjective minds. Truth, says Dewey, is that which conforms to the requirements of society's subjective actions.

Since an idea, in Dewey's theory, is a plan designed to deal with a concrete obstacle, the idea cannot to any significant extent be extrapolated beyond that concrete. Thus concepts, for Dewey, are not an important tool of knowledge. Integration through the use of abstractions is largely useless and can be harmful, he thinks, because it tends to draw men away from the complexities of the urgent present into an abortive search for some broad, inclusive principle that, precisely because it does abstract from differences, would be unable to offer the concrete guidance we need. No process of integration, he says, whether Platonic or Aristotelian, can cope with each day's uniqueness; to succeed in life, man must throw off the crushing burden of "principles," "incontestable theories," "necessary laws." Even Aristotle's logic, he remarks, having worked so well for so long, is overdue for a change.

Pragmatism is old-fashioned enough to offer an integrated approach to philosophy, albeit one that, like Kant's, rejects integration. A later stage of such rejection is found in Linguistic Analysis, a post–World War II movement often associated with Ludwig Wittgenstein. As its name suggests, the movement is concerned with difference, not similarity, with taking apart, not putting together.

Following Kant in their own version, analysts regard fact as outside the province of philosophy and concentrate instead on the study of mental structures. These structures are not, however, fixed categories nor a flux of plans, but people's "forms of speech"—that is, people's use in daily life of specific words and sentences. The task of philosophy, in this view, is the resolution of philosophic problems through language, mainly the "ordinary language" of the common man.

The practice of this task, analysts hold, does not rest on or lead to any system of philosophy. On the contrary, broad abstractions by their nature are almost sure to cause mental confusion, because they minimize or obscure the differences among men's actual, concrete linguistic usages. Philosophic problems, accordingly, should be dealt with only piecemeal—that is, as unrelated linguistic puzzles to be solved, or as they often say, "dissolved" in isolation. For the same reason, any attempt (such as these paragraphs) to give a unifying overview of the analysts' approach is to be condemned as "reductionist" or "simplistic." There are many linguistic analyses, but no philosophy of linguistic analysis, many of its practitioners say, and regard this absence as a key virtue.

In regard to ethics, Kant finds within his noumenal self another negation: an order binding on each man to sacrifice his values, all of them, because they *are* his values, and to do it not for any beneficiary, such as God or society, but as an end in itself. The pragmatists and analysts eschew ethical principles, even Kant's; as a rule, though not always, they advocate some form of concrete-bound social service.[11]

The Kantians' negations in regard to fundamentals are distinctively modern; there is no precedent for them in all the earlier centuries. In particular, the Critical philosophy, though it bears a seeming resemblance to skepticism, must not be confused with it. Skepticism is an ancient viewpoint that has come and gone repeatedly in the West, mainly on the fringes of philosophy; it has never defined any period of Western culture.

The skeptic holds that knowledge of reality is impossible to man, a conclusion that leads him to retire from intellectual pursuits, except to act as a gadfly exposing the illusions of other men. Hume, for example, having concluded that all conclusions are groundless, declared that philosophy is nothing but a futile amusement at odds with the requirements of practical life.

On every fundamental integrative issue, such a viewpoint clashes with Kant's. The skeptic seeks to gain knowledge of reality, then bewails the failure of his quest; Kant scorns the very attempt, rejecting reality because it *is* reality. The skeptic prizes the awareness of facts, but they elude him; Kant rejects awareness because it *is* awareness. The skeptic would welcome the discovery of connections among things, but cannot find any; to Kant, integration is the cognitive villain because it *is* integration. As to ethics, the skeptic says that he would gladly live by a rational code of values if anyone could define such; Kant demands that values be renounced because they *are* values. The difference between the two approaches is inescapable. One despairs because he cannot find objective truth; the other does not despair; he smashes the very idea of objective truth because it *is* truth.

Just as Kant is not a skeptic, so he is not a Platonist, although in this case the similarities go deeper. Kant's view that there are two worlds, with ours being inferior, is a reinterpretation of Plato; so is his view of the priority of concepts over percepts; and so is his view that morality is renunciation. For Plato, however, these ideas were an inspiration; they were the key to the transcendent, to enlightenment, to fulfillment. For Plato, they were salvation. For Kant, they are a hatchet.

Kant is the first and greatest nihilist in the history of thought. A nihilist is one who works to destroy man's mind and values as an end in itself, for the sake of the destruction. If he is not a philosopher, such an individual typically limits his activity to the ideas and values of a specific field.

Kant's nihilism is not an attribute distinct from his opposition to integration; on the contrary, each of these implies the other, because both denote the same process. Nihilism names the goal of the process; anti-integration names the means. The destruction of an entity—the nihilist's goal—is not the act of making it or its elements vanish into a void; rather, it is the removal of the *arrangement* of elements, which is what gave the entity its identity. What is left is disconnected bits, which no longer add up to anything. To wipe out, in other words, is to pull apart, and vice versa. This is why social observers who ignore the role of integration in culture are unable to understand the modern eruption of nihilism.[12]

A philosophy professor at the Stevens Institute of Technology makes eloquently real the connection between nihilism and anti-integration. I quote from a letter sent to me in 1998 by one of his students:

> An anecdote from his own life . . . He said that he sat his 5 year old daughter down on his lap one day and asked "Where's Daddy?" She responded by pointing to him. He said, "No, that's Daddy's body. Where's Daddy?" She looked perplexed and then pointed to his head. He responded, "No, that's Daddy's head. Where's Daddy?" This conversation continued for

some time until he had reduced his daughter to tears while she screamed "Where's my Daddy? Where's my Daddy?" I dropped the course very soon after that. . . .[13]

The above clarifies why I use the term "disintegration" in defining my hypothesis, rather than "non-integration." The latter term, if taken philosophically to denote a general mental policy, would apply to anyone who characteristically does not make connections, whether out of ignorance, indifference, laziness, low intelligence, and/or agreement with skeptics. By definition, these people, however great their number, hold no coherent ideas and have no cultural influence, except perhaps as echoes circulating the slogans of already established trends. The philosophic opponents of integration, by contrast, have changed our culture. They do not counsel mental inactivity, but wage an active fight to remove from cultural products any trace of the integrative work of their creators. Such men are the disintegrators in our midst.

Most people find nihilism to be so far outside the range of possible human motivations as to be unimaginable. One great artist, however, has left us an immortal concretization of the type; to my knowledge it is the first and only full-fledged presentation of a nihilist in Western literature. I am thinking of Iago in *Othello*, who works to destroy his heroic commander, knowing that he himself will gain nothing thereby; he is affronted by the great man because he is great, and seeks revenge against heroism because it is heroism. Iago is not a dictator, a capo, or an inquisitor who smashes others in the quest for power, loot, or the defeat of the devil. Iago smashes what he cannot help but admire, and does so for its own sake, expecting no reward.

An assault on the process of grasping or creating connections can leave in its wake only the unconnected—the Many without a One.

Basic Consistency of the Big Three

The writings of Plato, Aristotle, and Kant are not always consistent. Sometimes, even in regard to fundamental issues, they endorse contradictory ideas. Plato frequently writes as though he agrees with his contemporaries that the achievement of personal happiness on earth is man's proper goal, and also that knowledge is a product not of conformity to the transcendent, but of the individual's unaided exercise of his own mind. Ideas like these indicate a partial embrace by Plato of pagan worldliness and individualism, an embrace that contradicts his view that Nature, including individuality, is but a shadow from which men should flee.

Aristotle's books offer a greater number of contradictions. He describes the pinnacle of reality, for example, as a God that is form without matter; he seems to uphold some kind of (impersonal) immortality for a non-material aspect of man's soul; and even his theory of concepts, as we have seen, has Platonic implications. Ideas like these indicate a partial embrace by Aristotle of his longtime teacher's supernaturalism and rationalism, an embrace that is antithetic to his own fundamentals.

Kant affirms that his purpose is to defend faith by clipping the wings of reason. By limiting knowledge to appearance, he says, he makes religion invulnerable to scientific attack in regard to such ideas as the Christian moral code, along with the "God, freedom, and immortality" which, he says, a moral code presupposes. This embrace of religion is incompatible with his Copernican revolution, which tells us that reality, including its transcendent entities and attributes, if any, is inconceivable by any means, whether reason or faith.

Despite all this, however, Platonism is not paganism or even a mixture of paganism and idealism; just as Aristotle is not science plus Plato, or Kant the *Critique* plus Pietism. By its nature a philosophy, even a nihilist one, is not a potpourri of isolated ideas, like fortunes pulled from Chinese cookies; it is not a juxtaposition, but a whole, an <u>integration</u> of ideas— specifically, of the fundamental ideas on which all its other ideas depend. Within a philosophy, its metaphysics implies its epistemology and vice versa, and it is this unity that implies its ethics (and thence its politics and aesthetics).

What makes the Big Three great philosophers is that they are the only men in our history who have defined, whether validly or not, a *new* integration of fundamentals. The cultural and historical power they have had derives from this root. Plato, Aristotle, and Kant, each in his own way, tell us how to use our minds. Lesser thinkers then elaborate.

The above gives us one means by which to interpret contradictory statements in the books of the Big Three. If a tenet upheld in any of their writings is necessary to the author's <u>system</u>—that is, to his integration of fundamentals—then it is essential to his philosophy. By contrast, if a tenet, however prominent and even cherished in his writings, contradicts such integration, then it is worse than non-essential to his viewpoint; it is anti-essential. (A tenet with no effect on fundamental integration is irrelevant in this context.)

As one example, consider Aristotle's Platonic element. However extensive in his pages, it cannot be integrated with his own system; in fact, if accepted, it destroys his integration, because it clashes with every one of his fundamentals. Rejecting the Platonic element leaves Aristotle's integration intact, whereas rejecting even a single one of Aristotle's non-Platonic fundamentals destroys it. Take away Aristotle's notion of the Immovable Mover, for example, or his Platonic over-reliance on deduction, and he is still Aristotle, and even a better Aristotle for it. But take away his championing of Nature or the senses, and he is gone. The same principle is clear in the other two cases.[14]

Taken line by line, the Big Three are not free of contradictions; in a deeper sense, however, they are free, because their contradictions are irrelevant to their integration of fundamentals. A consistent set of fundamentals, I should add, may very well *imply* contradictions in derivative questions. Indeed, this is the fate of all systems reached invalidly, since it is impossible in any field to be consistently wrong. But this liability to error does not imply that invalid philosophies in regard to fundamentals are necessarily contradictory.

A great philosopher, by definition, is not a disciple, but an innovator. His philosophy is a feat not only of integration, but of new integration. This gives us a further means of defining essentials in the often tangled texts of the greats. One must identify a thinker's <u>new</u> ideas in regard to fundamentals, and determine whether they form by themselves a new integration of metaphysics and epistemology. If they do, then any older ideas in their books are at best irrelevant to their system, or at best mere elaborations of it. There will always be some older ideas, of course, because men build knowledge on knowledge, and so make integral to their thought many ideas discovered before them. In interpreting a great philosopher, however, one must bear in mind that his traditional ideas <u>as such</u> are not significant. Pre-existing ideas are merely what people believed before the thinker appeared; a "great thinker" who does nothing but echo his ancestors is neither great nor a thinker. In a great philosophy, the old may help the new, but it is not its substance, or the source of its influence. It was not Plato the pagan who inspired the Middle Ages, but Plato the anti-pagan. It was not Aristotle the Platonist who inspired the rebirth of secularism, but Aristotle the father of science. It was not Kant the Pietist who is everywhere today, but Kant the anti-everything.[15]

<u>A new integration of fundamentals</u>—this is the standard I use to identify the essence of a great thinker.

Although tradition does not define a great philosophy, it is often a significant factor in its influence. A new philosophy, by definition, arises only within a society governed by a different philosophy. Even if the new ideas are embraced by the society's intellectuals, therefore, the public at large may not be so inclined. Traditionalists may be ignorant of the new ideas, indifferent to them, or even feel threatened by what they see as an impending menace. Often, though not always, such traditionalism remains alive for long periods of time as a cultural background, even in the face of a powerful new philosophy. It is background because it is quiescent, intimidated by the new intellectual authorities, and only marginally influential on the society's course. But it can nevertheless be real, with the potential in the appropriate circumstances to come alive again in the public mind. Such a background is in effect a past in waiting—waiting for the new, ruling philosophy to be discredited.

Though tradition is irrelevant in defining a new culture, therefore, it is often essential to understanding what becomes of it. In this context, a philosopher's contradictory formulations can be important. An inconsistent nod to tradition may make him vulnerable to misinterpretation by friends and to attacks by enemies. Since contradictions work to blur the essential, they give people a chance to blur a philosopher and pick out as his essence some irrelevancy favoring their own cause. Even

Aristotle, many religionists are quick to say, sees that God is the end of all things.

Philosophic fundamentals have countless implications and applications, many, perhaps most, of which cannot be obvious to anyone at first. The innovator himself can hardly have the life span or the knowledge of the future required to perform such a monumental intellectual task—and then, in its light, to re-evaluate everything he believed before. However great a thinker, the full implications of his own achievement have to elude him. Hence the possibility of influence on Plato by his fellows or on Aristotle by his teacher or on Kant by his parents.

———

Here is a way to identify, in emotional terms, the appeal of each of the Big Three to their champions throughout the centuries. Plato appeals to soaring idealism scornful of the practical. Aristotle appeals to joyful realism on earth. Kant appeals to rage.

CHAPTER THREE

THE TWO MIXTURES

WESTERN PHILOSOPHY AFTER Greece is divisible into three periods: a Platonic era, from the Hellenistic centuries through the Middle Ages; an Aristotelian era, from the Renaissance through the Enlightenment; and a Kantian era, for the past two centuries. This progression has given rise to two further views of integration, both of which I call mixtures, as against the pure cases of the Big Three.[*16]

Worldly Supernaturalism

When medieval Platonism encountered the West's growing secularism, it mutated, bowing to the modern spirit. The new Platonists held on to the traditional idealism and rationalism, but they rejected the notion that these positions entailed the downgrading of this world to mere appearance and its corollary downgrading of sense experience. These new thinkers endorsed the long-popular ideas of Plato *and* the rebirth of the pagan Greek approach; they were champions of both religion and science.

This approach is a version of Platonism, but with an essential part of Aristotle's approach added. I identify this school as Worldly

---

* "Pure" here denotes simply the alternative to "mixed." It has nothing to do with the Platonic/Kantian meaning of "pure" as independent of sense. The context will make clear which meaning is intended at any given point.

Supernaturalism. Platonism in this form dominated modern philosophy for two hundred years, from the later Renaissance through the mid-eighteenth century. Some of its popularity derived from the fact that Worldly Supernaturalism had long been upheld by the ancient Stoics, who made a similar attempt to combine secularism and the transcendent.

René Descartes, the father of modern philosophy, was the most influential Platonist to embrace modern science. As a Christian, Descartes holds that God is ultimate reality, the only perfect being, and the source of all things, including our imperfect world. As a rationalist, he holds that knowledge is not gained inductively, from sense data, which he regards as confused; rather, it is gained deductively, through inference from the proper starting points, which he believes are intellectual intuitions "clear and distinct" to the mind apart from experience. In this view, the basic principles of thought, such as the laws of logic and causality, are given to us innately and do not refer primarily to this world. On the contrary, Descartes accepts them before he has discovered that there is a world, and he relies on them in order to discover it.

Directly or indirectly, he says, these *a priori* intuitions acquire their validity from God's character; we know they are valid because we know that their source, a perfect being, cannot be a deceiver. This is Descartes' version of the Augustinian principle that faith in God is the base of all knowledge. If we were to discard such faith and rely only on experience, Descartes holds, we would be trapped within our own consciousness. Without God's guarantee, a man can know only his own mind; the *cogito* by itself, we are told, takes us no farther.

Within this orthodox Platonic framework, however, Descartes takes a major anti-medieval turn. A physical object (*res extensio*) is real, he maintains, just as real as a mental object (*res cogitans*). So, although Aristotle was wrong to regard Nature as self-sufficient and all-embracing, he was right to regard it as fully real and its study as essential in man's quest for knowledge. The proper task of reason is to study both kinds of natural objects. In pursuing such knowledge, Descartes holds, a man is not sinking to the level of Plato's cave dwellers; rather, he is focusing on (part of) reality by exercising the rational faculty given him for that purpose by God. And he can be confident that the principles guiding his thought, because they are *a priori*, are absolutes everywhere, in this world as in the other.

Descartes' approach to science was soon overthrown by Newton's. But that does not alter the historic importance of Descartes' disagreement with Plato. Plato is eager to free the conceptual mind from the stultifying world of percepts, so that it can revel in the work of interrelating pure forms. Descartes, though he agrees that fundamental concepts are *a priori*, does not regard the organizing of such concepts as the essence of cognition. Although abstractions are rooted in a spiritual world, he holds, they nevertheless have an important application to the world of matter: They alone enable us to connect and explain the actions of observed concretes. That Descartes ascribes such earthly power to pure concepts suggests a broader reason he bases knowledge on God's goodness. If concepts apply to a perceptual world of which they are logically and genetically independent, this would seem to be possible only through some kind of divinely arranged harmony.

Just as the Worldly Supernaturalist accepts matter into his metaphysics, so he accepts the perception of matter into his epistemology. To him, the supernatural is not the enemy of the natural or of empirical data, but rather their source and illuminator.

Spinoza's philosophy is a striking example of this approach. As a pantheist, Spinoza holds that reality *is* God, whom he regards as an entity with infinite attributes, each of infinite extent; only two of these, mind and matter, are knowable by man. In this version also, Plato is held to be wrong, at least in part. Since the concretes of the physical world and the contents of the spiritual express God's nature equally, each of them is as real as He is. Neither may be viewed as a despised stepchild of some truer reality.

Because everything expresses God's nature, all existents for Spinoza are necessarily interconnected; their connections can be known only by a method modeled on mathematics. Spinoza begins his philosophy with *a priori* axioms certified by intellectual intuition, then deduces "geometrically" (his term) their logical consequences. The finished whole—in my view the greatest rationalist system of all—is a virtually all-embracing conceptual structure that subsumes experience but is not based on it. In developing his system, Spinoza goes beyond Descartes in his embrace of the *a priori*. God's nature, he deduces, is incompatible with any form of mind-body interaction; so it is not merely axioms that are *a priori*—all concepts, being mental entities, are independent of sense experience.

Like Descartes, however, Spinoza is a champion of scientific integration, who cannot rest content with a structure of pure concepts. Rather, he deduces from these a wide range of empirical facts, which he thus claims to have made intelligible. Like Descartes, he understands his obligation to explain why a system of *a priori* ideas should correlate with the events of a material world independent of it. And like Descartes, he invokes God as the correlator. In this issue, however, he does not invoke God's moral character. Rather, he reasons that since both mind and body express equally the nature of God, there must be a "psycho-physical parallelism": Every mental event, including every idea, must have its physical correlate and vice versa. This is the best attempt I have heard to explain the applicability to this world of non-worldly ideas.

Spinoza, some interpreters say, is really a naturalist, for whom "God" is but a synonym for Nature. Spinoza, say others, is a religious and even a "God-intoxicated" philosopher. I agree with the latter. Spinoza is a God-intoxicated man—who, living in the seventeenth century, welcomed Nature as a part, but only a part, of the realm that intoxicated him. As in Descartes, his Platonism is fundamental and his secularism derivative. He is another case of supernaturalism embracing the world.

Now let us take a look at ancient Stoicism which, despite some changes during its centuries of influence, offered the Romans a similar kind of philosophy.

In metaphysics, the Stoics, like Spinoza, were pantheists, though without his intellectual sophistication. To them, God or reality has but two attributes, the same ones that make up man; He is man writ large. The physical universe, God's body, is ruled by his omnipresent, quasi-personal mind, variously referred to as the world soul, logos, fire, reason, or (following Plato) the Form. This Form, regarded as the unseen ruler of Nature, is purposive and powerful; it shapes worldly events to fit its plan. We must not, therefore, disparage Nature. If matter is the body of God, then it must be fully real, just as real as soul or mind.

In epistemology, the early Stoics, contrary to expectation, rejected rationalism in favor of Aristotle's view that knowledge begins with percepts. Many of these Stoics, however, rejected Aristotle's demand for the next cognitive step: the conceptualization of percepts. Knowledge, they held instead, begins and *ends* with experience. This viewpoint left the Stoics vulnerable to caustic attacks by rival schools of thought, especially the skeptics. Stoicism, the skeptics insisted, cannot explain how, from experience alone, man can discover an all-powerful soul with an all-embracing plan—or more broadly how, from experience alone, man can access a dimension that transcends experience. Despite their early emphasis on the senses, therefore, the Stoics eventually came to regard empiricism as a liability, and rationalism crept in to replace it. At that point, their philosophy was no longer a juxtaposition of traditional elements, but became a *system*.

The Stoics' rationalism, when it developed, held that fundamental human concepts—the "common notions," as they called them, along with the basic concepts of science and philosophy—are *a priori*. They cannot be validated by experience, but only by a man's attentive contemplation of these concepts themselves and of their logical implications. Thus contemplated, it was believed, the true axioms of our knowledge will stand out as impossible to doubt; they will strike each man's mind, in the Stoics' term, as "irresistible." (Descartes' appeal to "clear and distinct" insights is a restatement of this idea.)

Though axioms are *a priori*, according to Stoicism, they should not remain detached from the world; the "common notions" and basic concepts are man's epistemological guide, the foundation of rational study and explanation of the observed facts of Nature. The Stoics pursued this task diligently, developing theories of physics, astronomy, cosmology, and much more. Such studies are possible, they held, because God has made the world logical and causal.

Their validation of the secular by the supernatural is illustrated in this school's ethical views, both in its ancient and modern versions. These thinkers counseled the individual to pursue earthly values for his own sake—in order ultimately to embrace the One and lose the self. On this point, too, Spinoza offers the fullest and clearest statement.

Worldly Supernaturalism is offered not as a juxtaposition of traditional elements, but as a new integration of them, a distinctive type of philosophic system made of known fundamentals connected in a new way. The essence of this integration lies in the <u>hierarchical relationship</u> given to its two elements: One is defined as the base and thus as primary, the other as derivative and secondary. For these thinkers, "that which is" is not divided into two antithetic entities—super-Nature versus Nature. Rather, super-Nature is conceived as the entity that makes Nature real and knowable. The medievals had held that Nature is as nothing because it is only a distant derivative, a shadow, of Him; these moderns counter that Nature is something *because* it is a derivative of Him. So *far* from God, sighed the one era; so far from *God*, smiles the other.

The distinctiveness of this approach lies in its claim that fundamentals widely taken to be logically incompatible are in fact compatible, and more: that each element logically entails the other. Secularism, the commitment to Nature, presupposes belief in a supernatural entity that makes Nature, and our knowledge of it, possible. Or: Plato's fundamentals are the indispensable base of Aristotle's. In the modern era, the commonest expression of this viewpoint has been the claim, for centuries considered axiomatic, that religion is the foundation of science.

From the perspective of Worldly Supernaturalists, such a claim is in no way illogical; on the contrary, they held, a philosopher's task is to apply this approach without contradiction to all the fundamental issues dealt with by the Big Three. By our earlier definition, the resulting systems *are* systems, because they present us with a structure of ideas that, whether right or wrong, is internally consistent.

Their internal consistency, however, has not led Worldly Supernaturalists to agreement in regard to the nature and method of integration. On the contrary, a number of incompatible interpretations of integration have been upheld by these thinkers, even though they all embrace the same mixed approach. Because of the importance of the approach in our history, this incompatibility is a fact we must understand.

Plato held that integration requires movement away from Nature; Aristotle, that it requires focus only on Nature. To both of which Worldly Supernaturalism on its face replies: Plato is basically right, but not so fast;

the pursuit of natural knowledge is a precondition of man's ascent up the ladder to God. If so, some within the movement wondered, how much worldly knowledge is necessary before we can leave science and start integrating our findings to the ultimate? The medievals, this group elaborated, had found God everywhere, leaping to Him from a single observation, but in our time this is clearly not enough; only a system of the physical world, like Newton's, can point us to the creator. Still not enough, said others; we cannot jump to the source of everything without a Theory of Everything (as it is now called). If so, some concluded, the earthly integrator must complete the fundamental task of science in purely secular fashion first, before he can use the knowledge to reach God. But if science is thus self-contained, others objected, how is it able to connect us to the transcendent? Besides, they added, to gain scientific omniscience would devour lifetimes or perhaps millennia, leaving men all the while ignorant of the most important integration, viz, man's connection to God.

As these men wrestled with one problem, another appeared: how to interpret the natural even when science has reached a highly advanced state of integration. Since natural laws are imposed by an Omnipotent whose plans we do not know, some said, the discoveries made by science are, to humans, mere descriptions of brute fact; in other words, to the purely secular mind without reliance on the *a priori*, inductive extrapolation is groundless. But, came the reply, this gives the victory to Skepticism; the answer must be that a perfect god has created a series of logical natural laws, which we can grasp to be necessary and intelligible in themselves, without the need to know God or his plans. But, countered other voices, if there can thus be certain knowledge of inductive law without reference to God, wouldn't that imply that the laws of Nature—and indeed Nature itself—are independent of God? And if they are, doesn't that make senseless the quest for the ultimate integration (of Nature and God) that we seek? On the other hand, without that quest, we may as well advise the integrator simply to forget science and turn straightaway to the transcendent, just as Plato said—or to do the reverse, as Aristotle said.

The argument went on for centuries; another of its forms pertains to the nature of the *a priori*. Since *a priori* ideas deriving from God are man's indispensable cognitive foundation, some said, the integrator should take these as his starting point, and proceed to reach scientific laws deductively, as in traditional rationalism. Others, however, unable any longer to envision scientific method as "geometrical," tended to minimize the scientific role of *a priori* ideas, relegating them to the status of general preconditions of thought, essential to all mental activity, but not specifically relevant to the scientist; in practice, these men urged the study of Nature through inductive methods independent of any *a priori*. Still others, developing this idea, went a step farther; they removed the *a priori* altogether from worldly thought, reserving for it a crucial role only in man's final, all-embracing integration.

As a last illustration here, there are the disputes about how to interpret the many apparent clashes between *a priori* and empirical knowledge— for example, Leibniz's deductive inference that "All is for the best," which was quickly followed by the disastrous Lisbon earthquake; or the biblical claim that Jesus walked on the waters and the Newtonian claim that gravity makes this impossible. If your *a priori* principle is correct, Plato would say, don't accept as an objection claims based merely on experience. If the *a priori* does not derive from observation, Aristotle would say, get rid of it. Perhaps, replied some of the reconcilers, we must occasionally reinterpret the findings of science in order to integrate them with the wisdom in the Bible (or some other repository of the *a priori*). But, came the retort, what then would be left of scientific method and thus of science? Well, then, suggested others, perhaps we should occasionally reinterpret the Bible to fit science. But, the more religious retorted, what then would be left of the absolutism of God's word?

Let me stress here that Worldly Supernaturalists do not regard the above questions and dilemmas as unanswerable. On the contrary, many of them have worked out their own answers, which in most cases form an internally consistent philosophy. My point is not that Worldly Supernaturalism is inherently unsystematic, but that by its nature it spawns <u>many</u> systems, each faithful to the mixture's fundamental principles, yet each incompatible with the others in its implications for integration.

As the disputes make clear, Worldly Supernaturalism subsumes a range of thinkers who, in regard to integration, differ not on fundamentals, but in degree—the degree of their tilt toward Plato or toward Aristotle. The tilt, of course, can go only so far before one of the two defining elements has been dropped, and the mixed viewpoint thereby abandoned. But within these limits, the mixed system by its nature cannot tell the integrator what philosophic role or importance to give to each of its elements: more or less to the study of Nature, more or less to reliance on sense-perception. Whatever the school's consistency in broad theory, the clash between Plato and Aristotle continually erupts in its representatives' thought about cognitive practice.

Render unto Caesar that which is Caesar's and unto God that which is God's. On this all the mixed thinkers agreed. But how much is God's, and when is it due? On this, the mixed men, being mixed, could not agree.

The above indicates an essential difference between the Big Three and the Worldly Supernaturalists. The philosophy of each of the Big Three does not lead to or allow for contradictory interpretations of integration. The fundamentals of the greats spawn no such clashes, which is why we find among their followers no similar proliferation of disputants. Within each of the three camps, thinkers give the same specific answers to the epistemological questions. How should man integrate? Should he focus his consciousness on Nature, or on God? Should he accept ideas only if based on sense data, or only if based on truths independent of sense data? (Or, for Kant, should he reject all of it?) These are either-or questions, which demand a yes or no answer. Reconcilers, by contrast, are the men of both-and; as such, they have been unable to escape differences in tilt—and the tilt is always toward one of the Big Three. By their nature, the Big Three cannot tilt.

I do not deny that there can be large and important differences among any theory's advocates when they come to apply their fundamentals to specific creative issues. As examples, to be discussed later, the same pure school of integration subsumes medieval teleology and Marxist dialectics; another pure school subsumes Sophocles and Hugo. Despite the obvious differences in each pair, the representatives within each camp, as we will see, are guided by the same approach to integration. Within a pure mode, thinkers face no insolvable epistemological dilemmas.

Worldly Supernaturalism accepts the worldly Many and their inter-connection through their derivation from a transcendent One. As corollary, it accepts observation of the Many as knowledge, since the empirical is validated by the One's *a priori* legacy. The philosophy thus affirms not the One without the Many, or the One in the Many, but, as we may call it, the Many from the One.

Knowing Skepticism

If one of the two modern mixtures represents a mutation of rationalism in the face of Aristotle, the other represents a mutation of empiricism in the face of Kant.

Early modern scientists, despite their frequent equation of Aristotle with the medievals, did accept in practice his integrative principles: Naturalism, the cognitive primacy of sense-perception, and scientific progress as the discovery of connections through the use of ever-broader concepts uniting ever-greater ranges of data. The early philosophers of modern empiricism, however, while they upheld Nature and championed the senses, believed that the root error of rationalism, their enemy, was its overreliance on abstractions. Hence they tended to downplay (though not to reject outright) the cognitive role of concepts.

When these Aristotelians manqués encountered Kant, they bowed to the *Critique*, but not completely. The post-Kantian empiricists agreed with Kant that reality is unknowable, but they did not agree that this conclusion turned empirical science, whose progress they admired, into a lowly recorder of mere appearance. Their new approach to philosophy, accordingly, is Kantian, but with some key Aristotelian tenets added. I identify this mixture as Knowing Skepticism, and here I do mean skepticism as against nihilism. The mixture was dominant throughout the nineteenth century, especially in England and America. Its first full statement was the positivism of Auguste Comte.

Comte begins by accepting, then extending, Kant's approach. Because our knowledge is relative to man's faculties, he says, it is subjective; so we can learn nothing about reality, not even that there is such a thing. Nor, by the same logic, can we learn anything about a pre-conscious world-shaping mind alleged (by Kant) to be real but unperceivable. Comte thus drops the idea of an unknowable noumenal world. What he is left with—as the total of that which exists and thus the only possible object of knowledge—is Kant's phenomenal world. The universe is no more than a stream of human experiences.

Mankind, says Comte, has evolved in three stages. The first was the theological, when men invoked supernatural causes to explain natural events. Next came a higher stage, the metaphysical, in which they invoked as explanation of what they observed entities that were allegedly worldly but nevertheless unobservable, such as "essences" or "ultimate causes" supposedly lurking within "external" objects. Finally, men have reached intellectual maturity with the development of positivism.

Positivism restricts cognition to the grasp of facts knowable by sense-perception. Any abstraction or theory involving unobservables is by its nature invalid.

The perennial questions of philosophy, accordingly, must be dropped. For example, "Do material objects exist independent of our experience?" is a metaphysical, and therefore invalid, question, since it cannot be answered by sense experience; no one can perceive a sense datum when he is not perceiving it. For the same reason, positivists do not stigmatize the natural world as mere appearance (or extol it as reality), because there is no sense-perception enabling us to differentiate what is called appearance from reality. All such questions and distinctions are literally meaningless, since their key terms have no empirical referents. Hume had attempted, in vain, to find empirical answers to some of these questions; positivism regards the attempt itself as wrongheaded. Nor, Comte says, does positivism undermine science; on the contrary, only if scientists take experience as a primary, dismissing questions about its source or status, can they achieve solidly based results, because only then are they restricting themselves to the knowable.

The corollary of positivism's restriction of cognition to sense data is its animus against conceptual knowledge, an animus that in several ways is without precedent in earlier empiricism. The animus is not a result of nominalism, the perennial view of skeptics that man cannot find any basis in reality for concept-formation. Here again the positivist position is not that we can't find such a basis, but rather that we shouldn't be looking for it. A concept, traditionalists had claimed, is an entity unifying and thus making possible knowledge of countless similar instances spread across all time and space. By definition, Comte notes, to invoke such an entity is to transcend possible experience and embrace the metaphysical.

An acceptance of concepts in the pre-Kantian sense would, therefore, be the destruction of science. Thus arose the first movement, not of weary skeptics decrying the futility of science, but of serious thinkers eager to advance science—science without metaphysics. It is in this way that integration—the great distorter of the mind, according to Kant—lost its final territory. Conceptualization became the enemy of empirical science. Concepts had now lost their status as cognitive tools in regard not only to the noumenal world, but also to the phenomenal.

It is difficult for the pioneers of a movement to see its full implications or therefore to carry their revolution all the way. In their earlier decades, accordingly, the Comteans retained concepts—including some quite broad terms—as a convenient, even inescapable, linguistic shorthand enabling men to segregate objects with observable and more or less similar features from the rest. But these groupings, they said, are not based on so-called "facts of reality," such as unperceivable "universals." On the contrary, the organization we impose is subjective and essentially arbitrary, since it reflects primarily men's needs and desires. And if the instances of a concept are subsumed under it arbitrarily, we cannot ask for their "necessary connection" (which anyway is another metaphysical term). Hence, Comte concludes, the laws science formulates and the classifications they presuppose cannot be described as necessary, or certain, or even true, in the sense of being necessitated by observation.

But, in the positivist's opinion, this conclusion does not sink science. It does not alter the fact that induction, which enables us to transcend the animals and predict future events, is a valid process and indeed the main task of science. In other words, generalizations are legitimate and even indispensable, though they have no objective basis in observation, which is our only means of knowledge.

The resolution of this seeming contradiction, according to positivism, lies in an observable fact: If we *assume* the uniformity of Nature even though we cannot prove it, and limit our inductions to our immediate, perceivable environment, many of our generalizations turn out, in Comte's words, to have "practical certainty" and "practical value," which is all men need in order to act.

Before Kant, a cognitive process based on a subjective, unprovable assumption would have been condemned by most philosophers as irrational and untenable, no matter what its practical results. A subjective assumption had been regarded by some as required for worldly action, but never on such ground as a form of truth or cognition; this was Hume's view, for example. After Kant, however, the subjectivity of an idea was no longer considered a bar to its acceptance; on the contrary, subjectivity was regarded as the very means of thought. The lesson of the *Critique* is that the needs of man's mind are the precondition and creator of human knowledge, perceptual and conceptual alike. If a subjective assumption is observed to be indispensable to science, therefore, it is by that fact to be regarded as knowledge. Such assumptions are merely a revised version of Kant's categories.

Thus for example, Comte views the idea of the uniformity of Nature as Kant does the category of causality—as *a priori*. It is not *a priori* in the manner of Descartes, who thought that the principle was a description of an external reality; rather, it is *a priori* in the Kantian sense, as the antecedent organizer of the world. As an empiricist, of course, Comte denies Kant's theory that such an *a priori* assumption is innate. Though not proved by observations, Comte holds, it is suggested by them, and in that way can be described as empirical. Comte applies his version of the *a priori* to several other assumptions he thinks necessary to science, but empirically unprovable; these include the laws of logic and the requirement that scientists be objective in the sense of understanding that their personal feelings do not affect the objects they study. Although scientists cannot pursue objective truth in the traditional sense, they seek instead what positivists call "interpersonal" truth.

Since concepts, in Comte's view, are merely tags that denote subjective groupings, we cannot expect them to perform miracles. We must aspire to modest integrations commensurate with the actual capacity of our cognitive faculty, remaining relatively close to perceptual experience and avoiding overly broad inductions. As a rule, positivists hold, the more abstract a concept, the more it is problematic. If one goes all the way in the quest for general principles, Comte sometimes says, that alone disqualifies the principles as irrelevant to science. Thus, though he demands consistency in science, he writes: "Anything that one could say about [logic] in the abstract would be so vague and so general as to have no influence on intellectual procedures."[17]

Positivists integrate, but unlike Plato and Aristotle they do not keep on integrating. They do not integrate their integrations. Rather, they stop the process at a comparatively much lower level of thought. Their goal and end product, evidenced in their work in science and in other fields as well, is not a broad unification of data, not an encompassing whole, but a number of unrelated sets of observed relationships. In this way, positivism does not reject concepts as such, but only in part.

Plato and Aristotle are commonly called "monists"—that is, they uphold the reality of a One, conceived as an integrating factor grasped by study of reality, a factor found, often in different forms, in most or all areas of existence. The Knowing Skeptics, by contrast, are called "pluralists." Pluralism upholds the primacy of the Many; in most or all areas, it says, the unconnectable will be encountered, elements that cannot be reduced to any kind of unity, natural or transcendent, and that are therefore closed to the process of integration. This view is held in different forms by pure and mixed Kantians alike. The Comtean version, conceived in the nineteenth century, is restricted in its pluralism; it accepts some connections and encourages some integration. Such pluralists, we may say, do seek unity—isolated <u>chunks</u> of unity, but not a broader One.

Along with his Kantian base, Comte upholds, in his own way, certain of Aristotle's fundamentals. Contrary to Kant (and to Plato), he holds that thinkers must be secular. Whether or not Nature is "real," he says, the realm we observe does exist and is the sole object to be studied. And in this study a proper scientist must reject the theory of innate ideas, agreeing with Aristotle that man without experience is a *tabula rasa*. The scientist must also agree to be objective and logical in his pursuit of causal relationships, albeit with the understanding that this goal and method of inquiry are mandated not by reality, but by a convenient *a priori*. In these ways, despite its Kantian foundation, positivism did not present itself as a negative outlook at war with the confidence of the Enlightenment; its very name features its purpose: to be a constructive guide to scientific progress. At last, Comte thought, empiricism had been made viable. Its cognitive aspirations had been reduced, but now they could be achieved. Though its wings were being clipped, it was still committed to fly.[18]

John Stuart Mill, an admirer of Comte, defends the same view of integration. He too regards knowledge as relative to human consciousness, reality as unknowable, the concept of "reality" as meaningless, metaphysical questions as irrational, and Nature as consisting only in the flow of sense experience. He defines "matter" as the "permanent possibility of sensation."

Mill accepts causality et al in the same manner that Comte did, but in his own variant. His validation of these principles rests on what he regards as the fundamental laws of the human mind—namely, the laws of association discovered empirically. These laws, he says, lead us to expect that patterns observed in the past will continue in the future. And these expectations of ours, he thinks, are sufficient to warrant our belief in causality and thus in the validity of science. Here again we see Kantian *a priorism*: something within our consciousness, some subjective structure or law independent of material objects, is what determines our cognitive process. Mill takes a similar view of logic; its laws, he holds, are suggested by introspective experience, and as such, like causality, are devoid of necessity. Nevertheless, logic, like causality, must be assumed by thinking men if thought is to be possible. Neither Comte nor Mill tolerates any theory ascribing to Nature the acausal or the illogical.[19]

Mill gives concepts the same degree of respect that Comte did, and places on their use the same restrictions. The traditional glorification of reason he sees as overblown; in particular, the praise heaped on Aristotle's syllogism derives from a failure to recognize the argument's uselessness. Occasionally, Mill voices his anti-conceptual animus in sweeping terms: ". . . I consider it nothing less than a misfortune, that the words Concept, General Notion, or any other phrase to express the supposed mental modification corresponding to a class name, should ever have been invented." This statement, however, is some generations ahead of its time; it is not consistently carried out in Mill's (or Comte's) own thought.[20]

In ethics, the most influential expressions of Knowing Skepticism are Comte's Religion of Humanity and the Utilitarianism of Bentham and Mill. Both variants reject the idea that values are based on God or on Nature. Being Kant-inspired, both regard elements within consciousness as the only basis for a distinction between good and evil. What Comte and Mill find within consciousness is not abstract moral principles, but people's concrete subjective desires—the satisfaction of which, therefore, must define proper action. Since these desires are the *a priori* source of value judgments, they themselves cannot be morally judged, but must be accepted as a given. Adapting Kant, most moralists within this movement claim that the satisfaction of such inner promptings is achieved largely by self-sacrifice—for the Goddess Humanity, for example, or for "the greatest happiness of the greatest number."

Like Worldly Supernaturalism, Knowing Skepticism is offered not as a juxtaposition, but as an integration of earlier viewpoints. And here too what makes the integration possible is a hierarchical relationship ascribed to the two elements. In this case, Kant's detachment of knowledge from reality is the base, which is held to make possible man's knowledge of Nature. In essence, the fundamentals of Kant justify (a significant part of) Aristotle. This viewpoint is internally consistent, but here again the reconciliation it attempts has given rise to a number of integrative problems.

Kant had said that an *a priori* conceptual framework precedes and makes possible our sensory experience. Aristotle had said that experience precedes and makes possible any conceptual framework. At the outset, Knowing Skepticism replies that to an extent both have a point. Aristotle is right in saying that empirical evidence is required to validate any truth, including the basic truths that enable scientists to know that the world they seek to study is lawful. But Kant is right in saying that the validation of basic truths is not empirical, but *a priori*. What, then, should a proper integrator take as his start—that is, as his primary cognitive data?

Clearly, many of the reconcilers said, the primary data must be empirical: it is only on the basis of suggestions gleaned from experience that one can discover the principles that are *a priori*. Impossible, replied others, we must start by discovering the *a priori*, since without this knowledge the integrator would be helpless; he could not know how to interpret sense data or which of the suggestions he gleans are reliable. Not true, said others, to accept principles apart from experience—isn't that rationalism? Not really, came the rejoinder; apart from the *a priori*, as Kant has shown, experience leads us nowhere; the integrator cannot interpret sense data if he does not know what kinds of connections to look for or rely on. How, for example, can experiences that a learner does not yet know to be causal lead him, apart from the *a priori*, to the notion that the assumption of causality is essential or even convenient to science?

Then there is the dispute about absolutism. Since the *a priori* is the base of our knowledge, some said, it cannot be undermined by new knowledge; so the integrator must regard the *a priori* principles as absolutes, rejecting any suggestion to alter them. But, others replied, if in fact experience is the primary that suggests the *a priori*, what could prevent experience one day from suggesting changes in it, even radical ones? Perhaps some absolutists answer, we are construing experience here too narrowly; perhaps the *a priori* is fixed because human evolution on purely biological grounds has, after eons of experience, entrenched in us certain assumptions. But then, came the counter, evolution might even now be preparing our minds for a new set of basic assumptions. No, many replied, let's drop Darwin and go back to Comte, contending that the answer lies in practicality—in other words, that the *a priori* consists of those principles that work, that make valid scientific prediction possible. No again, many claim in frustration; who is to determine what is useful to scientific results, but scientists; so the "practicality" answer gives experience the decisive word, and thus the potential to overthrow the *a priori*. Even patterns of empirical data that are constant apart from the *a priori* cannot be known as such, and so cannot be a precondition of knowing an absolute *a priori*. The dispute about absolutism took center stage in the twentieth century, when scientists began to claim that causality does not apply to subatomic particles, or logic to wavicles, or objectivity to parapsychology. This split the reconcilers into three broad camps. One told the integrator to accept such claims if defended empirically and rewrite the *a priori* accordingly. A second told him that, no matter what the claims of empirical support, he must reject these modern attacks on basic principles as an attack on science itself. The third, extending pluralism to new territory, rejected each of these answers as monist. Phenomena, they suggested, are divided into several mutually exclusive parts, each of which may require a different, even incompatible, set of *a priori* assumptions.

This last version of pluralism points us to another aspect of the dispute, this one pertaining to the breadth of *a priori* principles. Comte and Mill had interpreted them as applicable universally, to the entire phenomenal world. But, some argued, isn't it incoherent to ascribe to positivist man, self-restricted to sense data, a capacity to know universal principles, which subsume an unlimited and therefore unperceivable flow of phenomena? Shouldn't the integrator refuse to pontificate about non-verifiable universals and seek out more modest forms of unity to guide him—that is, narrower *a priori* rules? But if so, others retorted, by what means do we decide how much we narrow our principles? Since the *a priori* cannot narrow itself, wouldn't this approach end up turning the *a priori* into no more than an empirically based generalization, and a modest one at that?

As with Worldly Supernaturalism, we see here a variety of thinkers, each of whom is committed to a movement's distinctive mode of integration, yet who interprets it so differently as to offer incompatible answers to a whole series of inescapable integrative questions. Here too, I should add, most of them offer their answers in internally consistent form. The result is a wide range of viewpoints reflecting the relative importance given to each of the mixture's two elements: more or less to the *a priori*, more or less to sense perception. In other words, we see a range of tilts—some toward Kant, others toward Aristotle. And in this we see again the contrast between the mixed approaches and the Big Three, who do not tilt.

The Knowing Skeptics are pluralists who embrace integration, as long as it remains close to the perceptual level. They advise us to seek out unrelated chunks—each made of interconnected data. Such thinkers, we may say, uphold many Ones—many Ones in the Many.

I have chosen Descartes and Comte as the main spokesmen of the two mixtures, because these philosophers represented intellectual turning points, who brought the approaches to the fore. But this does not mean that all advocates of the mixtures derive from these two philosophers. Because the mixed modes open up a wide range of possible interpretations, the mixed advocates have been able to reach the approach by many intellectual routes, and in forms quite different from those of Descartes or Comte.

Integration that is only partially worldly, and worldliness capable of only partial integration. These are the lesser, yet philosophically significant, views to be added to our list of possibilities.

No Mixture Based on Aristotle

If there are mixtures taking Plato and Kant as their base, is there a mixture based on Aristotle? Since no one has ever interpreted Kant as a derivative of Aristotle, the only possibility would be a system justifying Platonism on the basis of Aristotle. This, some say, is precisely the great achievement of Thomas Aquinas in his philosophic upgrading of Nature and reason, which earlier had been despised as the antitheses of God and faith. There are indeed doctrines of Aquinas qua secular that seem to support the idea that his viewpoint is a mixture based on Aristotle. But Aquinas's philosophy, of course, has not only an Aristotelian but also a Christian element, and their conjunction seems inconsistent even internally. Nature regarded as a self-sufficient, inherently lawful primary can hardly validate or even tolerate the inference from its own existence to a super-Nature capable of obliterating it. Nor, if secular reason is man's faculty of knowledge, can an idea reached apart from this faculty be regarded as anything other than baseless fantasy, a conclusion that would deprive the tenets of faith of any cognitive standing. Mixed Platonists, by contrast, have no such problems. A super-Nature, precisely because it is above Nature and its laws, can easily be said to be the source of Nature or of anything else. Similarly faith, precisely because it dispenses with the need for evidence, may obey any—or no—cognitive method, so it can permit all forms of belief, including as one form those reached by reason.

Platonism in short remains internally consistent if reconcilers interpret Aristotle as a derivative of it, but the reverse does not hold. Super-Nature and faith leave plenty of doors open; Nature and reason close them.

Unlike both of the mixtures we have discussed, Thomism offers no hierarchy of the two elements. In fact, Thomas explicitly rejects a hierarchy in either direction: He denies that the fundamentals of Christianity rest on the Aristotelian philosophy, and he denies the reverse. What he offers, therefore, is not an integration but an intellectual division of labor amounting to a juxtaposition of two different systems. His heroic work sought to demonstrate the logical compatibility of these viewpoints, but not their necessary connection. In regard to the DIM theory of integration, therefore, Aquinas cannot be classified even as mixed, because he does not present an integrated view of fundamentals. He is both too secular and too Catholic to be Descartes.

Aristotle's main value to the mixed disciples of Plato and Kant is the ability he gives them to upgrade this world while still holding on to the basic philosophy of their anti-worldly mentor. Thanks to their Aristotelian element, the Worldly Supernaturalists could praise God *and* the scientific observation of matter, while the Knowing Skeptics could embrace *a priori* directives *and* objective knowledge of natural fact. Aristotle, in contrast to both, does not need to boost the metaphysical status of Nature or make room for the senses, because his essence is to give full and exclusive due to both. Any mixture on these issues would not expand an Aristotelian's horizons, but would destroy his mode of thought. If a philosophy endorses two worlds, such as the sensible world and the world of forms, or the phenomenal world and the noumenal world, it has the option of defining their relationship in a variety of ways. But this kind of option Aristotelians do not have.

Leaving aside theory now and considering only facts, it is a fact that in the history of Western thought, from Greece to global warming, we find many different kinds of philosophy, but only five modes of integration. I proceed on this basis.

CHAPTER FOUR

DIM AND THE HYPOTHESIS

IF THE ESSENCE of thought is integration, then the science that teaches men how and whether to integrate is the power that shapes men's thought—I do not yet say culture or history. It is philosophers who do this job, as we have seen, by defining the modes of integration entailed by their own fundamental principles.

The Definition of DIM

I use the term "mode of integration" (or simply "mode" or, mouthful as it is, "integrative mode") throughout to subsume any of the five possibilities, including the opposition to integration, and I refer to my procedure as "modal analysis." Further, instead of mode, I often use "method" of thought or other synonyms when these less technical, more generalized terms can serve the purpose.

The three fundamental modes correspond, as we have seen, to men's three basic integrative alternatives. Plato counseled a philosophic form of invalid integration; Aristotle, valid integration; Kant, anti-integration. This is the source of the trichotomy I define.

I call the Platonic mode "misintegration"—M.

I call the Aristotelian mode simply "integration"—I.

I call the Kantian mode "disintegration"—D.

In order to refer to all three modes together, I have coined the acronym DIM. The order of the letters is the reverse of the historical development and moreover might suggest that my theory reflects some loss of light or even of intelligence. But MID, to my mind, is even worse, because it might suggest that I favor middle-of-the-roaders or moderates. And no other combination of the letters can be pronounced.

I use these symbols freely throughout, whenever they facilitate brevity without affecting clarity. The symbols are used to refer to a mode in the abstract; or to the ideas of those who champion its practice within a delimited field; or to the champions themselves; or to the cultural products that reflect their mode. All of these are interconnected aspects of a single process that, when necessary, can be abstracted from the others for special study. Thus one can speak of a politician's M ideas, or of an I physicist, or of a D novel, or even say that "D claims . . ." and "M responds. . . ."

To accommodate the two mixed cases, I have subdivided D and M. I call the mode of the Knowing Skeptics D_1, as against the pure Kantian D_2; and I call the mode of the Worldly Supernaturalists M_1, as against the pure Platonic M_2. When used without a subscript, the letter D or M refers to the common denominator of its two variants.

The "$_1$," in both D and M, indicates fundamental agreement with the mode of the corresponding "$_2$," along with disagreement stemming from the acceptance of certain I elements. Unlike the D_2s, D_1 thinkers advocate some but not total disintegration; unlike the M_2s, M_1 thinkers regard integration as basically but not always a connection to the transcendent.

Given my symbolism, I myself can be identified, even ridiculed, as a DIM-wit, "wit" in the old sense of intelligence. I accept this designation and even boast of it on my license plate.

Before I can present my hypothesis, I must make clear in general terms to which kinds of people and practices the DIM categories apply, and to which they do not.

Since DIM categories presuppose basic philosophy, they cannot, strictly speaking, be used to classify it; the categories derive from the philosophy. Those who lay the foundations of methodical thought are not guided by definitions of method; on the contrary, they are the source and teachers of method. In a sense, though, one *can* validly apply DIM categories to basic philosophy, if one does so with an opposite meaning—not DIM processes as the source of such principles, but those principles as the source of DIM. Aristotle's system, for example, may be described as I in the sense that, by defining the basis and nature of the I mode, his system makes possible its deliberate use by others.

Since DIM categories identify a mind's chosen method of thought, each symbol denotes a person's epistemological commitment, no less and no more. In order to make such a commitment, the person must have a degree of intellectual bent and feel a need for some form of mental guidance. The bent has prompted an interest in questions of methodology; the guidance he accepts, which is what gives him a DIM status, is his answer to these questions. Without these factors, an individual cannot be subsumed under the DIM categories.

The reason is that no mode can be practiced by accident. A method of integration is too complex a mental phenomenon to be followed with any consistency unless one knowingly accepts it as his mental guide. The difference between the known and the not-known is essential here. By their nature, DIM classifications presuppose the distinction between epistemology and its absence, between viewpoint and ignorance, between policy and chance.

The fact that a practitioner of a mode must know what it is does not mean that he must be a pioneer or scholar of it. In regard to a cultural creator, it requires only that he embrace the mode in a form that enables him to follow its guidance in his own field. Considerable ignorance in this connection is possible: The creator may not know his mode's philosophic roots or implications; he may not be able to articulate the mode's various attributes with the clarity and detail of an epistemologist; he may even (within limits) misidentify its attributes when he moves from creation to analysis; and he may know the modal alternatives he has rejected only in the sketchiest terms. Thus even artists—as a rule the least articulate of cultural creators—know in some terms the modal approach that most of the time they follow. Though they may have little explicit idea of mode or of any non-artistic issues, as we will see, most of the culture-shaping ones know enough to be modally consistent in their work, and even to be vehemently articulate in their rejection of opposed modes.

Because the creative practitioners of a mode, whatever their field, are (in modern terms) "intellectuals" who have made a philosophical commitment, they are typically a relatively small group within a society, but one with a potentially great influence that may in time generate a large movement. As Jesus and Lenin have illustrated in different ways, the group that follows an innovator may grow exponentially. In such cases, which are frequent, certain modal principles become so entrenched that a broad public is able to understand and articulate the mode, and carry out in practice its essentials. Such followers are not cultural creators, and most have no interest in abstract philosophy as such, but they are not devoid of epistemological conviction, either; they are a mass of freshmen, so to speak, who have ingested the rudiments of a course on methodology. The fact that these people are mere followers does not place them outside of DIM classification. The criterion is not originality, but acceptance with enough understanding to make possible modal consistency in a person's own sphere of activity.

Since DIM categories are epistemological, their applicability to a given individual is determined not by his mind's content, but by its method— not by what he thinks, but by why he thinks it.

For example, the concept of D, to begin with that mode, does not apply to the countless people today who are merely non-integrators and know nothing about the issues of epistemology. Such people do not rise above the default state of consciousness—the observation of unrelated data given by Nature or by other people—and therefore come under no integrative category. Because of the nature of the human mind, of course, everyone (pre-historical men included) practices some kind of integration some of the time. But a great many people do not know in any terms that they are doing so, or that there are different ways of doing so, or that they have the power of self-direction in this regard. Instead, they merely absorb random snatches of someone else's way of thinking, prompted by untutored emotions, conformity, childhood habit, and the like. Such individuals have no epistemological identity.

The D individual, by contrast, is not passive or ignorant in the above sense. He is a person who, having grown up in a conceptual culture, rejects it, in part or in whole, practicing concrete-boundedness as a deliberate policy, turning out corresponding products, and justifying his approach on intellectual grounds. Examples of such products begin in the next chapter.

Similarly, an I type of man is not necessarily an Objectivist hero; the DIM symbols do not designate moral character, productive work, or even general rationality. For example, a rational businessman may pursue material wealth, enjoy his earned profit, and refuse to accept a balance sheet covered with the amount of each customer's purchases or with generalized projections said to come from intuition. In the great majority of such cases, however, the businessman does not or cannot identify his integrative process in any epistemological terms; in his mind, what is guiding him is past experience, "common sense," a nose for the practical, knowing how to read people. Such a man has no inkling that the mental steps he takes in his office are related to abstract ideas, or that they have application outside his office. He has knowledge about business, but no ideas about knowledge; he is a good worker in a civilization of whose roots he is oblivious. An I man, by contrast, knows what his mind is doing, and chooses to follow a rational policy as a matter of conviction. I have already given some examples, and will give more in due course.[21]

Most of the time Ms may be described in general terms as religious, but the M category does not subsume every adoption of religion. A vast line of people stretching back to the primitives has accepted sincerely the details, rituals, and leaders of some form of supernaturalism, but with no interest in ideas or in knowing intellectually what they are doing; these people fall outside of any DIM category. And, in the other direction, as we have seen, some individuals, such as Aquinas, have sought to prove God's existence through the use of purely secular logic; such an attempt, however mistaken its result, is not an example of M, but of I. Clearly, if religion—like any other outlook, statement, policy, achievement, or person—is taken out of context, then it cannot be classified in DIM terms; because such classification depends on the methodology, if any, used by the individual to reach his conclusion. An M in religion would see at minimum a connection between belief in a primary supernatural dimension and the need to accept ideas transcending the senses. His acceptance of dogmas and leaders would not be mere obedience, but would to him reflect a chosen mental direction, one built on God, faith, and the imperfection of the worldly.

Now let us note that modal commitment cannot be equated with moral or personal character. Each mode, even those predominantly favored by men of a certain type, has been adopted by many different kinds of men, for many different reasons—in some cases, even by men with opposite kinds of psychology. In regard to modal analysis, such differences are irrelevant.

It is to the modes publicly endorsed and culturally embodied that DIM applies, not to anyone's inner states as such. The latter do lead many individuals wordlessly to love or hate a certain kind of modal product. But an emotion as such has no power over the thought or action of one's society, not unless those who experience it find the words or products to give it definition and appeal. To concretize this point, let us consider for a moment a hypothetical justification of bin Laden given by some Muslim apologist, who explains that bin Laden bombed the United States only for political gain, but that secretly he loved Americans and hoped when in power to bring their system to the Mideast. This concoction, of course, is absurd, but the point is that even if this "inner" bin Laden had been real, nothing in Western history would have been affected. The horror of 9/11 would still have occurred, and its corpses would still be dead—while the method of thought that killed them is still alive.

For the reader's future reference, here are brief summaries of the DIM modes, each described in a few phrases.

Aristotle: Unity through: natural world/grasped by concepts derived from percepts.
I: One in the Many

Plato: Unity through: transcendent world/grasped by concepts independent of percepts; natural world is appearance, and percepts are untrustworthy.
M_2: One without the Many

Worldly Supernaturalists: Unity through: M_2 above, except: natural world is real, and concepts, some or all, must be applicable to percepts.
M_1: Many from the One

Kant: Unity impossible and undesirable; concepts and percepts alike are detached from reality.
D_2: Many without the One

Knowing Skeptics: Unity through: natural world/grasped in unrelated chunks by lower-level concepts.
D_1: Ones in the Many

The DIM Hypothesis

According to Aristotle, man is the rational animal; his mind is the source of his distinctive actions, including his creative ones. The process of creativity, in this view, does not consist in gaining a mystic insight or in reacting to a neural twitch; rather, it is a form of thought. If so, the thought of artists, scientists, and other cultural creators would be like that of men in other fields; it too would be guided by a method, by a mode of integration. And if it is, how can one identify the modes at work in the creators' minds except by studying the existential results of those modes—namely, the cultural products such creators bring into the world? This study defines the program of this book.

"Cultural products," as I use the term, are not academic treatises. Rather, they are things such as the *Aeneid*, the discovery of heliocentrism, Progressive education, the welfare state—i.e., entities that are familiar in some form to the people in a given society and that influence their lives uniquely, in both thought and action. Cultural products in this sense are not theories of aesthetics, but plays, concerti, the David. They are not philosophizing about science, but the publicly known conclusions of working physicists, who tell us about an absolute law of gravity or about big bangs and anti-causal quarks. They are not philosophy of education, but the curricula and teaching methods of the K–12 schools children attend daily. They are not political abstractions, but the behavior of actual governments wielding defined or purposely undefined powers. The sum of such products is the culture of a society.

Philosophy, according to Objectivism, is the fundamental shaper of human life, a role possible to it because it is the subject that deals with the broadest abstractions. But such broad abstractions have little or no reality in the minds of most people, who view them as empty talk. So the question arises: By what means do these abstractions gain and exercise their power over people?

One possible answer, the one I wish to explore, is that such abstractions gain their power through their influence in shaping the mental—integrative—processes of cultural creators; the processes then govern and so are reflected in the creators' products. This kind of influence can be real and sometimes epochal, even if many creators themselves do not know its deepest source. Thus the full definition of a DIM category: a mode of integration derived from philosophic fundamentals that, when it guides a creative cultural process, leads to a product recognizably reflecting it.

Now, at last, I can present the DIM Hypothesis, which is in fact two related theses. The first may be described as cultural, the second as historical.

a) The cultural thesis asserts that, since the Greeks' development of philosophy, cultural fields in the West have produced up to five but no more than five essentially different kinds of products, defined by their mode of integration. In other words, the DIM categories exhaust the alternatives in Western culture.

b) The historical thesis asserts that the West's mode of integration has changed several times across the centuries, and that this has occurred not by chance, but in substantial part because of the logic of modal progression. If we can gain an understanding of this logic, therefore, we will have a basis for a rational prediction about the West's future.

In short and in sum, if the essence of human cognition is integration, then, I hypothesize, an understanding of the West, past and future alike, requires us to identify and interrelate its dominant modes, from Greece onward. Can we find such modes through observation of a culture's products? And if we do find them, can we see a necessity in their historical progression? These are the questions we must answer not by studying DIM theory, but by inquiring into the facts—the cultural facts of real life.

I have said that there will be "up to five" trends in a given time or field, rather than invariably five. This is because cultural products do not spring up automatically, even when a given mode prevails. To originate a mode's application to a specific field takes effort, knowledge, motivation, and some form of independence; men with these attributes cannot be expected to appear everywhere at the same time. Sometimes, indeed, they do not appear at all; the field of education, for example, was stagnant for some four centuries in the modern era, and never reflected the mode of the eighteenth century. In such cases, I think, it is necessary for me to characterize the missing products, at least to the extent that their distinctive DIM category could be objectively recognized if they ever did appear. Otherwise, the DIM analysis of the field would become in this respect vague and inconclusive.

In the historical thesis I state that the West's historical progression occurs "in substantial part" because of the logic of modal progression. This formulation is intended to exclude any deterministic interpretation of history, such as Hegel's; in my view, modes do not progress in some pre-ordained sequence independent of human choices or worldly events. Non-modal factors are indisputably essential to historical change. This fact limits the ability of modal theory to make predictions; but though it limits, it does not destroy that ability, as we will see in part four.

My conclusions at each stage of this study are reached by the only method appropriate to generalizations: induction. Following Aristotle's advice, I start in every era with observed facts in particular fields, and proceed to the lower-level generalizations they warrant; on this basis and in accordance with an ever-growing body of inductive data, I come to ever-broader generalizations at each stage. Only at the end of the inquiry do I reach my hypothesis and claim that it has been proved.

The fact that induction rests on observation does not imply that theory is unnecessary to it; on the contrary, an advanced inquiry must rely on a theory to guide the inquirer. The theory tells him what questions to ask, where to look for answers, and how to know when he has found them. In developing the DIM Hypothesis, my own guide has been the I method of thought—which alone makes possible the very idea of DIM as a means of cultural understanding. A D analyst, who denies the need to identify and integrate essentials, finds within a given field dozens or even hundreds of different viewpoints, most of equal importance to him; he brushes aside broad similarities as empty generalities. An M type dichotomizes: since he recognizes only two real alternatives—the pro-God voices and the anti-God materialists—the differences between D and I are to him insignificant.

Whether the I approach does enable us to answer our questions credibly is something that at this point we do not know. Only induction from observation can tell us that.

By the nature of this book, I must delimit my inductive undertaking (see the preface). I have chosen four fields that I regard as representative of a culture and thus as reasonable test cases for the DIM Hypothesis. Two of these fields pertain to individual thought and reveal the modes of integration practiced by those who mostly create their products alone. The other two pertain to social action and reveal the modes practiced by those whose joint product is the policies and actions of large public institutions.

For the first two, I have chosen from the broad area of arts and sciences, which, apart from the professional schools, constitutes the entire college curriculum. In the arts, I have chosen literature (poems, plays, and novels), because it is the only art whose medium is concepts (words), and thus the only one that provides explicit evidence of its creator's mode of integration. In science, I have chosen physics—or when necessary its precursor or substitute—because physics is the broadest science, the one that studies the nature and universal laws of matter, and thereby provides the base and direction of all the other sciences.

For institutions, I have chosen the fields of education (K–12) and politics. There are more practitioners in these fields than in any others, and these two alone impact incalculably every member of a society, from birth to death.

There are many other fields in which the DIM Hypothesis could be tested, including most of the other arts, humanities, social sciences, and natural sciences. But these other fields, however interesting in themselves, introduce nothing new in regard to the method or results of modal analysis; anyone who applies the method to such fields can discover this fact on his own.

Despite its scope, the DIM theory does not apply to all human endeavors. The main reason is the crucial difference between cultural and what we may for a moment call physical or material products. As Ayn Rand has demonstrated, industrialists are men of the mind who produce wealth primarily by a process of reason and who, therefore, are guided at least implicitly by the teachings of Aristotle. Seen from this perspective, jet planes and computers are every bit as spiritual—every bit as intellectual and philosophical—as the plays of Sophocles or the equations of Einstein.

Although both types of creativity reflect a view of thought, however, only the cultural creators build that view into their products, and thereby express the view in observable form; only cultural products can communicate to us, though not necessarily in words, a <u>philosophic</u> content. By contrast, a physical object as such—however profound the thought of its creator—does not deal in viewpoints and cannot transmit them. For example, the influence of education on children is through curriculum and pedagogical method, not school buildings or machinery, even though these latter make the education possible. Similarly, if science influences people's outlook on the world, it is the proclamations of physicists that do so, not their laboratories or cyclotrons. A revolutionary philosopher like Ayn Rand, it is true, can infer the profound intellectual meaning of a material creator's work, but neither she nor anyone else can acquire such knowledge simply by knowing the product, however thoroughly. In the cultural cases, the intellectual meaning is available to anyone, philosopher or otherwise, who attends to the product intelligently. A cultural product speaks volumes. But even an eloquent material creator can give us only a mute product.

If it were otherwise, the great technological progress of the West since the Industrial Revolution would not have been as impotent as it has been in shaping our course. The automobile replaced the horse and buggy; the computer drove out the typewriter and much else. Each of these achievements, like many others, is in a sense revolutionary; each has changed just about everything in our lives—except the nature of our society and the direction in which it is moving. The automobile takes us more rapidly and comfortably to destinations farther away, but it cannot tell us what destinations are worth reaching; a work of art can. The computer makes a thousand tasks, including communication, easier, faster, cheaper, but the hard drive or the mouse does not tell us *what* to communicate; a fifth-grade teacher does.

There is another reason why I do not apply DIM to the material professions. By the nature of the job, their practitioners are virtually required to have a rational perception of reality; both M and D types would soon be evicted from these fields on economic grounds. The specialized concern of these professions is not abstract meaning, but the concretely practical; so performance in them can usually be judged by direct observation. For example, one can see and even feel the negative effects of a bad dentist; any dentist who ignores individual teeth in order to treat the mouth "holistically," or who casts aside medical and dental principles on the grounds that every tooth is unique, would soon lose his patients. Contrast this with the freedom of a philosopher, whose abstractions are so far removed from experience that virtually no one can identify their practical results; he can embrace whatever mode of integration he chooses and do so without penalty and even with widespread admiration.[22]

Mode Hunts

The first step in modal analysis is not to seek an overview of a culture, but to be specific—that is, to determine whether each individual product we consider does reflect the guidance of one of the five modes. Only if the evidence provides a broad range of positive answers can we go on to identify general cultural patterns.

A product's modal character, if it has one, is to be sought in its essential attributes—specifically, in the method by which its elements are (or purposefully are not) related. I do not define "essential" here by reference to DIM theory—which would be circular reasoning—but independently of it. In fact, in this regard I am deliberately unoriginal, taking as essential only the attributes that creators and observers through the ages have agreed are necessary by its nature to a certain kind of product. For example, in literature I take as essentials story, characters, and theme; in politics, I consider the functions of a government, the source of its authority, the role of the individual, and so forth. If *all* of such essential attributes in a specific product, including their interrelationship, reflect the same one mode at work, I classify the product under that mode.[23]

Since a mode defines a broad abstract category, any given mode, as I must keep repeating, can be applied in different ways by different creators, and thus come to include seemingly unrelated or even opposed products. But differences as such, however abundant or striking, are not relevant to the discovery of mode; only differences with modal implications are significant in this context.

Nor, to repeat, is modal analysis concerned with evaluation. Cultural products can vary enormously in their value, even when they fall within the same mode. In literature alone, as we will see, there are great D_1 novels along with minor or even trashy ones; there are M_2 masterpieces as well as state-dictated tracts; and there is *Atlas Shrugged*, along with a spectrum of Is going down to the pulps. Such differences in value are real and important, but they are not what we are seeking to discover—which is the method of a creator's thought as reflected in his work, not the extent of his skill, genius, or mediocrity.

If we are to use our analysis in the interpretation of culture and history, we must know more than a product's DIM category. The product must also be representative of its era. It must embody something distinctive to a given cultural period, as against being a mere carryover of an earlier tradition. And, of course, to be representative it must be embraced by one or both of the two social powers relevant here: the people and/or the intellectuals—as against being peripheral, unknown, or rejected. In choosing representative cases, I am again being deliberately unoriginal; the products I look at are not esoterica, but the *Divine Comedy*, absolute monarchy, string theory, and the like.

As we seek out modes, we must keep in mind the possibility, discussed in chapter two, of a society with two incompatible modes: one being its new, defining essence, the other a no-longer-defining but still lingering background tradition. We must also keep in mind another fact mentioned earlier—namely, that some signs of the older viewpoint may still be apparent in some products of the new. As in our analysis of the Big Three, however, so here: The essential is what is necessary to the new product's integration; traditional hangovers as such are irrelevant. A continuity of tradition may be highly relevant to understanding why and how a new culture changes, but it does not tell us what the new culture *is*.

In identifying a product's mode, it can often be helpful to consider the views of its defenders, but only if the product is given primacy—that is, only if we first observe and modally analyze the product itself. Any claim of its defenders that contradicts what the product itself reveals is thereby invalidated. Much of the time the defenders are forthright and in agreement; their main value in this context is that they often identify explicitly a relevant but otherwise unstressed or merely implied aspect of a product. Sometimes, however, its defenders misrepresent a product in order to whitewash it, as when totalitarians describe their secret police as agents of freedom. And sometimes the defenders, most often artists, are sincerely in error.

Besides helping to identify a product, its defenders (and detractors) also have historical importance; their assessments are usually factors in people's evaluation of the product, and thus of its longevity and that of similar products. A firm defense or attack, sincere or otherwise, may generate a society's enthusiastic response, even if the evaluation is dead wrong. A weak defense, by contrast, can prove fatal even to a noble cause. Even the silence of commentators can be a factor, if it prevents a potentially popular product from gaining or keeping public attention.

Since I offer the DIM theory as applicable to the West from Greece to the present, that is the time span I shall survey. I am doing it in reverse, however, starting with the post-Renaissance era, from the seventeenth century to the present. My reason is that cultural facts are more fully available in the modern era and more widely known by today's public; so I am using these centuries as a kind of primer. Then I will turn to its prequel, from Greece to the Renaissance.

When our survey is complete, we will have learned something about what (in the existential sense) men have done, but a whole lot more about what they have said. Only a handful of my pages touch on existential events, like the Peloponnesian Wars or the latest presidential election, although these are of undeniable importance. The bulk of the book takes a microscope, or modoscope, to things like the *Iliad*, the theory of relativity, the Declaration of Independence, and the manifesto of Summerhill.

The popular bromide, which has its uses, tells us that actions speak louder than words. But in regard to understanding culture and history, does it still apply? Indeed, is it possible that the bromide is in reverse?

Let the mode hunt begin.

PART TWO

DIM IN MODERN CULTURE

CHAPTER FIVE

LITERATURE

BY LITERATURE, I mean works of fiction presented by means of language, such as poems, plays, and novels. The serious artworks of this kind to which a society responds are eloquent evidence of its soul. Since the modern world was ushered in by the rediscovery of the ancients, it is hardly surprising that the dominant school in seventeenth-century literature, classicism, extols the ancient classics. After centuries of medieval mediocrity, writers in this period could not but feel "nostalgia for . . . [the] order and reason" of past greatness.[24]

The men of the Renaissance had greeted the new secular treasures with an excited anticipation of further achievements to come in their own time. In this first post-Renaissance century, however, the nature of literary ambition changed; the classics, it came to be thought, could never be equaled, let alone surpassed. The artist's function then is to imitate the Greeks and Romans by adhering to the aesthetic values and principles embodied in their works.

Classicism

Since a work of literature consists in essence of events enacted by characters, usually with an overarching theme, a literary school's mode of integration is to be found in its treatment of these three aspects.

In classicist dramas (for example, those of Corneille and Racine), there are few events for the audience to observe. As a rule, any action takes place offstage, and the audience learns of it only from a character's narration. Moreover, in the name of good taste and serenity of outlook, many kinds of actions, however dramatic they might be, are rejected. There can be no violence onstage, no fights, no crimes, not even a crowd scene.

The central concern of these plays is not the characters' physical action; it is their mental state, such as their feeling of romantic love, rage at injustice, passion for liberty, or despair at the decrees of fate. These feelings are not dramatized onstage. There are no events like a balcony scene in which a woman is wooed and seduced before our eyes; instead, there is a man's recitation of love poetry. And even the poetry for the most part is delivered without much emotion; the passion proclaimed is always polite and decorous. The speeches are clear, logical, precisely worded, and elegant. They are the poetry of love or despair, but not its reality.

To the extent that there are events onstage, there is not much progression among them, because, according to classicist rules, the play as a whole must be set in a single location and must occur within a twenty-four-hour time period (these rules were based on the classical unities of place and time). So the viewer gains virtually no knowledge of how or why the characters have reached their present desires and conflicts. We come in only at the climax, watching without context as the protagonist's desperate struggle is stated, elaborated, and resolved. In effect, the audience sees the end of the story, but not the beginning or middle. "We see on the stage," writes the anti-classicist Victor Hugo, "only the elbows of the plot, so to speak; its hands are somewhere else." "Nothing really happens . . ." English professor Paul Landis sums up, "only endless talk, some impassioned duologues and soliloquies, and more long analytical confessions to characterless confidantes. . . . In a sense these plays do not really tell a story at all."[25]

The themes of classicist plays are indicated by the kind of struggle that is typical of the main characters. Almost all of these are torn by the same, agonizing conflict: their sense of honor versus some beloved personal value that, they believe, cannot be countenanced by their honor. The theme is the conflict between virtue and desire, between duty and selfish-ness. Being highly moral, as their authors understand the concept, the heroic characters usually struggle against the lure of self-assertion, in order finally to embrace the rigor of overcoming the self.

In some cases, the hero, even though he chooses duty over desire, nevertheless does gain his desire; so the ending is happy. More com-monly, he is stoic in the face of tragedy. Either way, however, the hero, especially in Corneille, *is* a hero; he is self-directed, responsible, unflinchingly courageous, and proud of his ability to be guided by his rational faculty, rather than by baseless feelings.

In their depiction of both events and characters, classicists uphold the values of simplicity and concentration. Their plays almost always present a single situation; subplots are not allowed. The characters reveal their torture in that situation and their strength in wrestling with it. Since the range of a man's qualities and the details of his situation cannot be included in a work thus concentrated, the playwright cannot portray them. The result is that both events and characters, though in part con-cretely real and even compelling, are also, insofar as they are "simple," the opposite of concrete. Largely, we see the same abstract type of character facing the same abstract type of problem, in plays that in these ways do not vary significantly from one another—not, for example, as *King Lear* does from *Othello*.

This tilt toward abstraction was not regarded by classicists as a flaw, but rather as another aesthetic requirement: universality. In their "Intro-duction to Neoclassicism," the English department at CUNY elaborates: these artists "consciously emphasized common human characteristics over individual differences . . . [aiming] to articulate general truth rather than unique vision. . . ." Universal characterization of this sort often gives abstractions in their plays primacy over concretes. For instance, the uni-versal conflict of man—their theme of duty versus desire—often strikes one as the real protagonist of the proceedings, which is reflected in the individual players' goals and behavior, not the other way around. Such an impression is heightened by the fact that the substance of the play is a flow of beautiful concepts (language) largely unrelated to perceived action.[26]

Classicist writers defended their approach by reference to a set of values that in their eyes defines artistic excellence. These values, though suggested to them by the works of antiquity, were regarded not as inductive generalizations from these, but rather as objective requirements of art validated not by inference from percepts, but by intellectual intuition—that is, by rationalist deduction from *a priori* self-evidencies. Besides those already mentioned, the values thus intuited included order, clarity, reason (the Apollonian element versus the Dionysian), balance, symmetry, idealism, nobility, dignity, and unity. The analogy to the prisoner in Plato's cave is apparent: Prompted by observation (in this case, of the works of antiquity), one ascends to the Forms (the concepts defining aesthetic merit); intuition, appealing to these abstractions independent of observation, finally clarifies and validates the progression.

Plato's prisoner proceeded all the way to the Good. Classicist playwrights, however, do not typically deal with religious topics. Rather, they are concerned with applying their abstractions to their own concrete aesthetic creations. Here they faced a version of the problem faced by Descartes and Spinoza: how to apply concepts independent of the worldly to worldly art; or how to infer dramatic specifics from floating abstractions. The answer given was: by deduction from them. By this method, "emotional restraint" led them to the deliberate avoidance even of vivid imagery. "Unity" led to the confining unities of time and place. "Dignity" required an elevated style of writing that eschewed commonplace words such as "knife," "cow," and "dog." (The French were shocked by the appearance in *Othello* of a handkerchief.)

The most eloquent statement of the classicists' general viewpoint lies in their own official definition of it; their credo is the elevation of form over matter. In this context, form denotes the rational, abstract, and immutable rules that logically precede and govern a play's matter; matter denotes the flux of worldly emotions, struggles, and events that the abstractions of form integrate. The playwright, accordingly, was cautioned always to follow the abstract rules, even at the expense of artistic individuality and originality; to disregard form, in this view, was to embrace the non-objective, the non-beautiful, and the non-rational.

The classicists are not pure Platonists. Despite their fundamentals, they do not dismiss concretization as trafficking in unreality. To these moderns, the perceptual world conveyed by the dramatist, though structured and made intelligible by transcendent rules, is still an important reality. These artists do not write medieval morality plays; they do not present onstage hypostatized concepts, but rather try to dramatize the role of these in the lives of observable men and events. Although their Platonism, as we have seen, subverts such an attempt, it does not fully negate it. So far as they can, given their base, the Classicists do show us onstage living, feeling individuals.

Platonism as the ground of an earthly embrace—in my language, that is Worldly Supernaturalism. The classicists do achieve unity in their works, by means of retaining the Many occurrences and characters onstage, but subordinating them to *a priori* form. Thus the M_1 approach: the transcendent One leading to and ultimately integrating the earthly Many.

The classicist approach, renamed neoclassicism, dominated eighteenth-century literature as well.* In England, its most famous representative was Alexander Pope. The historian Will Durant tells us that, in Pope's *Essay on Criticism*, "he laid down with magisterial finality the rules of literary art," which Durant says are in essence, "to make the goblet more precious than its wine."[27]

Although French playwrights are the most eloquent exemplars of the period's literature, other writers combine their admiration of the pagan classics with a different kind of commitment, such as a passion for Christianity. The greatest of these, part classicist and part Puritan, was John Milton, whose epic *Paradise Lost* was from its first release a sensation.

No one could describe this work as decorous, static, or emotionally restrained. I consider Milton here to illustrate a principle often discussed earlier: that there can be striking differences among examples within the same modal category. I want to concretize this fact once, at the beginning of our mode hunt. But since I am not writing an encyclopedia, this is the last time. I do not again offer such a repetition of any modal analysis.

---

* Since I classify trends by their epistemological fundamentals, I ignore any "neo" or "post" prefixes attached to the name. In my context, they are always irrelevant.

From the outset of *Paradise Lost*, we know that Satan is doomed to lose his war against God, who is supreme, immutable, the source of all existence, and, like Plato's spiritual sun, invisible, even, Milton says, "[a]midst [His] glorious brightness. . . ." As in Augustine, however, God is not static, but an active being with an all-encompassing plan. Besides these descriptions of God in terms of abstractions without perceptual content, the epic also suggests that God experiences a few emotions related to concretes, such as His passion for obedience, His demand for revenge, and His love for his Son. These emotions, although stated more than dramatized, give this Platonic entity some quality of human personality and thus of specificity; we may fairly describe Him not as a pure abstraction, but as a quasi-abstraction.[28]

Of the Son we are told even less; he is introduced only as "The radiant image of [God's] Glory . . ." and stresses the fact that he has no desires of his own. Repeatedly, this 99 percent pure abstraction, more devoid of specifics than His Father, declares that he is nothing but the executor of whatever God wants. Of course, these divine entities and their interrelation, as Milton recognizes, can be known only by faith.[29]

The most astonishing character in the poem is Satan. This defiant demon—who rebels against God in the name of freedom from tyranny, of "Hard liberty before the easy yoke / Of servile Pomp"—is presented by Milton the Puritan as the incarnation of evil, and at the same time by Milton the heir of the pagans as admirable and even heroic. In concretizing Satan's evil, Milton mentions but does not stress the demon's pride, malice, and guile. But in concretizing Satan's virtue, Milton does not pass over it quickly; he stresses Satan's strength, his intellect, his inventiveness, his courage, and even his sense of morality, shown by his regret over the necessity, inherent in his war against God, to seduce Adam and Eve. This character surely is the protagonist of the story, the initiator of the action at each turn, whereas God is passive; in effect, He puts out fires and voices disapproval from the sidelines.[30]

Given so full a portrayal of his thoughts, feelings, and actions, Satan in the poem is the opposite of any kind of floating abstraction; he is not "sinfulness," but a worldly, conflicted individual and individualist. Adam and Eve, though lesser characters, also earn Milton's approval for their earthly concerns and success: They are happy at work, relish their food, revel in the beauty of Nature, and are blissful when making love. The portrayal of these two is so detailed that even their hairstyles are described. Of course, in the end, they and all their issue are stripped of their love of life. But even so, they are not crushed by the expulsion, because, Milton tells us, though Paradise for them was no more, after Paradise "The World was all before them. . . ."[31]

Despite all this secularism, of course, God in the epic is still the fundamental reality: the creator, the ruler, the judge, and the winner of all contests. But from this, Milton (though with some inner conflict) comes to the opposite of the medieval conclusion: If this world is a creation of God, man must love it. Indeed, he muses at one point, Earth may not be so different from heaven after all: "what if Earth Be but the shadow of Heav'n, and things therein Each to other like, more than on earth is thought?"[32]

The epistemological counterpart of Milton's metaphysics is his view of the relationship between worldly observations and religion's *a priori* abstractions. The Christian's non-experiential framework, Milton holds, must be tied to men's actual experience; we must come to understand how that framework explains what we see around us, especially the many evils we see. This in fact was Milton's stated purpose in the poem: to justify the ways of God to man. A pure supernaturalist can simply write off human experience, including worldly doubt and evil; a Worldly Supernaturalist cannot.

There are obvious contrasts on all these issues between the French classicists and Milton. One approach minimizes physical action in favor of spiritual life, while the other revels in physical and even violent action, because it ultimately reveals the supremacy of the spiritual. One offers characters who are partly but not fully melting into abstractions, while the other paints richly detailed characters ruled by divinely pure abstractions. These two approaches obviously do not conceive the One and the Many in identical terms. But they do agree in regard to their basic principle of integration: The Many are real and connected, because they derive from an *a priori* One.

M$_1$ literature in this period displays many other versions of Worldly

Supernaturalism, with many different answers to such questions as: How extensive and restrictive are the rules of form, and to what extent should importance, albeit secondary, be ascribed to content? What is the proper balance in a literary work between physical events and abstract moral issues? How specific can a character be and still be universal? Such disagreement, we may say, reflects a classicist's tilt: toward the transcendent or toward Nature. Given our discussion of mixed modes in chapter three, this is just the kind of variation we would expect. I cannot say who is the most Christian of the post-medieval M_1 writers, most likely an early Renaissance figure. But Milton, with his admiration for the worldly and even for Satan, would appear to be the end point in the other direction, after which there is M_1 literature no more.

Romanticism

It was against classicism that the Romanticist writers rebelled. Their approach dominated Western fiction from the late eighteenth to the mid-nineteenth century, and some of it still exists today, albeit in an antagonistic cultural environment. Although there were many famous Romanticist playwrights (for example, Edmond Rostand), the movement's best showcase is its novels, such as those of Victor Hugo and, later, Ayn Rand. (The novel by this time had become the leading form of literature.) The Objectivist view of Romanticism has been stated in detail by Ayn Rand. I shall indicate here only those aspects necessary for a DIM analysis.[33]

The Romanticists rejected authority in aesthetics, classical or divine, in favor of the independent judgment of the artist. "As for himself," writes Hugo, the great Romanticist spokesman, "he prefers reasons to authorities; he has always cared more for arms than for coats-of-arms." The long tradition of classicism, which claimed to embody reason, is thus to be rejected—in the name of reason. Clearly, Hugo's view of reason is not that of the classicists.[34]

The most obvious anti-classicist features of the new literature are drama, excitement, and emotion that is *not* restrained. But this does not provide Romanticism's definition, merely a lead to it. Emotions are not a primary; they presuppose value judgments, which in turn presuppose a man's choice of values. Such choice is possible only because man has the faculty of free will. Thus Ayn Rand's definition: "Romanticism is a category of art based on the recognition of the principle that man possesses the faculty of volition."[35]

Romanticists reject the idea of determinism—of man as a puppet, whether of outer or inner, material or spiritual forces; they regard the individual as self-made and self-directed. Since he is ruled by values he has chosen, he is the master of his own destiny, in the sense that nothing inherent in his own nature or in the nature of reality can threaten this mastery. He is an efficacious being with at least the potential to triumph in his pursuits.

The classicists, too, held an uplifted view of man and did not think that he was a puppet. The differences are that man's freedom to choose values is not the basis of the classicists' approach, but merely an important attribute of their protagonists, and that their hero typically fights to *defeat* a desire of his regarded as unchosen. The Romanticist hero, by contrast, is intoxicated by his own goals; he is defined by his wholehearted use of his faculties to gain and keep what he desires.

Romanticist characters are often articulate in identifying their goals, their reasons for them, and the obstacles they face. But they reveal their values primarily by their actions. Like those of Rostand's Cyrano, their speeches, even when poetry, are not poetry to be savored as an end in itself, but statements, however elegant, that lead to or flow from *action*, whether in a play or in a novel. Action here pertains primarily not to the classicists' inner emotional conflicts, but to existential conflicts fought against opponents in this physical world. Typically, internal conflicts in a Romanticist work do not lead to agonized paralysis, but are resolved in the arena of physical action.

Although the Romanticist writers, in their exercise of art's new freedom, throw aside the traditional rules of form, their works do have a definite structure. To dramatize a man's commitment to his chosen values, the author typically presents us with a purposeful character, who then encounters antagonists and mounting obstacles that he fights righteously, with every power at his command, until his final triumph or defeat in the climax. Since the factor shaping the action and outcome is the characters' choice of values, the climax does not depend on chance, but follows logically from the earlier choices already presented.

Ayn Rand finds the distinctive attribute of Romanticist works not in their characters or themes, but in their plots. A plot, in her definition, "is a purposeful progression of logically connected events leading to the resolution of a climax." So the author of a plot, she says, must devise

> a sequence in which every major event is connected with, determined by and proceeds from the preceding events of the story—a sequence in which nothing is irrelevant, arbitrary or accidental, so that the logic of the events leads inevitably to a final resolution.

Aristotle makes a similar point; a proper story, he says, must have "all the organic unity of a living creature." The pattern of an ordinary story, Ayn Rand (paraphrasing E. M. Forster) once told a class, is: The king died, and then the queen died. The pattern of a plot is: The king died, and *because of it* the queen died. The second event did not merely happen to follow the first; rather, given the context, it *had* to happen. The first case exemplifies juxtaposition, the second integration.[36]

As the quote from Aristotle indicates, plot is not exclusive to the works of Romanticism, which is a nineteenth-century movement. In chapter nine, we will see some of its important predecessors.

The protagonists in Romanticist works are often described as larger than life; they are certainly not the folks next door. These writers have no desire to present the world as it is—which to them is not much more than the product of the undistinguished or even decadent choices men happen so far to have made. The Romanticists are moral idealists; they present things not as they are, but, in Ayn Rand's words, "as they might be and ought to be." "Might be" means that the work cannot flout the laws of reality; "ought to be" means that it cannot dispense with values. Aristotle, Ayn Rand observes, was the first thinker to state this viewpoint: "The distinction between historian and poet," he writes, "consists really in this, that the one describes the thing that has been, and the other a kind of thing that might be. Hence poetry is something more philosophic and of graver import than history. . . ." I should mention in passing that Dostoevsky—a negative Romanticist, if you will—expresses moral idealism by presenting and denouncing what ought *not* to be.[37]

How can Romanticists create a hero who is larger than life, if they know men only from observation? They cannot turn for guidance to the Form of Man offered by Plato, who regards individuality as unreal and human heroism as hubris. Nor, as artistic rebels, can they turn to establishment models. They have no option but to follow the method of Aristotle: abstraction from sense experience. The Romanticist separates out one attribute (or more) from his observations of people as they are, an attribute that in the real world coexists with many others that are irrelevant to it, or may even contradict it. Then, setting aside these irrelevancies as non-essential, the writer is able to embody the selected attribute (good or evil) in his characters in purer, more consistent form than is found in life. He *stylizes* his characters; in accordance with the needs of his plot, he presents the traits that flow from their choices. Thus are heroes created by observing non-heroes.

Because these writers are committed to observation of their fellows and to individualistic heroes, their characters, though created conceptually, are not interchangeable giants, but unique concretes. Contrast Francisco d'Anconia in *Atlas Shrugged* with Jean Valjean in *Les Misérables*, and both with Cyrano de Bergerac. Then, in regard to the issue of unique versus semi-generalized, contrast all three to the protagonists of Racine's *Phaedra* or of Corneille's *Cinna* or even his *Le Cid*.

Romanticist literary works typically exhibit three interrelated forms of unity. Events have the unity of plot; characters, the unity of stylization; and the work as a whole, the unity of <u>theme</u>.

To Romanticism—at least during the height of its period—a writer's abstract meaning, his work's theme, however wide or narrow, is what guides him consciously or subconsciously in the process of selection; he chooses the characters and events necessary to communicate his meaning. The characters and events are the work's concretes, while the theme, the guiding abstraction, is what unites them into a whole. Most artworks

of cultural significance—even the disjointed chronicles of old, with their
hit-and-run praise of some leader—have had themes of some kind, but
these have often been rather loosely (and sometimes virtually not at all)
connected to the concretes of the work. Only Romanticism uses theme as
an all-encompassing integrator, which it could not do if the events of the
story and the traits of the characters were viewed by the writer merely as
juxtapositions.[38]

Classicist dramatists also offer themes—for example, that honor is
superior to love. But for them themes do not have a comparable integrative role. The reason is that the content of the play—its events, characters,
and even its meaning—though presented as necessary, is regarded as secondary. Theme, in this view, may be important, but it belongs to a play's
matter, not its form, and matter is not what creates classicist unity. For
the Romanticist, the reverse is true. If the free choice of values is what is
to shape a play, then its matter—what the characters do and what that
means—has primacy over its form, which is conceived now not as ruler,
but as derivative, merely as the means by which the matter is presented.
Form, in the Romanticist view, follows function. In Hugo's words, form
"has no laws to impose on the drama, but on the contrary should receive
everything from it. . . ."[39]

A novel, Hugo states, is a secular undertaking, based on the observation of Nature: "There are neither rules nor models; or, rather, there are
no other rules than the general laws of nature. . . ." As an approach to
literary art, this means that Romanticism does not rely on the supernatural. Most Romanticists did believe in some form of the divine, but this
was irrelevant to their method of interrelating the elements of their
books. The connector of their events was not divine purpose, but the logic
of natural cause and effect as men observed it. The source and connector
of a character's traits was not grace, but earthly free will. The theme was
not an abstraction uniting semi-abstract characters, but an abstraction
whose concretes the audience grasps from the body of specifics that these
works present. Even when, as in Dostoevsky, a Romanticist's theme is
deeply religious, it is presented in this secular fashion: not by floating
abstractions, but by offering observations of men—observations stylized,

then integrated by the inner logic of a plot structure into a broader meaning; his message is unworldly, but his method is not.[40]

Romanticism in literature is a consistently Aristotelian approach to the relationship of the One and the Many. The work is its content, made of the real Many concretes in the novel or play; but it is a Many so connected by the author as to be a One, a secular One created by man's integrating process. Such a One has no transcendent connotation, and no reality apart from the Many. It is a One in the Many—the I formula.

Naturalism

Although the integrative method of the Romanticists was rational in the Aristotelian sense, these artists did not identify their work in this way. Accepting as their explicit philosophy the Platonic dichotomy of reason versus emotion, which they had inherited from the classicists (among others), they tended to equate their rebellion, their own emphasis on values, with an embrace of emotionalism, subjectivism, even Oriental mysticism. This is a classic case of a mode's practitioners buying into the claims of an opposite viewpoint, and thereby trying to justify their own mode in reverse. Such a defense of Romanticism soon led to its predictable result: the rise of the next dominant literary movement, Naturalism, which held sway in the West from the mid-nineteenth century well into the twentieth (and is still the mainstay of non-genre popular literature). Its writers range from Tolstoy and Balzac (Realists, in the earlier terminology) to Zola, Flaubert, Somerset Maugham, and many others.

Naturalists, rejecting emotionalism, identify their works as the embodiment in literature of reason, though not in the classicist sense. If novels and plays are to be expressions of reason, they hold, they must be empirical descriptions of people and their behaviors as they actually are. The author should regard himself as a recorder, a camera, a reporter. "A novel," said French novelist Stendhal as early as 1830, "is a mirror walking along the road." Or in Zola's famous phrase, the function of a novel is to present a "slice of life."

The standard by which literature is to be judged, therefore, is fidelity to observable fact. The artist is to present his material without imposing on it preconceptions, selectivity, or moralizing; as many of the later writers put it, he must emulate the scientist, aiming at the same unbiased, value-free objectivity. So he must dispense with the traditional artist's purpose of uplifting his audience, whether by poetry or by heroic action. On the contrary, if truth is the standard, then every aspect of life should be presented without comment, including the sordid and the ugly. As Chekhov put it: "To a chemist nothing on earth is unclean . . . he must know that dungheaps play a very respectable part in a landscape. . . ."[41]

The Romanticists' basic principle—that literature should be based on the fact of man's free will—is dead wrong in the eyes of Naturalists. To them, free will is an empirically groundless, metaphysical concept, and thus an anti-scientific one; the same conclusion applies to the concept of value, which was held to have no basis in sense perception. The truth, say the Naturalists, is that men are moved not by choices or values, but rather by forces outside their control. These forces are almost always construed as social in nature.

To Naturalists, characterization is the essential task of literature; the theory, however, leaves room for a spectrum of different interpretations of this task, according to the width of abstraction regarded as legitimate. Thus we find such diverse writers as Tolstoy and Sinclair Lewis, Balzac and Upton Sinclair upholding the same Naturalist principles, while offering themes such as the timeless and universal plight of the adulteress as against some specifics of small-town American life in the 1920s—or the essence of France as manifested across decades in its every class and corner as against the conditions of the American meatpacking industry at the turn of the century. As a rule, the more universal writers regarded the narrower ones as trivial, while the narrower regarded the more universal as detached from reality.

The Romanticists, stylizing their characters, presented only essential traits. Naturalists, by contrast, whether they favor wider or narrower abstractions, do not distinguish the essence of a character from accidental or irrelevant features. The concept of essence, too, is metaphysical. To sense perception alone, a man is simply everything he does, feels, and says; since all of these are equally real and observable, all of their instances deserve the same attention from the writer. The literary goal, therefore, is to reproduce factual detail on a scale far beyond anything that previous schools had found worthwhile or, indeed, had ever imagined.

Naturalists reject the idea that writers must explain their characters, beyond reproducing without comment whatever reasons the subjects themselves sometimes give. The idea of a unifying explanation lurking beneath the observed data is again metaphysics; a photograph does not explain its subject, but merely records the visible surface. In Naturalist novels, there are no necessary relationships among a character's various ideas, traits, and actions. He acts as he does only because "that's the way these particular people are." Since most men, however, do have some underlying motive(s) binding some aspects of their behavior, Naturalists generally do present or imply some logical connections between their characters' traits and actions, albeit within a framework of disconnected, irrelevant facts. This makes their characters recognizable figures and not merely collages of details.

Naturalists regard action in a story primarily as a peg on which to hang characterization. They reject the concept of plot, regarding it as incompatible with the artist's task. The carefully worked-out structures of the Romanticists are seen as artificial and contrived. Life as it really is, they say, is not neat and logical, but messy and random, and this is a fact that honest literature must record. What we actually observe in our lives is merely human events that follow one another; we see juxtaposition, not necessary connection.

Despite these disclaimers, most Naturalists do tell a story, by including in their books, as part of their observations, some essential connections among events; unlike the Modernists, they do not offer a stream of alogical or acausal occurrences. But just as there is no essence of a character, so there is no essence of their story lines—that is, no logic dictating a progression from beginning to middle to end. In Turgenev's novel *On the Eve*, for example, a young fighter for freedom prepares to do battle, falls in love, has the bad luck to be caught in the rain, and before he can set out for the war, dies from pneumonia, at which point the novel ends.

Turgenev's justification of such a sequence of events is simply that these things have happened.

Naturalist theory opposes the idea of theme. The writer is not to bring an interpretive or evaluative framework to his art; he should disdain propagandists, proselytizers, and purveyors of "messages." In many cases, however, the beliefs of Naturalist writers are passionate and do show up in their work; this amounts to offering a theme. When a consistent naturalist does present a theme, however, it is intended not as an expression of the author's value judgments or selectivity, but simply as a description of empirical fact. Such a theme cannot be used methodically as a guide to the writer in his selection and integration of the work's elements; in his hands, a theme is merely a fact he has observed among all the other facts. When he lights on a broad enough fact, however, a naturalist's theme *can* serve to integrate some aspects of his book's elements—that is, he integrates in chunks, and thus provides his book with a certain level of abstract meaning.

Sinclair Lewis, by no means the most anti-conceptual of these writers, states the Naturalist viewpoint in regard to literary style. "The generic concept" of style is "metaphysical and vain" because of its breadth. Stylistic issues can be judged only in terms of particular sentences, without reference to general standards.[42]

Naturalism represents the first modern rebellion against the requirement, upheld by classicists and Romanticists alike, that a work of art be a fully integrated product. Like the positivists in philosophy, Naturalists repudiate—in regard to characters, story, and theme—the quest for a full integration. They too uphold only partial conceptualization—integration in chunks, as I have called it—within the framework of an otherwise random flow of people and events. Here again—as with classicism, but in a different form—we see a spectrum of tilts: "Some integration" poses the question, "How much?" Such a spectrum is impossible to any school whose aesthetic requirement is full integration.

Naturalists hold that "reality" is a metaphysical term, concepts are suspect, and explanation is impossible; but they also contend that they can discover and depict objectively observable truths about men. This is

Knowing Skepticism. The Naturalist avows his allegiance to the Many, certain aspects of which are connected by a number of unrelated Ones.

Naturalism represents Ones in the Many—the D_1 mode.

Modernism

The Modernist movement, although rejected by the public, has dominated Western culture for more than a century now. (Most American intellectuals, lagging behind Europe, did not embrace it until the 1930s.) So-called postmodernism, which arose after World War II, is, as others have observed, merely Modernism carried further; since there is no philosophic significance to this "post," I ignore the distinction. Among many acclaimed Modernist figures, too well-known today to need identification here, the most eminent, I would think, is James Joyce.

Modernists reject all previous approaches to art—classicist, Romanticist, and Naturalist alike. The features required by traditional literature, in John Barth's words, are "naive pretensions of bourgeois rationality." The rejection of such pretense, a trio of Canadian academics notes, means "the rejection of plot and character as meaningful artistic conventions; and the rejection of meaning itself as delusory." [43]

Modernist writers are contemptuous of books that tell a story. They regard as artistically worthless any presentation of man in purposeful action in the world, whether by a Romanticist or a Naturalist. Plot, an English professor at NYU explained to my daughter in 2004, is a contrived editorial intervention on the part of the author. Instead of imagining some progression of events, many Modernists turn inward to offer unstructured collages of their own or their characters' mental contents—for example, stream-of-consciousness novels, replete with a flow of moods, memories, literary allusions, dreams, images, and the like.

To the extent that Modernists' books do include existential events, these are virtually devoid of connection and offered even out of intelligible sequence. Connections are castigated as "linear," and are replaced with juxtapositions, frequently in defiance of both logic and causality. For example, in one play by Georg Kaiser, an Expressionist popular in the Weimar Republic, a man's refusal to eat his pork chops leads without explanation to his mother's immediate death. The movement's rejection of connection is not merely implicit; it is stressed explicitly. If a work of literature were to have a beginning, middle, and end, Gertrude Stein observes, then the work "would be of necessity and in relation and that is just what a master-piece is not." Thus even the Naturalist's delimited chunks of integration disqualify his work from consideration; in art, connection as such means "pedestrian."[44]

"The 'theatrical principles' of Absurdist drama," English professors Donald Heiney and Lenthiel H. Downs elaborate,

> are primarily reductive (not only anti-Aristotelian like Brecht but anti-play): . . . plot is minimal if there is any, place and time are often reduced to any place and any time, language or dialogue is minimized, made absurd, close to being eliminated. . . .[45]

Modernists use several other techniques to eliminate story. They may present an event simultaneously from multiple perspectives, with no indication of which, if any, is correct. They often reject chronological progression, so that the reader cannot know even the order, let alone the interrelationships, of events, if any. They blur dream and reality. They deliberately inject irrelevant elements—such as etymological information—in the midst of a dramatization, in order to kill a story while telling it.

The same Modernist approach rejects characterization as well. Again, there are many techniques of elimination, including characters with no attributes, such as Kafka's nameless cipher, and characters whose behavior is unreal because it is bizarre, such as Hans Castorp in Thomas Mann's *Magic Mountain*, who feverishly adores the X-ray of the tubercular lungs of the woman who has spurned his love. For Naturalism, the unanswered question is: Why does a character act as he does? For Modernism, by contrast, the reader asks: Who is acting and what is he doing? Is the narrator the child of a dead father or is he the father of a dead child or is death supposed to be unreal or is it the only reality?[46]

If one were to try to abstract from Modernist works a recurrent theme of some kind, it would have to be their campaign against man—specifically, against the depiction in art of man, whether heroic or average, as a being who pursues values. On the contrary, these writers hold, the man who lacks values or, better, who embraces anti-values, the depraved man, is literature's proper subject, and he is all of us—not the man of achievement, but the man who is barren or even psychopathic; not confidence, but disorientation; not beauty, but the repulsive. So the universe men inhabit, as we are regularly shown, is a hell of pain and doom.

In describing these ideas as Modernists' themes, I am contradicting their own stressed rejection of theme. A literary work, they often say, is not a telegram; it should not have a message to convey, any more than events or characters. In place of theme, these writers often disperse random non-objective symbols and obscure literary allusions throughout their books, which only literary insiders can decode. The fact that their symbolism is unclear is not a problem for them, but a virtue; only philistines ask what a book is about. To be serious, Modernism holds, an artwork must be ambiguous, elusive, enigmatic, indeterminate, opaque, all of which words are indispensable in the lexicon of literary praise today.

Opacity is most distinctively achieved by Modernist writers through their use of language. Alone in the history of literature, they reject the rules of rational linguistic usage, often down to the need for capitalization and punctuation. Amidst known words, they are wont to insert neologisms; instead of linguistic continuity, they feature non sequiturs; scornful of grammar and syntax, they often come up with random juxtapositions of sounds, known as word salads. A much admired example of these techniques is the soliloquy of Molly Bloom, a previously silent character, at the end of Joyce's *Ulysses*. Her utterance consists of a single sentence without punctuation that runs to about 2,500 words.

Their embrace of opacity indicates the extent of the Modernists' opposition to integration. Works made of unrelatable non-elements cannot be grasped by the conceptual level of consciousness—or even by the perceptual level, which at least gives us, as it does an animal, a world of clear-cut entities. What the Modernists seek to evoke in the reader's mind is a flow of the purely unintegrated—that is, of a newborn's random, momentary sensations.

At times, Modernists sound a bit like classicists when they say that style or form is what counts in art, and that that is why they dismiss content. For the classicists, however, form has primacy because it is what determines the proper presentation of content, and it can do this, they believed, only because the rules of form are logical and objective. For the Modernists, the supremacy of form means the elimination of content in the name of the illogical and the non-objective. The difference is: form respected as a rational guide versus form flaunted as a sanction for destruction.

Destruction is the essence of the Modernist creed. What these writers acclaim and produce are negatives: non-story, non-hero, non-character, non-meaning, non-grammar, non-language, non-objective, non-representational, non-intelligible, non-rational. This is not a mixed viewpoint, attempting to blend Kant with the conceptual orientation of the Greeks, but an uncompromising declaration of war against the Greek method of thought.

Disintegration, writes Ayn Rand,

> is the keynote and goal of modern art—the disintegration of man's conceptual faculty . . . [T]o reduce man's consciousness to the level of sensations, with no capacity to integrate them, is the intention behind the reducing of language to grunts, of literature to "moods," of painting to smears, of sculpture to slabs, of music to noise.[47]

A nihilist, we have said, is one who works non-venally to destroy man's mind and values, who smashes not weeds but roses, and does it for the sake of smashing, who elevates nothing above something as an end in itself. If he directs his actions to a specific field, he works to eliminate all the essential attributes of that field's product, leaving in their place nothing but the smashed remnants. The contribution of Modernism to literature is the demand for non-literature.

If one grasps the connection between Modernism and disintegration, it will come as no surprise that the father of Modernist art is generally recognized to be Kant through his *Critique of Judgment*, his treatise on art. For Modernism, following Kant's anti-conceptualism to the end, there is no longer a One, not in any version, but only a militantly unrelated Many. Modernism, as Barth observes, represents the "frustration of conventional expectations concerning unity"; its exponents prefer the disjointed to the unified—D_2.[48]

Socialist Realism

The literary schools discussed so far developed during the freer centuries of the modern era. In the twentieth century, a different school of thought with its own distinctive position on art arose primarily in Russia and Germany: totalitarianism. Although the two versions of this approach agreed on essentials, the Communists were by far the more intellectual; for example, they defined literary standards and required writers to follow them, whereas the Nazis, as has often been noted, mostly preferred to burn books rather than to write them. This kind of difference helped to make the Communists far more influential and long-lived in the West. In every field, accordingly, my analysis of the totalitarian mode will be drawn from the Communist version, with only occasional reminders of its Nazi counterpart.

The official literary theory of Communist Russia, Socialist Realism, was conceived in the 1930s by Maxim Gorky; its acceptance by writers was quickly mandated by Stalin. For fifty years, any other form of literature was prohibited.[49]

Socialist Realism, like Modernism, presents itself as a rebellion against all previous literary movements. Unlike Modernism, however, what it condemned was not representation or objectivity in art, but rather the thing it regarded as the root of all evil, "bourgeois individualism." The school of Romanticism, therefore, with its praise of the heroic individual, was seen as thoroughly false; so was Naturalism, with its aim to describe impartially the average individual; and so was Modernism with its subjectivism, which this movement interpreted as the unleashing of a writer's individuality. In place of the individual, the socialist realists' primary was the group; in place of impartiality, they required the writer to make value judgments; and in place of subjectivism, they upheld what they called "realism."

Plato was the first to regard art as a didactic tool, to be evaluated by its effectiveness in the task of creating a better society. The Communists accept this viewpoint, and apply it to their own concept of a better society. The purpose of art, they say, is the dissemination of socialist thought. A proper work, in Gorky's view, must conform to three criteria: It "must represent the interests of the people . . . further the cause of the Party, and . . . have sound ideological content." Novels and plays must be designed to energize the proletariat in its class struggle, extol the Communist Party, and develop in people a social consciousness to replace individual consciousness.[50]

Writers thus become social engineers, working with and for the state to create an unprecedented kind of idealism; their idealism is their enthusiastic desire to be absorbed into the group. Even if some individual does achieve a great feat, therefore, it is counter-revolutionary to write a book about it, or perhaps even a sentence. For example, when seven fliers rescued passengers from an icebound ship in the Arctic, *Pravda* asked: "Is it necessary to repeat the names of the seven . . . ?" For Communists, *Pravda* explained, "The main character in Soviet literature consists of people," people in the mass, "not heroic archetypes from nineteenth or early twentieth century literary tradition."[51]

Despite the above, Socialist Realism did sometimes endorse what it regarded as larger-than-life heroes. But these men were not the individualists of Romanticism; they were super-Communists in body and soul. For example, the Stakhanovites were said to perform superhuman feats of labor precisely because they were not mere individuals, but rather perfect embodiments of the collective strength; as such, they were also perfect exemplars of "selfless devotion ('predannost') to the bolshevik party."[52]

The stories told in socialist realist works were not expected by the state to be original; on the contrary, a few approved stories were regularly repeated, often with only the names changed. These stories almost always begin with class struggle, against either world capitalists or their local remnants or, during World War II, against the Nazis, who were regarded as capitalist agents. The struggle presents the grievous exploitation of the proletariat and culminates in its triumph and revenge after a heroic battle. The collective, the stories made clear, is able to triumph because of the support and guidance of the party. These stories were often described by official commentators as optimistic, because the proletariat always wins; the party suffers no defeats.

In fact, however, the party did suffer defeats, some of which were publicly acknowledged by Russian leaders during regime changes, but this fact did not disturb these realists. They found little difficulty in reconciling party omnipotence with party failures—even while still claiming to be realists. Their explanation of this feat lies in their concept of realism. Like Plato, though in their own variant, the Soviets distinguished two kinds of events: those pertaining to daily life, and those pertaining to reality; the two realms, they believed, may contradict each other. Thus even when it appears that Communists are losing, that is only appearance; in fact, they may *really* be winning. (I will explain their version of this view in chapter eight.)

Characterization for this school is the depiction and praise of an exploited collective, which feels and acts as a unit. In a story by Aleksandr Fadeev entitled "Young Guard," one character, who has performed a good action on his own, confesses his error: "It was a bad thing to act the lone wolf. Brave and clever, but by yourself, bad." Individuals who did appear in a story were given no distinctive characteristics, no motives or traits that would make one character stand out from the others. Rather, all were depicted as having a single, ideological concern: to bring about the triumph of their political system. Often, the language of these characters sounds not like dialogue, but like the reading of a government proclamation; sometimes, as part of a story, an actual Kremlin speech was read aloud, then distributed to the audience. For characters of this kind, a choice between the self and the social is no choice; they are fascinated by the industrial development of Siberia, but indifferent to their own lives or to anything the West would regard as personal. Thus the wisecrack by an anti-Communist that the essence of this literature is "girl meets tractor."[53]

The characters in these stories have often been criticized in the West for being cardboard or unreal. This charge is valid if reality is conceived in Aristotelian terms, as a realm made of concrete, perceivable entities. But that is not the realm these characters inhabit. Devoid of individuating attributes, they are presented as the opposite of perceivable concretes, as indistinguishable fragments of a collective entity transcending its individual components—that is, an entity that is an abstraction transcending the perceptual world. The story then consists of abstractions in battle. An unperceivable entity, the proletariat, collides with another such (the bourgeoisie), and does so in order to attain still another such (the "withering away of the state"). Novels and plays with such content do not present the actions of people; they present a ballet of Platonic forms.

Although the protagonists of classicism are part abstraction, they nevertheless retain a real element of individuality, because we see that they have personal desires and are torn by personal conflicts. They are concretes subverted by Platonism but only up to a point. In the case of Socialist Realism, however, abstraction takes over completely.

The products of Socialist Realism, by definition, feature a philosophical theme. In many works of earlier centuries, a writer's theme functioned as his guide in selecting and integrating the concretes in his work. In the Soviet books, by contrast, the theme does not integrate concretes because, in truth, there are none; rather, the theme integrates abstractions into a defense of the ruling ideology. In this sense, the socialist realist work is the meaning that it conveys; put otherwise, the theme is the work. Whereas Modernism rejects the idea of theme, Socialist Realism rejects everything but theme. The Modernists throw out conceptual integration of sense data, and are left with disconnected sensations. The socialist realists throw out, as counter-revolutionary, reliance on sense data, and are left with a system of connected floating abstractions—the One without the Many, M_2.

————

From this point on, I refer the reader to the chart at the back of the book, which can profitably be consulted as an aid to memory, and as a help in grasping the interconnections of the increasing number of results of our mode hunt. The chart indicates those results tersely by offering a name or phrase, not as a definition but merely to assist the reader in bringing back earlier material. I include a time frame for the dominance of the different modes, with the understanding that such temporal estimates are ballpark approximations, so that within limits there is a range of legitimate options. But this detail is irrelevant in the context of a broad historical perspective.

CHAPTER SIX

PHYSICS

THE FIRST SYSTEM of physics after the Renaissance was that of Descartes, whose approach dominated science in France and Germany, and to a lesser extent England, from the mid-seventeenth through the early eighteenth century.

The error of science like Galileo's, the Cartesians said, was its reliance on induction. To generalize from observation, they argued, is merely to describe what we perceive without explaining it, whereas the latter is the true purpose of science. So science must proceed in the opposite direction. It must begin with axioms stating first causes—that is, with axioms identifying the fundamental elements and laws of the physical universe—and then deduce from these axioms the facts we observe. A physicist interested in gravity or light, for example, should not begin by conducting experiments, but rather by answering basic questions, such as: By what physical mechanism does the gravitational force propagate? Or, what is the fundamental nature of light? The answers to such questions, the Cartesians held, are *a priori* and self-evident; we know the truth of these axioms intuitively because they are "naturally implanted in human minds."[54]

The resulting physics is a variant of the later Plato's Pythagoreanism: Descartes attempts to explain the physical world as a derivative of pure mathematical quantities. Taking as axioms several such *a priori* principles—including, for example, the principle that matter is composed of three types of elementary particles differing only in size, shape, and movement—Descartes deduces, in his words, the "explanation of absolutely every phenomenon that we observe in the heavens above us," along with the explanation of sublunary phenomena ranging from earthquakes and volcanoes to magnetism and the tides.[55]

In physics as in philosophy, Descartes elevates the transcendent and the conceptual *a priori*, but holds on to the reality of this world and to the importance of using concepts to explain our perceptual observations. After the explanations, the world of the physical Many, in his view, is united; it is so because the physical Many and the conceptual system necessary to grasp them are derivatives of an antecedent, nonphysical One.

Clearly, Descartes' physics is M_1. It is not, however, the actual beginning of modern science, but rather its short-lived precursor. We will soon encounter an M_1 physics incomparably more sophisticated and influential.

Newton

Descartes' physics was given a deathblow at the turn of the eighteenth century by the man universally regarded then and since as the creator of modern science: Isaac Newton, whose physics, in both method and content, ruled the field for two centuries. Among his many achievements, Newton was the first to identify three fundamental Laws of Motion along with his best-known discovery, the Law of Universal Gravitation.

The method by which he made his discoveries, Newton writes, is induction, the method Descartes opposed. Induction for Newton is essentially generalization validated by two processes: experimentation and then the mathematical interpretation of its results. Although each of these had been necessary to Galileo's work, and implicit in that of a few others, it was Newton who first identified the combination explicitly, and who first declared the two processes, if used together properly, to be necessary and sufficient to define the method of science. Newton thereby banished from physics any attempt to reach truth by deduction from *a priori* ideas, which in his view were arbitrary, subjective, and non-scientific. It was Newton who committed science exclusively to the study of fact: empirically based, precisely quantified, and therefore objectively demonstrated.

In Newton's interpretation, each of the two crucial processes is a form of uniting percepts by the use of concepts. Experimentation is based on, though it is not the same as, observation; mathematics is an interrelating of concepts, but not of pure concepts. Given this union of body and soul, as we may put it, it is not an accident that Newton's famous inventions include calculus, to expand the power of the mind, and the reflecting telescope, to extend the range of the senses.

Before Newton, most empirically minded investigators regarded science as the passive observation of physical regularities; the task of the scientist was to record (and then by speculation try to explain) the data manifest to anyone simply by inspection. Such an approach, though it involves language and even theory, may be described as perceptual-level, since its provable content does not extend beyond perception. Experimentation, by contrast, requires not merely sense perception, but also an antecedent process of creative thought. On the basis of past experience, a scientist conceives a question unanswerable by obser-vation alone, then conceives a physical procedure by means of which, through observation, he can wrest the answer from Nature. The experi-menter reaches such answers by the control of variables, which enables him to eliminate irrelevant factors and thereby isolate the cause actually at work. In this way, past percepts make possible a conceptual develop-ment that then makes possible the extraction from percepts of a fuller meaning.

For example, interested in the relation between white light and the colors, Newton eschewed the popular rationalistic answers. Instead, he beamed sunlight into a small circular hole and thence through a prism onto a wall. Surprisingly, he saw no white circle on the wall, but rather an elongated spectrum of colors, which had been refracted by the prism. Newton concluded that white light is a mixture of the colors, which are the primary forms of light. This fundamental discovery, which he verified by other experiments, is inaccessible to perception alone or to thought alone. It was made possible only by a complex interrelating of concepts and percepts.

In the early stages of experimentation, as of observation in general, only qualitative information can be gained. For such information to lead to knowledge of scientific law, Newton held, it must be identified in abstract and in particular mathematical terms—specifically, as a relation of quantities expressed in equations. Once such equations have been established on the basis of observation and experimental data, Newton showed, the scientist, by mathematical reasoning alone, can extract from those data many otherwise inaccessible implications—which sometimes reveal laws so new to us that the experimenter himself, apart from the mathematical interpretation, could not even have imagined them. To Newton, in short, science is essentially a form of conceptualizing observational data.

The best-known example of the power of such conceptualizing is Newton's discovery that the force of gravity between two objects diminishes according to the square of the distance between them. How could one reach such an unexpected conclusion? Newton started with observations of the planets and his first two Laws of Motion, experimentally established; then, using nothing but geometry and differential calculus, he deduced an equation, the Law of Circular Acceleration, then combined it with one of Kepler's empirical laws of planetary motion. At this point he was able, using algebra alone, to demonstrate—though not yet completely—his revolutionary Law of Gravity. Later he demonstrated that the law applied not only to the planets circling the sun, but also to the moon circling the earth, as well as to the apple falling to the ground. The law, he induced, applies not merely within the solar system, but everywhere.

Descartes too had regarded mathematics as essential to science, but Newton is no rationalist, and there is nothing pure about his equations. Mathematics, in his view, is only a tool devised by men to help answer questions about matter. Equations, accordingly, are scientific only because they are not pure. It is only because mathematics is not transcendent—only because it is a description of relationships among physical objects—that it can enable us to predict their actions.

The number of facts that Newton's approach enabled him to explain is legendary. To explain for Newton means to integrate facts to their causes. Relying for the most part on his Second Law of Motion combined with the Law of Gravity, he did this repeatedly, thereby making understandable for the first time phenomena ranging from Galileo's discoveries to the cycle of the tides to the movement of comets, and much more. Facts that had appeared to be disconnected were seen to be necessary parts of a growing cognitive whole.

His method, Newton sums up,

> consists in making Experiments and Observations, and in drawing general Conclusions from them by induction . . . and in general, [proceeding] from Effects to their Causes, and from particular Causes to more general ones, till the Argument end in the most general.[56]

Newton was often told that his confidence in induction was misplaced. Any inference from some to all, his critics held, is illogical, since there is always a possibility of instances yet unknown that differ from the ones so far encountered. Newton's famous answer was: "I frame no hypotheses." By hypothesis, Newton does not mean an idea suggested but not yet proved by observational evidence; he himself regularly began his inquiries with such ideas. Rather, he means an idea lacking *any* observational basis. Such ideas, by definition, are arbitrary, since they are concepts unrelated to percepts. As such, they have no relevance to science, because they defy the essence of scientific method. It is only the acceptance of such hypotheses, Newton holds, that can render induction suspect. The critic tries to undercut a generalization not by adducing relevant data, but by saying, in effect: "Maybe something somewhere contradicts it." But his "maybe" rests on nothing but baseless imaginings. Newton had no patience with this mentality:

> We are certainly not to relinquish the evidence of experiments for the sake of dreams and vain fictions of our own devising . . . [I admit] of no Objection against Conclusions,

but such as are taken from Experiments or other certain
Truths . . . if no Exception occur from Phaenomena, the Conclusion may be pronounced generally.[57]

Science, in short, is not a tentative local map, but a launching pad to
rocket man through the cosmos.

Living in the seventeenth century, Newton believed firmly in God,
thereby introducing a major contradiction into his writings. As we did in
interpreting the Big Three, however, we must strip away such traditional
carryovers in order to grasp the essence of his thought. The proper standard of classification, as we have seen, is new integration; by this
standard, the essence of Newton the physicist is clear. With a few exceptions, Newton himself grasps the difference between his science and his
religion, and holds that physics and the transcendent are not only separate, but also *independent*: "neither affects the other," he writes; "God
suffers nothing from the motion of bodies; bodies find no resistance from
the omnipresence of God." A God who does not affect physical motion is,
to the science of physics, an irrelevancy.[58]

Newton called his secular One his "System of the World," the Many
motions so far known being connected by a few interrelated universal
laws. And those laws, far from creating the physical Many, exist only as
similarities among them.

Here again, this time in the area of physics, we see the I perspective.
The One is real, but only as the One in the Many.

Positivism

The first challenge to the Newtonian approach, positivism, developed in
the mid-nineteenth century, and influenced physicists through the early
decades of the twentieth. It was even more popular among chemists; the
standard textbooks were unanimous in treating the new viewpoint as
uncontroversial. Two of the movement's best-known representatives are
Ernst Mach (physics) and Marcellin Berthelot (chemistry).

The positivists regarded Comte's epistemology as the definition of scientific method. The world consists of sense data; percepts are the only means of knowledge; the unobservable is metaphysics; concepts, including those of mathematics, are merely a convenient shorthand; science is the description of regularities that happen to occur, but not because they are "necessary."

The scientist, therefore, must delimit the questions he may legitimately consider. He can ask how things happen, but not why; the "how" is observable (it pertains to the phenomenal world), but the "why" is not (it would pertain to the now rejected noumena). As historian Benjamin Brodie states the theory: "We cannot ask what water is, only what it does, or what it becomes. We have no means of grasping the underlying reality of things, and so should content ourselves with the accurate description of what things do. . . ."[59]

The idea of a reality underlying a world that is made solely of appearances is a contradiction. As David Harriman puts it, "it makes no sense to investigate appearances that do not appear." The first thinker to make this point, unsurprisingly, was Kant: "Natural science," he wrote, "will never reveal to us the internal constitution of things, which, though not appearance, yet can serve as the ultimate ground for explaining appearances. Nor does . . . science need this. . . ." Science, therefore, must abandon the age-old quest for explanations; our experiences must always remain an unintelligible given. This is true, Mill adds, even when, as Newton did, we have discovered universal laws of Nature, because: "What is called explaining one law of nature by another, is but substituting one mystery for another. . . ."[60]

"All positivist theories," notes Russian philosopher Igor Naletov, "invariably started from some sort of denunciation. . . ." Such denunciation was regarded as a means of housecleaning; every room of science had to pass the test of empirical purity. In 1835, Comte had written that since we can never perceive the chemical composition or true mean temperature of the stars, these are outside the province of science. For the same reason, all the fundamental entities once upheld as explanatory were denounced by the Comteans, including the "forces" of Newtonian mechanics and the "waves" of electromagnetism. The Naturalists in literature rejected the attempt to look beneath the psychological surface; positivists rejected the attempt in regard to the physical surface.[61]

The bête noire of the nineteenth-century positivists was the still-developing atomic theory. As the German chemist and positivist Friedrich Kekulé expressed their view:

> The question whether atoms exist or not has but little significance in a chemical point of view; its discussion belongs rather to metaphysics . . . from a philosophical point of view, I do not believe in the actual existence of atoms. . . .

"Who has ever seen a gaseous molecule or an atom?" asks French chemist Marcellin Berthelot. ". . . I do not want chemistry to degenerate into a religion; I do not want the chemist to believe in the existence of atoms as the Christian believes in the presence of Christ in the communion wafer."[62]

If all knowledge is perceptual, what if any is the role in physics of concepts? Conceptual frameworks, Ernst Mach stated—if taken as a means of knowledge beyond sensations—are fictions. But such fictions may in the early stages be useful as an aid to memory; their value is mnemonic, not cognitive. But, Mach adds, however helpful in the beginning, abstractions must soon be discarded: "The object of natural science is the connexion [sic] of phenomena; but theories are like dry leaves which fall away when they have long ceased to be the lungs of the tree of science." In this context, Mach recollects that when he was fifteen, Kant's *Prolegomena to Any Future Metaphysics* made "a powerful and ineffaceable impression upon me, the like of which I never afterward experienced in any of my philosophical reading."[63]

In rejecting forces, atoms, fields, energy, and the like, the positivists were rejecting the quest for broad integration in science, since such integration had never been possible apart from a basis referring to these unobservables. Only the "metaphysical" scientists had been able to interrelate a wide variety of data, data that had earlier seemed to be obviously unrelated. By contrast, non-metaphysical scientists had no basis to look for or even imagine a connection between the course of Halley's comet and the shape of the earth, or between falling bodies and magnetic repulsion, or between the Law of Multiple Proportions and the laws of electrolysis.

Having written off universal laws, though, the positivists did not give up the quest for any physical law; instead, they restricted science to the discovery of relatively narrow generalizations on or close to the perceptual level. They did not deny that the scientist could discover some linkages enabling them to unify some delimited segment of observed data—as long as these chunks of unity were modest in scope and understood to be unconnected to other such chunks. The lawful segments, in short, must not be taken as elements in some general system (which they equated with rationalism). Many chemists at the time insisted on such non-connection; for example, they held that it would be a huge error to try to integrate chemistry and physics.

Since the positivists allow a level of generalizations less than all-inclusive but more than non-existent, it is no surprise that there are many differences among them as to the proper scope of scientific laws—in other words, as to the extent of the connections we can discover among percepts. Positivists like Comte and Mill believed that they had found certain universal laws; Mach and Carnap, by contrast, regarded such claims as invalid, because impossible to a consistent positivist. And there were many variations in between—just the kind of variations we would expect within a mixed mode.[64]

Although positivists in science dismiss reality and seek out only relatively narrow generalizations, they do require that the discoveries scientists make be objective. Qua Aristotelian, they demand that the conclusions reached by science be demonstrable not by appeal to any supernatural entities (including pure numbers) or to anything innate, but by reference to observed facts. Qua Kantian, these physicists and chemists are skeptics.

Positivists champion the Many while still finding unity, in the form of internally related chunks, each unrelated to the others. Their formula is: the Ones in the Many—D_1.

Einstein

The positivist movement did not last long. Abstract theory, physicists came to believe, is indispensable to physics; it is not a cancer to be removed, but the heart of the subject. But the proper theoretical approach, these moderns hold, is not necessarily Newton's. The most influential of the new theoreticians, the giant in the twentieth century's radical reshaping of physics, was Albert Einstein.

Einstein was a champion of integration, always looking for fundamental principles expressed in the widest abstractions. In later years he sought, though unsuccessfully, to find a Unified Field Theory, which would subsume everything known in physics. His aim, he said, was "to obtain a formula that will account in one breath for Newton's falling apple, the transmission of light and radio waves, the stars, and the composition of matter."[65]

Einstein's first major step in this direction was his theory of special relativity, which illustrated, as early as 1905, the nature of his break with Newton. Special relativity begins with the observed fact that lengths, times, and masses, as measured by an observer, vary according to his motion relative to the body being observed. Hendrik Lorentz had earlier attempted to explain these variations by hypothesizing physical factors operative in these contexts. Einstein rejected this approach, and instead formulated a series of mathematical equations. These equations, he said, are not empirical, but nevertheless from them the observed variations in measurements can be deduced. So observed numerical relationships (physical measurements) can be derived from antecedent and different numerical relationships—that is, from abstract equations that are not physical entities. This, in Einstein's view, is sufficient to explain the physical data; explanation by reference to physical causes is unnecessary.

The same tilt toward abstraction is evident in the foundation Einstein gives to special relativity. Besides the physical discoveries of Newton and of his great descendant James Maxwell, which Einstein accepts, he introduces into physics a new, axiomatic fundamental: the constancy for all observers of the speed of light. Again, he seeks no physical explanation of this fact, and offers for it no empirical basis. He does not even invoke the groundbreaking 1887 experiments on light performed by Michelson and Morley. His method of validating the axiom is to relate it not to fact, but to other ideas, and he does this in essence by consulting aesthetic criteria. For example, Maxwell's electromagnetic equations, he says, would be simpler and more beautiful if combined with the light postulate; so on that basis alone the postulate deserves to be part of the foundation of physics.

Despite his tilt away from perceptual data, Einstein in 1905 had not yet fully escaped the positivism of his earlier years. Since, according to special relativity, each of us can know length and the other attributes only as they appear to him relative to his state of motion, all such attributes, he concluded, are subjective. Length in itself thus became unknowable (noumenal) and so a dispensable idea; the only objects real to us are objects as measured (phenomenal). Although positivism was never fully cast aside by Einstein, it did not take him long to reject anti-conceptual and subjectivist conclusions such as these.

In 1908, Hermann Minkowski introduced the concept of space-time, which, purely by mathematical inferences from the light axiom, he proved to be invariant—that is, the same for all observers regardless of their state of motion. This chain of deductions reinstated for Einstein an objective physical world. Thereafter, Einstein described himself not as a phenomenalist or positivist, but as an objective realist.

Here again, we see Einstein using the method of deduction from *a priori* axioms. In this case, such deduction is man's means to discover the very existence of physical reality and also to correct the deceptive appearances that seduce us on the purely observational level.

Combining special relativity with the classical legacy in physics, Einstein went on to deduce an extension of his theory; by applying it to accelerating frames of reference, he reached general relativity, which deals with gravity. The new theory subsumed the earlier, which was now merely one of its instances.

General relativity exhibits the same philosophic orientation as its predecessor, because gravitational attraction for Einstein is not in essence physical. Newton was wrong to think that there is a force of gravity pulling things this way and that, he says. Rather, gravitation results from an interaction between the two constituents making up Nature: matter and space. Combining Newton's observation-based laws with a set of *a priori* mathematical equations, Einstein deduces that space is not characterless, as Aristotle had held, nor the same everywhere, as Newton had held. Instead space has a geometrical (curved) structure, which both affects the movement of matter and is affected by it.

On the one hand, the structure can cause material objects to accelerate, which is what we identify as gravity; on the other, a body large enough can warp the space around it, thereby requiring other bodies to follow the new curvature. According to Einstein, all these interactions are knowable, because all of them can be derived from mathematical axioms. From his equations, he says, he can deduce the structure of space at any time and place, and one can then deduce how space and matter will affect each other. These deductions are possible, according to general relativity, because space is a non-physical entity. It does have definite attributes, but all of them are quantitative in nature and can be stated as a set of equations. Space in Einstein's sense is not reducible to relationships among physical objects; it is not a sum of places; it is a purely geometrical entity, a form of mathematics.

Clearly, Einstein and Newton disagree fundamentally about the nature of mathematics. For Newton, mathematics is a tool created by man. For Einstein, mathematics (space) is half the universe. For Newton, mathematical equations are valid because they describe physical facts learned ultimately by observation. For Einstein, mathematical equations are valid because they belong to a certain self-contained, *a priori* system of numbers. For Newton, to explain an event is to discover its physical cause. For Einstein, to explain an event is to discover its equations.

Physical causes, according to Newton, have the power to explain an event only because they are the antecedent factors that produce it. Presumably, then, equations can explain a physical fact only because _they_ are the antecedent power. This sort of metaphysics—which would reflect the perennial connection of *a priorism* and idealism—seems to be implicit in

Einstein's viewpoint and often explicit. It is especially evident in his theory that space has causal efficacy in regard to motions. Since space, in his
view, is a form of mathematics derived from a series of equations, its
causal efficacy means that equations are an essential factor in creating
motion. So numerical relationships are not only a precondition of knowing the physical world, as in special relativity, but an active constituent
within that world.

The world of Nature is still regarded by Einstein as real. But in his
theories, we see the beginning of the takeover of Nature by mathematics,
which means: the subordination of perceptual fact to a transcendent
realm of concepts. Since this implication is the antithesis of positivism,
Einstein soon described himself as a rationalist.

Einstein defines rationalism in traditional terms. "Physics," he writes,
is "an attempt to grasp reality as it is thought, independently of its being
observed." "There is no inductive method," he says, "which could lead to
the fundamental concepts of physics. . . . Logical thinking is necessarily
deductive. . . ."[66]

What if reality as it is thought should conflict with reality as it is seen?
"The demonstrations [of physics] are so certain," wrote Descartes, "that
even if our experience seemed to show us the opposite, we should still be
obliged to have more faith in our reason than in our senses." Einstein was
once asked what he would have done if a certain prediction of general
relativity, already confirmed at the time, had been mistaken. He replied:
"Then I would have been sorry for the dear Lord—the theory *is* correct."
There is a jocular element in this answer, but also, I think, something a
bit more serious.[67]

Einstein disagrees with the view, held by earlier rationalists, that the
foundational postulates of scientific deduction are intuitively self-evident,
given to man either by God or by Nature. On the contrary, Einstein holds,
the scientist has no absolutes to guide him. He chooses his starting points
from an array of possibilities, and does so not by a process of cognition,
but by an act of will; the "basis" of physics "can only be attained by free
invention." Even "the great Newton," he remarks, did not grasp this truth.
One necessary test of the validity of these free inventions, Einstein holds,
is their ability to make accurate empirical predictions, but this is not a

sufficient criterion, because predicting a fact is not the same as under-standing it.[68]

The additional requirements of axioms are mathematical (the simplic-ity and unity of one's equations) and aesthetic (the axioms' beauty, ele-gance, symmetry). It is remarkable how similar Einstein's criteria for physics are to those of the French classicists for art, remarkable until one considers their modes. Whatever Einstein's criteria, however, his free inventions, by his own statement, cannot be proved. As physicist-philosopher Max Jammer, one of his admirers, observes, Einstein's phys-ics is ultimately "supported by an attitude that is 'akin' to religious faith."[69]

One of the major rationalist problems, as we have seen, has always been to understand how it is possible to derive percepts from concepts independent of them. In Einstein's version, the question takes the form: Why do conceptual structures adopted by will, without reference to the physical world or even to mathematical necessity, have the power to explain the world? Einstein does not evade this problem: "the eternal mystery of the world is its comprehensibility."[70]

If Einstein had denied the reality of the physical, he could have adopted a purely Platonic solution to the problem. His favorite philoso-pher, however, was not Plato but Spinoza. However much Einstein ele-vates theory above observation, he remains a scientist. As such he accepts the reality of Nature and the importance of understanding it. It is the facts we perceive, he often tells us, that he is trying to derive from his postulates. His rejection of empiricism is not a rejection of empirical data; on the contrary, like his forebears in the Cartesian tradition, he views it as a crucial part of his task to connect his *a priori* framework to the world of sense.

The danger in rationalism, Einstein states, "lies in the fact that in the search for the system one can lose every contact with the world of experi-ence." "Why," he asks elsewhere, "is it necessary to drag down from the Olympian fields of Plato the fundamental ideas of thought in natural science, and to attempt to reveal their earthly lineage?" His answer: "In order to free these ideas from the taboo attached to them [by Hume and Mach], and thus to achieve greater freedom in the formation of ideas or concepts." That Einstein "drags down" to earth his fundamental ideas is

his otherworldliness; that he believes it is necessary to do so is his secularism. And that he seeks to combine these two elements—that is the
evidence of a mixed mode at work.[71]

Here again a mixture leaves open a range of incompatible interpretations, varying according to tilt. Thus we see significant differences among
physicists, each of whom remains faithful to the Einsteinian approach.
There are differences as to how many and what kinds of free inventions
to permit; how the criteria of valid axioms should be defined, some plac-
ing more emphasis on mathematical or aesthetic requirements, others on
empirical fruitfulness; and whether the axioms are impervious to future
empirical developments or not.

And there are differences in regard to the place in the universe of matter itself. Whereas Einstein had regarded space (the mathematical-
Platonic element) and matter (the secular-Aristotelian element) as entities
equal in metaphysical status, many of his later followers pushed this balance in the Platonic direction. Why not, they asked, make space the primary and construe matter as a mere derivative of it? At this point, M_1 was
moving perilously close, but not yet all the way to M_2. The "concept of
space," writes one historian of physics, has "seized totalitarian power in
a triumphant victory over the other concepts in theoretical physics."[72]

The One, in Einstein's physics, is a transcendent system of *a priori*
equations that underlie, interrelate, and explain the Many real concretes
of this world. Like that of Descartes, though in a very different way, Einstein's mode is the Many from the One—M_1.[73]

Quantum Mechanics

Although Einstein's early positivism was a major influence on the next
movement, quantum mechanics, he rejected the central ideas of its leading exponents—Niels Bohr, Werner Heisenberg, and Erwin Schrödinger.
Despite this fact, quantum mechanics dominated mid-twentieth-century
physics and is still regarded by those in the field as an essential compo-
nent of any physical theory.

At the turn of the twentieth century, light, which had earlier been conceived as a wave and thus as continuous and spread out, was found to exhibit the discrete nature of particles. Similarly, electrons, earlier conceived as particles and thus as discrete entities with a specific position, were found to have some of the characteristics of waves. Thus arose the wave-particle duality: Waves, it seemed, have some attributes of particles and vice versa, which by the definitions of each seems to be a contradiction.

To deal with this problem, Bohr in 1927 put forth the principle of complementarity: Even though wave and particle are incompatible descriptions of an entity, they complement each other, and together provide the entity's full description. The two perspectives, in the words of historian of physics Dugald Murdoch, though "mutually exclusive," are jointly complete. In making a measurement or interpreting an experiment, therefore, a physicist is free to use either perspective; one model, he will find, works in some situations, the other in others. Since each model thus applies only within its own delimited context, Bohr concludes, no contradiction is involved in using both.

But how, traditionalists asked, can the same entity have mutually exclusive attributes? Which is it really—a wave, a particle, or something else? These questions, Bohr replied, are invalid; they arise from the attempt to visualize or in some other way physically interpret subatomic phenomena—and physics has no means of doing such a thing.

What physics in this theory can do is implicit in Heisenberg's uncertainty principle, according to which subatomic measurements are necessarily vague. The reason is that the physical interaction required to measure a "wavicle" changes its measurements. In the best-known application of the principle, two types of measurement become, in effect, adversaries: The more precisely a scientist measures the position of a subatomic entity, the vaguer his measurement of its momentum, and vice versa; he can never know both these attributes precisely at the same time.

A physicist, Heisenberg goes on, agreeing on this point with positivism, cannot in principle go beyond the perceived. The positivists of an earlier period, however, were old-fashioned; still working largely within the traditional framework, they had rejected only specific unobservables, such as atoms, but not the entire classical outlook. Quantum mechanics has no such ties to tradition. If a precise position and momentum at the same time cannot be measured, Heisenberg holds, then the idea of such a thing is metaphysical and anti-scientific. So if a moving electron is known to be somewhere definite at a given moment, its velocity at that moment is neither zero miles per hour, nor 186,000 miles per second, nor anything else. And if a definite velocity is known, then the particle is not here nor there nor anywhere. Similarly, if the particle is measured at one position and then at another, but there has been no observation of the path it took from the first to the second, then, says Heisenberg, to claim nevertheless "that the electron must have been somewhere between the two observations and that therefore the electron must have described some kind of path . . . would be a misuse of the language. . . ."[74]

By the same reasoning, these physicists do not hesitate to affirm many other anti-Newtonian possibilities, such as: A particle can dart to and fro at the same time; a particle can be at two different places at the same time and can interfere with itself; a pulse of light can leave a chamber before it enters; the trajectory of a particle is equivalent to the reverse trajectory of its anti-particle going backward in time. Part of the revolution of quantum mechanics, remarks Bohr, is its "overthrow of our ordinary spatio-temporal models. . . ."[75]

Since subatomic entities are vague, predictions in this realm can never be certain; they can have only a degree of probability. Nor, for the same reason, can science accept Aristotle's Law of Identity or its corollary Law of Causality, since these are ways of affirming that entities are the opposite of vague—that they have specific, determinate natures. Thus the other name of the uncertainty principle, which identifies these rejections of Aristotelian metaphysics and of the process of induction based on it: the principle of indeterminacy. In regard to the subatomic world, this principle declares, the idea of causal law must be discarded in favor of rule by chance. (Einstein rejected this idea, remarking famously that "God does not play dice with the world.")

Since the only thing men can know is probability apart from determinate entities and causes, that is all there is. Uncaused probabilities, called "probability functions" or "probability waves," are the ultimate constituents of the universe. Although they cannot be explained by science, physicists, according to the theory, can learn to predict them.

According to Heisenberg, unactualized probabilities, though they are the constituents of the physical world, are not yet real; in his own words, each is "something standing in the middle . . . a strange kind of physical reality just in the middle between possibility and reality." Aristotle's Law of Excluded Middle, therefore, is also mistaken. As Heisenberg says elsewhere, we must sometimes modify the law of either-or in order to allow for a third possibility.[76]

For the traditional physicist, probability is an epistemological concept; it identifies the incompleteness of our knowledge in a given issue, but this is knowledge that in principle we can obtain, after which in that issue we are certain, and probability is no more. Probability for quantum physicists is a different animal; it does not pertain to a lack of knowledge, but to the nature of things. Even if men were omniscient, probability, in this theory, would be unaffected, because it defines reality itself apart from man.

By definition, a world made up of unactualized probabilities is, in actuality, nothing in particular. Quantum physicists stress this conclusion by referring to Nature as a limbo. The most famous example here is Schrödinger's 1935 thought experiment imagining a cat placed in a radiation chamber under these conditions: If a uranium atom inside decays, the cat will die, and if it doesn't, the cat will live; either way, the outcome will be a matter not of causality but of chance. David Harriman provides the quantum interpretation of this setup:

> After the box has been closed for an hour, the theory describes the system as an equal mixture of two states, one in which the cat is dead, and one in which the cat is alive. Physicists claim that such a description does not reflect our ignorance of the actual state of the system. It is the actual state. Quantum Theory says the cat is in a state of limbo between life and death—it is both and neither at the same time.[77]

"Until we look inside [the box]," writes physicist John Gribbin, an advocate of the theory, "there is a radioactive sample that has both decayed and not decayed, a glass vessel of poison that is neither broken nor unbroken, and a cat that is both dead and alive, neither alive nor dead." "[E]ven in the most precise part of science, in mathematics," writes Heisenberg, "we cannot avoid using concepts that involve contradictions." "Our classical ideas of logic," echoes quantum theorist David Finkelstein, "are simply wrong in a basic practical way."[78]

Despite the contradictions lurking in the box, when we open it, all agree, the limbo has turned into something definite: We see the cat either alive or dead, never both or neither. This transformation illustrates another tenet inherent in the indeterminacy principle: When we measure the indeterminate, it becomes determinate; so when we measure the contradictory, it becomes consistent. Our measurements, in short, are what confer identity on the limbo. "Only with measurement," says physicist Paul Davies, "will the entire pyramid of quantum 'limbo' states collapse into concrete reality."[79]

Astonished by their discovery that the measurement of nothing can make it something, quantum physicists came to call such an occurrence the "measurement miracle." It is doubtful whether Kant would have found it astonishing, since the quantum theory here is but a reformulation of his distinctive form of subjectivism, his principle that the world we perceive is created by our mental apparatus operating on the unknowable. As Murdoch states Bohr's obviously Kantian view here:

> the observed properties of microphysical objects [are] subjective in the sense that they are artefacts of the process of observation. . . . An experimental statement, if true, is true not absolutely, but only relatively to the conceptual point of view which we human thinkers adopt.[80]

If measuring, a form of thought, is what creates the perceived world, then concepts are logically prior to percepts. If so, the physicist's conceptual framework (his mathematical formalism) is not based on observation. On the contrary, it is created independently of empirical data.

Einstein, too, had regarded basic concepts as *a priori*, but as we have seen he agreed with traditional rationalism that such concepts nevertheless describe objectively the real world. The exponents of quantum mechanics, however, are far from being rationalists; a conceptual framework not derived from experience, these empiricists say, is neither true nor false, and as Bohr had said, should not even be physically interpreted. In itself, therefore, any mathematical symbolism is acceptable, because all of them are subjective and arbitrary.

The equations of physicists, these innovators proclaimed, do not identify natural laws or describe physical facts. On the contrary, writes Murdoch, they may be regarded as "fictions," artifices of our imagination—but fictions that work. By suitably interpreting and manipulating these fictions, the physicist is able to predict, with some probability, the mass behavior of subatomic particles. His equations do not tell us anything about the nature of matter. They are merely "recipes" (Bohr's term) to facilitate empirical predictions. Quantum mechanics is not concerned to explain why some recipes apply to the indeterminate world and others do not; or why mutually contradictory frameworks work (for example, the Copenhagen interpretation, the path integral interpretation, the multiverse theory). Such "whys," the theory holds, are metaphysical; the only question one can ask in this context is: Does a given fiction predict or not? Does the recipe deliver?

Having detached their equations from Nature and the particles of Nature from identity, what do these specialists in the subatomic realm claim to have learned about it? What is the real nature of particles like the electron and the rest? Murdoch gives Bohr's answer: In the classical sense "strictly speaking nothing falls under the notion—not even macroscopic bodies such as billiard balls—and hence there are no such things as particles. . . ."[81]

The positivists had held that, since there are no atoms, there can be no study of them. The quantum theorists tell us that they have made a lifelong study of the atom's constituents, which has taught them that there aren't any. If Einstein dilutes the physical world, quantum mechanics dismisses it, substituting for it detached formalism presiding over limbo.

"If to-day," wrote astrophysicist Sir Arthur Eddington in 1929,

you ask a physicist what he has finally made out the aether
or the electron to be . . . [he will point] to a number of symbols
and a set of mathematical equations which they satisfy. What
do the symbols stand for? The mysterious reply is given that
physics is indifferent to that; it has no means of probing
beneath the symbolism . . . it is necessary to know the equations which the symbols obey but not the nature of that which
is being symbolised.

"Physics," Eddington concludes, deals "with shadows and illusions,
not reality." It is Plato's cave over again, but, since concepts now have no
tie to reality, it is a barred cave, from which there is no escape.[82]

Classical physics had studied material reality in order to discover objective, causal laws. Throw it all out, says the quantum credo. Reality is limbo;
objectivity is pre-Kantian; causality can't compete with Heisenberg; sensations arise by miracle; concepts are a detached formalism; mathematics is
arbitrary; probabilities exist but not yet; Aristotelian logic is wrong; matter
is passé; the science of physics does not investigate the physical. And quantum particles, whose study leads to all of this, do not exist.

"Quantum theory," Bohr quietly sums up, "represents an essentially
irrational element. . . ." It is this element that the movement uses to negate
every concept and principle that makes physics—or any form of mental
functioning—possible. This is the eruption of full-blown nihilism in the
hitherto rational field of science. Confronted by such a spectacle, the mild
Einstein could not stifle his reaction: If this is physics, "I would rather be
a cobbler, or even an employee in a gaming house, than a physicist."[83]

As with all ambitious disintegrators, quantum physicists leave behind
them only the Many—in this case, a juxtaposition of sensations, probabilities, and equations—a Many without a One, and thus reflect the D_2 mode.

String Theory (Theory of Everything)

By the mid-sixties, physics was in a state of disarray. Four unconnected
kinds of forces, along with dozens of kinds of particles, were being

hypothesized and interpreted on the basis of the two unrelated (and sometimes mutually contradictory) theoretical frameworks of Einstein and quantum mechanics. This situation was intolerable to some physicists—among them, John Schwarz, Ed Witten, and Brian Greene—who demanded that their science once again be integrated on the basis of fundamentals. Their goal, states science writer George Johnson, was "'grand unification'—recovering the primordial symmetry in the form of a single law—a few concise equations, it is often said, that could be silk-screened onto a T-shirt." When discovered, these equations would be the completion of physics, because they would make possible a Theory of Everything.[84]

The new unification begins with a new analysis of matter, string theory. The basic constituents of reality, in this view, are not particles or fields, but one-dimensional strings or membranes that vibrate in ten dimensions, a setup that allows for a great number of different kinds of vibrations, most of them impossible in a three-dimensional world. All the differences among the forces and particles we know, the theory continues, along with such essential physical attributes as charge and mass, are associated with different kinds of these vibrations (their different modes or resonances). The seven extra spatial dimensions are much too small to be experienced. Nor can they be defined by using concepts derived from experience; they are simply too different from anything men have ever known or even imagined.

If we are to reach the all-encompassing explanation we seek, most of these physicists say, we must recognize the validity of a certain popular physical theory and then interpret it in terms of string physics. Since we are seeking to derive everything that exists from an antecedent state, the theory argues, we are led back ultimately to the only state that could precede existence: nothing. But if a realm of nothing is our cosmic ancestor, there must at one point have been a cosmic eruption, a creation of existents *ex nihilo* but without a creator, a big bang, as the cosmologists have long called it, in which the primordial nothing turns into something. What this latter turns into is the sub-microscopic world of strings.

In the beginning, the universe was a pure state of energy in eleven-dimensional space-time (eleven, because time is added here). The numbers required by string theory to elaborate this idea are unprecedented—the initial energy, for example, is said to be twenty orders of magnitude greater than anything measurable by an experimentalist on earth. During this instant of super-energy, there existed only a single kind of particle and a single kind of force associated with it; the world at this point was a unity. The unity, however, did not last, because the world at once started to expand and cool, which led to a process of cosmic splintering called "symmetry-breaking." The primordial particle broke into many different kinds, and so did the primordial force, which turned into gravity, electromagnetism, and the nuclear forces, strong and weak. All but three of the spatial dimensions curled up into sub-microscopic structures.

Since the central concepts of this theory, such as "string" and "ten spatial dimensions," cannot be interpreted physically, they are defined only as mathematical entities—essentially, as sets of non-empirical equations. The goal of understanding everything thus becomes the project of deriving from these equations all the important equations already established in physics. The requisite starting equations were accordingly invented, and the equations both of Einstein and of quantum mechanics were in fact deduced from them. This was a unification widely hailed by physicists, though some dissenters claimed that such deduction is possible to anyone using any mathematical formalism, if he is allowed to start with invented premises, however fantastic.

The physical world, in this new approach, is not a primary, but a derivative of a non-physical realm consisting of pure mathematics. As Leon Lederman, a philosophically similar though somewhat earlier Nobel Prize–winning physicist, said: "I think there's a universe because somewhere, way back, there were the laws of physics. The laws of physics said there had to be a universe. The laws of physics were there." Or as George Johnson puts it, these physicists object to the Aristotelian idea "that it is the equations that flow from nature instead of the other way around"; on the contrary, to them nature is "crystallized mathematics."[85]

The advocates of this viewpoint are not quantum theorists; they regard their equations not as "recipes," but as truths. They reject Kantian subjectivism in favor of idealism—specifically, though in far more sophisticated form, in favor of Plato's attempt to deduce the physical world from the five regular solids of geometry. They also accept Plato's philosophical downgrading of this world. Physical disorder, they believe, increases with distance from the primordial unity. Therefore, the world we perceive is metaphysically inferior to the world of equations—it is multiple, complicated, "messy," as they put it, a distraction from ultimate truth.

Lesser scientists, they say, can deal with the chaos of sense data, but in doing so they are wasting time on trivia. Solid-state physicists, for example, are ridiculed as "squalid-state" physicists or as "dirt" physicists. What physics needs instead is a fundamental reorientation. Rather than studying observable objects, physicists should focus on the initial state of perfection. Their urgent concern should be to probe the first fraction of the first second of the first something (that second's first 10^{-30} part); this knowledge will enable us to discover the equations that govern the moment of super-high energy. From these equations in turn all else can be derived.

Einstein, though a rationalist, accepted the reality of matter, and almost always required that a theory make empirically verifiable predictions. The string physicists, by contrast, take rationalism all the way; they are avowedly not concerned with the empirical; nor has their theory so far led to empirical predictions. In the words of theoretical physicist Lawrence Krauss, their theory is "still without a shred of empirical evidence . . . [is] yet to have any real successes in explaining or predicting anything measurable . . . [and is] a thus-far empirically impotent idea. . . ." To the more consistent of these men, this kind of "impotence" is not a reproach, but an asset. Up to now, says physicist David Gross, accomplishments in physics have been "based on data forced down our throats by our experimentalist friends. Now we're in a situation where there are no experimental clues, just a feeling that the theory must be right."[86]

Not all of these moderns rely on "just a feeling." The movement offers a variety of traditional rationalist norms, both intellectual and aesthetic, including the ability of a theory to integrate ideas (sets of equations). As physicist Sheldon Glashow puts it, "Superstring theorists pursue an inner harmony, where elegance, uniqueness and beauty define truth. . . . Do mathematics and aesthetics supplant and transcend mere experiment?"[87]

The universe of the Theory of Everything is an unworldly monist's dream: a transcendent, *a priori* One (a single set of equations) from which flows the unreal Many— unreal in physics, because banished from it as irrelevant. This exemplifies the M_2 mode in physics.[88]

CHAPTER SEVEN

EDUCATION

THE HUMANISTS OF the Renaissance, "reborn" after a thousand years of faith, looked for inspiration and guidance to Greco-Roman culture. They embraced it not as educators, but as students going back, as they said, to the only rational school that ever existed. By the seventeenth century, however, their descendants in the field of education, as in art, had turned admiration of antiquity into their fundamental principle, which defined value in every cultural field. Thereafter, what is called classical education (or, as in art, classicism) ruled Western schools for three centuries, fading away only in the later nineteenth. The movement's intellectual supporters span these centuries and occasionally beyond, ranging from Erasmus and Melanchthon to Mortimer Adler and Allan Bloom, and including even such figures as John Locke and Benjamin Franklin.

Classical Education

According to the classical approach, proper education is the study of the culture and society of the ancients, including their languages, especially Latin. Greco-Roman civilization, these new educators held, was not merely great; it was immeasurably superior to anything else (religion apart), including whatever educational ideas might emerge in times to come. In this view, as in that of the classicist playwrights, the ancients were no longer regarded as the key to unlimited human progress, but rather as treasured authorities from whose culture any deviation was not progress, but degeneration. According to Erasmus, write two British scholars (Boyd and King), mankind should

> derive both the substance of its knowledge and its linguistic media from the great literatures of Greece and Rome. It was not only that he found in the language of the best Latin writers a more admirable means for the conveyance of every form of human thought than any existing language; but he [also] . . . believed that all essential knowledge on the main concerns of life, whether in law, medicine, or science, were to be found in their writings.[89]

Centuries later, Benjamin Franklin, though a frequent critic of the approach, still affirmed that

> the finest Writings, the most correct Compositions, the most perfect Productions of human Wit and Wisdom, are in those [ancient] Languages . . . [and] that those Languages contain all Science. . . .[90]

By definition, classical education favored the traditional over the modern; the arts and humanities over the often suspect observations of natural science; and the student's intellectual development over vocational and technological training, with its usual result moneygrubbing. As these educators saw it, the schools had to choose between two incompatible realms: the profound or the worldly, the theoretical or the practical, the spiritual or the materialistic, the timeless or the trendy.

Perhaps the boldest claim of the classicists was that only a study of the classics could achieve a crucial secular value: the development of a student's rational faculty. In their words, only classical study "sharpens a student's mind"; it does so by instilling in his mind the method of logic, the rigor of mental discipline, and the ability to think clearly while using broad abstractions. An essential element in the learning of these skills was thought to be the study of Latin, whose grammar and syntax were widely regarded as uniquely logical. A teacher aiming to sharpen minds in this way must present his material, including Latin, not as a miscellany of data, but as a structured progression of principles. Ultimately these principles, having been shown in various areas to be logically interrelated, will form for the young mind a system linking all the knowledge it has gained.

In structuring the curriculum, classicists adopted a long-standing practice of the medievals, who themselves had derived it loosely from the later Romans: They started the child with the trivium. To them this meant the child's exclusive immersion, during his youngest, most formative years, in three subjects taught in Latin, each presented as a precondition of the next: grammar, logic, and rhetoric. Grammar studied the relations of words to one another; logic, the relations of sentences to one another; rhetoric, the methods of gaining one mind's consent to the sentences of another. After these studies had been completed, the child's mind was regarded as molded, and he could then deal rationally with more advanced subjects, such as geometry, astronomy, and others. Because the mastery of Latin grammar was thus the foundation of the curriculum, the subject was taught intensively for a period of years, starting with children from the age of six or younger. This is why classicist schools, despite the broader curriculum they offer to older students, are called grammar schools.

The classicist study of grammar, taken virtually intact from the ancient Romans, taught students how to connect words unrelated to experience. The teachers were not concerned with the role, if any, of these words and rules in the student's life—for example, with their relevance to a boy's actual mental process in understanding observed fact and organizing his conclusions. On the contrary, the focus was on the connection of words to other words, not to the world, on texts apart from experience. Non-empirical words, in short, are taking the role of tradition's pure forms.

The same purity was evident in the classicist's method of teaching. Years were spent on mechanical drills in the rules of Latin, which were commonly presented as self-contained and even as self-explanatory.

Often the rules were taught before the student had read anything in Latin. Even vocabulary lists were sometimes presented without reference to the perceptual objects denoted by the words. After Latin was presumed to be known, the curricular horizons broadened, but the linguistic approach typically was retained. The focus was not on the truth or falsehood of the ideas of a great thinker, Greek or Roman, but on the sentences he used to express them—their structure, clarity, inner logic, elegance, and (in the later period) on the methods of achieving proper translations into the vernacular.

Throughout his formative years, the student lived and thought primarily in a world of rules, sentences, names—that is, in large part a world of pure abstractions. Whereas the Renaissance humanists had been passionate about the empirical content of the pagan works, the seventeenth century, as the *Britannica* points out, soon shifted from content to form—in education as in literature. Form apart from content is, of course, the definition of Platonism.[91]

Comparatively few students worked up much enthusiasm for the task of learning the assigned forms by rote, but rebels were reminded that school, being the opposite of dens of worldly enjoyment, required arduous discipline. Now and then, reformers would propose a means of simplifying Latin grammar to make its study easier, but their ideas were rejected by the classicist educators on the grounds that it was a good thing for students to find Latin difficult, because this taught them a lesson even more important than Latin: how to bear hardship. If the lessons still did not get across satisfactorily, the schools had a further recourse: in Colonial America, notes the International World History Project, "Learning [in elementary school] consisted of memorizing, which was stimulated by whipping."[92]

Classical schools provoked continual, though largely ineffectual criticism from empirically minded reformists. Our schools, said the educational pioneer John Comenius, are "the slaughterhouses of minds," since understanding comes "not in the mere learning the names of things, but in the actual perception of the things themselves." Without empirical content, wrote John Locke, students might as well throw away their books as "containing nothing but hard Words, and empty Sounds. . . ." The classicists rejected such criticisms. Empiricism, they believed, leads to relativism and amorality, whereas a teacher should teach absolute philosophical principles and universal values.[93]

Since the student could not for the most part understand or prove these principles (many from the Bible), he was usually asked to accept them on faith. The teachers did not intend this as an approval of unreason, but rather as a preliminary of reason necessary for children, who would eventually outgrow the need for a non-rational introduction; the emergent adult would then come to see the logic of what he had earlier accepted apart from logic. He would see the logic because he would now be able to deduce the principles from self-evident axioms grasped by intuition. As in classicist literature and in Einsteinian physics, the criteria of axiomatic truths include the standard rationalist values: balance, symmetry, harmony, order, and the like. The error of the modern empiricist educator, writes David Hicks, a contemporary classicist, is that he "looks upon observation, not reason, as the starting point. . . . [Such an educator has] a too lofty regard for the experimentally verifiable. . . ." The educator should look for guidance not to Nature, but to another realm:

> . . . the secondary school student's mathematical curiosity should not be bound by the rule of material applicability, for there is a beauty in numbers, perhaps a mystery, suggesting the ideal and touching the transcendent. This awesome sense . . . should never be sacrificed in early learning for the purpose of making mathematics the scullery maid of the technological sciences.[94]

While the classical educators greatly admired the ancients, they were also pious Christians, who could hardly equate paganism, even in Platonic form, with the religion of Jesus. Hence their conviction that education must have three hierarchically related purposes: to foster a student's intellectual development, and on this base his moral virtue, and on this base his love of God. Although the first two were seen as steps toward the transcendent, each, in the classicist view, also entailed a worldly commitment, which is what essentially distinguishes these moderns from their medieval predecessors.

Intellectual development leads the student upward, but the teachers spent a good part of the time after the trivium analyzing and praising the "downward"—the secular culture of the pagans. *A priori* absolutes, the teachers said, are the means of moving toward a knowledge of God, but also, in learning them, the student sharpens his mind and is thus able to cope effectively with the otherwise confusing world of daily life. Similarly, virtue is a commandment from God, but the classicists said when the West's development demanded it, the thing that God often demands is self-reliance and the pursuit of earthly happiness.

The classicists offered the student a journey from the lower abstractions of grammar to the ultimate, but they were not in the medievals' hurry to get there. First, they held, men have to perfect their human faculties, learn to feel love for the works of human greatness, come to understand the world and even enjoy it. The movement, in short, is Worldly Supernaturalism.

As with the other cases of a mixed mode, classicism opened the door to a range of incompatible interpretations, each adhering to the same fundamentals, but differing in tilt. There were classicist schools eager to remove any suggestion of impiety, which retained a fair amount of medieval content; increasingly, there were also schools that minimized medievalism, believing that scientific study and even vocational training could be a step toward God, if pursued within a classical framework. In the classroom, many of the teachers were martinets in the name of inculcating obedience to God; many, however, considered this behavior educationally destructive. Although it was the rule to demand memorization with or without understanding, some teachers did try to promote understanding by discussing in class some empirical examples and scientific discoveries. Despite such differences, however, all these variants continue to implement both sides of their mixture: The more religious were still proud to be modern; the more secular were still proud to be Christian.

For these educators, the Many—a school's goals, its curriculum, its method of teaching—are realities interconnected because they all derive from a supernatural One—the formula of the M_1 approach.

Progressivism

According to the *Britannica*, "Concepts of teaching and learning—and school practice—have changed more since 1900 than in all preceding human history." The reason for this lies in the Progressive movement, which began in the late nineteenth century, took over American schools in the 1920s and 1930s, and still remains influential here at all levels, from kindergarten through college. Europe adopted Progressive elements a few decades later, and only in part. Leaving aside its many precursors, the preeminent creator of this approach was John Dewey, whose general philosophy I sketched in chapter two: Reality is indeterminate (like the limbo of the quantum physicists); man is primarily an actor, not a thinker; an idea is a plan of action designed to remove obstacles from an actor's path; and the idea's truth or falsehood lies in whether or not the plan works, an outcome that cannot be known in advance, but only after the action has been taken.[95]

If action has primacy over thought, the Progressive educators say, then that is how a child must learn: "by doing." "Doing" here subsumes a wide array of activities, including making things, growing plants, looking around, collecting pictures, touring the neighborhood, sharing experiences, cooking, playing, and looking things up in a book when necessary. This activism, the Progressives stress, requires that the traditional classroom apparatus be scrapped. There are to be no more texts (classical or otherwise), no lecturing by the teacher, no structured presentations forcing someone else's logic on the child—indeed, no lesson plans at all. So we will no longer have to see what the intellectualist schools produce: passive, tuned-out students confined involuntarily to their seats, trapped into listening, reading, memorizing, and test taking. Instead we will see youngsters actively and enthusiastically pursuing their interests, projects, experiments. Education, in this vision, is no longer the process of transmitting acquired knowledge to the child in order to prepare him for life. On the contrary, education is "participation in, rather than preparation for [life]."[96]

Yesterday's teachers, Dewey holds, pretending to be cognitively superior to their students, were given to spouting in class a stream of alleged certainties, intellectual and moral. But, Dewey believes, the teacher, just as much as his students, is an uncertain actor who does not know what is coming next. At most, therefore, he can serve as "a helpful guide for the children's chosen activities." For example, he can make non-compulsory suggestions to his young colleagues, moderate their discussions, and even answer concrete questions, such as the spelling of a certain word.[97]

The same approach soon led to a new view of the role of parents, who learned that it was no longer their responsibility to build their child's character or to discipline him. They must cease to regard themselves as overseers or even protectors of their offspring; instead, summarizes a reviewer of John Holt's book *Escape from Childhood*, "let them thrust themselves—when they feel like they want to—into the real-life world."[98]

The new watchword, at home as at school, was the child's "self-expression," with "self" denoting a repository of interests, desires, and impulses. Since a child matures by a process of internally directed self-development following its own individual timetable, it was held what the child needs most is *freedom*, not as a privilege, but as his birthright. According to A. S. Neill, the founder of Summerhill, one of the leading Progressive institutions of the twentieth century, the child needs freedom not merely at home, but also in school—even the freedom to ignore schoolwork. Education, Neill says, requires the complete freedom to play, "to experience the full range of feelings, free from the judgment and intervention of an adult." "Learning," said Aristotle—and educators through the centuries after him—"is no amusement, but is accompanied with pain." No more.[99]

The Progressive child does not, however, enjoy the same independence in relation to other children. Self-expression, though still important, is transcended by a more important goal: adaptation to one's peers. The child must learn to see himself not primarily as a separate entity pursuing personal desires, but as part and servant of a larger entity, which after graduation he realizes is society as a whole. The fundamental goal of education, says Dewey, is not that of traditional individualism, not sharpening minds, nurturing selves, or stuffing the student with knowledge, but developing in children a social spirit expressed in the desire for social service.

To achieve this end, one common Progressive innovation was group learning, in which students are assigned a project to be done in and by a group, and for which each member will receive the same grade, regardless of the quality or quantity of any one individual's contributions. Often the grade is decided by the rest of the class, through majority rule. The purpose of such assignments is to let the student absorb by experience the lesson that, even when using his own mind, he cannot function successfully without melding into a body of other people.

A similar lesson is taught by a Progressive school meeting, in which school rules and policies are decided by a vote of students and teachers alike, each person, whether age four or seventy-four, having equally a single vote, with the students, of course, far outnumbering the teachers. In these meetings, states one Progressive describing a Canadian school based on the Sudbury model, "we can trust even the youngest kids to spend the school's money and hire and fire the staff." Since the meetings determine the penalties for behavior unacceptable to the group, as well as the teachers' career prospects, the child soon learns another aspect of social adaptation: that his peers collectively have near-absolute power over him.[100]

Progressives do not regard their twin goals, self-expression and social adaptation, as logically incompatible. During the years that we leave the young child free to seek selfish gratification, they say, the school is gradually reshaping him so that he is unable to gain much satisfaction on his own. Eventually, he comes to identify with the collective unit. Thus his earlier self-expression turns into peer expression; in a sense, his self becomes the group. This idea reflects the early Dewey, who started as a Hegelian metaphysician. But Dewey qua Progressive is a modern empiricist, who rejects metaphysical entities; for him, therefore, the group is not some truer reality underlying the individuals we observe. On the contrary, the child's peers and teachers alike, for Dewey, are merely a collection of uncertain actors deprived of contact with an independent reality, and thus left with no option but to make decisions together, by consensus. Even so, Dewey acknowledges, it is possible for a dissenter to sway his peers and even overturn their consensus on some point, in which case adaptation to the consensus takes an appropriately new form. The individual, in short, must identify with the collective, but he is not wholly swallowed up by it.

Since thought is of value only if it helps remove concrete obstacles that interfere with the pupils' concrete doings, the children do not hear much in school of abstractions. To teach principles, natural laws, scientific theories, and intellectual systems may sometimes have an auxiliary role. But as a rule these are just words to a student, because they are irrelevant to his immediate projects. The real problems of life, the student learns, are too complex for any neat set of words to be able to deal with. So the traditional curriculum, too, must be scrapped.

"Formerly," write Boyd and King,

> when mind was supposed to get its content from contact with the world, the requirements of instruction were thought to be met by bringing the child into direct relation with various masses of external fact labeled geography, arithmetic, grammar, etc.[101]

But now, the Progressives say, we see that it is harmful to the student to divide data into arbitrary categories dictated by some broad abstractions. Such general classifications are unrelated to the concrete requirements of today's action. Often, these teachers say, a child doing his specific project needs some piece of information from several different academic subjects. The schools can no longer be subject-centered; they must be child-centered. "We don't teach history; we teach Johnny," they say—and we teach him (when he asks) only the specific data he needs today, no matter from what alleged "subject" it comes. With this approach, it is said, school is no longer yesteryear's dreaded house of rote, but rather a center of relevance, curiosity, and enjoyment.

Insofar as Progressives do teach traditional subjects, they apply consistently their commitment to the concrete as against the abstract. In reading, they reject phonics in favor of the whole-word method. In the latter, the student learns to read a word without knowing the sound of its individual letters; he learns the whole word as a concrete—usually through associated pictures and/or memorized spelling. He is offered no principle to explain the sound of the word or to relate its sound to those of other words. Phonics, by contrast, is regarded as unreal by the Dewey-ites, because of its focus on individual letters, each grasped by selective attention, abstraction (measurement-omission), and then integrated with other, similar letters—that is, phonics is rejected because it is the conceptual-level method of teaching reading.

A similar approach guides Progressive schools in advanced subjects, too. The teaching of science, for example, consists largely of hands-on science activities—that is, concrete experiments performed by the children usually without any theoretical context or general conclusion offered by the teacher. One Progressive-minded authority, F. James Rutherford, CEO of the American Association for the Advancement of Science, chastised his more traditionalist colleagues for being "too serious [in class]. We insist on all the abstract stuff. We need to relax and let the children learn their own neighborhood."[102]

As to mathematics, that onetime citadel of abstractions is now almost unrecognizable. According to Anemona Hartocollis, a *New York Times* reporter, one Progressive offshoot, constructivism,

> has led to the schools' widespread rejection of textbooks, in favor of exercises using blocks, beans and other materials. One popular program, MathLand, suggests that students count a million grains of birdseed to get a feeling for the size of a million.

One "reactionary" mathematics professor at Harvard, Wilfried Schmid, was incredulous when he discovered that his daughter was "reduced to drawing 39 little men to solve problems like 39-14."[103]

Traditionalists often object that the Progressive student does not learn, that he does not graduate knowing the body of facts and truths that are the cognitive legacy of earlier generations. Progressives reject this criticism as "old-fashioned intellectualism"; on the whole, they consider their opponents' description of the Progressive child's lack of learning to be accurate, but they dismiss the negative evaluation of this fact.

Communicating knowledge, they explain, is a secondary and relatively unimportant purpose of education. "If students enjoyed working with science-type materials such as magnets or mirrors," says a science teacher, "I really don't care if they learned anything." Dewey goes further; communicating knowledge to a student, he holds, may be not only unimportant, but downright harmful. "The mere absorbing of facts and truths is so exclusively individual an affair," he writes, "that it tends very naturally to pass into selfishness. There is no obvious social motive for the acquirement of learning, there is no clear social gain in success thereat."[104]

The Progressives' program for the schools is not reform, but demolition: of subjects, facts, lessons, texts, structure, intellect, teaching, and learning. Above all, the movement represents the equation of education with the perceptual-level mentality. It is the anti-conceptual mentality embracing the pre-conceptual child and training him to remain in that state for life.

Education without teaching and learning is not "education for democracy." It falls in the same category as literature without story and characters, and physics without matter and laws. It is nihilism.

In their thoroughgoing concrete-boundedness, the Progressives, like all nihilists, recognize only a Many, a Many without a One—the formula of D_2.

Pluralism (in Schools)

For generations now Progressivism has been a major influence in America, and to a lesser extent in Europe. But most of our educators do still accept many traditional elements; they have not gone all the way with Dewey, and are best described as pluralists. Pluralism in this field, as in others, means the elevation of the Many above the One; this approach is by far the top choice of our teachers today. Out of all the educational possibilities, it alone is institutionalized across America and publicly financed.

Classical educators aimed at mind-sharpening through exposure to antiquity. The Progressives denied the validity of imposing adult goals on children. The pluralists, in contrast to both, believe in pursuing educational goals, but not in the single-tracked, monistic fashion of past centuries. Instead these educators endorse a wide variety of goals—some regarded as optional, some as indispensable, some as interrelated, but none regarded as an element connected with the others to form a hierarchy or system resting on some ultimate base. The proper goals of educators, they say, are an irreducible multiplicity.

Since schools cannot pursue all possible goals, pluralists admit that we must choose only the most worthwhile among them. But since, according to the empiricism they accept, values cannot be perceived, the basis for our choices can be only our desires. The goals of education, therefore, are those that satisfy people's desires; in a democracy, the pluralists add, this means the desires of all the community's diverse and relevant social groups. None of these groups is thought of as having any special knowledge as to how "really" to run a school, but this is irrelevant because "really" is a metaphysical concept. Since the American public, for example, still demands some academic training in the schools, the pluralists, contrary to the Progressives, willingly comply. As pluralists, however, they do not regard this goal or any other as fundamental; a student's learning of traditional subject matter is merely one goal within a diverse world, merely one out of many.

Political conservatives often allege that our schools are not really pluralist, since they seem to have a single mission: to disseminate leftist propaganda. This charge overlooks the fact that the majority of our teachers are not ideologically trained and in fact insist that they deliberately avoid proselytizing. From my own observations, it is certainly true that the schools are in the hands of egalitarians, multiculturalists, environmentalists, and other similar groups. As they see it, however, the teachers are simply expressing, in piecemeal fashion, what they regard as obvious truths, newspaper truths, when they seem relevant to a class. Such a mentality, however widespread, does not affect the epistemological nature of the American approach to education. If and when proselytizing did become the schools' primary purpose, that would signify the end of free speech and of America as we still know it.

Classical educators asked their classes to study the relatively small number of subjects dictated by their ultimate goal. The Progressives reject the teaching of subjects. Again, the pluralists stand in contrast to both; recognizing how many goals the public or various subgroups within it cherish, their schools offer for credit a historically unprecedented number and variety of subjects. Besides the standard academic material, one finds in their curricula—in some, most, or all of them—courses in such subjects as holistic health, environmental stewardship, happy marriage, auto tune-up, racquetball, marketing, leadership, wood technology, flexibility, beginning photography, intermediate acting, racial tolerance, self-esteem, and "joy and humor." In 1994, the National Education Commission on Time and Learning "found that American students spent only about 41 percent of the school day on basic academics."[105]

A former high school teacher, now a harsh critic of the school system, described what this type of curriculum meant in his classroom. Asked by a parent whether "there is some system to it all and it's not just raining down on them," John Gatto replied:

> *The first lesson I teach is confusion. Everything* I teach is out of context. I teach the un-relating of everything. I teach disconnections. I teach too much: the orbiting of the planets, the law of large numbers, slavery, adjectives, architectural drawing, dance, gymnasium, choral singing, assemblies, surprise guests, fire drills, computer languages, parents' nights, staff development days, pull-out programs. . . . What do any of these things have to do with each other?[106]

The concrete-boundedness of today's teachers begins with the schools of education, especially with the courses on methodology. Jacques Barzun, the famed Columbia educator and a critic of Progressive education, has identified what students learn in these courses. There is no one proper method of teaching, the aspiring teacher hears, but rather many methods.

> There is a method for supervising schools and another for being a principal. Every subject matter taught has its special method. Even janitorial method can be learned, and the

method of teaching janitorial method also. Methods grow like fleas on one another ad infinitum.[107]

Teachers thus trained soon acquire a disdain for broadly integrating principles and usually even for lesser generalizations. They come to seek multiplicity not only in the goals they endorse, but also in how they deal in class with the content of any given course. For example, if a history teacher covers the American Revolution, he likely tends to dismiss as vague or empty an explanation in terms of the colonists' view of individual rights and their consequent opposition to tyranny. Instead, his students learn that this view is simplistic, because in fact there were many causes at work

> including the big landowners' desire to preserve their estates, the Southern planters' desire for a cancellation of their English debts, the Bostonians' opposition to tea taxes, the Western land speculators' need to expand past the Appalachians, etc.[108]

In a course on "introduction to scientific method" at a well-regarded Southern California public high school some years ago, the students were given a printed handout stating the course's topics and the order of their coverage. Here, to the best of my memory, was the list: Franklin's kite experiment, Newton's laws, atomic theory including some twentieth-century particles, colors, cellular structure, valence, Mendel, and magnets. I heard later that time ran out before they could get to the solar system and batteries.

Students of such teaching—whether in history, science, or elsewhere—Barzun observes, "make heroic efforts to memorize . . . they provide themselves with five causes for this and ten results of that. They bulge with factors, forces, and trends. . . ." Because of the material's disintegration, however, most of them cannot understand or even retain for long the data filling their notebooks. Again, as in naturalist art and positivist science, the creators of the product offer description without explanation.[109]

As all the above indicates, our schools are abandoning concepts in favor of perceptual-level education. The clearest illustration of this fact can be observed on the perceptual level: the rising use in the classroom of videos and digital pictures, and the fading interest in books. Textbooks are increasingly filled not with words, but with pictures. In one learning test, the state of California instructed eighth graders to answer an essay question about Einstein; as the tools by which to express their idea, the test offered the students a choice: "symbols, images, drawings, and/or words."[110]

Despite all the above, pluralists, though much influenced by Dewey, are not Progressives. They still regard as essential some organized presentation of subject matter, involving some degree of integration. Rather than leaving percepts deliberately unconnected, they do teach causes and generalizations, though on a lower level than that of their traditionalist predecessors. Their students, therefore, grasp some order and connection in the content they are taught, but it is connection in chunks, unrelated to other chunks in other topics and subjects. Unlike the Progressives, the pluralists do present facts and truths; but these are presented, in effect, as a flow of atoms without much molecular structure to bind them together.

As one would expect, pluralism in education, being a modal blend, subsumes a number of variants that are committed to the same fundamentals—but which confront the teacher qua integrator with a variety of incompatible guidelines flowing from the variant's tilt: toward the Aristotelian or toward the Kantian. Some emphasize what man can know, and tilt to the teaching of traditional academic disciplines, while still allowing for the need, even in these areas, for self-expression. Others emphasize what man cannot know, and tilt to Progressive "life skills" classrooms, while still allowing for the need for some traditional subject matter. Some are amenable to the teaching of relatively broad abstractions; others distrust broad abstractions, though not the conceptual level as such. Some offer a curricular structure (even including compulsory courses) devised by adults; others favor more, though not complete, student power. Since all these alternatives are made possible by the governing mode, that mode itself can make no evaluations and offer no advice in these issues.

Despite their differences, all pluralists agree that—in purposes, subject matters, and methods—educators face an irreducible Many. But it is a Many among which unrelated Ones can be found—the D_1 formula.

Totalitarian Education

Turning away now from the theories of the relatively free West, we find a last twentieth-century viewpoint: totalitarian education, which rests on the same basic principle as totalitarian literature. Being self-proclaimed materialists, the Communists extolled workers and soldiers while deprecating intellectuals and the mind. Despite this, however, they held and enforced definite ideas as to how the minds of their youth should be developed.

Totalitarian educators regarded Western schools as disseminators of fragmentation, skepticism, and immorality, all of which they saw as the corrupt legacy of groups such as the bourgeoisie (or in the Nazi version, the Jews). Instead, the schools should work to advance the goal long dreamed of by mankind but never before achieved. They must work to turn out ideal men, men unprecedented in moral character, aspiration, and thought. The essence of such a man, they said, is defined by his ideology; he is the man who has become a true Communist. "The entire purpose of training, educating, and teaching the youth," wrote Lenin, ". . . should be to imbue them with communist ethics."[111]

As in art—which in totalitarian theory is but a form of education—students from the earliest age must be taught the primacy of the group. "Textbooks," writes Nadezhda Krupskaya, a pioneer in socialist education, "must be thoroughly *permeated with the spirit of collectivism . . .* so that children could get accustomed to *view themselves as parts of a whole.*"[112]

To carry out this program, the content of virtually every school subject had to be reconceived. In history, for example, the traditional idea that a child should learn facts about the past and then draw generalizations from them was rejected as counter-revolutionary. Rather, the trends and even the details of history are to be taught as products of antecedently known ideological generalizations—which tell us of the class struggle, the evil of the capitalists, and so on. Even such concretes as Beethoven's symphonies have been explained in such terms.

In other fields dealing with the nature of man, such as psychology and biology, the Soviet teachers celebrated Pavlov and especially Lysenko. The theories of these two were regarded as scientific confirmation of the Communist belief in the infinite malleability of human nature, and thus in the possibility of the state's creation of a new man. (Under the Nazis, school subjects "became a study of the different races to 'prove' that the Nazi belief in racial superiority was a sound belief.")

Even in math, ideology played a role for the totalitarians, albeit a lesser one. One exam problem during Hitler's rule told students the weight of an outgoing aircraft's body, fuel, and bombs, and then required them to calculate the plane's final weight—once it had returned from bombing Warsaw. As for the study of logic, both the Communist and Fascist versions of totalitarianism agreed that there is no group-free neutral logic, but rather many logics (polylogism). Proletarian logic, the Communists taught, being superior to that of the bourgeoisie, has little difficulty in refuting the enemy's conclusions.[113]

As in art, there can be no question of a totalitarian citizen appealing to "objective fact" as the basis on which to validate or challenge a theory in any field. Theory is not a derivative of fact, but the standard by reference to which facts are to be determined. Students thus taught have no way to question the theories of their teacher; they cannot attach significance to apparent discrepancies between fact and theory. Nothing in the student's experience is relevant in assessing such freestanding (floating) conceptual entities.

Totalitarian education was a thorough epistemological retraining of the student; as such it was an indispensable factor in the state's ability to maintain total power. This is our first example of a system of floating abstractions being used as Plato did—that is, as a means of achieving thought control. Totalitarians, I should add, did not construe thought control as entailing passivity or fear; their aim was to turn out not cowed puppets, but impassioned zealots.

In the totalitarian schools, course content, like observed fact, ultimately reduces to an *a priori* system of concepts—as do the students themselves, merged as they are into a collective defined as real only because it manifests the same system. In the end, therefore, in the Communist schools, only the ideology, the One, was real—the One without the Many, M_2.

An I Approach

I can find no I (or any other) approach to education in the modern era— no one like Aristotle in philosophy, Hugo in literature, or Newton in science. Certain educators do suggest an I approach, notably Maria Montessori, but her works, while Aristotelian in essentials, are not a full theory of education, but only an anticipation of one, focused on guiding pre-school teachers. So I must here suggest my own, Objectivist projection of an I approach (a quite different, ancient version of I education will be considered in part three). An I approach would not be oriented to classics, doings, a lot of things, or ideology. Its focus, in my view, would be on the student's use of his conceptual faculty—the faculty that is basic to every aspect of human life that depends on cognition, including survival.[114]

As I have discussed in chapter one, the conceptual faculty does not operate automatically. It may be directed to reality or detached from it; it may be treated as dependent on observation or as independent of it; it may be applied to all areas of life, only to some, or to none. Man's basic tool of survival, in short, may be properly developed—or derailed, stunted, even destroyed. This sets the single ultimate purpose of the I educator. His task, across years, is to teach the perceptual-level toddler how to become a rational, conceptual-level thinker. As in any theory reflecting an Aristotelian foundation, an I school would be secular; its content and methods do not rest on supernaturalism or on *a priori* cognition. The teachers are concerned only with thought that is derived from and applied to the world in which we live.*

The content of an I education is uniquely delimited. Beyond the three Rs, the curriculum includes only four subjects: science, mathematics, history, and literature. Science, especially physics, teaches the basic known facts of Nature and the laws that integrate them—a knowledge necessary to a student's full grasp of the connection between concepts and percepts. Mathematics, besides being necessary for science, teaches many of the most important requirements of a thought process and does so in a unique way, exhibiting thought separately, apart from a specific content. History presents the known facts about man's actions through the ages, and is thus the primary, empirical workshop in the study of human nature; in due course, this knowledge will be essential to conceptual thought in the humanities and social sciences, and also in the students' choice of values. Art, according to Ayn Rand, is the concretization of a philosophic view of life; as such, art (and especially literature) acquaints the child with the highest level of abstraction. It thus serves as the integrator of the other subjects; the concern of art is not merely the world or man, but man in the world.

The above curriculum, obviously narrow, does not include many other subjects worth knowing. It deliberately excludes these as time-consumers undercutting the school's ability to achieve its complex mission. If parents wish their offspring to learn music, foreign languages, and the like, they must make their own private arrangements; in the I school, such topics are covered only peripherally, as aspects of history or literature. Similarly, the curriculum excludes college-level material—such as politics, economics, psychology—in which the student has not yet learned the facts and methods necessary to think rationally. So far as the student can understand them, the teacher does give him the concretes and enable him to grasp lower-level generalizations that, on the college level, will become the

---

* Here is the essential difference between the I and M_1 approaches to education. M_1 also values the student's conceptual development. But concepts interpreted in Aristotelian fashion lead to a curriculum and pedagogy that are in fundamental ways opposite to that which follows from M_1's Platonic interpretation.

bases he brings to these advanced subjects. Similarly, the teacher does not present philosophy in class except, like the other advanced subjects, in the form of preliminary data.

The I teacher is hired as an expert in subject matter and in the method of its presentation. His primary activity in class, accordingly, is not to moderate uninformed discussions, but to lecture. To achieve his purpose, he must carefully select and logically structure the topics he covers.

Logical structure in this context is a form of integration; it means hierarchical structure. Since advanced concepts in the Aristotelian view are rooted ultimately in perceptual fact, the teacher, in any area, must present his material accordingly. He must teach not only facts, but facts forming a connected chain—a chain going from perception to lower-level concepts and generalizations to the more abstract, underlying principles, so far as the student at any given stage can understand them. The students are not given the arbitrary or the floating, but the inductive and the objective.[115]

If students are to achieve a proper cognitive development, other forms of integration must also be taught. In my experience, the most important skill for them to learn is how to identify cross-relationships—that is, relationships between points taught in one area and those in others. I regard this aspect of teaching as critical, especially when the points and areas at first appear to be completely unrelated. Not all issues are related, of course, but the conceptualizing student should learn to see (or at least seek) connections everywhere—for example, between King Tut and George III and Othello, between the inverse square law and Thomas Jefferson, and even between Mr. Spock and geometry. Gradually, the child so taught comes to see the world not as a juxtaposition, but as a whole. In my experience, the champion in teaching this particular skill, who achieved breathtaking results even with toddlers, was the great Chicago educator Marva Collins.

In following the above principles, the I teacher provides the students with knowledge not only of factual content, but also of the proper method of forming and using concepts. He does not, however, lecture on so abstract a subject; on the contrary, through his lectures on content he presents the method of rational thought concretely—that is, in the context of specific cases; the student thus learns the method implicitly and gradually. The teacher, in short, does not expound a proper epistemology; he exemplifies it. The I teacher, even though highly directive, recognizes that it is essential, if he is to produce a thinker, that he not proselytize. Years later, when a student has become intellectually independent and sophisticated, he can choose to study questions of method explicitly and come to his own conclusions. (The same approach is used in teaching values.)

The above is what I see as a possible I view of education. Its Many—the specific goals, the subjects, the methods—are integrated by a single One, its ruling purpose. And that One has its being not in the transcendent, but in the worldly schools themselves creating it. So it is a One in the Many.

CHAPTER EIGHT

POLITICS

FROM THE LATE Renaissance to the mid-eighteenth century, the political system accepted almost universally in the West was absolute monarchy, famously exemplified in the rule of Louis XIV, the Sun King of France. The more philosophical among those regarded as its defenders were Thomas Hobbes and Jean Bodin.[116]

Absolute Monarchy

The basic principle of absolute monarchy is that the king alone is sovereign and thus has unlimited power. Without needing the consent of any other person, he is the legal authority in every matter of state, including but not restricted to taxation, property, infrastructure, economic issues in general, the justice system, the police, the military, and the life or death of any individual or group. As James I of England declared in a speech before Parliament in 1609:

> Kings are justly called gods, for that they exercise a manner or resemblance of divine power on earth. . . . They have power to . . . make of their subjects like men at the chess—a pawn to take a bishop or a knight—and to cry up or down any of their subjects, as they do their money.

Such a ruler cannot be challenged by his subjects nor asked to justify his actions; on the contrary, it is the subjects who, being his inferiors, owe an accounting to the king. Like the masses in Plato's politics, the subjects are regarded as inferior, because, as monarchists put it, they are unable to comprehend "the greatest politic actions and motions of state. . . ." They are mere children in relation to the king, who is their father—a "headless multitude," helpless by themselves without the only head available. The duty of such uncapitated bodies is "to be submissive and obedient. . . ."[117]

The king's actions were not intended to be an expression of whim; on the contrary, it was held, they had to be governed by a system of law. But a law in this system is a creation of the king, resting on his unique authority and serving his chosen purpose. Such a creation cannot limit the king, since he always retains the power to annul an offending law. "[T]he Prerogative of a King is to be above all Laws," concludes Sir Robert Filmer, a defender of the English monarchy. In the words of Edward McNall Burns, a deservedly eminent historian, Louis' *"L'état, c'est moi"* "was not just the brazen boast of a tyrant, but came close to expressing the prevailing conception of government—in Continental Europe at least."[118]

Since all human powers, in this system, are grants from God, this must be especially true in the case of unlimited power. Thus the standard defense of the system: the divine right of kings. According to this theory, writes Jean Domat, a then famous jurist who championed it, ". . . it is from Him that all those who govern derive their power and all their authority, and it is God Himself Whom they represent in their functions."[119]

In addition to this metaphysical argument, the monarchists offered what they regarded as more specific evidence: God's own words as recorded in the Bible. Bishop Jacques-Bénigne Bossuet, widely influential at the time, sums up this line of thought in the title of his book *Politics Drawn From the Very Words of Holy Scripture*. The most common reference cited was Romans 13 ("The authorities that exist have been established by God"). Other popular passages were the story of God awarding Adam supreme dominion over the earth, and the commandment to honor thy father. Filmer adds that there is no text in the Bible giving people the right of self-government. During the seventeenth century, of course, biblical appeals were not often challenged. Thus, according to Cornell philosopher George Sabine, in my opinion one of the best historians of our time, the divine-right theory "was believed with religious intensity by men of all social ranks and all forms of theological belief."[120]

The intellectuals defending political absolutism did not base the theory on perceptual data; rather, Sabine writes, "The imposition of divine authority upon the king is essentially miraculous and must be accepted by faith . . ."—the same faith that grasps the infallibility of divine revelation. The epistemology of political absolutism, in other words, equates fundamental knowledge with *a priori* truth and inferences therefrom. When men of an empirical bent objected, pointing to observed facts in conflict with the divine-right theory—facts such as the many non-monarchical systems God had allowed in the past or the destructive actions, counter to God's will, of many past kings—the rationalists were unmoved. The justification of absolute power, they replied, has nothing to do with the facts of history or the practical needs of men; the king's supremacy rests solely on his transcendent pedigree.[121]

Living in the early modern period, the absolutists claimed that their ideas, though resting on God, in no way demeaned the material world; on the contrary, they pointed out, the king's role is precisely to be God's *secular* agent, which implies the reality and importance of this world. In contrast to the medieval popes, whose duty had been to prepare men to escape from this life, the king's duty is to promote men's success in the world, mainly by expanding his nation's wealth, trade, and power over competitors. In this way, as has often been noted, absolute monarchy was a usurpation: It was the (partial) wresting of divine right from the Church, its longtime possessor, in order to award it to the palace, a worldly institution. Even some of the kings (though not the public), it seems, viewed the monarchists' claim of God's backing as no more than a strategy to reduce the power of the Church by taking over its basic intellectual defense.

The upshot of this struggle was a division of power between the ruler of man's spiritual life and the ruler of his material life. The Church was the acknowledged authority in matters of faith and morals, and thus was free to criticize a king for any action it deemed counter to God's word, but it was not to attempt to enforce its view by physical means. The king was the authority in practical life, with the right to enforce any decrees that practicality, in his opinion, required; this included the right to criticize and even act to oppose the Church, but not *ex cathedra*—only when, in his view, the religionists were attempting to muscle into his territory, by vetoing a war he favored, for example, or supporting a sect he regarded as traitorous. The king, in short, was a political, but not an ethical authority. Each of the two masters was held in some sort of check by the other. In practice, the division lacked a clearly defined hierarchy and left many issues undefined. The citizens, accordingly, enjoyed substantially more freedom than the term "absolute" monarchy implies; in relation to some twentieth-century regimes, one would have to say incomparably more freedom.

Like Descartes in science, the absolutist movement, though rationalist, was not indifferent to the perceptual. On the contrary, to discover the successful practical policies decreed by God, the king sought out a great deal of empirical information about other monarchs, navies, prices, and the like. Moreover, since the king was not an ethical authority, lawabiding citizens, within limits, had the right to criticize his chosen policies—partly on religious grounds, as ungodly and immoral, but increasingly on empirical grounds, i.e., by citing the observed worldly effects of a king's actions. The absolutist system, in short, did not dismiss percepts any more than it did the world itself; it sought to relate harmoniously the *a priori* and the observed, or the conceptual and the perceptual. Transcendence gives men their basic framework of values and validates their earthly leader and his mission; observation is what shows whether and how that mission is being carried out.

As with all instances of a mixed mode, there are many variations among absolute monarchies: disputes about the limits of the king's power; where specifically to draw the line between Church and state; what to do when political decisions have ethical implications and vice versa; whether empirical data are merely suggestive or have the power to teach us truth. As we would expect, the disputes arise from a difference in emphasis: a tilt toward Platonic medievalism or toward the new secularism. But within these variations, the same mode rules. The absolute Church was no more, but, despite his claim, only a semi-absolute ruler had taken its place.

In this politics, the worldly One is the king, who is the state uniting the citizens, the Many—and this worldly unity flows ultimately from a transcendent One—the M_1 approach.

Capitalism

In the eighteenth century, absolute monarchy was succeeded to varying extents by a new system, one that, in the opinion of James Madison, had "no parallel in the annals of human society." In the nineteenth century, its opponents named the new politics capitalism. Its main intellectual source was a long line of freedom-loving Englishmen stretching from the nobles under King John to the philosopher John Locke, and culminating in the Enlightenment figures who are its best spokesmen, the American founding fathers; these men not only accepted Locke's theory, but created a country based on it.[122]

Throughout history, although the forms of the state have varied widely, its essence has not; the state, to quote from a book of mine, has always been regarded

> as the ruler of the individual—as a sovereign authority . . . to which he must submit. The Founding Fathers [by contrast] . . . started with the premise of the primacy and sovereignty of the individual. The individual . . . logically precedes the group or the institution of government. Whether or not any social organization exists, each man possesses certain individual rights.[123]

And among these, according to a New Hampshire state document at the time, "are the enjoying and defending life and liberty; acquiring, possessing, and protecting property; and in a word, of seeking and obtaining happiness." These rights were regarded not as a disparate collection, but as a unity expressing a single basic right; in the words of Samuel Adams, they "are evident branches of, rather than deductions from, the duty of self-preservation, commonly called the first law of nature." Self-preservation requires that an individual have the liberty to think, to act, and to keep the products of his thought and action. Before the Enlightenment, these rights, had they been conceived, would have been regarded as sins if not crimes, because they represent and protect the opposite of service to authority, whether king or God. Individual rights enshrine self-assertion, not self-sacrifice; the quest for material wealth, not poverty ennobling the soul; the profit motive, not the heaven motive; independence, not obedience; the pursuit of happiness, not of duty.[124]

Man's rights, it was agreed, are inalienable, and their source is not society or government, but Nature. "Natural" here means based on the facts of reality—that is, on laws of Nature discovered by man scientifically; "inalienable" means eternal and immutable—that is, absolutes which no one may properly infringe. In both respects, it was said, there is no difference between these newly discovered laws of politics and the universally revered laws of Newton.

And "to secure these rights Governments are instituted among Men, deriving their just powers from the consent of the governed." These powers, therefore, are limited. Government is forbidden to take any action that would infringe individual rights because, in Adams's words, "the grand end of civil government, from the very nature of its institution, is for the support, protection, and defense of those very rights. . . ." An agent of individuals, in other words, can exercise only the powers they have delegated to it.[125]

Capitalist theory, consistently interpreted, requires a "wall of separation" between Church and state, just as it does between economy and state. The government may not establish religion or any other ideology; nor may it redistribute wealth or regulate any other aspect of the economy in this system. A church may gain spiritual power over man, and a business economic power, but neither can exercise political power—that is, neither can advance its goals by seeking special government action. The whole apparatus of the absolute state—and implicitly of the modern welfare state—is thus swept away. The government is nothing but a policeman charged with arresting criminals at home and abroad. The state, in

Jefferson's words, is to concern itself only with that which "picks my pocket or breaks my bones."

Since this view of government, being a corollary of the principle of individual rights, is viewed as an absolute, no segment of the population can properly pervert it—neither a politically established clique of nobility nor the sentiments of a majority, however large. Proper law is not aristocratic or democratic; it is objective, because the right to liberty is based on fact, not on anyone's arbitrary desire. As Locke puts it, men are "not to be under the will or legislative authority of man, but to have only the law of nature for [their] rule."[126]

Europeans at the time believed that a nation with so limited a government could not survive; a strong man was considered necessary to preserve order, by keeping in check the innate sinfulness of human nature. But the founding fathers, being Enlightenment believers in progress, rejected the idea of original sin. Since each individual possesses the powerful faculty of reason, they held, each has the ability to know reality, to pursue rational goals, and to grasp the importance of being self-made and self-sustaining; so the individual does not need brutality to keep him peaceful, but only freedom. If virtue did require the grasp of an ineffable supernatural, as Platonism held, then morality would be impossible to the worldly masses; but if Platonism is wrong, as this period thought, then a people's virtue requires only their exercise of their worldly minds to achieve worldly goals. In this system, seeing is not at war with believing, and everyone can deal with a world he can see.[127]

Secularism, though most widespread in America, was a defining attribute of the Enlightenment throughout the West. Everywhere thinkers in this brief era praised science, while rejecting the demand for faith, making fun of dogma, and heaping contempt on organized religion, especially Christianity. Nor, especially in the New World, was this merely a trend among intellectuals. Only one in fifteen of the Colonial population were churchgoers, and Christians here were often fearful for the very survival of their faith. Mankind, observed Reverend Charles Backus, is in "great danger of being laughed out of religion. . . ."[128]

It was in this philosophic atmosphere that the capitalist system of government was born. Their revolutionary documents, the founders stressed, were secular declarations, and they were castigated for this by their opponents, who regarded the independence movement as an un-Christian evil. During the Constitutional Convention, William Williams of Connecticut moved to enlarge the Preamble to include language that today would be considered uncontroversial rhetoric; he wanted some mention of the country's belief in "the one living and true God . . . His universal providence and the authority of His laws. . . ." The motion was voted down. In the same year, the Senate ratified unanimously a treaty that included the statement that the U.S. government "is not in any sense founded on the Christian religion. . . ." Again in that year, when someone asked Hamilton why there was no reference to God in the Constitution, he answered cheerfully: "We forgot."[129]

A stranger wrote to me recently to see whether I agreed with him about the philosophy of capitalism. I cannot recall his name, but I cannot forget his best sentences: "Capitalism is not God's way for fallen man. It is man's way for fallen God."

Like Aristotle, the thinkers of the Enlightenment were not atheists. Mostly they were deists, who believed in God but cut His connection to life on earth. In this view God has a plan, but it is irrelevant to us, since we receive no communication from Him. The supernatural, they conceded, created Nature and its immutable laws, including man's rights and the laws of politics, but these rights and laws are discovered by our unaided reason and—since they *are* immutable—not even God can change them.

For the medieval popes and even to a great extent for Louis XIV, we might say, God writes, casts, directs, and judges the political show, continually demanding changes from the wings. For the founding fathers, God builds the theater and its personnel, then takes off, leaving man alone to write the scripts and stage the production. A god so silent and powerless (in these ways, just like Aristotle's) is not a factor in human life, but merely a fading echo of an earlier age. He is no more relevant to capitalist politics than to Newtonian mechanics. In Jefferson's words, "our civil rights have no dependence on our religious opinions, any more than our opinions in physics or geometry." The Enlightenment's references "to God or a divine being seem purely perfunctory," sums up J. M.

Kelly, fellow of Trinity College, Oxford; "reason is in the foreground, the Divinity or the Creator hardly more than a decorous adjunct. . . ."[130]

In applying its secularism to epistemology, the Enlightenment generally followed Locke—not Locke the nominalist and budding skeptic, but Locke the empiricist, who had followed Aristotle in rejecting any claim to *a priori* ideas. Knowledge, thinkers held at the time, rests on experience. On this basis, men can then abstract, generalize, deduce—that is, they can conceptualize their observations, and thereby discover truth with certainty.

Secularism without skepticism—this was the essence of the Enlightenment philosophy, as it had been for its progenitor, Aristotle. As to rationalism with its claim to intuitive insight, the period tended to agree with Locke's barb that it is easy "to be sure without proofs, and to know without perceiving"; men turned their backs here on *a priori* deductions in order to grasp actual fact—by experience. Jefferson, for example, urged the young to study history on the grounds that it would give them "the experience of other times and other nations . . ."; only this kind of knowledge, he believed, enables us to know the nature of man and the causes of happiness. More important here, Jefferson presents the Declaration of Independence not as an expression of *a priori* insight or pure thought, but rather as knowledge that "all experience hath shewn." "Experience," write Madison and Hamilton, "is the oracle of truth; and where its responses are unequivocal, they ought to be conclusive and sacred."[131]

All the key features of the capitalist state—its validation, its powers and limits, the prerogatives and interrelationships of its citizens—are unified, because all are derived from a single principle: the worldly self-preservation of the individual. In this view, the state is a form of connection among the Many—a connection made by the Many, and real only through *their* agreement. Here we see not a One transcending the Many, but a One in the Many. Or, putting Thales into Latin, *e pluribus unum*—the I formula.

Pluralism (in Government)

During the second half of the nineteenth century, the intellectuals of the West increasingly rejected capitalism. A new political approach had taken hold in Europe by the 1880s, starting in Germany under Bismarck; a generation later, the Progressive Party brought it to the United States. Following many political scientists, I call this approach pluralism, although in different contexts it has two better-known names: the mixed economy and the welfare state. The exponents of this viewpoint have included a wide diversity of influential thinkers; in America alone, they were prominent among Social Gospelers, utilitarians, Keynesians, and pragmatists, to say nothing of the fact that the viewpoint has been endorsed by every president since Theodore Roosevelt and Woodrow Wilson through the two Bushes.

The pluralist in politics denies that government has any single purpose, such as carrying out God's will or protecting man's rights. There are many proper governmental goals, he holds, and these are not connected by or deducible from any abstract formula. Under the right circumstances, a proper government may and/or should, among other things, prevent monopoly and unfair competition; ensure full employment, obscenity-free TV, and safe drugs; protect civil rights; prohibit insider trading and racial discrimination; protect free speech and a free press; prohibit abortion and prayer in the schools; conscript the young; nationalize health care; protect the citizen from unwarranted intrusion by the government; redistribute wealth; and safeguard patents and copyrights.

By its nature, pluralism does not prioritize these functions. In its commonest, democratic form, it leaves the evaluation of any particular program to the people (at least, that is the theory). As in pluralist education, so too for these empiricists; they do not claim people's desires to be objectively valid—that is, to be based on an external reality, whether Nature or God. On the contrary, desires are taken as proper guides to action simply because they exist, and that is all we have to go by. Hence, in the words of William James, "So far as [a man] feels anything to be good, he *makes* it good."[132]

The pluralist state is not frozen in the capitalist role of watchman, forbidden by "inalienable rights" to expand. Since the concept of rights, natural or divine, has no basis in experience, Comte wrote, the term in its Enlightenment sense is "metaphysical." Rights properly understood derive from that which alone in this context is observable: society. As

American journalist Walter Lippmann put it, rights are "creations of the law, and have no other validity except as they are ordained by law." Laws, of course, can be changed when people want them to change.[133]

Although most of these anti-capitalist pluralists have endorsed an ever-increasing growth of government, they deny that they seek to establish an omnipotent state. Over a century ago, Washington Gladden, congregational minister and crusading Social Gospeler, gave the position one of its clearest statements. Although he himself was working to bring about bigger government, he wrote, he did not wish the state "to be turned into a good fairy" who would "empty the horn of plenty at every man's door. . . ." The pro-capitalist, he went on, would have government fill *none* of man's wants (aside from police protection). The socialist would have it fill *all* of them. By definition, however, the pluralist shuns "none" and "all"; rather, Gladden says, the government should fill "*many* of [people's] wants and provide for *many* of their necessities. . . ." To a pluralist, the Many here as elsewhere are not linked by necessary interconnection.[134]

One of the great virtues of pluralist government, say its defenders, is its ability to adopt the good features of capitalism *and* of socialism, while avoiding the evils caused in each by its monistic inflexibility. The pluralist society can combine individual freedom with caring government; property rights with redistribution of wealth; the citizen's independence with his interdependence. Gladden sums up: pluralism, he says, can combine "liberty and love." When the exponents of capitalism or socialism criticize these combinations as self-contradictory, pluralists reply that they reject the extremism of the monists in favor of moderation, balance, or centrism.

When the monists ask for the ideology validating their moderation, pluralists reply that the question brings out another virtue of their approach: It needs no ideology to validate it, it depends on no system, it cannot be defined or implemented by reference to sweeping generalities.

This feature of pluralism, its exponents say, is what enables its government to deal with the real issues of political life. Life is concrete, so the proper political agenda is a compilation of concretes, of specific, changing answers to specific, changing problems, each of which must be dealt with not by reference to some overarching conceptual scheme, but singly, empirically, and piecemeal.

Colonel Gian Gentile of West Point once illustrated this approach in regard to foreign policy, in a statement pointing out (I think favorably) that American forces in Iraq were deliberately pursuing measures chosen on an ad hoc basis without an overall objective. In a memorable phrase, he calls this approach a "strategy of tactics."[135]

Those who uphold the old-fashioned approach, Dewey says, agreeing here with the pluralists, cannot give us practical guidance. Capitalists and socialists, for example,

> suffer from a common defect. They are all committed to the logic of general notions under which specific situations are to be brought. . . . [Their theories] are ready-made principles to be imposed upon particulars in order to determine their nature. They tell us about *the* state when we want to know about *some* state.[136]

Here again we see the concrete-boundedness of pluralists—but here again we can also see their moderation. Within limits, pluralists in politics often do seek out empirical generalizations and causal connections, the knowledge of which they typically do regard as an important or at least relevant factor in resolving policy disputes. The generalizations they reach, however—sought out as they are to deal piecemeal with unconnected problems—are much narrower in scope than those of their intellectual predecessors, and are of course avowedly not absolutes. "[N]o particular set of tenets," writes Edwin Seligman, a Columbia economist, "can arrogate to itself the claim of immutable truth, or the assumption of universal applicability to all countries or epochs."[137]

Since political pluralism is a mixed mode, there are substantial differences among its exponents. In content, there is a wide range of opposed views in regard to how, when, and whether a given government should grow. Although all these men reject capitalism and socialism, there are still many significant incompatibilities between, say, FDR and Ronald Reagan, or in general between liberals and conservatives.

Epistemologically—leaving aside Christian fundamentalists, who are not pluralists—there are the pluralists' many differences in regard to the value and scope of principles as practical political guides. Some believe that the American founding principles, even if not absolute, are the best we have, but that now they must be restated in less sweeping a form to accommodate the unique conditions of modern life. Others attach more weight to such conditions, and interpret the founders' philosophy as a set of important but more or less toothless generalities—still useful, but only when converted into volumes of more specific generalizations. These differences reflect differences in tilt within the mixed mode. The more pro-capitalist side tilts to the Aristotelian politics of the Enlightenment along with its view of concepts. The more anti-capitalist and anti-conceptual side tilts to the new master of the times, Kant. Despite their often fierce contention, however, they all uphold the same political mixture; they all practice the same mode.

Modern pluralists in politics are skeptics in regard to basic principles, but knowers in regard to lower-level generalizations. They advocate the Many interspersed by unconnected Ones—the formula of D_1. This is one reason why the Republicans and the Democrats, despite their rhetoric, so often seem indistinguishable.

Totalitarianism

Both Communists and Fascists describe themselves as socialists, since unlimited power over the economy entails unlimited power over everything, and vice versa. Socialism, however, is a narrow term, referring primarily to economics. The broader term, which covers the state's power over everything, is totalitarianism. More than any others, the philosophers who directly generated this type of state in both its modern forms were Hegel and Marx. For reasons already given, I focus here on Communism.

As the name "totalitarianism" (coined by Mussolini) implies, the powers of the proper state are unlimited. The leadership can tolerate no dissent, whether based on religion, morality, or any other entity once regarded as independent of government. The state is to control not only art and education, as we've seen, but every detail of a man's life; the only prerogative of the citizen is obedience. As to personal liberty, private ownership, inalienable rights—all these are remnants of a decadent past, which must be obliterated. "The only person who is still a private individual in Germany," declared Robert Ley, a member of the Nazi hierarchy, "is somebody who is asleep." As we saw earlier, the beneficiary of such a state and the mover of history is the (chosen) collective, which is the only human reality. The individual extolled in the past is but a myth; it is wrong, writes Marx, to "postulate an abstract—*isolated*—human individual. . . . *My own existence* is a social activity."[138]

Mankind has matured across centuries, according to Communists, through the interaction of economic classes. A society's material forces of production, it is said, inevitably come into conflict with the property relations it has established, a conflict that leads to class struggle until the exploiting class is overthrown and a new economic order established. In time, however, the new system spawns a new version of the same basic conflict, which leads to a new form of class struggle and resolution, which is then followed by another such cycle and then another. Every social system thus contains the seeds of its own destruction, and history in essence is no more than the record of these economic rises and falls.

So economic forces determine everything about human life. All the other alleged causes of human behavior—such as ideas, free will, morals, law, religion, and philosophy—are mere "superstructure"; they are historically impotent rationalizations usually designed by the exploiters to protect their own class interests. "It is not the consciousness of men that determines their existence," writes Marx, "but, on the contrary, their social existence determines their consciousness."[139]

The reason that history is a continual progression of struggles, the Marxists hold, lies in the basic law of reality: the dialectic process, a concept originated by Hegel and taken up by Marx. In this view (touched on in chapter two), reality by its nature unfolds itself in a succession of triads: one entity (the thesis, A) necessarily generates its contradictory (the antithesis, non-A); then the two are united in a synthesis, which is an identity of opposites (A and non-A). But this fuller synthesis entails a higher thesis that generates a higher antithesis, etc. First off, therefore, Aristotle's logic must be wrong; the true law of reality is the opposite of the Law of Non-Contradiction. "In its proper meaning," Lenin observed, "dialectics is the study of the contradiction within the very essence of things." Although Marx accepted Hegel's dialectic theory with its embrace of contradictions, he rejected Hegel's idealistic interpretation of it (as a progression of ideas); in fact, Marx held, the dialectic process entails materialism, the opposite of idealism, because the dialectic's elements are not ideas, but material (economic) factors.[140]

In Hegel's view, the dialectic flow is a process of reality's maturation, which ultimately reaches its final stage in complete and perfect self-development; at this point the progression of contradictions ceases. The Marxists follow Hegel here as well, again in economic terms. History, they agree, is teleological; it has always been moving toward a final and perfect conclusion. In the Communist interpretation, history reaches this climax in two steps: the preparation and the culmination; or the dictatorship of the proletariat followed by the classless society; or, as the Communists liked to put it, socialism and then Communism.

During the first of these, the state must have total power, so that it can eradicate every trace of the pre-Communist mentality. Even the proletariat, Lenin found, were seriously infected ideologically and needed re-education. Thus arose the need for a political party of ideologically sound teachers who would be, in Lenin's words, the "vanguard of the revolutionary forces in our time." Since by the nature of its role the vanguard is the necessary expression of reality's self-development, since it is reality at this stage of history, it follows that the decrees of the party are infallible. The decrees of the party are too well-known to need rehearsal. The main enemies, it was held, were not intellectual dissidents, although they too must be eliminated, but the bourgeois exploiters, however powerless they may seem at present.[141]

When it arrives, the final stage, the classless society, will be the first truly moral society in history, according to the *Communist Manifesto*; the reason is that nothing then will be left of "naked self-interest," "egotistical calculation," or "callous 'cash payment.'" Instead, the ruling principle will be: "From each according to his ability, to each according to his need." These moral values, Marx observed, are "as old as the Judeo-Christian tradition. But their acceptance for social organization—their social realization—would be new. . . ." In other words, the difference in moral values between Christianity and Communism is that the Communists intend really to live by the principles that the Christians merely preach.[142]

Once these principles have been internalized by the citizens, Marx concludes, all will want nothing but to serve the group. So there will be no further need for a coercive state and the whole apparatus of totalitarianism will "wither away." Lenin regarded the details of this withering-away—when, where, how—as unknowable. Nikita Khrushchev did have one idea about it; the period of time required to reach the classless society, he said, "will be a very long one."[143]

As avowed materialists and empiricists, the Marxists held that they could validate their system, including its Hegelian base, scientifically, through observation; *a priori* ideas, they said, are merely unscientific vaporings. It would, however, be a daunting task to prove any rationalist's theories by empirical means, let alone the theories of Hegel—and there is little evidence that the Marxists even attempted to do so.

One sympathetic writer, Louis Dupré, illustrates this point in regard to the principle of dialectic progression.

> In Marx's view the dialectical principle is much more than an empirical description of the relations between man and his world. It has an essentially *ideal* character. . . . It is precisely this ideal, rational character which gives the dialectical principle a quality of necessity which a purely empirical description always lacks. A mere empirical study of facts can provide a hypothesis, or at most a theory, but it can never predict with the absolute confidence which gives Marxism all its power and influence.[144]

Again, in regard to the notion of teleology—that is, of reality moving purposefully toward motionless perfection, with its corollary that whatever is, is right—Hegel tried to validate this idea and the conservatism it implies apart from observation, by means of his own rationalist framework. To my knowledge, no revolutionists of any stripe have claimed to validate it on the basis of observation. Indeed, Marxists themselves have always found and decried a great many evils in "whatever is."

Sabine questions the empirical base of still another Marxist essential: the seemingly straightforward division of bourgeois society into two economic groups, capitalists and workingmen. What about farmers, he asks, and independent artisans, the professions, white-collar workers, and others? Marx, he says, "merely lumped" all these forms of production into a miscellaneous "petty bourgeoisie," which was then written off as historically insignificant. "No empirical sociology," Sabine concludes, "would count independent artisans and office workers as having the same type of work experience." For Marx, however, a society with only two contenders is a deductive necessity mandated by his dialectic theory, which requires social thesis and antithesis.[145]

The above is merely a sample of Marx's non-empiricism, which the interested reader must investigate on his own; in my judgment, the sample is representative. The fundamental principles of the Communists, I conclude, are not based on observation; they are accepted as *a priori* truth. This applies not only to the admitted Hegelianism in their metaphysics, but to their materialist interpretation of it as well. An idea is *a priori* not through content, but through method; it is *a priori* if its validation is independent of experience, whatever its subject, including matter and economics. Marxists do cite observations as a starting point in justifying their theories, including their materialism and economic determinism, but few rationalists from Plato on have done differently. What makes a thinker a rationalist is what he does after the starting point. What he does is turn away from observation in order to uphold a discovery inaccessible to experience or to scientific inference from it. This, it seems clear, was the procedure of the Marxists when they jumped from an ideology-driven analysis of a handful of past societies to the all-embracing metaphysical principles of materialism and economic determinism.[146]

A realm known by percepts and another known by concepts—the sensible world and the world of ideas—this is the Platonism of the Marxist metaphysics. It is unmixed Platonism, since in Marx's view (as in Hegel's), the ideal world is the true, unified, immutable reality, as against its transient worldly stages, which are all that has ever been available to our experience. As in Hegel, these stages may not be regarded as reality, because each is only a partial and fleeting manifestation, soon to be contradicted and vanish into the next.

Conceptual reality versus deceptive appearance is, of course, not the formula of materialism, but of its opposite, as Sabine points out. Marx's claim to be a materialist, he writes, "in no way displaced the Hegelian assumption of an underlying force which is the hidden reality behind a multiplicity of more or less ephemeral manifestations and appearances." A succinct elaboration of this point—by Sir Karl Popper, British philosopher of science—is deservedly famous. Marx, he writes,

> replaced Hegel's "Spirit" by matter, and by material and economic interests. In the same way, racialism substitutes for Hegel's "Spirit" something material, the quasi-biological conception of Blood or Race. Instead of "Spirit," Blood is the self-developing essence; instead of "Spirit," Blood is the Sovereign of the world, and displays itself on the Stage of History; and instead of its "Spirit," the Blood of a nation determines its essential destiny.
>
> The transubstantiation of Hegelianism into racialism or of Spirit into Blood does not greatly alter the main tendency of Hegelianism. It only gives it a tinge of biology and of modern evolutionism.[147]

Since percepts, in this view, are mere appearance, a thinker has the right and even the duty, if observations challenge the established *a priori*, to reinterpret or reject them. This is the philosophic explanation of the totalitarians' elevation of ideology above fact both in literature and education. According to Sabine, the same elevation applies to science; Marx, for example, gave little weight to Newton's mechanistic explanations of events, since Marx regarded them "as belonging to a lower form of logic because it deals with a lower stage of reality." For the same reason, the Party is infallible, because an unreality cannot contradict the vanguard of reality. In this issue, Friedrich Engels's work is perhaps the most clear; Engels, Sabine writes, "attributed rationality to nature in exactly the Hegelian sense. The real or rational cannot be equated with existence because much of what exists is irrational and therefore unreal; for example, in 1789 the French monarchy existed but was not real."[148]

The equivalent of such an utterance would have been possible for the medievals, but not for the earlier modern mind. In the twentieth century, however, it became possible again.

In totalitarian thought, there is no longer a philosophic justification for a division of political power, such as between Church and king. The one true reality is grasped by the one unified party in the form of a unified system of ideas—a system that elevates the collective, and regards the individual and ultimately all worldly entities as unreal appearance. So: the One without the Many—M_2.

Egalitarianism

In the decades after World War II, a new approach became increasingly evident on the ethical-political scene: egalitarianism, which for the first time has made explicit an idea long implicit in Western thought, notably in the teachings of Christianity, Kant, and Marx. The non-academic representatives of this viewpoint are usually concerned not so much with theory as with its application to some delimited area. But the pioneering source of this movement in our time is an academic: Harvard philosopher John Rawls.

Egalitarianism is the view that equality is the fundamental moral value and, therefore, the standard of good and evil. Equality here does not refer to equality before the law; although this principle, introduced by capitalism, is endorsed by most of these thinkers, they regard it as merely a minor instance of morality. Nor does equality mean equality of opportunity, a social condition advocated since FDR by welfare statists, who argued that society should equip all men equally from the start with the knowledge and goods necessary to achieve success in life, but thereafter should leave men reasonably free to compete, some ending up winners and others losers. To this viewpoint, egalitarians reply that, owing to factors beyond their control, some men are doomed to fail no matter what society does. If the fundamental moral value is to be achieved, they conclude, society must concern itself primarily not with the start of a man's endeavors, but with the end. The moral principle is not equality of opportunity, but equality of *result*.

Egalitarians differ, at least linguistically, in their interpretation of equality, but not on its essence. In regard to any value of significance, all agree, every man is equally entitled to have it. It is immoral, therefore, for men to compete with one another, each attempting to gain for himself or his loved ones an unequal share of the good things of life. Instead, writes Peter Singer, Australian philosopher and an intellectual founder of the animal rights movement, each of us should "go beyond 'I' and 'you' to . . . the standpoint of the impartial spectator. . . ."[149]

The value most often discussed by these theorists is material wealth. If equality is the definition of justice, then any disparity between rich and poor is self-evidently unjust. Egalitarians acknowledge that some men produce material values (and thus gain an income) that are superior, sometimes incomparably so, to those produced by others. Further, contrary to the Marxists, the dominant voices acknowledge that such producers usually succeed through their own character and consequent actions, such as disciplined thought and hard work. But none of this, they say, justifies the conclusion that producers have *earned* their products or deserve to keep them. The reason is that a man's intelligence, his character, and all his other productive attributes are a result of luck: his luck in the "lottery of nature," which gave him his superior brain; and/or his luck in being born and raised in a superior environment, which gave his brain the means to develop.

The actual creator of a product, therefore, is not its so-called producer, but the Nature/society combination that produced *him*. Since he is moving through life courtesy of factors he did nothing to earn, he cannot claim moral credit for his work, mental or physical, or ownership of it either. To the windfalls of luck, every person has equal claim. Justice does not allow us to reward the lucky or to penalize the unlucky—this last, because unproductive and immoral men, too, are not the authors of their actions. In the ancient world, Theophrastus, a student of Aristotle's, stated a viewpoint then regarded as obviously true: "It cannot happen that a good man is not angered by evil . . . the better each person is, the more irascible he will be." Not anymore.[150]

In place of the traditional idea of justice as giving every man his due, which implies that some are due more than others, we must implement a new definition of justice—justice as fairness. Fairness here means the elimination of the results of Nature's *un*fairness.

Besides inequality of wealth, there are many other sorts of inequality that egalitarians in various areas condemn as unfair and seek to remove. Today's ethnic leaders, who regard opponents of the new fairness as racist, seek not old-fashioned civil rights, already long gained, but equality for their minorities in regard to all the values enjoyed by the majority. Feminists seek equality with males—in income, status, power—through liberation from "sexism." Age activists, fighting "ageism," want equality with the young. The physically handicapped, fighting "ableism," want equality with the healthy. The ugly, fighting "looksism," want equality with the beautiful. The multiculturalists, fighting "imperialism," want the West to acknowledge that its culture is no better than any other. The animal-rights activists, fighting "speciesism," want us to recognize that man is no more important than any other creature.

So *any* standard or practice that divides men (or creatures in general) into better or worse, winners or losers, must be eliminated—for example, offering merit pay, awarding the Nobel Prize, or holding beauty contests. The only way to eliminate all these injustices, said the egalitarian former director of the Van Cliburn International Piano Competition, is to "stamp out the concept of the better."[151]

Rawls is concerned that, in practice, bad consequences might flow from his theory, especially from its advocacy of the redistribution of wealth. He argues, therefore, that some inequalities are justified—but only if and to the extent that they benefit the unluckiest men, the "most disadvantaged" members of society. In other passages, however, Rawls emphasizes his conviction that consequences of any kind are not relevant to ethics, which is not a recipe for achieving goals, such as men's happiness or the welfare of the poor. On the contrary, he says, ethics is an injunction to obey unconditionally one law: the moral law itself, the principle of equality. This inconsistency of Rawls has been deplored by the movement; the moral man's concern, many pointed out, is not quality of life, but equality. One cannot, therefore, place standard of living or any other consideration above it. To the moralist, they now agree, practical results do not matter.

Egalitarians acknowledge that, as a matter of fact and in virtually every respect, men are unequal. But their theory holds that in order to be just we must not only ignore this fact, but reverse it—that is, we must act (including redistribute values) as though its opposite were true. Men are not equal in reality, granted, but they *are* equal in our moral theory. These moralists do not claim to be working for the eradication of human differences; to make all men equally intelligent, honest, attractive, etc., is a task they spurn as utopian. Rather, they want us to make moral choices as if the differences <u>had</u> been eradicated.

Rawls, the most philosophical of them, explains why. Men's differences, he says, though real, are not morally relevant; we can reach a man's moral essence only by imagining him stripped of his attributes, because all of these are but effects of his unearned (and thus non-moral) natural/ social endowment. The moral man, in other words, is what is left after the man we see has been stripped of his brain, body, knowledge, memory, character traits, desires, skills, etc. From this perspective, Rawls concludes, all men *are* the same. If men were placed under what he calls a veil of ignorance, so that each were ignorant of any attributes distinguishing himself or anyone from anyone else—that is, if each became in thought his pure self, stripped of all non-moral features—then, having no basis any longer to judge any man, himself included, as more deserving of anything than any other man, he would have to choose egalitarianism as his moral viewpoint.

A moral claim, in this theory, is one made by an attribute-less man— which means: by a man who is nothing in particular, by an existent without identity, i.e., by nothing. Men are equally deserving not because of what they think, feel, or do, but because at the core they are equally zero. Kant, as we have seen, was the first philosopher to elevate nothing above something; in his ethics, nihilism took the form of his theory that each man has an unknowable, noumenal self—and that this is the authority demanding unlimited sacrifice by his worldly self. Rawls's approach is a variant of this: Egalitarianism is to be obeyed because it is demanded of phenomenal man by his real self—that is, by his unknowable, identityless negation. His own theory of justice, Rawls notes, "is highly Kantian in nature. Indeed, I must disclaim any originality for the views I have put forward."[152]

Since Kant's ideas cannot be defended by empirical means, as he himself insisted, and since most egalitarians, as empiricists, reject his noumenal world and his quasi-rationalist embrace of the *a priori*, the majority, unlike Rawls, simply brush aside the issue of validating their viewpoint. If asked why equality is desirable, writes Kai Nielson, a Canadian philosophy professor and an egalitarian,

> it is difficult to know what to say. . . . Reason . . . is not sufficient to provide an answer. . . . I do not know how anyone could show [egalitarianism] to be true . . . or in any way prove it or show that if one is through and through rational, one must accept it.

The egalitarian principle, such philosophers seem to suggest, has no objective basis; it is justified neither inductively, as a means to an end, nor deductively, as an inference from intuitive self-evidences.[153]

An ethics thus detached from perception and conception alike offers little guidance in regard to selecting a specific course of action. Since all demands for equality are by definition meritorious regardless of merit, and since consequences are irrelevant, some interpreters say that inequalities anywhere should be fought against equally. But some inequalities are more egregious, say others, and thus more deserving of society's immediate concern.

Few egalitarians attempt to resolve such disagreements. Since they cannot prioritize inequalities by reference to a theory—that is, to conceptual thought—most dismiss these questions as pointless abstraction. People, they say, know what they want, so no hierarchy of importance is required. The moral man needs no intellectual system to guide him. He starts anywhere, singling out for crusade the specific injustice about which he feels strongly; he is moved by emotionally charged concretes in the here and now. His eyes are not on a vision of an ideal human future, but on a perceptual-level flux of social sores—inequality of health insurance, of gender pay, of wheelchair access, et al—sores to be picked up piecemeal, fought against, and, if the emotional charge runs down, dropped piecemeal. Here again we see, but more consistently than in the D_1 case, the method of strategy through tactics.[154]

Whatever the injustice egalitarians strive to eliminate, their method of dealing with it does not vary. Since the unlucky losers, the bottoms among men, are by definition helpless, they can gain the values equality requires only if the tops are cut down—that is, only if they are deprived not merely of their greater money, but also of their unequal share of respect, admiration, rights, and power. These values, too, must be—and are now being—redistributed.

In the affirmative action programs, jobs and college admissions are awarded regularly to unqualified applicants at the price of being denied to the qualified. In many schools, grading students and even scorekeeping in games are being dropped, so that the superior performers, being unidentified, do not enjoy admiration for their feats, while the inferior ones gain self-esteem, since they are free now not to know that their betters are better. On many elite campuses, the civil rights of boys charged with rape are being redistributed: To bring equality to women, seen as victims of male aggression, the presumption in trials now is not the innocence of the accused, but the probable truth of the accusation—especially, at Stanford, if the accused acts "persuasive and logical." On the handicapped-lib front, one group a few years back, during Christopher Reeve's fight to regain normal functioning after his tragic accident, denounced his fight as hurtful elitism, since it implied that a normal man is superior to a paraplegic.[155]

Big business is increasingly told that community or environmentalist activists, though without capital or business experience, should have a seat on the board or at least a real voice in corporate management, so that today's unfair distribution of power can be replaced with equality of decision making. In our foreign policy, we see the United States, though on the verge of bankruptcy, lavishly (and sometimes apologetically) redistributing its wealth and often even its soldiers to dozens of relatively primitive cultures, including some that embrace murderous enemies of this country. We do it now not on biblical grounds, but mostly because it is politically correct: There are no enemies, there are no better or worse cultures, only some unlucky losers, who for that very reason have a right to share in the fruits of the lucky ones, such as the West.

The ambition of the egalitarian theory is all-encompassing; its target is not merely art, science, and education, but values as such, in any realm. Those who succeed in the pursuit of a value are to see the products of their action, spiritual and material, "spread around" to the non-succeeders, *because* they are non-succeeders. Value achievement leads a man to loss; non-achievement leads him to gain.

Peter Singer sums up the point memorably. It is essential, he writes, that we bring down the "high flyers."

Bringing them down, egalitarians concede, may cause suffering among men, even among the losers at the bottom, since, by the theory's own statement, they can survive only through the work of the "flyers." Nevertheless, consequences are irrelevant to morality. "[J]ustice," writes Marshall Cohen, professor of philosophy at Columbia, "requires the elimination of . . . inequalities, even if their elimination inhibits a further raising of the minimum." By the same reasoning such elimination is required even if it plunges men down to disaster level. The acclaimed humanitarian Albert Schweitzer, avant-garde in this issue, confessed the dilemma that often tortured him as a doctor: Since both are equal, should he save the man and kill the virus, or vice versa?[156]

The dictator of Cambodia, Pol Pot, an eclectic mix of Communism and egalitarianism, had no hesitation in mandating the result implicit in the ideal he had learned from the French: "After the first year of Khmer Rouge rule, to take just one example, foraging for food was denounced as a manifestation of individualism. Some might wind up with more than others. Better that all should starve equally."[157]

There is only one name for a theory that starts with a zero in man's soul and uses it to create a zero out of mankind: nihilism.

Although I have now given the same level of detail to egalitarianism as to its predecessors, I cannot ignore one more variant of the theory, because this one is the most consistent to date, and by far the most influential in our culture. Since the instances of a mode often come and go with ease, this particular instance is not necessarily here to stay; nevertheless it does make the nature of egalitarianism even clearer than the other variants do, and thus provides a unique key to understanding today's intellectual establishment.

Since moral respect is merited by existence apart from identity, this movement holds, there is no reason to deny such respect to inanimate Nature; since it exists, it has the same moral status as man, and must be treated accordingly. So the social redistribution of wealth discussed earlier is not true egalitarianism, as it turns out, because wealth is created by our species' assault on this moral equal. In the act of production, men necessarily violate the rights of Nature; they gain their survival and standard of living by molesting rivers with dams, tearing open the earth and looting it of its coal and oil, driving whole species into homelessness or extinction in order to build shopping malls; etc. To abolish these immoralities, writes Roger S. Gottlieb—a philosophy professor at Worcester— we must stop hoping "for a continually better life for ourselves and our children, defining 'better' as 'richer, bigger, faster, more.'" The moral alternative is a life that is poorer, smaller, slower, less. To achieve this, consumers must come to understand the evil of "all those long drives, all those appliances, all that stuff we've bought. . . . What kinds of lives are we living if we continue to shop, drive our cars, fly ozone-destroying jets . . . ?" The fact that "all that stuff" may contribute to men's happiness is morally irrelevant. The moral standard is not happiness, but fairness, and by that standard, people must learn not to accumulate, but to give up their enjoyments.[158]

Since man is but a fragment of Nature, these egalitarians contend, rights are not possessed only by humans; the environment, too, has rights. "Distinguishing between ourselves and nature," says one, "reflects a self-centered arrogance." It is wrong, therefore, to be "interested in the utility of a particular species, or free-flowing river, or ecosystem to mankind." In this view, man must give up not merely "excessive" wealth or the use of "dwindling resources," not merely jet planes and oil, but all material products, everything acquired by interfering with natural entities and thereby violating their rights. If men do not comply with this obligation, they are moral monsters and a threat to the planet.

Specific political measures to achieve the environmentalist agenda are often presented to the public as a practical means of averting some catastrophe to human life. Since the desirability of such catastrophe is inherent in the theory, however, the appeal to practicality is disingenuous—a fact further evidenced by the parade of ever-changing and often mutually contradictory disasters predicted by the movement. (In one recent series of weather-centered menaces, "nuclear winter" gave way to "global warming," which seems to be giving way to an undefined yet ominous "climate change.") The predictors of all these disasters claim the support of science, in part through the use of skewed and ever-changing computer models; in part by excluding from academic outlets the many scientists whose research contradicts their claims; and in part, as the newspapers have recently revealed, through shocking fraud at the top of the climatologist hierarchy in England. It seems obvious that the environmentalists, like the Marxists and many other groups, invoke science selectively, when it seems useful to their cause.

The enemy that makes man's rape of Nature possible on today's scale, the most philosophical among the environmentalists hold, is the industrial revolution. The movement's efforts to eliminate this enemy are concretized and analyzed in Ayn Rand's *Return of the Primitive*, especially in the chapter entitled "The Anti-Industrial Revolution."

One example of the environmentalists' animus here is the establishment's policy in regard to energy: its campaign to slow up or shut down every form of energy (unless it is green and useless), including coal, oil, nuclear, natural gas, and even the dams of hydroelectricity. This campaign reflects a commitment to choke off the lifeblood of an industrial society. Three main methods are being employed to achieve this goal: cutting the consumption of energy, cutting its production, and changing people's psychology.

The first is stated by Paul Ehrlich, a pioneer in the movement writing years ago, who explained, "Giving society cheap, abundant energy at this point would be the moral equivalent of giving an idiot child a machine gun." The second method, usually presented in gradual, unscary form, is illustrated by one of the current administration's *non*-controversial ideas, here described by Bret Stephens, an editor and columnist at the *Wall Street Journal*. President Obama, he writes, "wants to cut U.S. greenhouse gas emissions by 83% from current levels by 2050, levels not seen since the 1870s—in effect, the Industrial Revolution in reverse."[159]

The third method aims to teach an individual to consider his personal life not from a selfish but from a conservationist point of view. A nice, if untypically extreme, example here was provided by the Web site of the Australian Broadcasting Corporation in a "fun" program aimed at a young audience: Children are invited to click on an icon of a skull and crossbones in order to "find out at what age you should die so you don't use more than your fair share of Earth's resources!" A seven-year-old girl named Suzie discovered that she deserved to die years ago because she had already used up her "fair share."[160]

As there should be no trespassing on a neighbor's property, the environmentalists sum up, so there should be no trace of man's existence in the world of Nature, no "environmental footprints." A patient way of removing these footprints was reported decades ago by *Newsweek* magazine: ". . . a number of today's environmental reformers conclude that mankind's main hope lies not in technology but in abstinence—fewer births and less gadgetry." For those impatient to cleanse the globe now, biologist David Graber has an idea:

> Human happiness, and certainly fecundity are not as
> important as a wild and healthy planet . . . it is cosmically
> unlikely that the developed world will choose to end its orgy
> of fossil-energy consumption, and the Third World its suicidal
> consumption of landscape. Until such time as Homo sapiens
> should decide to rejoin nature, some of us can only hope for
> the right virus to come along.

It is mass death being welcomed here, for its own sake, with no war or shortages or social needs to justify it.[161]

Even though a minority of egalitarians are conservatives, those influential in politics stress the need for government action to achieve equality. As history has shown, they say, human beings left alone will always treat one another and/or Nature unequally. Only a state with the power of coercion can reverse this evil, and in performing this moral task there can be no limitation on its power. But, the egalitarians go on, they do not advocate a totalitarian state. If liberty is taken to be the inalienable right to ownership and action regardless of the effects on equality, then of course liberty will be abolished by their government. But, they say, freedom of a different kind, as a matter of degree, is compatible with the egalitarian state—freedom in the form and amount society deems proper at a given time; of this kind of freedom by definition everyone will enjoy an equal amount.

The precursors of today's egalitarians preached equality in theory, but always postponed its practice. For example, the medieval Christians and the modern Communists, each in their own fashion, held out as their goal and result the final triumph of the deserving and the banishing of the wicked. In this cause, they righteously rewarded their supporters and punished their enemies; they elevated those who knew the truth and cast down those who did not. In short, they were staunch defenders of moral and epistemological *inequality*—a fact expressed in the political hierarchies prominent in both movements. Both did champion the value of equality. But the Christians preached it as an ideal realizable only in the next life, and the Marxists as an ideal realizable only in the ever-receding final stage of Communism. Each group understood that the end of the "better" would mean the end of their movement.

The egalitarians have a different viewpoint. They want equality now, with all the zeros that entails. It has been said that the greens are Communism reborn, merely a name change for the reds. But this is not true. The egalitarian movement rejects certain of the fundamentals of the Communist mind. It does not work for or promise a better life for a better man—but rather no life for any of us.

The true color of the environmentalist movement is not red or green, but black.

In the nineteenth century, men entered the race of life at different starting points, according to whatever assets they were given or had created; fairness, it was held, is men's equal freedom to run. In the twentieth century, we heard that the race is fair only if everyone, through government aid, starts at the same point. Now, in the twenty-first century, we hear that, to be fair, the men leading the race must have their legs broken so that the losers can catch up.

As the archetype of the anti-integration mentality in social-political issues, egalitarianism clearly upholds the Many without the One—the formula of D_2.

PART THREE

DIM IN PRE-MODERN CULTURE

CHAPTER NINE

GREECE

SO FAR, WE have hunted for modes by following four subjects across a succession of modern cultures, considering each subject as an isolated discipline. The next step is to study the four subjects together—that is, as they exist at the same time in a single culture—and see what relationships their modes bear to one another. If the products are representative and we find a mode common to all four of our subjects, that mode may validly be taken as defining the mental processes not merely of individual creators, but the method of thought of the culture as a whole.

The three Western cultures not yet considered are Greece, Rome, and the Middle Ages.

Literature

In the field of literature, the works most beloved by the Greeks were the epics of Homer and to a somewhat lesser extent the plays of the great dramatists, Aeschylus, Sophocles, and Euripides, who were much influenced by Homer. There are, of course, many differences between eighth-century B.C. epics of largely unknown origin and the fifth- and fourth-century tragedies, especially since drama was a newly created art form with its own (religious) origins and development; nevertheless the essentials of Homer's works are the same as those of the great Greek dramas. The most Homeric of his poems, many think and I agree, is the *Iliad.*

In presenting the epic of Achilles going on strike because of the injustice done to him, Homer is concerned above all to tell a story. The main figures do reveal their inner lives and often speak poetically and with passion. But the primary content of the work is the actions and results in the physical world brought about by their inner lives and public speeches: expropriation, revenge, strategy, battle, death, victory. "In a play," as Aristotle later explained the Greek approach, ". . . they do not act in order to portray the Characters; they include the Characters for the sake of the action . . . the first essential, the life and soul, so to speak, of Tragedy is the Plot. . . ."[162]

Aristotle's view of plot is essentially that of the nineteenth-century Romanticist movement: a progression of necessarily connected events, as in the *Iliad,* moving logically from problem to climax to resolution. Or as Aristotle puts it, plot is a progression with a beginning, a middle, and an end. Although there were sporadic rudiments of plot long before Homer, his epic is the first work we know of to present a plot that integrates a story's events from start to finish. His plot is simple, and the epic, transmitted for centuries only by oral means, is somewhat digressive. This does not, however, diminish its distinctiveness. The practice in earlier cultures had been to tell stories about the gods' arbitrary behavior, or chronicles reciting past events however illogical, or comedic patter aiming to produce laughter, or tales of omens aiming at fear. None of these literary expressions were concerned with logically connected narrative.

The gods' interventions in the action, and the characters' obeisances to Zeus's unlimited power, are all over Homer's story. Despite this, however, the gods have no real effect on the story. For example, Zeus, who is supposed to have ordained the war's outcome, is a pathetic omnipotence. At one point he complains that he doesn't know what to do; at another, he is seduced and drugged by his nagging wife, who denounces him to his face as a tyrant. Meanwhile the primary concern of the lesser gods is rivalry over their status in the divine pecking order. It is hardly a surprise, therefore, to see a human character now and then openly defying the gods when their whim gets in his way, and doing so without a moral qualm, without penalty, and with Homer's seeming approval.

The gods, in the distinctively Greek view, are physical entities, parts of Nature like all else, and subject to its laws. As gods, of course, the Olympians have superhuman—though not supernatural—abilities, but even these are limited in all respects, including knowledge and power, as even Zeus is in the story's action. The removal of omnipotence from deity explains why the Olympians are not movers of or even players in the story, but detached spectators, more like kibitzers. The essence of Homer's gods, comments Richard Jenkyns, the distinguished Oxford classicist, lies "in the lightness of their emotions. On one level they are keenly caught up in the great game of the war, but deep down they do not care a whit." The historian Will Durant rates the gods' role a step lower: "[T]he Olympians have essentially the function of comic relief. . . ."[163]

The Greek plays with which I'm familiar follow Homer in regard to plot. They too are concerned primarily to present action, action that is not only physical, but often violent (albeit offstage)—for example, a son sleeps with his mother and blinds himself, a wife murders her husband and is then murdered by her son, a mother wreaks vengeance on her husband by killing their children. Such events occur as or within a carefully structured progression; they follow from previous events and lead to inevitable consequences. The events are not juxtaposed, but united into a plot. A number of stories, it is true, do feature chance, as in the use of *deus ex machina*; but this is not typical. Most of the tragedies do live up to Aristotle's demand that dramas have "all the organic unity of a living being." And most, in Homer's fashion, present homage to gods who "do not care."[164]

The Greek writers usually present the generating problem of their story as of divine origin; the gods, so to speak, write the prequel, and the humans take it from there. This is culturally significant, as we will see shortly, but it is not modally significant, because this use of the gods is not relevant to the writer's mode of integration within the work. It does not alter his method of interrelating its elements. If the "divine framework," as it is commonly called, were removed from these works, the essentials of the epic or play would be untouched. An obvious example is the irrelevance of the gods to the instigation of the *Iliad*'s action. Paris's lust for Helen and Menelaus's passion for revenge are common human emotions that need no prompting from a jealous goddess; this kind of triangle goes back to pre-history and forward to Hollywood.

Epic action requires epic protagonists. The archetype presented by Homer is Achilles, the mighty warrior who is also much more. "The Homeric hero's ideal," says Jenkyns, "is to be 'a speaker of words and a doer of deeds. . . .' [He is a man] honouring sharpness of mind alongside strength of arm. . . ." So Achilles is also an intellectual, as demonstrated by his speeches, an impassioned moralist, an artist at the lyre, a wit, and a true lover of his friends. What integrates all these traits is the Greek ideal: self-fulfillment through the development of one's rational faculty and physical skill, the reward for which is eudaemonia, happiness on earth. That it must be on earth Homer tells us unequivocally in the *Odyssey*. When Achilles finds himself in Hades, the Greek version of the afterlife, this is his opinion of it: "I would rather be plowman to a yeoman farmer on a small holding than lord Paramount in the kingdom of the dead."[165]

Just as the gods have little effect on the story, so they have little effect on the characters; in particular, they do not subvert human self-confidence or moral stature. The same is true, as Durant writes, of the dramas:

> Not one of [the gods] could bear comparison with Odys-
> seus in intelligence, with Hector in heroism, with Androm-
> ache in tenderness, or with Nestor in dignity. Only a poet of
> the sixth century, versed in Ionian doubt, could have made
> such farcelings of the gods.

The gods' inability to debase man, like their inability to defy Nature, stems from their finitude; because of this, a man can grasp and deal with the divine by using his own unaided mind. Contrary to man's helplessness before Plato's ineffable, Homer's characters possess a storehouse of divine information. They know the gods' location, desires, rivalries, pettiness, disguises, weaknesses, strengths, musical tastes, preferred hijinks, lineage, etc. Gods who are thus concretely accessible to us and judgeable by secular reason cannot, on a fundamental level, subvert human independence, logic, or self-esteem. In spirit if not in fact, the Zeus worshiper does not fall to his knees, but ambles through perfunctory rituals, then goes about his earthly business.[166]

Homer, in my opinion, is the least tragic of the non-comedic writers; he focuses on man's stature while indicating without emphasis his protagonists' flaws. The later tragedians for the most part feature a man's flaws as essential to their story. But this does not affect their mode of characterization or even their fundamental view of man, both of which remain Homeric. The characters are presented as unified; their traits flow from a fundamental attribute integrated to their actions. And whatever the playwright's pessimism, it did not lead him to the idea of original sin; on the contrary, he was still concretizing onstage the Greek view of man, but in negative form—that is, not by exhibiting man's virtues, but by condemning his betrayal of his potentially noble human nature. In their basic estimate, pessimists and optimists alike agreed. "Many wonders there be," wrote Sophocles, "but naught more wondrous than man."[167]

Most Greek protagonists are concretizations of an abstraction that is their fundamental, integrating attribute—rebellion against injustice, fidelity to a moral principle, rage at a cheating spouse, power lust—but they are not reducible to that abstraction. Achilles, Antigone, Clytemnestra, Creon are not more or less interchangeable reciters of elegant verse or ideological lessons; they are individual men and women who burn with desire, tear their hearts out in grief, go mad with rage, are buried alive for their convictions. Such passion—precisely because it connects to everything else we know about them and motivates their often cataclysmic actions—conveys to an audience not floating abstractions or meaningless concretes, but real individuals whose lives have universal meaning. In this way, the characters reflect the union of the perceptual and the conceptual.

The same union applies to the author's method of creating a character. He observes and then stylizes on the conceptual level. The tragedian, Aristotle explained, "should follow the example of good portrait-painters ... [representing] the distinctive features of a man, and at the same time, without losing the likeness, make him handsomer than he is."[168]

A logical progression of events enacted by conceptually unified characters must convey a general idea of some sort, a theme that the writer conveys through his selection and integration of the work's elements. Homer's selectivity in creating the *Iliad* has long been praised as a historic turning point. Contrary to the chroniclers, who would recount all the battles of a war simply because they happened, Homer wrote only about the eleventh year of the twelve-year Trojan War. That was the year that provided him with the kind of conflict necessary to convey the theme of interest to him. As I interpret it, the theme of the *Iliad*—the meaning that integrates its elements—is the dependence of humanity on the strong, and thus the disastrous result of injustice to them.

When the theater emerged, a playwright was expected to follow certain conventions regarding a play's length, number of characters, observance of the unities, etc. Contrary to seventeenth-century classicists, however, the Greek writer did not regard these formal requirements as aesthetic primaries or standards of value. It was not the rules he followed, but the content he dramatized that was the Greek writer's passion. To him, matter, not form, was the fundamental in art.

The abstract themes of the Greeks were not presented as a string of concepts—words and speeches. Rather, a theme was presented through concretes, of specific people and events available to the perceptual level. Such a union of abstractions and concretes is essential to their work. Theme without story they would have regarded not as art, but merely as an idea belonging to ethics or philosophy, while quarrels and battles unrelated to meaning (like today's action movies) they would have regarded as senseless.

Given the secularism evident in Greek literature, some scholars have interpreted the Olympians out of existence. In one version, the divine framework is merely a technique by which, in the era before philosophy, a play was given metaphysical significance: "[W]hat Homer calls 'the plan of Zeus,'" remarks H. D. F. Kitto—professor of Greek at the University of Bristol—is what "we should call the inevitable working-out of events." Poet-scholar Robert Graves and others, from another angle, regard the use of mythology as no more than a convenient means of worldly expression, a purely secular form of allegory, satire, political polemics, and the like. This kind of interpretation is certainly consistent with the modal essence of the works, but it errs, I think, in denying the importance to the Greeks of religion—a lesser consideration, perhaps, in regard to Homer, but more significant later.[169]

That the gods capriciously inflict on man the problems with which he must struggle does not dictate his stature or the steps of his struggle. But it does suggest a metaphysics that—while not guiding the thought of the artist qua integrator—nevertheless is real in his work. According to this metaphysics, the universe does not have the rationality depicted within the writer's own play, because, as the human species seems always to have believed, men are at the mercy of forces they cannot control, and against which any struggle, however reasonable and good it may seem, is doomed. So: The hero is great, his passion is real, his actions are logical, but, comedies aside, the end of it all is his loss, failure, death.

I have referred earlier to the phenomenon of a method of thought placed on the back burner—a background mode incompatible with the distinctive new mode guiding the creators, yet still a lingering presence within their world, evident even in most of the advanced thinkers. Typically, the old mode is not much evident in intellectual form; one sees it, rather, in the form of automatized emotions carried over from the past. Such creators are unwittingly in conflict: drawn to the new thought and also to some part of the old. The products of these men, accordingly, usually reflect both these contradictory factors.

If this was true of ancient Greece, it would be an example of the broader concept that Ayn Rand calls "sense of life." She means by this a philosophy held actually though not consciously—held not in words, but as a subconscious emotional appraisal of man and existence. A sense of life may be consistent with or contradict the conscious convictions and creations of a man or culture. All in all, it seems, there is evidence that such a contradiction existed in ancient Greece—not in every area, perhaps, but certainly in literature.*

---

* There is also the possibility, as we have seen in regard to the Big Three, that a creator can consciously accept and articulate the old, without seeing that it contradicts the new. In such a case, the conflict does not spring from unidentified emotions. But this does not alter the fact that the contradiction exists, emotionally and/or intellectually.

The hero fights purposefully for his worldly passion, but he does it in a world of whimsical powers who demand obedience and portend doom. In effect, the writer carves out a logical realm within a universe he feels (not so much Homer) to be illogical. The creator's method of thought expresses a new view, man as the wondrous being; but the creator's feeling about life is the age-old sense of man as helpless.

It is hard to imagine this kind of conflict being avoided in the centuries when the new mode of thought was just emerging, when its full definition and implications could not yet be clear. At that early stage, a clash between the subconscious and the just discovered was hardly remarkable. It is understandable, perhaps inevitable—and yet in a way still astonishing: an unprecedented culture defined by a brilliant new method—used to convey a diametrically opposite view of life. As always, however, the former—the method—is what primarily concerns us.

Nineteenth-century Romantic literature and ancient Greek literature express the same mode. Artistically, their major difference lies in their sense of life. The Romanticists, reflecting the Enlightenment's disdain for religion, broadcast man's liberation, political and metaphysical, and therefore his freedom to choose his own goals and achieve them in an unobstructed universe. But most of the time even these writers, because of their Christian moral code, could not project a hero who was fully efficacious and triumphant. Only with Ayn Rand did Romanticism achieve consistency in this regard. The tragic endings of so many Romanticist works are but another form of the conflict expressed by the Greek tragedians.

Whatever their differences from the Romanticists, however, it was the Greek writers who paved the road for them two and a half millennia later. Both schools represent neither the One without a Many nor the reverse, but the One in the Many—I. Greek literature thus carries on the revolution of Thales.

Science

Science, like drama, started in Greece. From the sixth century B.C. through the Hellenistic era, an unprecedented approach to gaining knowledge of Nature was developed by many illustrious figures. Among the better known are Thales, Euclid, Hippocrates, Archimedes, and Aristarchus. Their method of gaining knowledge of the physical world was the same: observation of facts, then the use of man's rational faculty to reach a secular interpretation of them.

Thales, who started the whole enterprise, began with sense experience—water, he noted, can assume all three forms of matter, liquid, solid, and gas; in river deltas, it turns into earth; in evaporation, into air; and it is essential to life. From such observations he drew a secular and in his case universal conclusion. Centuries later, when considering a disease that the Mesopotamians had attributed to displeased gods, Hippocrates was using the same method. "I am about to discuss the disease called 'sacred,'" he writes. "It is not, in my opinion, any more divine or more sacred than other diseases, but has a natural cause, and its supposed divine origin is due to men's inexperience. . . ." It is not enough, he writes elsewhere, simply to make up theories: ". . . one must attend in medical practice not primarily to plausible theories, but to experience combined with reason. . . . I approve of theorising also if it lays its foundation in incident, and deduces its conclusions in accordance with phenomena."[170]

Most of the Greek scientists were too early or their interests too narrow to seek an overall system of physics. The only thinkers to attempt such a task were Plato, Democritus, and Aristotle. The first two, however, being rationalists, were not representative of the long line of Greece's scientific pioneers. That is why it is Aristotle who is still called the father of science.

Since we already know Aristotle's underlying epistemology, I turn now to Aristotle the practicing scientist. He identifies physics as the study of Nature and more specifically of moving objects. He observes six types of motion: substantive change, coming to be, passing away, quantitative change, qualitative change, and change of place or locomotion. In pursuing this study, Aristotle takes, as his paradigms of change, living action and distinctively human action—for example, an acorn becoming an oak, or an educator teaching a lesson. He chooses such examples deliberately, rejecting the idea that all motion is reducible to locomotion. He is seeking to reach a theory of motion that will apply to all types of motion.

A theory derived only from its simplest form, locomotion, will leave the more complex types unexplained; whereas a theory that explains the complex will have no difficulty in explaining the simple as well.

Aristotle begins his study with a generalization he regards as based on a great wealth and variety of observations: that the course and outcome of any given natural process is consistent—i.e., that the process continually takes place in the same way. The acorn regularly grows into an oak, not a bunch of daffodils; the teacher transfers his knowledge to his students, rather than sitting silently to promote their creativity (he wrote before the twentieth century); water, if unimpeded, always moves downward until it reaches its stopping place next to the earth, but fire moves to the sky.[171]

We can explain this consistency, says Aristotle, only if moving entities are goal-directed—that is, only if, inbuilt in each, there is a conatus, a "striving" to reach its natural state. For Aristotle, such teleology has no transcendent implication. He is not suggesting that conscious purpose is what causes motion; on the contrary, he rules that idea out as irrelevant in this context—except, of course, in the case of a moving entity that possesses the faculty of consciousness. For example, he distinguishes man's pursuit of art from the striving of physical elements or of vegetables.[172]

The meaning of Aristotle's theory, as he interprets it, is that each entity has a certain nature and, if not disturbed, acts only in accordance with that nature, reaching thereby only one possible outcome. In Aristotle's terminology, each entity has a definite, limited potentiality to actualize, and must therefore act—move—accordingly. When the actuality—an oak, an educated boy, water in its natural place—has been reached, the relevant motion ceases.

The enduring essence of this view, long accepted by scientists who dropped the idea of natural strivings, is that the world is ruled by natural law, so that there are no chance events and no miracles. As John Herman Randall Jr., longtime philosopher at Columbia and distinguished Aristotelian scholar, put his view: "Every process involves the operation of determinate powers. There is nothing that can become anything else whatsoever. A thing can become only what it has the specific power to become, only what it already *is*, in a sense, potentially." Even though

Aristotle's statements on this topic are not always consistent, his theory is the first attempt in Western history to formulate, validate, and apply a universal Law of Cause and Effect, and to do so in purely secular terms.[173]

Apart from what Aristotle calls "violent" action, the source of a natural object's movements, flowing as they do from its own conatus, lies within itself. This does not mean that objects take off in pursuit of actuality independent of the things around them. On the contrary, an external cause in physical contact with an object is a necessary condition of its movement toward self-actualization. As Aristotle famously puts it, every change has four observable "reasons why" it occurs: the material cause, the object at the start of a process, with a potentiality to change; the formal cause, the object at the finish, which is the actualization of that potentiality; the efficient cause, the event that by mechanistic means makes the change occur; and the final cause, the end for the sake of which the change occurs. The end, in short, cannot start motion; only the mechanistic cause can do that and thereby unleash the power of the object to move itself toward its end. In natural change, therefore, both teleology and mechanism are necessary, and they always cooperate. Like form and matter, the two interpretations of motion are not antagonistic, but integrated.

This dual approach, Aristotle holds, is the only one true to our observations, as proved by the theories of his two leading opponents. He dismisses Plato's version of teleology because it places the explanation of Nature in a realm of motionless, disembodied forms, which Aristotle regards as nonexistent—and anyway by definition irrelevant to understanding motion. Nor, he thinks, is Plato's physics improved by its writing off of Nature, and thus of mechanistic causation, as unreal.

Aristotle dismisses Democritus's atomism because it rejects teleology and recognizes only mechanistic causation. This, as Empedocles explained, means that "There is no 'nature' of anything, but only a mixing and unmixing of mixable things." But, Aristotle replies, if there were no entities with natures, but only random atomic collisions and rearrangements, then we could not explain—indeed, there could not *be*—the orderly world that we do, in fact, observe. Democritus had also claimed that atoms possess only quantitative attributes—that is, they are devoid of sensory qualities, which accordingly are unreal. But, Aristotle objects, this theory arbitrarily denies one observed aspect of Nature in favor of another, whereas the proper conclusion from the evidence is inescapable: We see qualities just as much as we see quantities—both are real.[174]

Plato and Democritus, each in his own way, did not derive their conclusions from observation; rather, they proceeded dialectically—that is, by combining into an *a priori* theory what they regarded as the logical implications of the ideas of their predecessors, especially Parmenides and Heraclitus. "When he looks at nature," sums up Columbia philosopher Frederick J. E. Woodbridge, another distinguished classicist, Aristotle

> does not see atoms moving necessarily in a void; he does not see heavenly essences reflected in a refracting mirror; he sees the obvious and insists that nature must first be defined in terms of the obvious before we proceed to any theory of nature.[175]

Aristotle's approach to science is further illustrated in his treatment of four issues crucial to physics and often used by rationalists as a springboard to another dimension: the issues of space, time, infinity, and mathematics. An object's place, Aristotle holds, is the boundary of its container; space is merely a relationship of natural objects qua occupying different places; absolute space is a myth; the universe is not in space; space is in the universe. Similarly, time is a relationship among objects; it is a measurement of motion, not a bodiless stream; the universe is not in time, but the reverse. As to infinity, it cannot exist actually, but only potentially, as the capacity for indefinitely repeatable mathematical processes such as addition or division; these processes can continue without limit, but the quantity reached at any point—the number of integers or segments—is always finite. And most important in this context, mathematics is as naturalistic as physics; both sciences study and describe, from different perspectives, the same worldly objects: Physics studies objects as a whole; mathematics abstracts their perceived quantitative aspects.

Nature for Aristotle is thoroughly natural. There is no room for the mystical within it, and there is no without, no dimension waiting to take in the absence of objects.

I repeat once more that a mode hunt does not yield Oscar nominations. My obvious approval of Aristotle is not relevant in this context; nor are my many disagreements with him.

The Greek physicists sought to gain a conceptual understanding of the observed world. They sought not the unity that comes from discarding the Many, but the One discoverable only by study of the Many—the One in the Many—the I formula.

Education

In Greece at its height, a child's education was determined by his parents. Typically, younger boys were not taught in a group setting; the individual child learned alone, from a series of tutors each qualified in a different subject (this approach encouraged many educational variations). In addition, there was a significant change in emphasis from the fifth century to the fourth, when the "Old" education (600–450 B.C.) was replaced by the Sophist-influenced "New" (450–330 B.C.). Despite these differences, however, there are basic common features throughout.

Greek education was monistic. Within the knowledge and resources available to them, a single fundamental goal dictated all of education's essential attributes, including curriculum and teaching methods. The goal was training for manhood—that is, to enable the boy to achieve the full realization of his distinctively human potentialities. Such realization required his achievement of arête in every important part of life. In general, "arête" means excellence; in a man, writes Kitto, it means excellence "in the ways in which a man can be excellent—morally, intellectually, physically, practically." The Greeks did want their children to become good citizens and good warriors. But they believed that these practical advantages were consequences that, to be fully achieved, required the child first to spend years pursuing the primary, non-practical purpose of education: all-around self-development.[176]

In the Greek view of education, there are three relevant human attributes: body, character, and mind. These three, being necessarily connected, cannot be trained independently of one another. Rather, it was held, the perfecting of each makes possible and/or reinforces that of the others. The curriculum, accordingly, must consist of three forms of training, three subjects, as we would say: for the body, gymnastics; for the character, music; for the intellect, literature. Training in professional or mechanical skills was regarded as irrelevant to education, since the teacher's purpose is to make an excellent man, not an excellent doctor or carpenter. (For those who cared to pursue them, such callings required specialized study elsewhere.)

Although gymnastics was regarded as a valuable start of military training, the latter was not its main purpose (at least in Athens as against Sparta). Primarily, gymnastics was the means of developing the boy's body and physical skills so that he could achieve arête qua physical being. Such a program bore little resemblance to today's pluralist phys ed courses, with their seemingly limitless array of sports and workouts. The Greek training was highly restricted; it included only those activities regarded as essential to the fundamental goal. The pentathlon, for instance, a grueling sport eagerly competed in by virtually all the young men, tested running, jumping, throwing the discus and the javelin, and wrestling. These activities, it was thought, do not merely foster specific skills; they train a boy's very capacity for action, promote his health, and teach him the critical qualities of poise and grace in posture and movement. Boys thus brought up become men who are strong, confident, courageous; physically, they have become men in the full sense. Such men became heroes to the younger boys, who heaped adulation on them—rightly, in the adults' eyes. A good part of the admiration for the hero was for the element most obviously instrumental in his feats, his body. Thus all participants were naked during gymnastics; in the Greek view, the boys were thereby unveiling and learning to idealize male beauty, along with the effort it presupposes and the virtues it represents.

Since gymnastics was a part of the pursuit of arête, the Greeks would never have allowed into their program such modern sports as golf, tennis, basketball, football, et al—all of which they would have viewed as narrow specializations and/or pointless amusements, not as activities necessary to the development of the perfect body and the whole man.[177]

In building character, the second part of a boy's training, the teachers were again concerned to nurture virtue in the Greek definition. They taught the boy about the personal happiness he would enjoy by living the good (Athenian) life, which, as Durant puts it, is "the fullest one, rich in health, strength, beauty, passion, means, adventure, and thought. . . . [The ideal man] combines beauty and justice in a gracious art of living that frankly values ability, fame, wealth, and friends. . . ." In this subject too, the boy learns to love the good in part through hero worship, by reading about and striving to emulate the great men of his nation's literature and history, such as Achilles.[178]

Although it requires some intellectual training, however, the Greeks held that arête in character does not derive primarily from reading or lectures. The teacher's primary moral tool here is music—not music in the broad sense of the fields covered by the Muses, but in the narrower sense of auditory art. Based on their experience, the Athenians, including both Plato and Aristotle, believed that music has a great effect on character, that certain melodies and rhythms tend to uplift the listener and make him a better person, whereas others tend to coarsen and debase him. (We might think today of a child raised on Brahms or Chopin versus one raised on grunge rock or death metal.) From the boys' earliest years, therefore, they were exposed to the appropriate selections; they did not merely listen, but also learned to sing to the music, to accompany it on the lyre, and in later times even to dance to it. From such musical immersion, according to Plato, the boys were expected to "become more civilized, more balanced, and better adjusted in themselves and so more capable in whatever they say or do, for rhythm and harmonious adjustment are essential to the whole of human life."[179]

Developing the student's intellect, the third part of the educational process, was the most important part, because, to the Greeks, reason is the greatest of man's attributes.

In their early years, boys were taught the three Rs. Reading, according to Plato's *Republic*, was taught by what we today would call the phonetic method. Since reading and writing are indispensable tools of intellectual growth, the teacher demanded excellence in both—that is, mastery of Greek vocabulary and of the rules of its grammar and syntax. This task, however, was considerably lightened by the fact that, in the pre-Hellenistic era, the rules were still being formulated and had not yet been codified in comprehensive treatises. As to elementary mathematics, including arithmetic and geometry, it too had not yet been fully conceptualized, but the teachers passed much of what was available to students.

Greek education on the more advanced level was highly limited; subjects that we now take for granted—such as science, history, and higher mathematics—were just being created *de novo* and, with some exceptions, such as astronomy, were not yet ready to be offered in the schools. (A minority of boys went on to the universities, learning from Plato's school the cutting-edge discoveries in mathematics, and from Aristotle's, those in science and history.) For the majority of students, intellectual education was concerned mostly with one area: literature—in all known genres, including lyric poems, dramas, passages from important political thinkers, Hesiod, and—by far the most important—Homer.

On Homer, the Athenians were all but unanimous: What skill in gymnastics was to the body, the grasp of Homer was to the mind. Since writing materials were still scarce, and since the only way to understand poetry was to hear its meters and rhymes spoken aloud, the only practicable method of teaching Homer was by oral means. The boys had to memorize the epics. The teacher would read aloud, the boys would learn by heart, then recite, discuss, and compete, testing the quality of one another's recitation and understanding.

For the Greeks, writes Kitto, Homer "enshrined all wisdom and all knowledge. . . . Homer held and nourished the minds and the imaginations of Greeks for generation after generation—of artists, thinkers and ordinary simple men alike." This description is not exaggerated; the teachers used every aspect of Homer—characters, events, themes, and style—as their workshop and guide in morality, aesthetics, logic, language, and rhetoric.[180]

In morality, they started not with abstract exhortations but with Homer's graphic depiction of the good or bad consequences of different human attributes and actions; this led eventually to discussions about the broader implications for man's life. In aesthetics, they started not by studying artistic techniques in the abstract, but by analyzing the specific stylistic means used by Homer to achieve his powerful effects; later, they could point out common denominators at work. In logic, students were asked to identify the arguments used by the different characters, and to explain which ones were convincing—training in how to think clearly about other subjects as well. They learned their Greek not by struggling with general principles of grammar, but by starting with the linguistic specifics they already knew. They learned rhetoric not by memorizing rules of eloquence, but by studying specific speeches, mostly Homeric, with an eye to finding out what made a speech effective and how best to tell a story, thus paving the way for their future understanding of general rhetorical rules.

In every area, the Greeks' method of fostering intellectual development was first to present concretes and then to integrate them by abstractions. Their teachers did not treat percepts and concepts as independent of each other or as opposed to each other. When principles were taught to the boys, as Boyd and King put it, they were "principles expounded and illustrated by their master. . . ." Nor were the principles, once illustrated, left unrelated; the goal was to interconnect them to the extent possible at the time. "Mathematics and geometry were central," says classicist John Lewis, "to emphasize the abstract connections between things—for example, between music and astronomy, each regarded from a mathematical perspective." As a result, the student's observations were not in his mind a miscellany of unrelated data, and his broad abstractions were not a floating castle.[181]

Apart from the references to the Olympians, there was no religion in Greek education—no periods of worship, no sermons, hymns, prayers, or sacred text. Such things either did not exist (e.g., a sacred text) or were thought to be irrelevant to the pursuit of human excellence. The Greeks did venerate Homer, but they did not deify him; they were always free to criticize and even ridicule him without reprisal, as a few did. The culture was passionate about Homer's art, but indifferent to his credentials in some other world.

During the New period, the Sophists, rebelling against traditional views, argued that education should primarily be practical, not intellectual; that it should equip the student for social and political success, rather than concentrating on cognitive and character development. In this view, logic and rhetoric should become the essence of the curriculum, teaching the student how to influence people while being indifferent to truth or values, as the teachers themselves often were. Even among these skeptics, however, many retained traditional subjects and goals (and certainly Homer), albeit in the new updated form. The emphasis was changed, but the schooling, even at its most practical, remained highly intellectual as compared to that of other cultures.

The educational approach of the Greeks differs from the education for conceptual development that I sketched earlier as a possible example of the I mode. But content, as always, is not relevant in this context. The modal character of these two approaches is the same: a monistic and purely secular curriculum flowing from a fundamental view of man, and taught as an interconnected whole by means of integrating percepts and concepts. "A sense of the wholeness of things," writes Kitto, "is perhaps the most typical feature of the Greek mind." Greek education is an example: It is whole because it is an interconnection of parts. It is the One in the Many—the I mode.[182]

Politics

In politics, as in other areas, the distinctively Greek approach arose in Athens. Among the famous representatives of democracy were Cleisthenes, Solon, Pericles, and Demosthenes.

Greek democracy upheld two values as fundamental: a man's self-determination—that is, his freedom to make his own choices and direct his own actions—and a man's relation to his fellows, conceived primarily as his ability to appreciate Greece's cultural treasures and thus to participate fully in the life of his community. These two values, it was held, imply each other: A creature thrust into a group without choice and ordered to adapt does not have the autonomy of a rational being, but rather the impotence of a slave; a creature who shuns the minds and achievements of a rational culture is in effect discarding reason and turning himself into an animal. Neither one is actualizing his distinctively human potential—which was the ruling goal of the Greeks' politics, as of their education.

In seeking to implement their political values, the first question in the Greek mind was population size. On the one hand, they observed, there are social units such as a family or a village that are too small to support or defend themselves. On the other hand, there are empires such as those of Persia or Egypt in which the individual is but a speck of sand engulfed by a continent of other such specks—who can form a functioning whole only through despotism. There is only one valid alternative, they concluded: the city-state or *polis*, whose citizens usually numbered in the low five figures. Only three of their cities had more than twenty thousand; a *polis* of a hundred thousand, Aristotle said, would be absurd. (Women, slaves, and foreigners had no role in government.) Because of the relatively small number of its citizens, the government of a city-state was comparable to a private club or extended family, whose members generally knew one another personally.

A *polis*, the Greeks held, can achieve its values only if it has the right kind of ruler. Here again they weighed observed possibilities. Under the rule of kings or oligarchs, the citizens are clearly not free. Nor are they free in representative democracies, which, it was held, are merely another form of tyranny: Certain men allegedly speaking for constituents actually discard the constituents' interests in order to advance their own. Only direct democracy, they concluded, preserves freedom. Only if all the citizens rule together—that is, only if, in any issue, each man's vote has the same weight as that of any other—only then does each man enjoy equal power with the others in determining the outcome and his fate. To ensure this equality in practice, each citizen had an equal opportunity of holding office and of trying to change the minds of his constituents; so even if a man lost one vote, he might very well win a later one.

Thus the Greeks' way of reconciling freedom with the prerogatives of the state: To them, as Kitto says, the idea of freedom is "to rule and to be ruled in turn," with each citizen having an equal chance at each role. For the Greeks, I should add, equality is a value only in this delimited context; in the words of the *Oxford Classical Dictionary (OCD)*:

> the equality advocated by the democrats was that all should have an equal opportunity to participate in politics . . . especially an equal opportunity to speak in the political assemblies . . . and that all must be equal before the law. . . . The concept of equality was purely political and did not spread to the social and economic sphere of society.[183]

As to the other fundamental value of politics, a man's participation in the life of his community, this required the performance of his political obligations, such as attending the monthly assembly meetings, debating policies, and casting votes—along with immersion in Athenian culture, including the arts, the games, and the discussions among the educated, who were fascinated by the questions raised by the new studies of matter, man, and philosophy. With this agenda, citizenship obviously demanded time and effort. The *polis* was not merely a political entity, but an education for adults in arête; in Kitto's words, it was "an active, formative thing, training the minds and characters of the citizens. . . ." Thus Aristotle's famous line, "Man is a political animal," by which he means: an animal who reaches full actualization only in a *polis*.[184]

The values a man gains through equal voting and cultural participation are not enough in the eyes of the Greeks to qualify him as a free man. Besides man within the *polis*, there is man alone; besides the requirements of the citizen, there are the requirements of the individual. In this capacity, too, a man pursuing arête must seek fulfillment—a necessary condition of which is individual freedom.

An Athenian was thus expected to combine in his life two elements, with neither outweighing the other. As the *OCD* puts it: "the fundamental democratic ideal was liberty . . . [which consists of] political liberty to participate in the democratic institutions, and private liberty to live as one pleased." Like the American founding fathers, the Greeks did not fear that free individuals, living as they pleased with no dictator to restrain them, would run amok. Since men are rational beings, they can on the whole be trusted to pursue their goals and run their government rationally, respecting one another's prerogatives. For the Athenians, Sabine writes: "Government is no mystery reserved for the Zeus-born noble. The citizen's freedom depends upon the fact that he has a rational capacity to convince and to be convinced in free and untrammeled intercourse with his fellows."[185]

The individualist side of the Greeks was prominent in both intellectual and economic matters. They upheld the principle of free speech, for example; according to the *OCD*, they even regarded it as "the most important aspect of liberty." Nor, most of the time, were they merely "moderate" in this regard. No modern democracy—writes C. M. Bowra, renowned classical scholar—would allow "the reckless, scurrilous, and often ill-natured [speech]. . . . even in anxious times of war" that the Greeks typically allowed and even enjoyed.[186]

As to material possessions, Durant writes,

> the [Athenian] law of property is uncompromisingly severe. Contracts are rigorously enforced; all jurors are required to swear that they "will not vote for an abolition of private debts" . . . and every year the head archon, on taking office, has proclamation made by a herald that "what each possesses he shall remain possessor and absolute master thereof."[187]

Concerned that their form of government might permit encroachments on individual liberty, these democrats established many institutions and procedures to prohibit or limit such unwanted behavior, and especially to discourage hasty, mob-inspired legislation. There were several kinds of committees and officials who, among other duties, could often dismiss proposed measures, and declare at the start of a meeting that certain types of legislation were officially prohibited. Since their political ideas were formulated millennia before the concept of individual rights had been identified, the Greeks made little attempt explicitly to limit the powers (as against the procedures) of government. In general, they thought, members of the closely knit *polis* did not need to be much concerned with enumerating limits on themselves.

Despite its commitment to free speech and private property, therefore, there was nothing in the political system to prevent the continued growth of the Athenian state. In time and among other things, it came to run a substantial welfare program, impose conscription, and occasionally to maintain morals by exiling or even killing men whose ideas were deemed harmful to the *polis*, even though the victim may have violated no law (for example, the fate of Socrates). In each such case, it was argued, the policy was observably necessary to safeguard the values of the *polis*, while it was not unduly (or at least not undeservedly) harmful to its victims.

Though the Greeks upheld majority rule, they did not believe that any particular majority decision was necessarily rational or just. The fact that society approves a statute or even a whole political system, in their view, is irrelevant to its validity. Politics must be based not on men's arbitrary wishes, but on reality. "Greek political and ethical philosophy," Sabine points out,

> continued along the ancient line already struck out by the philosophy of nature—the search for permanence amid change and for unity amid the manifold ... the substance of the physical philosophers consequently reappeared as a "law of nature," eternal amid the endless qualifications and modifications of human circumstance.

So political action cannot be judged objectively merely by reference to votes in the assembly. The reverse is true: The votes are to be judged by reference to natural laws independent of men. In the early Greek years, these laws had been regarded as divine in their origin and validation. But as early as Hesiod, the defense of these laws became their reasonableness in human life, with the divine pedigree receding into the background. In the end, observes Durant, "[T]hesmoi, or sacred usages, became *nomoi*, or man-made laws. In these codes law freed itself from religion, and became increasingly secular. . . ."[188]

The Greeks' theory of natural law is the first appearance in the West of an idea essential to the later Lockean defense of individual rights and limited government. In the development of this theory, we see again the Greek mind at work: The facts of Nature in politics, as in physics, are not a juxtaposition of unrelated concretes. On the contrary, the whole body of *nomoi* can and must be organized into a system and then written down for all men to grasp and follow. In other words, we see the emergence of the first society in history to cherish, in Aristotle's immortal line, "a government of laws and not of men."

It is difficult to classify Greek politics using modern terminology. Their viewpoint is not individualism, because it places no limits on state power. But it is not collectivism either, because it regards the individual as the only real political entity and his personal arête as his proper ultimate value. And the Greek system is no version of the mixed economy, trying to combine individualism (of which they were ignorant) and collectivism. In the Greeks' view, their own approach is the opposite of a mixture. It is a principled approach defined by objective values and the social forms necessary to achieve them—all of it based ultimately on observation of fact.

In my own view, Greek politics is as individualistic as it was possible to be in the absence of modern Enlightenment political theory. The Greeks (and to a lesser extent the Romans) took major steps toward the American approach, but left other major steps for posterity to take. Posterity took two millennia to show up.

Greek politics is a system upholding unity, a unity whose reality consists of a certain kind of connection among individuals—which they themselves have created. In regard to mode, therefore, despite their many differences, the politics of the Greeks and of the founding fathers are the same: the One in the Many—the I approach.

————

Greek ideas and institutions were in many respects incomplete and/or inconsistent. But in our four areas, the Greeks across the board spoke with one voice. Theirs was an I culture.

After classical Greece, Western thought was a semi-Greek epilogue that lasted for three centuries, dating from the deaths of Aristotle and

Alexander. During this Hellenistic period, the Greek heritage, increasingly diluted, spread across the civilized world, after which Rome, long on the rise, took over. Because I consider it essentially similar to Roman culture (covered in the next chapter), I will give the Hellenistic period only a glance.

There are many obvious differences between the Hellenistic and Roman cultures. By definition, the Hellenists were more like the Greeks and therefore more intellectually active, whereas the Romans emphasized the pursuit of practical goals. Both cultures were religious, but the Hellenists could be traditionalists or receptive to freewheeling Oriental mysticism, whereas the Romans, at least before their decline, endorsed a decorous, state-sponsored polytheism. The Hellenists, though closer in time to the life-savoring Greeks, were the ones who began the West's centuries-long failure of nerve, as it is called; the more duty-bound Romans carried it further, eventually turning the West over to Christianity. These differences and others, though real, are of degree rather than essence.

Greece and especially Homer had a profound influence on the Hellenists and on Rome, while Stoicism, a Hellenistic product, was a leading philosophy in both periods. So a mix of life-savoring and life-denying feelings was approved by both. Even in religion, the two finally converged when in Rome's later years Jupiter was ousted in favor of Isis, Jesus, and the rest.

We cannot compare the serious literature of the two cultures, because the Hellenistic writers, contrary to those in every other Western period, did not write epic poetry or serious drama, but rather comedy, pastoral poetry, and the like. Contrary to the overall picture, the Romans in this area were far more active and creative.

In our other areas, however, the Romans essentially took over and adapted the cultural products of their Hellenistic predecessors. In science, both groups offer recapitulations of post-Aristotelian physics. In education, the Hellenists created what we now call classical education, of which Roman education was "only an adaptation," according to the sorbonne's H. I. Marrou. And in politics, writes Edward M. Burns, a historian at the Free University of Berlin, "The dominant form of government in the Hellenistic Age was the despotism of kings who represented themselves as at least semi-divine." The Roman parallel here is obvious.[189]

In a period stretching from Alexander to Constantine (in 315 he made Christianity Rome's official religion), and embracing a culture eventually spreading to the whole civilized world, we must expect to find innumerable variations in virtually every facet of a society. But in these centuries, I think, the variations are a flux of surface details, while the same underlying method of thought is still at work. Many German scholars who agree with this interpretation identify these six centuries by one name: "*hellenistisch-römische Kultur.*"[190]

Since it was in its Roman form that this culture was passed on to the medieval and modern worlds, only a study of the Roman version is necessary to understand the development of the Western mind.

CHAPTER TEN

ROME

Literature

During Rome's most distinguished artistic period (ca. 100 B.C. to A.D. 100), serious literature, following that of Greece, was first and foremost epic poetry. Virgil's *Aeneid*, the most famous of the epics, was intended to be a Roman counterpart of the *Iliad*; it was to be Homeric in form while embodying the Roman rather than the Greek spirit. The work was an instant success; the intellectuals of the empire embraced the epic almost as passionately as the Greeks had embraced Homer, and its study was soon made compulsory in the schools. In regard to literature, therefore, the best way to discover the distinctively Roman mind is to examine the contrasts between these two great poets.

Virgil employs the same divine machinery as Homer. His characters, too, heap praise on the gods, study omens, and affirm the gods' power over men. But while the Homeric gods are morally flawed and ultimately indifferent to men, Virgil's Jupiter is flawless, an august being who is deadly serious about his plan for human beings. The plan is nothing so parochial as resolving a local enmity, but rather flows from a much more ambitious purpose: "In the *Aeneid*," writes Philip R. Hardie, a classicist at Cambridge, "the stakes are higher. . . . It is the will of Jupiter that Rome shall be founded and conquer the world: by a bold stride of imagination, Virgil makes the Roman dominion . . . a central part of the cosmic world order." Jupiter's plan thus bears a similarity to that of the Christian God: Each ordains a historical progression that culminates in the birth of man's link (Rome or Jesus) to ultimate reality.[191]

Given the scale and importance of his plan, Jupiter is portrayed as much more hands-on—much more active and detail-oriented—than is Zeus in the *Iliad*. He is so powerful that he makes the achievement of his purpose and every step leading to it inevitable. In the face of such power, independent human purpose or efficacy is a myth. In the words of Aeneas, human beings are under the rule of "Fortune, that no man can resist, and Fate, that no man can escape. . . ." Zeus can be put to sleep, but Jupiter is always watching.[192]

Although the stories of Homer and Virgil both contain digressions, each author nevertheless presents a sequence of events with an inner logic. But that logic takes a different literary form. Homer selects a historical incident, then unifies his events into a plot by dramatizing specific human choices and actions related to the incident. By contrast, Virgil's purpose is not to select but to include, to cover the whole line of events leading from his own time to the Rome of the future, the Rome regarded in the epic as still millennia away. On the secular level, no logical connection among these events is presented; there is no explanation of their sequence in terms of the goals or actions of men. Aeneas himself, quite aware of this, tells us regularly that he is baffled by what is happening.

The epic's progression does have its own kind of logic, but one that eludes Aeneas, because it is not a human but a divine logic. In other words, the unifier of the story's elements is not men's purpose but God's. The earthly actions required to achieve this purpose are presented by Virgil as necessarily connected, but only because they enjoy a transcendent origin and mandate. For Homer, the divine is an expression of Nature and as such obeys its laws; for Virgil, Nature is an expression of the divine and as such obeys <u>its</u> laws. "It was mind," Virgil says in a profoundly anti-Greek declaration, "that set all this matter in motion."[193]

While the removal of Homer's divine machinery would not affect the essence of his work, the opposite is true of the *Aeneid*. Without the divine planner, there would be no story at all, but at most only city planners seeking a site for their future capital. It is not an accident that Dante, looking for a figure to serve as his first guide through the next world, did not think of Homer, but chose instead the poet he thought of as the "best of the pagans."

The characters of the *Iliad* and the *Aeneid* differ as their respective stories require. The secular hero, Achilles, acting in a knowable world, is confident of his rational faculty, and so can be independent, passionate, egoistic, proud. Aeneas, by contrast, viewing reality as fundamentally (though not exclusively) divine, regards the Greek hero worship as self-deception—because man is a being who, as Jenkyns puts it, "has to cope with a world which has become in some ways incomprehensible. . . ." Whereas Homer knows his gods as well as he knows his characters, Virgil stresses that *he* doesn't. "As Aeneas enters the underworld," Jenkyns goes on,

> Virgil prays to the gods that he may be permitted to speak
> of what he has heard and reveal things hidden in deep earth
> and darkness. . . . He puts into our minds the notion that it is
> very difficult to say anything about such matters . . . [and sug-
> gests that to Aeneas himself the] revelation of things unseen is
> a special dispensation; and even so, though much is revealed,
> much remains unexplained.

Man, a Sybil in the poem pronounces, is "commanded to obey, not to understand. . . ."[194]

In describing the underworld, one might add, Virgil does not present Homer's repellent room of the dead, but rather the admirable home of justice, where divine rewards and punishments are meted out.

To some extent, Aeneas is given the strength and character of a Homeric hero. But what Virgil stresses is not his hero's similarity to his Greek forebears but his difference. Aeneas is admirable not because he sets the course of his action and brooks no interference, but the reverse: because he is an obedient servant of Jupiter. In his own oft-repeated self-definition, he is "Aeneas the dutiful," a definition poignantly dramatized in his affair with Dido. Despite their passionate love for each other, when a word from the duty-giver, even though inexplicable to them, reminds him of his duty, he at once ends the relationship regardless of the agony—sympathetically depicted by Virgil—this action causes Dido and himself. Similarly, when Aeneas meets the ghost of his beloved dead wife, Creusa, with only a brief moment to talk, they use it not to talk about personal concerns or feelings, but about the divine. The idea here that a moral life requires indifference to worldly desires is the Stoicism so popular in Rome.[195]

As we have noted in discussing classicism, it is difficult for an author to make characters without personal desire fully real, a fact increasingly evident in the development of Aeneas. In the words of Richard Rutherford, an Oxford classicist, we gradually see

> a kind of dehumanization. That the hero seems less acces-
> sible, less of a "well-rounded character," in the second half of
> the poem is surely part of Virgil's design: Aeneas has made the
> transition from being an individual to his true role as leader
> of a people. Characterization is here shaped by ideology.[196]

In this case, we see not an individual given an abstract meaning, as in Homer, but an abstract meaning beginning to usurp the reality of the individual. We see not a man living by a creed, but the creed beginning to devour the man. In other words, the messenger is in process of turning into the message.

As with God, so ultimately with Aeneas: Neither is presented as an observable individual. In the end, the story is largely about an abstraction (the dutiful) serving an abstraction (the almighty). A more extreme use of abstraction to displace concretes, we may note, is evident in the plays of Seneca, centuries later, which are the only complete Roman tragedies to have survived. In these plays, writes British classicist C. J. Herington, we typically "begin with a Cloud of Evil, then witness the defeat of Reason by Evil and finally experience the Triumph of Evil. . . ."[197]

Although his work regularly extols the divine, Virgil does not reject this world. He regards Nature and man's perception of it as derivative but nevertheless as real and valid respectively because they <u>are</u> derivative from the divine. Earthly, even earthy, behavior is depicted in some detail, and the author clearly approves. Aeneas's goal is to reach not the city of God, but the city of Rome. And the characters, despite their commitment to duty, believe that some of their worldly desires come from God and should therefore be guiltlessly satisfied, even to the point of gluttony. Thus they relish extravagant banquets, described by Virgil in loving detail, not only on earth but also after death. They do not chant or make ethereal music in the next life, but instead hold athletic contests, dance to and sing the songs of their former life, own swords and horses, take the same joy in chariots and armor as when they were alive, and have great feasts in the grass. If we judge by these passages, Virgil seems to believe that life after death is pretty much the same as life before it, but merely moved to a different location.

A similar respect for the worldly is evident to an extent even in Apuleius's *The Golden Ass*, the only even partly serious Roman "novel" extant. When the hero finally reaches his cherished salvation in one of the proliferating Oriental cults of his time, the divine Osiris tells him what to do next. His advice is not to mortify the flesh or become a monk, but rather: "Go home and practice law."[198]

Virgil, like the other serious Roman writers, is a Worldly Supernaturalist. He achieves unity among his work's concretes through a transcendent purpose to be achieved on earth by characters with their heads merging into the world of forms, but their feet still on the ground. This is the mode of M_1.

Physics

By either the Greek or the modern definition of the field, there is no distinctive Roman physics. Although Romans did make some relatively narrow scientific discoveries, they generally regarded broad theories of Nature as unimportant because impractical; as in many other cultural areas, those interested in the subject took their ideas from the Greeks, usually from Hellenists. Characteristically, they rejected the theories of Plato and Aristotle as being difficult to understand and without practical payoff. Instead, most—for example, Cicero, Seneca, and the sometimes contradictory Varro—embraced the physics of the Stoics. Their chief competitors, not nearly as popular, were the atomists, the most famous of whom was Lucretius.

The Stoic physicists distinguished three objects of study: the world, its elements, and the causes operative within it. Being rationalists and pantheists, they rested their conclusions not on sense experience, but on *a priori* ideas, using observation merely as an auxiliary support. They held (following Heraclitus) that the substrate of Nature is fire, from which all things evolved. God or the gods, Nature, and fire, therefore, were ultimately the same and, in Cicero's view, constituted "the active force responsible for the existence, activity, and rationality of the universe." In elaborating this viewpoint, the Stoics followed Aristotle in one important issue: Their physics combined mechanism and teleology, though in their own distinctive manner.[199]

The motions of matter/fire, they held, can be properly (though incompletely) described as mechanistic. Any given state of the universe, solely through the actions and interactions of physical elements obeying physical laws, leads necessarily to the next; using Aristotle's terminology, only "efficient causation" is a source of movement. Further, many Stoics reasoned, if the universe is finite and one picks any one moment in time as a starting point, eventually all the possible combinations of elements will have been exhausted, so that a universe identical in all respects to the one at the start will reappear; and since matter always obeys the same laws, the same cycle will be repeated without end. The universe will forever oscillate between the Nature we see and a cosmic conflagration in which Fire has consumed everything. In this doctrine of "eternal recurrence," everything that happens in the universe (including in human life) has happened already countless times in the past, and will happen again countless times in the future. Free will, therefore, is an illusion. Thus Marcus Aurelius: "[E]verything which happens, always happened so and will happen so, and now happens so everywhere. . . ."[200]

But to understand the motions of objects, the Stoics held, mechanism is not enough. The laws of mechanics themselves must be explained—by understanding that such laws and the events they govern are a product of God in his pursuit of a long-range and beneficent purpose. The divine, in other words, is a providence whose plan makes the world rational and orderly. Nor in their eyes is the power of the divine mysterious. God is not only the Nature we observe; he is also an all-powerful spirit within it. He is to the universe what man's soul is to his body; in both cases, the purposes of the spiritual are what move the physical.

Aristotle had posited an observation-based teleology, according to which an entity's course of action is entailed by its identity and therefore immune to otherworldly intervention. The Stoics, by contrast, upheld a transcendent teleology in which an object's identity is not the source of its action; rather, natural things qua natural are regarded as passive and plastic, moved ultimately only by the source of natural law: the supernatural.

> Do you not know [writes Epictetus] that, just as the foot . . . viewed apart will cease to be a foot, so you will cease to be a man? For what is a man? A part of a city, first a part of the City in which gods and men are incorporate, and secondly of that city [Rome] which has the next claim to be called so, which is a small copy of the City universal.

The copy does have a claim to reality, but only as a copy. It is real because this world *is* God.[201]

As pagans, the Stoics did not defend their *a priori* premises by an appeal to faith. On the contrary, since all things come from God (or the gods), they held, so did man's faculty of reason; and if so, he intended us to use it. Although the Stoics did substantial empirical research in several fields, they did not base their fundamental philosophic ideas—fire as the primary element, pantheism, teleology, cyclical conflagrations—on observation. Instead, to use reason, the Stoics thought, one must construct deductive chains flowing from axioms expressed as pure abstractions. Whitney J. Oates, professor of classics at Princeton, gives an example:

> The Stoic argument [for monism] seems to have run in some such way as this: Holding firmly to the notion that

"self-sufficiency" is of supreme value, a conception to be found in Plato, they insisted that any theory that the cosmos was radically dualistic was not tenable. The universe, if it is of any value at all, must be self-sufficient; hence if self-sufficient, it must be untainted with dualism, and therefore monistic. If then the universe is self-sufficient the whole must be good.[202]

Historian Stewart C. Easton sums up Stoicism fairly as a "semi-religious philosophy" (what I call Worldly Supernaturalism). The religious element is obvious in the Stoics' view of the primacy of a transcendent entity known through an appeal to concepts divorced from percepts; but the "semi" is also valid because of their equation of God with the world and their view of observation as necessary and valid in regard to truths not open to rationalist deduction.[203]

The series of worldly events, wrote Marcus Aurelius, "is not like a mere enumeration of disjointed things . . . but it is a rational connection . . . the things which come into existence exhibit no mere succession, but a certain wonderful relationship." The Many, in other words, are realities, but they form a connected whole through the power and purpose of a transcendent One—M_1.[204]

Although Lucretius opposed teleology and the idea of hidden spiritual forces at work in Nature, he made his own distinction between Nature and a hidden realm that moves it. This last is the realm of the atoms, which are without sensory qualities and therefore unperceivable. This is the true reality, he held, as against the derivative world of colors, textures, et al, which appears to us in sense perception. Lucretius defended atomism not by reference to empirical data (which did not point to atoms until two millennia later), but rather by restating Democritus's rationalistic inference from the premises of pre-Socratic philosophy. Given this *a priori* basis, Lucretius works to explain a great variety of observed facts, including the path of the sun, the mortality of the soul, the origins of mankind, thunder, magnetic attraction, and even the great Athenian plague.[205]

Our world is real but secondary, and experience is valid if interpreted in the light of the *a priori*—the same mode as the Stoics, M_1.

Education

Roman education underwent many changes during its thousand-year history. Broadly speaking, it was practicality-oriented and anti-intellectual in the early centuries; practical but also intellectual at its high point (ca. 100 B.C. to A.D. 100); and intellectual but non-practical in the empire's final period. Despite these changes, however, and despite the continuing influence on Rome of Greek culture, there was an enduring and distinctively Roman approach to education upheld by Quintilian, Tacitus, and many others. Its fundamentals, implicit in the earlier years, became fully explicit only in the last stage. This stage, despite its inferiority to its antecedents, was by far the most influential one on the later West. The views of the late Roman educators on curriculum and pedagogy were the only educational ideas of the ancients to be picked up and carried on through the ages, waning only in the mid-nineteenth century.

As we have seen, Greek education was value-oriented, both in goal and method. In order to help the child become the human ideal and gain a life of personal happiness, he was taught the supreme value of heroism, independence, and self-sufficiency as exemplified by Achilles. Further, most boys were taught by or with teachers and fellow students whose knowledge, character, and/or athletic feats the boys naturally came to admire and seek to emulate.

Roman education replaced value with duty. The child was not placed in a world of heroes and admiration; rather—at least in the early, trend-setting centuries—he was left to learn from his parents; in the earliest years, his teacher was his mother, later his father. A father was not presented to his son as a hero; the child was told that his father was entitled to respect not because he was Achilles or strong or brilliant, but simply because he was his father, regardless of his traits. What was required of a Roman child, he was told, was not admiration, but obedience to duty—duty not only to his father, but also to his family, ancestors, gods, the men in authority, and, above all, the state. His highest duty, he learned, was the duty to support and protect the enduring supremacy of God-blessed Rome, regardless of any personal opinions he might hold on the subject.

As the centuries passed, a boy's parents were replaced by professional teachers, but the centrality of duty remained. "If ancient Greek education can be defined as the imitation of the Homeric hero," says the *Britannica*, "that of ancient Rome took the form of imitation of one's ancestors." Roman boys, of course, were also taught to admire illustrious figures—not as a means of promoting self-realization, however, but rather self-abnegation. Aeneas, for example, was esteemed in classes as a more or less impersonal figure symbolizing renunciation for the fatherland. As against the "wild and imaginative Homeric hero," writes H. I. Marrou—a superlative historian of education—Roman "heroism never had any particular individual character; it was always strictly subordinated to the public good and the public safety. . . ." Indeed, Marrou goes on,

> . . . we must realize the absence of anything behind the Latin tradition comparable to Homer's [secularism] . . . there was never a time when Roman education did not single out as examples to be followed men of honour who had put divine right before their country's immediate interests. . . . Roman patriotism itself believed that it was essentially religious.[206]

Roman education, like Greek, was monistic. But since its ultimate goal was different, so was its curriculum, which did not include two of the three Greek subjects: gymnastics and music. The public nudity of gymnastics, the Romans believed, was unmanly and immoral, while its athletic competitions were unserious. A boy did need physical education, they conceded, not for personal reasons, however, but for purely practical ones: to learn hygiene and military preparedness. As to music (and most arts, aside from literature), Roman teachers for the most part regarded it too as impractical. In particular, they disliked the spectacle—to their mind frivolous—of boys in school singing and dancing.

The essence of the developed Roman curriculum was the third of the Greek subjects: literature and language, a bilingual study now, since

Roman boys were taught Greek as a matter of course. To a large extent, the Romans' approach in this area was similar to that of the Greeks. The boys studied fiction, primarily epic poetry, along with noted Roman speeches and other non-fiction writings. Besides the three Rs, they were taught some history (mostly Roman), science (much neglected), and also music, medicine, astronomy, mythology, geography, religion, and other subjects. Generally, as with the Greeks, facts and ideas were introduced piecemeal, when the teacher thought that some point was relevant to the study of the literary work under consideration.

Whereas the Greeks, however, had featured the study of great writers primarily as an aid to the child in achieving arête, the Romans, always interested in the practical, sought through the study of literature to turn out men who were politically effective. If a boy became adept in oratory and rhetoric, if he learned to write an eloquent sentence, to argue with compelling logic, to present his views persuasively—the very skills, they held, that were taught by the great poets—then, when he spoke publicly as an adult, he would be heard and more likely to be followed. Knowledge of literature, in short, was a necessary means to success in life. Thus one idea of Greek education, the one introduced by the Sophists, became the ruler of the curriculum, as it had been during the Hellenistic period.

If a teacher today were told that his curriculum should include only practical subjects, he would probably drop grammar first of all. The Romans took the opposite view. Expertise in thought and action, they believed, requires expertise in words, including their interrelationships and rules—in other words, it requires a knowledge of grammar, the subject, according to Quintilian, that imparts "the knowledge of correct speaking and writing. . . ."[207]

In Athens, as we have seen, grammar had not yet been fully developed. In the Hellenistic era, by contrast, lengthy and comprehensive grammar texts had appeared in abundance, and the Romans embraced them. A knowledge of grammar, they came to believe, was invaluable not only in regard to practical politics; it was a prerequisite of success in virtually every field, since all fields depend on the use of language. The subject, therefore, must be taught from the boy's earliest years. Thus did the practicality-minded Romans become the creators of the modern world's practicality-disdaining "grammar schools."

Apart from proper names, words are abstractions. When the mastery of words as such becomes the basic concern of the schools, the study of the entities and actions that are the words' referents becomes secondary and relatively unimportant. Especially for the younger boys, it was commonly thought, this kind of study is largely a waste of time. We have encountered this education-through-words approach before, in connection with modern classicist education, which was taken from the Romans (then tweaked to satisfy Christianity). Now let us see what the creators of the approach did with it themselves.

Their method was implemented in the first days, when the boys began to learn their letters. First the boy was taken forward from A to X,

> and then [writes Marrou] backwards from X to A; then in pairs—AX, BV, CT, DS, ER—then jumbled into different combinations. After the letters came the syllables with all their combinations, and then single names. These stages came one after the other, and there was no hurry to get on to the next. The little school boys were known as *abecedarii*, *syllabarii* and *nominarii*. . . . rare words . . . the most difficult sayings to pronounce . . . were deliberately chosen for these first reading lessons.[208]

Then the child was immersed in word relationships—that is, grammar. As in the Hellenistic era, Marrou writes,

> grammar still meant essentially the same abstract analysis . . . and the same meticulous distinctions and classifications: "nouns" . . . were studied according to the six accidents—quality, degree of comparison, gender, number, figure and case; and common nouns were separated into twenty-seven classes—corporeal, incorporeal, primitive, derived, diminutive, etc.[209]

After completing these preliminaries, the child learned to use the knowledge as his guide to a proper reading of the classics. Priscian, a late-empire author of a substantial treatise on teaching literature, illustrates the grammatical method in the form of dialogues between master and student. His whole book covers only twelve lines of verse, the first line of each of the *Aeneid's* twelve books. In his study of the first sentence of the twelve, the student was asked, among a great many other things, to scan the line; to number, name, and locate the caesuras; to number its figures and their division into different kinds of rhythmic patterns, along with the names of each kind of metric foot; to identify how many nouns, verbs, and other parts of speech—and then, in regard to the first noun, its quality, kind, gender, and so on.[210]

What the educational system at each stage worked to achieve in the boys' minds was in essence the same at each stage: alphabetic expertise, the ability to distinguish and manipulate symbols; then grammatical expertise, the ability to analyze and manipulate words; then literary expertise, the ability to find these analyses and manipulations in the work being studied. In the final centuries of Roman education, the teachers dropped the promise of political practicality. In the late empire, the training of political orators had lost its purpose and the long implicit became explicit. The teaching of grammar as the primary study did not stop, but now the teachers, still clinging to language, turned away from the world. They became, as the Columbia historian of education I. L. Kandel puts it, "out of touch and sympathy with reality." In this "scholasticism in education," as he calls it, schoolboys competed in debating such subjects as—Tacitus's examples—"deflowered virgins . . . the licentiousness of married women . . . ceremonies to be observed in times of pestilence," etc. These were subjects of which the debaters knew little or nothing, a fact of no importance to them or their teachers. The concern was not with the content of what the boys said, but with how they said it—whether it was polished, grammatical, well structured, internally consistent, rhythmic, stirring, and so forth. As Henry Nettleship, Latinist at Oxford, sums it up, they "were called upon to admire, not the adaptation of language to thought, but the language itself."[211]

The study of language as a self-contained world at the base of learning means the primacy in education of form over matter, of rationalist logic over observation, of concepts over percepts. This means floating abstractions as the ultimate educational reality. Roman culture, while certainly not Christian, was always more religious than the Greek, and it was increasingly so in the empire. This was a trend to which the teachers, whether they were for or against Christianity, were receptive. They had little difficulty in uniting their grammar with their gods. To their mind, both represented the same metaphysics: the supremacy of the spiritual over the material.

Despite its Platonism, however, Roman education was still pagan, at least for some centuries into the empire. As such, students were not taught contempt for the material world or for its ruling city; on the contrary, the schools aimed to produce Roman patriots. Even during the final stage, it was claimed, at least officially, that education served this purpose, not so much anymore by teaching oratory, but by enabling the student to be inspired by the texts depicting the great feats performed by great men in this world. In this way the floating concepts the boys learned were still intended, however inadequately, to be put to use here and now—that is, to connect to and illuminate the events given us by our senses. The teachers' goal was not to climb Plato's divided line and disappear, but to stay up there as long as necessary so as eventually to return to the earthly delights Plato himself scorned.

Roman educators achieved unity in their field by holding that the Many are connected because their source is a transcendent system of abstractions known *a priori*. This is another case of Worldly Supernaturalism. It is the Many from the One—M_1.

Politics

Roman politics, both republican and imperial, rested on three interconnected ideas: collectivism, duty, and law.

Whereas the Greeks' goal in politics, as in education, was in substantial part individualistic—to foster each man's self-development and personal fulfillment—the Romans' goal was collectivistic. The purpose of the citizen, as Virgil had said and as all knew from their early schooling, was to promote not the welfare of the individual, but of the Roman state—to promote it and, when called upon, to sacrifice himself for it. By this standard, most of the Greek values—such as abstract science, idealistic admiration, and even rollicking laughter—the Romans judged to be insignificant or even selfish. Instead, a citizen's life, especially his public life, should exemplify whatever traits strengthened Rome: love of hard work, self-control in thought, seriousness, frugality, piety, and public spirit. The good citizen practiced these virtues not as a means to his happiness, which was morally irrelevant, but as an end in itself, simply because they were his duty.

But duty—in politics as elsewhere—the Romans stressed (at least in earlier centuries), cannot be imposed by anyone's whim. Rather, acts of the government must be guided by law, in regard to both substance and procedure. Building on the Greeks' pioneering work, the Romans turned the early narrow codes into an organized, comprehensive, and therefore massive system of laws. Since the laws were explicitly stated, widely publicized, and generally respected, Roman governments took them seriously (until the imperial degeneration).

The political problem of the republic, as the leadership saw it, was class warfare. In Greece, too, there had been clashes between rich and poor, but they were ameliorated to an extent by the fact that the citizens regarded themselves as members of the same, relatively small family, each of whom, whether rich or poor, possessed equal political power. The Romans, however—on their way to becoming the ruler of the world, with a corollary flood of immigrants to manage—could hardly model their own state on a system designed for a pitifully (to them) small *polis*. To deal with class warfare, they concluded, the active unit within the government could not be the individual.

The Romans recognized three classes: the aristocracy, the equestrians, and the plebs. The first were men from a special tribe or family with money and prestige; the second, businessmen rich enough to afford a horse; the third, the masses without status or money. The primary goal of politics, the creators of the republic held, was to establish a system within which these groups would stop fighting and instead agree to coexist peacefully.

The means to this end, it was decided, was to divide political power among the classes, and to codify every aspect of the division by defining a set of laws agreed to by all. The laws would specify precisely the functions, prerogatives, procedures, and officials pertaining to each class. The home of the aristocracy was the senate; of the plebs, the assembly.

Polybius and Cicero argued that this system was a logical inference from Greek political experience. Monarchy, the rule by one, they said, led to despotism; aristocracy to oligarchy; and democracy to mob rule. By contrast, Polybius writes, the great virtue of the Roman system was that it rejected all three in favor of an integration of elements drawn from each (the Roman consul was regarded as their equivalent of a monarch). Such a system had to be enduring because it was "in a state of equilibrium thanks to the principle of reciprocity or counteraction [checks and balances, as we say]."[212]

Although the republicans, as Polybius indicates, defended their political system by praising its practicality as proven by historical experience, they did not regard this argument as their system's fundamental validation. It was practical, they held, because their kind of government and laws was ordained by the divine. And, for that very reason, their system was not of merely local application, but was required in all proper societies. Details could be altered, but only within the framework of principles made absolute by their divine source. Natural law, in Cicero's words, is "valid for all nations and all times," because of "one master and ruler, that is, god, over us all, for he is the author of this law, its promulgator, and its enforcing judge."[213]

The Roman commonwealth, sums up its great admirer Polybius,

> ... to show its superiority most decisively ... in that of religious belief. Here we find that the very phenomenon which among other peoples [the Greeks] is regarded as a subject for reproach, namely superstition, is actually the element which holds the Roman state together. These [religious] matters are treated with such solemnity and introduced so frequently both into public and into private life that nothing could exceed them in importance.[214]

God as a transcendent factor antecedent to this world is, as we know, an object accessible only to pure thought; he is an abstraction or series of them independent of observation. This primacy of abstraction runs throughout the Roman approach to politics. For example, their view that Rome eternally serves God's plan regardless of what we observe about its citizens' behavior is clearly an *a priori* idea. So is the idea of classes being autonomous entities distinct from their individual members. Here again we see the common union of God and floating abstractions or of religion and rationalism.

The best example of Roman rationalism known to me—specifically, of their predilection for proof through *a priori* deduction—is found in Marcus Aurelius.

> If our intellectual part is common, the reason also, in respect of which we are rational beings, is common: if this is so, common also is the reason which commands us what to do, and what not to do; if this is so, there is a common law also; if this is so, we are fellow-citizens; if this is so, we are members of some political community; if this is so, the world is in a manner a state.[215]

Soon enough, by this method, Aurelius, many centuries before Hegel, reaches the same conclusion: "[E]verything which happens," he writes, "happens justly. . . ." Epictetus articulates another epistemological feature of rationalism: "[E]very one has come into the world with an innate conception as to good and bad . . . happiness and unhappiness . . . what is right to do and what is wrong."[216]

The strategy of the republicans to mute class warfare by building it into the very structure of government worked, or seemed to, for a long time. As a rule, the aristocracy was the dominant power—the republic is now commonly described as an oligarchy—but periodically the rich felt it necessary to pay off or otherwise pacify restless plebeians. In the end the vaunted equilibrium of the system, after a century of devastating civil war, broke down. A government based on class war was finally consumed by it. "The very form of the republic," Easton comments, "carried within itself the seeds of its downfall."[217]

During the civil war, the Durants say, republicans started to call for a "legitimate dictatorship" to keep order during periods of "national chaos or peril." By the end of the war, both classes were working openly to get this job, demanding that the proposed dictator be given "almost complete authority over all persons and property. . . ." It did not take long for Augustus to accept the republicans' invitation and thereby make them obsolete. In their place, the emperor introduced a new form of government.[218]

Like Hellenistic predecessors and his Roman successors, Augustus claimed and exercised absolute power, unhampered by any individual or group. He had the power to run politics, economics, foreign affairs, and his citizens' very lives, both in public matters and in private. He enjoyed "the right to initiate legislation in the Senate or the Assembly, and the power to veto the action of any official in the government." He had no hesitation in demanding from his subjects moral behavior, as he defined it. The Durants cite his marriage laws as an example.

> Marriage was to be obligatory upon all marriageable males under sixty and women under fifty. Bequests conditional on the legatee remaining unmarried were made void. Penalties were imposed upon celibates: they could not inherit, except from relatives . . . and they could not attend public festivals or games. . . .[219]

Perhaps the emperor's best-remembered policy is his creation of a welfare program along with an array of public entertainments—a combination satirized by Juvenal as "bread and circuses." Relatively few intellectuals criticized the emperor by reference to the once revered natural laws. "By Hadrian's time," writes Easton, "it was recognized that the word of the emperor was the true source of law for the empire. . . ."[220]

In the history of the civilized West, the deification of the all-powerful ruler dates back to the fall of Athens—to the religious cult of Demetrios, whom the Athenians at the time accepted as their master. The same kind of adulation was demanded by Alexander the Great, who proclaimed that his actions flowed from God (whom he sometimes equated with himself). And it was demanded by the long line of Hellenistic successors who were worshiped by their subjects as god-kings. This practice ceased in the comparatively less religious republic, but was picked up again in the empire. Since he came so early in the empire's development, Augustus at first muted the attempt of his cult to deify him, but then found an alternative. According to Easton, he "permitted his [own] Genius to be worshiped. . . . Later this indeed became the worship of the living emperor as god, a state cult to which all had to subscribe on pain of treason." The worshiper, of course, did not judge what he saw, but submitted. As Sabine puts it, it was "an age in which all the servility of oriental despotism had apparently been transplanted to Rome."[221]

Despite their claim to absolute power, the Roman emperors did not attempt to exercise it in every area. They had no ideology to impose, so philosophy (within limits) did not much concern them, and they did face certain entrenched obstacles—among other things, they had to respect certain long-revered Roman traditions, to keep on good terms with important pressure groups such as the military, and at least outwardly to obey the morals of the state religion. Further, although the collectivism of Roman politics offered men less individual freedom than did the Greeks, the Romans did pride themselves on protecting—even from the emperor if necessary—certain individual rights for the first time. The most famous of these was their declaration of the equality before the law of every man, no matter where or when he lived—an approach opposite to the Greek division of men into Greeks and barbarians. The Roman emperor, in short, however debauched and brutal, was no totalitarian. He can be compared to Louis XIV, but not to Hitler or Stalin. "[T]he official cult of the [Roman] king," Sabine observes, "had a constitutional significance, not altogether unlike that which the theory of divine right had in the monarchy."[222]

Despite his character as god-man, the emperor, like his counterparts in the seventeenth century, was regarded by most Romans as having primarily a secular function: not to lead men away from this life, but rather to use his unique gifts in guiding men's worldly endeavors, especially those pertaining to the glory of Rome. Exemplifying the Romans' commitment to such endeavors are their unprecedented feats in architecture and engineering. In epistemology, too, because of their overall emphasis on practicality, reverence for an abstract realm, while crucial, was not enough for them. Thought in their view must be connected to the world of Nature and experience.

> Rome as a civilization and an empire [writes historian Steve Jolivette] is unique in the feebleness of its religion. This does not mean that the Romans were not religious, in the sense of believing in all kinds of magic, taking rituals seriously, etc. They were religious in this regard in a way in which the Greeks were not. But it does not mean that the Roman State was anything like the Egyptian or the Persian.

In other words, in politics, too, the Romans were Worldly Supernaturalists.[223]

In the Roman state, the political Many—the citizens, laws, and officials—are integrated into a system in virtue of a divinity who endows it with purpose and authors its laws. The change from the republic to the empire took place within this approach; it was not a change in method of thought, but in application of the same method. In both versions, Roman politics reflects the Many from the One—M_1.

———

In all four of our fields, Roman culture, like that of the Hellenistic era before it and through a history four or five times longer than Greece's, consistently exhibits the mode of M_1.

CHAPTER ELEVEN

THE MIDDLE AGES

IN THE HIGH Middle Ages, mainly the thirteenth and fourteenth centuries, the seeds of a lengthy preparation bloomed into a full-fledged and distinctive culture.

Literature

In literature, the towering achievement was Dante's epic *Divine Comedy*, which is to medieval Christendom what Virgil was to Rome, and Homer to Greece. On the popular level, the most famous of the medieval morality plays is *Everyman*.

Achilles peeked into the underworld and found it repellent. Aeneas made a longer visit, found the afterlife awe-inspiring, but then came back to pursue his earthly goal. Dante's epic, in contrast to both, is set in the afterlife from start to finish. Earthly things have been left behind with relief, of use only if they helped to convey a non-earthly meaning—beasts, mountains, and such being used as symbols to express the idea that true reality is timeless, spaceless, non-material, and perfect.

At the start of the poem's tour of the next world, Virgil guides the poet through the lowest part, showing him the agonizing punishments that obstinate sinners have merited from God. Then the two move on to see the fierce struggle of the penitents in Purgatory, who have not yet been forgiven. Then Beatrice, a non-pagan, takes over as guide and leads Dante through the different grades of virtuous souls joyful in Paradise, a progression moving ever nearer to the climax of being, God. It is the climb up Plato's divided line, with the Christian God at the summit.

Since humans enter the other world only after their lives have been completed and judged by God, the poem presents no physical action—no massed armies, no storm-tossed fleets, no conflicts among the principals, no act of revenge, no act of politics, no mission to win a war or found a city. Earthly actions are regularly mentioned, mostly as the explanation of a sinner's suffering. But the actions are not dramatized; they are merely recalled. Nor are the actions of one sufferer connected to those of others. The epic presents not what was done in the past or is desired in the future, but what reward or punishment a given soul is experiencing now, and why. The conceptual analysis of sins and their interrelationships—these abstract issues typify what the work focuses on primarily.

The leading character, Dante himself, is the opposite of Achilles and Aeneas. He is a spectator, even a straight man, who, until his epiphany in the final canto, experiences much the same emotions as a tourist at an exciting new locale: wonder, sympathy, appreciation, etc. One of his stronger interests is in rehearsing standard theological riddles such as the Trinity, the Incarnation, and the necessity of the Son issuing from the Mother and vice versa. As to Dante's distinctive personal reactions, the most we hear about is his love for Beatrice, which is portrayed as no more than a sincere but empty generality, albeit an often repeated one. There are no love words or notes, no stolen kiss, no electrifying touch, no hint of desire, let alone of temptation. For Dante, of course, all these would be signs of profane love.

We must, Dante affirms, be "from all these [worldly] things released." Our affections should be "aflame only in the pleasure of the Holy Spirit. . . ." The epic's marked interest in worldly matters (such as Italian politics) is no contradiction of its unworldliness, because for Dante politics, science, and history have meaning only insofar as they can help lead us away from themselves and toward God. Any independent interest in the things of Nature is a sign of spiritual immaturity or worse—probably worse, since all such interests, including his love for a woman, drop away from Dante as he nears the top of the hierarchy. At that point, the near-abstract spectator encounters pure abstraction.[224]

In this regard, Beatrice outdoes Dante. According to a description I heard years ago, but whose author I have forgotten, the only information we get is that she is gracious, beautiful, smiles sweetly, talks a lot of theology, and changes clothes when she is near God. When she first arrives, she is hidden by a veil; later, she suddenly disappears. No one could recognize such a person physically or psychologically; she is not an individual or even a human being, but an abstraction—not a character, but a symbol. According to various interpreters, she is Jesus, or "Theology or Sacred Science itself," or "Revelation and Grace," etc. Aeneas felt personal desires keenly, but then painfully sacrificed love to duty. Beatrice and Dante, however, are without temptation or inner conflict; they eagerly throw aside any remnants of personal identity so that they may be absorbed into the infinite. Both characters are abstractions, in this case used didactically, to present the essentials of a philosophy—that is, of a whole system of abstractions. In this way the epic _is_ its theme; that—not story or character—is its only real content.

Homer's characters, being concretized abstractions, are real to an audience because they pursued personal values with unflinching passion. Virgil's characters, being semi-concretized abstractions, come across as less real because they pursued personal values but without commitment to them, willing when called upon to throw them aside in service to God. Dante's Christian characters float because they have no personal desires. The only desire, shared by all but the unrepentant, is to leave this world.

Dante's elevation of abstraction above concretes is clearest at the climax of his tour. He grasps God by a mystic experience about which he offers only a few more generalities, such as the joy and inspiration He creates in the blessed as His non-physical "light" streams forth. But whatever Dante's God is, it is clear that He is the antithesis of the material world. To Dante, this world is not merely corrupt; it is corrupt metaphysically and thus of necessity, because it is the opposite of reality. It is unreal—nothing but a distortion, an unsubstantial reflection, a Platonic appearance:

> That which dieth not [writes Dante], and that which can die, is nought save the reglow of that Idea which our Sire, in Loving, doth beget; for that living Light which so outgoeth from its Source that it departeth not therefrom, nor from the Love that maketh three with them, doth, of its goodness, focus its own raying, as though reflected, in nine existences, eternally abiding one. Thence it descendeth to the remotest potencies. . . .[225]

Immortal and mortal things alike, in other words, are nothing but the "reglow" (reflection) of God's Idea. They are nothing but the light that, leaving God and breaking into separate rays, never does leave God; always abiding with God, it does but shine into the darkness, into the absence of light—that is, into a negative, a realm of non-being, which is the world of matter.

Faith in Christianity, note two Dante scholars, requires one to free himself "from those limitations of corporeal sense organs." But given the articles of faith and the faculty of deduction from them, Dante writes, we can grasp many "deep things": things "from the eyes of them below so hidden that their existence is there only in belief, whereon is built the lofty hope . . . and from this belief [in deep things] needs must we syllogize without further sight. . . ." To "syllogize without sight"—a nice definition of rationalism.[226]

Since the essential content of *The Divine Comedy* is an integrated philosophy, the epic is fully unified. This unity is ultimately possible to Dante only because the poem on all its levels is an integrated movement from the void toward the all-absorbing light, the One without the Many—the M_2 mode.[227]

Everyman does not pretend to be high art, but rather presents in simple terms a theme common in the thirteenth century. Everyman discovers it while preparing to meet a summons from Death to face the day of judgment.

Each of the characters promises to accompany the frightened man on his journey, but then forsakes him, each in his own way succumbing to a desire for worldly values, such as riches, feasting, drinking, making good cheer, dancing, and consorting with lustful women. All these traitors, "drowned in sin," are presented as abstractions and named accordingly— Fellowship, Kindred, Strength, Beauty, Goods, etc. Unless taking a walk is an event, there are no events in the play, which presents not a story, but a sermon warning the audience to cultivate abstinence. As Good Deeds puts it: "[A]ll earthly things is but vanity."[228]

The author of *Everyman*, however unsophisticated, suggests in his story the epistemology essential to his religion. Among Everyman's supporters, Five Wits (the senses) is portrayed as less reliable than Knowledge, since he forsakes Everyman much sooner, and even Knowledge is defective, since he cannot reach all the way to God. Here again, in rather primitive terms, we see the M_2 mode at work.

Science

Science, largely unknown to the medievals, was of little interest to them. Truths about the soul, religion, eternity, they believed, were incomparably more important than truths about the body, Nature, or the temporal, since these latter pertain only to the darkness that constitutes this world. Only a handful of individuals across the centuries, therefore, gained fragments of new scientific knowledge. No medieval thinker produced or even upheld a theory of the physical world as a whole, not even in rudimentary terms. It was an era without physicists. Whereas the Romans had tended to brush physical theory aside as impractical, the Christians condemned what little they knew of it as immoral. To them, it was not insignificant, but a threat; such a worldly interest might provoke God's wrath and endanger one's salvation.

Despite their animus against science, the medievals' metaphysics did imply a general view of physical events—a view one might call supernaturalist teleology. In this view, physical entities are and do what God wills them to be and do in order to fulfill His all-embracing plan, thought of as the divine Idea. Theologians sought to validate this approach by an appeal to religious authority, including the Bible, the Church fathers, and the saints. In the received opinion of the period, these sources give men substantial although limited knowledge of the Idea. They tell us, for instance, of the incomparable importance to God of the Incarnation and the Resurrection, but they do not tell us God's ultimate goal or its meaning. Such things are not knowable, not in this life.

There are no natural laws to stand in the way of God's plan. Some regularities in Nature can be observed, but they will persist only until God annuls them, for a reason and at a time we cannot know, and mandates a different sequence of events. Since Omnipotence is what creates natural entities and their powers, it cannot by definition be restricted by them. Thus we see the medievals' untroubled acceptance of the most experience-defying miracles—ascribed not only to God but also to Satan and many others. The Greeks had believed in natural laws that even the gods had to obey; the Christians, regarding Nature as unreal, could not think of it as a check on the supernatural. To the medieval mind, accordingly, the proliferation of non-material entities with miraculous powers, good and evil, was uncontroversial and to be expected. Even the most acute thinkers did not doubt that at least some of these entities were real; Aquinas, for example, undertook to systematize the subject of angelology.

Although man cannot understand much about God's plan, the medievals often referred to it. A proper explanation of some event, they believed, was one that identified, so far as possible, the event's role in the divine scheme. "There is not an object nor an action, however trivial," writes Johan Huizinga, renowned Dutch medievalist, "that is not constantly correlated with Christ or salvation. All thinking tends to religious interpretation of individual things. . . ." Easton illustrates, using the hypothetical case of mistletoe seen growing on an oak tree. The medieval, he says, when asked "the purpose of the mistletoe in the household of nature . . ." [would answer that] "no investigation would be necessary. His mind could speculate freely." He might, Easton goes on, come up with the idea that God's purpose was to cure the tree of evil humors if it were sick, or keep the tree population down if the tree died, or serve as an example to man of the evils of parasitism, or be a useful medicine given to man by a merciful God, or any number of other possibilities.[229]

The whole of the medieval view of the physical world, from metaphysics to mistletoe, rejects sense experience in favor of *a priori* ideas gleaned ultimately from faith. Percepts are worldly; ideas (concepts) are not. The fully matured expression of this dichotomy was reached in the period's universities by the Scholastics. These rationalists—as Carl Stephenson, a Cornell medievalist, puts it— "under the influence of St. Augustine, remained Neo-platonic. So the orthodox generally held that all knowledge is based on divine ideas implanted in the human reason by the Creator. . . ." By far the most famous example of medieval rationalism is Saint Anselm's ontological argument, which claimed to prove the existence of God without reference to sense experience, purely by logical inference from a definition (a being "than which nothing greater can be conceived").[230]

To our knowledge, there were a dozen or so thinkers who were more secular than their culture and who can be said to have carried science some small steps forward; but they, too, being medieval Christians, embraced idealism and rationalism. Abelard, for instance—one of the least submissive, most worldly, and most logical thinkers of the period— nevertheless developed a new version of systematic theology widely regarded as essential to the Scholastic curriculum; its methodology "was deductive, being essentially the development of general principles taken from authoritative sources." Roger Bacon, another such example, was perhaps the leading champion of experience as the base of knowledge— but he distinguished two kinds of experience: "that gained through the senses and that gained through the inner faculties by divine inspiration." Hence this "empiricist," as he is sometimes called, could and did believe that all knowledge had been revealed to Seth, the son of Adam, then to Solomon; that it had been diluted in the process of being transmitted from these great men to the pygmies of his own time; and that a good moral character was the first prerequisite for receiving a revelation from God.[231]

In regard to the Many, Meister Eckhart, though unorthodox in several ways, sums up correctly the viewpoint held for all these centuries: "Whoever sees two or distinction does not see God." What makes integration possible is the fact of an all-absorbing reality—of the One without the Many—M_2.[232]

Education

From the fall of Rome to the Renaissance, the Church controlled education in Western Europe, at first partially, but during its culminating period officially and completely. Arthur Francis Leach, a pioneering scholar in the history of education, describes education in these latter centuries: "[T]he law of education was a branch of the canon law . . . until 1540 all schoolmasters and scholars were clerks, or clerics, or clergy. . . ." Medieval education, in other words, was designed for religious professionals. Although there were changes across the years, especially after the rise of the universities in the twelfth and thirteenth centuries, the essence of the distinctively Christian approach remained the same.[233]

Most theorists of education today, assuming they value a study involving broad abstractions, postpone it until a relatively late stage of the student's development; they think that during the formative years schools should concentrate on subjects more suited to the mind of a young boy. The medievals took the opposite view—namely, that there is one and only one purpose of schooling: to instill in a boy the right ideas, the right philosophy, and thereby, so far as possible for sinful man, to turn him into a true Christian in thought, feeling, and behavior.

Since, according to the consensus, all important truth has already been given by revelation, the medieval student soon realized that it would be foolish to seek out such truth on his own or to question the truths he was taught. The boy's task was to accept the body of established wisdom, and try to understand those parts of it accessible to the human mind. As to the parts he could not understand: "Not my will, but Thine be done."[234]

Whereas the pagans had conceived education as a preparation for life, the Christians conceived it as a preparation for life after death. So the teacher cleansed his lessons of any taint of worldliness; the worst carriers of this, it was held, were the remnants of the pagan writings. Even the more innocent of these were dismissed as superfluous, because the truth man needs is already in the Bible. Therefore, "abstain from all heathen books . . . which subvert the faith of the unstable," said the *Apostolic Constitution* in the fourth century. "For what defects dost thou find in the law of God, that thou shouldst have recourse to those heathenish fables?" (After Aquinas became a tolerable presence, the Church dropped its all-out rejection of pagan texts.)[235]

In regard to curriculum, medieval educators adapted some ideas of the later Romans. They taught seven main subjects: the trivium (grammar, logic or dialectic, and rhetoric), thereby preparing the student for the quadrivium (arithmetic, geometry, music, and astronomy), all of which prepared him, at the universities during the final centuries, to study the supreme subject, theology.

Following the Roman model, grammar was regarded as by far the most important subject in a boy's early years (reading, writing, and some literature were included under it as adjuncts). For years, after a boy turned six or seven, he spent most of his school time taking dictation on elaborately developed categories and rules of grammar, then memorizing all of it. To the youngster, much of this material must have seemed pointless and often unintelligible—for example, when his teacher, carrying out a sixth-century idea, presented grammar to a class as "divided into eighteen parts, of which sixteen deal with accidence and two with syntax."[236] Immersion in such floating abstractions shaped the boys' thought processes from the outset. The Romans (much of the time) had defended such immersion as a means to worldly success, and the classicists as a means to understanding ancient greatness. The Christian educators' purpose was the opposite. A perfect knowledge of Latin acquired in an environment of disdain for the world, they thought, would enable a student to copy, preserve, and so far as possible understand the language of the sacred texts. Logic, too, was taught not as principles to guide Nature-oriented thought, but as another means of moving the student toward God. In the child's early years, for example, he learned how logic helped him to detect and thus reject ideas that contradicted Christian belief.

The primacy of abstractions—especially mathematical ones—is evident in the quadrivium as well. In this more advanced stage, too, as a ninth-century council decreed, the teacher's goal should be religious; he should teach the "principles of the liberal arts, because in these chiefly the commandments of God are manifested and declared."[237]

Thus in the first years, the students of arithmetic were taught only the rudiments needed to calculate religious occasions, such as the date of Easter Sunday. Then, as the subject advanced, concretes were dropped; mathematics, as in Pythagoras and Plato, became the study of pure number theory. The study of music was not of music as we know it; music was taught as the branch of mathematics pertaining to the numerical ratios between the notes of the scales. Astronomy (after Ptolemy) was presented as a study not of the heavenly bodies, but of the mathematical relationships among them. "[A]rithmetic," in one apt current summary, "was pure number, geometry was number in space, music number in time, and astronomy number in space and time." As to a nonmathematical subject, such as history, it was little taught except for the axiom that the course of man's past and its climax in Jesus are the expression of God's plan. The teaching of science consisted of giving the students a list of mostly undefined "scientific" terms to memorize.[238]

Medieval thinkers learned rationalism at school, especially at the universities, which specialized in developing this type of thought. "The data of Biblical revelation," as Easton says, "were the axioms, and were implanted in the human mind in the same way as geometrical truths," and the rest of knowledge was deduced therefrom. One of the most valued skills taught in this connection was the art of disputation. One student would advance a theoretical argument in favor of some conclusion, and another its counter-argument—each claiming that his basic premises were inherent in the faith and that his opponent's contradicted it. The dispute was then resolved by logic and/or by authority, but not by observation.[239]

Thus the scholar, as the *Britannica* puts it, might debate about "how many angels could stand on the head of a pin, but he did not question the existence of angels." He did not question, because any challenge to the accepted axioms was regarded not only as anti-Christian, but also as senseless on its face. If the Christians *a priori* is what makes possible all our knowledge, then by definition no so-called worldly fact can contradict Christianity. A creature cannot contradict its creator, any more than an object of knowledge can contradict the faculty of knowing it—or any more than a theorem can contradict its axioms.[240]

Medieval education is monism of the unworldly type: a curriculum of abstractions united, in content and method, by the pursuit of a single goal—to move ever closer to the transcendent unifier, which alone is real. In other words, the One without the Many, M_2.

Politics

The base of medieval politics was the Church's demand for all-inclusive papal rule, rule both in the spiritual realm and in the material. The vicar of Christ must be the final authority within the Church and without, in the secular kingdoms headed by Christian kings and, as far as possible, in the lands of the infidels as well. The pope, according to Innocent IV in the thirteenth century, must have control over the mind and body of "all human beings, whether Christians or not." "[A]ll governments," Gregory VII had said three centuries earlier, "should accept a place in a world state of which the pope should be the head. . . ." "Both swords, the spiritual and the material . . ." wrote Boniface VIII in the fourteenth century,

> are in the power of the Church; the one, indeed, to be wielded for the Church, the other by the Church; the one by the hand of the priest, the other by the hand of kings and knights, but at the will and sufferance of the priest. One sword, moreover, ought to be under the other, and the temporal authority to be subjected to the spiritual.[241]

Since, as Augustine had declared, the pope was "the final arbiter of human affairs," there could be no concession to any desire for individual or group autonomy. Thus the first famous attack in the West on the right to liberty, in 1215. Innocent III excommunicated the nobles who had wrested from King John the rights granted in the Magna Carta, while absolving John of guilt for repudiating the oath he had taken to obey the document's provisions.[242]

The Church's quest to control the temporal world was regarded as fully consistent with its scorn of that world; indeed, it held that the scorn entailed the control. Secular factors, being inherently materialistic, were always a seduction to immorality. Moreover, even the modest level of material goods necessary for the Church's mission would be jeopardized if worldly work were irreligiously managed. An independent temporal power would thus be a constant threat both morally and practically. One cannot control men's souls, these Christians concluded, unless one controls their bodies as well.

Despite the Church's preeminence after the fall of Rome as the West's acknowledged moral authority, it took centuries of bitter struggle for Christians to achieve their political goal. The Church had to battle not only the decentralized feudal system along with its own loose organization and some irrepressible remnants of the pagan mind, but above all, in practical terms, the secular kings. This battle was protracted, even though the kings never had a chance, because the Church had an invincible power: ideas that all, including the kings themselves, agreed were sacred. The perfection of God versus the evils of this life, and thus the exalted status of the priest with his eye on men's salvation versus the ungodliness of the rulers coveting worldly corruptions—none of this was disputed, not even by the kings.

The kings, being secular figures, had to lose because they were secular. They had no answer to give Everyman when he said, "There is no emperor, king, duke, nor baron / That of God hath commission / As hath the least priest in the world being. . . ." "Who," asked Gregory VII,

> does not know that kings and rulers took their beginning from those who, being ignorant of God, have assumed, because of blind greed and intolerable presumption, to make themselves masters . . . being incited thereto by the prince of this world, the Devil?[243]

Given such a philosophic setting, the overthrow of the kings was largely a result of intellectual strategy, at which the Church was expert.

To mention one example, the pope could (and did) threaten excommunication, and extend the threat to an entire nation, with the result that its citizens feared that they would be shut out of heaven. But the nation could still be saved, the Church declared, if the people rebelled against the errant king and substituted for him a true Christian. Besides the power of religion, I should add, the Church did make limited use of military force, mostly through temporary alliance with a friendly king, but this tactic was not of much significance. In essence, the Church conquered the West not by physical but by spiritual means—that is, by the power of its ideas over men's minds and souls.

From the twelfth to the fourteenth centuries, the Church was able to establish the theocracy sought by the religious for so long. Although its rulers lacked the technological necessities of total power, they came as close to it as unbreached dogma and unopposed passion could achieve. At its height, the papacy officially controlled—though at times only in part—not only matters pertaining to dogma and morals, but also treaties between nations, treatment of widows and minors, war and peace, the legal system, disposition of property, marriage and divorce, usury, the universities, libel, wills, sex, sorcerers, and more. In Sabine's words, Innocent III, a striking example of the medieval aspiration in politics, "conceived the papacy as having a general power of review which could be extended at need to practically any sort of question, the ecclesiastical authority itself being the judge of the need." Even with such papal power, this system's defenders point out, it was permissible for a Christian to object to a pope's ideas and/or to accuse him of sin, even of mortal sin. But the charge could apply only to the pope qua human, since, qua agent of the divine, he was infallible in matters of dogma and morals. The pope alone, however, decided in each case which of his two personae had been attacked.[244]

Since the success of the Church rested on an intellectual foundation, the greatest threat to its mission was not political rivals or priestly scandals, but ideas—ideas that deviated from orthodoxy. Such heresies might spread among the ignorant, it was feared, undermining their faith, subverting their loyalty to the Church, and thereby annulling their only real asset: the hope of salvation. To stamp out this kind of evil, the authorities agreed, was a divine imperative for both philosophical and practical reasons.

To our knowledge, there were no agnostics in this period, no atheists, no Christian sects with competing visions. The heretics pursued by the Church were devout Catholics who had no intention of subverting Christian dogma, but sought merely to correct some relatively insignificant doctrinal wording or official behavior. But the Christian leadership regarded any such innovation, however minuscule it might seem to us, as the vilest treason against Christ. Intellectual independence on any level, they understood, could not coexist with unquestioning faith.

For many centuries, going back to the fall of Rome, Christians had regarded heresy as a crime, but had no power to impose punishment; now they had the power. They argued that their campaign, including its methods, had the sanction of Jesus himself, as revealed in the Gospel of St. John (15:6): "[I]f anyone abide not in me he shall be cast forth as a branch, and shall wither; and they shall gather him up, and cast him into the fire, and he burneth." [245]

To catch a heretic, one must first find him, which requires that one make inquiries. To find a mass of heretics, one needs a mass of inquirers. The Inquisition was little concerned with a heretic's capacity to effect what we call regime change, which in that era, if conceived at all, would have been understood to be impossible. Nor was the motive primarily to punish crime. Their goal, the Inquisitors stated, was not to harm their enemies, but to express in action Christian love—not only their love of God, but also of each heretic himself. If the Inquisition could change his thinking and turn him into a true Christian, it would thereby ensure his salvation. So torture was merely an ephemeral infliction of pain on the errant, necessary for them to reach in the very near future an eternity of joy.

Fundamentally, the Inquisition was not motivated by power lust, hatred, or sadism. It was instructed to inquire only about Christians, not Jews or Moors, who were regarded as divorced from God by nature and irrelevant to human life. The personnel and supporters of the Inquisition viewed themselves as healers—healers of the soul—and by the evidence I have found, a substantial number held this belief sincerely. Nothing else seems to explain their unique treatment of their victims. The best-known examples of it are the cases of a condemned man being led to the fire, a man who had been tortured and sentenced for being invincibly unrepentant. The man was not then confronted with indifference, gloating, or even disapproval by his executioners (though he often was so treated by an unruly mob). On the contrary, from the moment of sentencing, the victim's confessor, showing a kind of tender concern, stayed next to him and prayed, beseeching him to repent. The prayers and pleas continued until the last moment, when the pyre to which the heretic was bound had been lit and the flames had begun to rise. If the man even then had nodded his head in a gesture of repentance, he would still be incinerated, but his soul, everyone knew, would have been saved.[246]

Every sacred tenet of the Church behind the Inquisition is *a priori*, from the belief in the pope's power to close the heavenly door to the dogmas of the Immaculate Conception, the Incarnation, the Trinity, and the rest. To a philosophic-political system based on faith, observation is valid only insofar as it conforms to faith. We may *see* only wine and wafer, but the holy intuit the bodiless in the body and the bloodless in the blood, just as they see the non-man Jesus in the man Jesus.

In chapter eight, I distinguished two versions of statism: absolutism, as in a seventeenth-century monarchy, versus totalitarianism, as in a Communist or Fascist state. The one approach mostly leaves man's mind alone, seeking rather control of his actions, and "inquiring" into beliefs as an auxiliary, if and when a belief is regarded as a practical threat or a personal affront to the ruler. The other form of statism seeks total control, control not only of action, but of every aspect of man's life, including above all his thought. By these definitions, Christianity in its centuries on top was a theocratic form of totalitarianism, both in theory and in practice.

The medieval Church not only exemplified totalitarianism, it *invented* the system. It is this Christian creation that became the model inspiring its twentieth-century heirs—the only model they had to guide them, spreading out before their eager eyes the essential ideas, the practices, and even some of the details necessary to implement their own (modernized) versions of papal supremacy. The logic leading from God to the Inquisition opened the door, and then we saw our contemporaries salute the logic leading from the dialectic to the gulags.[247]

Medieval politics is clearly a form of Platonism. Individuals are as nothing because, metaphysically, they are unreal, merged ultimately into the *corpus Christi*, "one mystic body, of which body the head is Christ, but of Christ, God"—the One without the Many—M_2.[248]

In literature, science, education, and politics alike, medieval culture is modally consistent.

We have now seen an I culture (Greece) followed by an M_1 culture (Rome) followed by an M_2 culture (Christendom). Combined with the knowledge we gained in the study of modern cultures, we now have plenty of data, from which we will soon draw conclusions.

The Renaissance

To bring our historical survey full circle, we must take a look at the Renaissance, the period from about 1400 to 1600, in which a secularist breakthrough was the new cultural element existing alongside the continued veneration of religion. No Western society has ever before (or since) faced such a cultural conflict: a mode of thought accepted by all for a millennium as self-evident—confronted seemingly out of the blue by a new, incompatible mode that men were finding impossible to resist. Widespread skepticism was one result of the tumult, but that is not a philosophic viewpoint. So let us now, as far as possible, try to identify the operative modes in our four fields.

In literature, the towering figure was Shakespeare. His plays are secular, and his depth of characterization and scale of theme are rightly acclaimed examples of his power of integration. In regard to these two elements, Shakespeare, in more sophisticated form, continues the tradition of the Greek playwrights. In regard to his stories, however, the case is different. Although they have a generalized logic, the events onstage do not have the inexorable, step-by-step connection of the typical Greek (or, later, Romanticist) work. On the contrary, as the Shakespearean expert A. C. Bradley points out, Shakespeare "in most of his tragedies allows to

'chance' or 'accident' an appreciable influence at some point in the action."
Perhaps such chance events are intended to indicate man's metaphysical
helplessness. Or perhaps, as has often been said, characterization is
Shakespeare's real interest, and events are included not for their story
value, but rather somewhat randomly, when judged as helpful in illuminating the characters. On the other hand, while there is "appreciable
chance" in his work, Shakespeare does not feature chance; he does not
extol this form of non-integration as a virtue. In regard to story, it seems,
Shakespeare has no consistent mode of integration; and since story is so
fundamental an element in literature, I can only conclude that Shakespeare's work as a whole is outside of DIM classification. There are several
other such Renaissance writers—Cervantes, for example, who presents
characters in terms of fundamentals and unites his material by broad
themes; he also gives us sequences of events much more chance-driven
than anything in Shakespeare.[249]

Other Renaissance authors are more consistent. In *Dr. Faustus*, for
example, Christopher Marlowe depicts an admirably passionate scholar
righteously disobeying God in order to acquire knowledge; he is a hero
who sells his soul to the devil in order to develop his mind, but in the end
suffers the punishment of eternal damnation. All the elements in this play
are integrated; the events are integrated not in a secular context, but by
the assumption that whatever happens does so necessarily because it is
required by God's plan. This play is a Renaissance precursor of *Paradise
Lost*, in which we see noble disobedience—an enticing earthly reality, but
one subordinate to the transcendent, which is the essence of an M_1
product.

The case of <u>science</u> is simpler. Although Renaissance man could create
literature for the ages, he did not yet grasp clearly the difference, let alone
the clash, between science and supernaturalism, or between conclusions
based on observation and those deriving from astrology, alchemy, magic,
the Bible, the occult. Hence the striking contradictions of some of the
great Renaissance pioneers of science.

Copernicus is one example of this combination, but Francis Bacon,
champion of empiricism and oft-claimed father of the inductive method,
outdoes him in this regard. Alongside his valuable scientific ideas, he

believed in astrology, divination, and witchcraft, and even praised the church father and avowed irrationalist Tertullian, declaring that "the more absurd and incredible any divine mystery is, the greater honor we do God in believing it."[250]

These part-fledged scientists did not attempt to integrate their views. Science in this period was merely a generalized aspiration along with a few specific discoveries. It was not yet regarded as a distinct cognitive field that had to be integrated with other fields or even within itself. In regard to science, it is too early for any DIM category to apply.

Education gives us the clearest case. As we have seen, the seventeenth-century classicist system is in essence a recapitulation of the late Roman approach, which was much admired by the early Italian humanists. By the later sixteenth century, the Roman system was fully reborn and widely practiced. As in ancient Rome, teachers were again building their curricula and methods on linguistic mastery. Once again, the study of language apart from experience—especially Latin, and especially its grammar—was regarded as the key to intellectual and perhaps also practical success.

Once again, the ruling principle was form over matter—the traditional M_1 mode.

In the politics of this period, papal totalitarianism having faded, we see virtually everywhere the emergence of absolute monarchy. The defenders of monarchy, however, had no agreed-upon intellectual base on which to stand. Some upheld monarchism on practical grounds, as the only workable system; some pointed to precedents in Roman law; some claimed that God favored the system. No one doubted that God's blessing was a necessary condition of a king's legitimacy, but there was no appeal to the divine right of kings, an idea that had not yet been formulated. So it was not clear at the time which, if any, of these justifications was regarded as primary or how they were related—another sign of the period's indeterminacy. It was not until the seventeenth century that a whole system of politics gave God the primacy.

To sum up:

Literature: major works—inconsistent or M_1.

Science: no DIM description.

Education: M_1.

Politics: M_1 rule without a coherent base.

For two hundred years Renaissance intellectuals faced a culture that, in DIM terms, combined a weakening M_2 with a rising but still far from ascendant I. They could not go backward to the Middle Ages; nor, even if it had been possible, would most of them—still highly religious by today's standards—have gone forward to the Enlightenment. The result was consistent, often brilliant cultural products in some fields, but no distinctive, culture-wide mode of integration.

The most suitable category for this period, which would seem to give its due to both God and Nature, would be M_1. And in many respects, as we have seen, the dilemma was being dealt with by moving in this direction. But the philosophy that would explain in contemporary terms how to resolve the dilemma had not yet been created. With Descartes, the two hundred years of confused creators were shown, at last, how to find "clear and distinct" answers. The transitional mind became the modern mind.

Hereafter, I treat the Renaissance as outside of the DIM categories, though in certain defined contexts, I acknowledge its M_1 tendency.

PART FOUR

THE FUTURE

CHAPTER TWELVE

IDENTIFYING A CULTURE'S ESSENCE

SO FAR, I have been using the DIM approach, offered only as a hypothesis in chapter four, as a guide to cultural analysis. My analysis has conformed to each of the standards of objectivity set forth in that chapter. The DIM approach, we have seen, enables us to discover the essence of the products within our four fields in each era. Now we must move in the other direction—not from hypothesis to products, but from the observed facts about products to hypothesis. Using the cultural evidence, we must identify the generalizations it supports and determine whether we can now claim that the DIM principles are objective, inductively established truth.

Philosophy and Cultural Products

As Ayn Rand and I have argued at length, a society's philosophy is what shapes its actions and future. The DIM Hypothesis, as I have pointed out several times, presupposes this viewpoint as its necessary foundation. Despite its causal primacy, however, philosophy taken by itself does not enable us to identify the essence of any particular society. The reason is that a society's philosophy cannot be discovered <u>directly</u>, simply by asking its people—whether the intellectuals and/or the general public—what they think in regard to fundamental questions.

Most intellectuals, even in the humanities and sciences, are—often understandably—too caught up in the specialized problems of their field to be explicitly concerned much with philosophic abstractions. Some thinkers, of course—the more philosophic minds of a period—are concerned with fundamental ideas, and may indeed formulate some new ones that could at some point become influential in shaping the society. But to determine the extent of such influence, if any, we must discover to what extent these ideas are accepted or at least tolerated by people outside the intellectual world. A philosophy, brilliant or otherwise, that is unknown or intolerable to the public as a whole may still have future potential, but it does not reveal the society's essence in the present.

For example, Plato and Aristotle were the two most powerful intellectual forces with prestigious schools in ancient Greece, but only one was indicative of the culture's essence, and this fact could not be ascertained merely by a study, however thorough, of the ideas of the two. Historical development is usually a time-consuming process. Occasionally it is a matter of years, but often of generations and sometimes even centuries, for new basic ideas to move from the status of esoteric theory to public mind-set; during these periods, there is often a prolonged dichotomy between these two.

Polling the public is no more helpful. Most non-intellectuals—aside from some usually small, ideologically self-conscious groups—cannot state their philosophical views, even to the extent they hold such. Mostly they discuss abstract ideas—when they do—incoherently, inconsistently, and as unrelated to one another. So it is common for them to change a stated view on the spur of an emotion or a headline and then, with some new headline, change again. From such ephemera we gain at best inconclusive leads.

Moreover, even if we could by Q & A somehow compile an accurate list of a society's philosophic principles, this knowledge would not enable us to make *specific* predictions about its future. By their nature, philosophic principles are universal in scope. Their unique power rests on the fact that they are not limited to any one society, but rather identify the nature of man's requirements—and of the results of contradicting them—everywhere. From general principles alone, however, one can infer only other general principles. Identifying a society's philosophy, I repeat, is a precondition of identifying the basic causes at work in it. It is necessary, but not sufficient—not if one's goal is to find out in less abstract terms "what's next."

Let us take as an example the Objectivist principle that the rise of unreason in a society leads, if unchecked, to dictatorship (a principle on which I based an earlier book analyzing Hitler's takeover of the Weimar Republic). And let us suppose we know by some means that a substantial part of a given society increasingly accepts unreason. Philosophy by itself would then tell us the ultimate political fate of that society if it did not change its ideas. This is certainly not a vague generality, but a definite and frightening prediction. Despite this fact, however, the philosophic prediction as such necessarily leaves unanswered several questions of great interest to those living in a particular society. What kind of dictatorship will it be? Is any group in the still-free period the most dangerous threat to freedom-lovers now, and thus the most important enemy to fight? If so, is it necessarily an obvious group, such as statist politicians and their Hollywood retinue? Are there better people now among us to be recruited, and are they necessarily to be found on the right? Is there still time for us to reverse direction, and if so, by what specific means can we do so? Or has our society reached the point of no return, and if so, how long does it have? And how probable are all these assessments?

My idea, put forth in chapter four merely as potentially illuminating, is to find the answers to these kinds of questions not by ignoring philosophy, but by looking for it everywhere—in a form specific enough to give us the specific answers we seek. And the vehicle of this specific form, our survey has shown, is cultural products.

To reach and direct the minds of the general public in any era, philosophy has to take the form of <u>concretes of a special kind</u>: concretes that incorporate and communicate fundamental abstractions, but do so largely by implication—while in explicit terms they engage people's interest and assent by offering them specific items of knowledge and/or value they do understand and desire. Only cultural products perform this dual task. They alone present philosophy in a form accessible to minds oriented to concretes, concretes such as the stories people enjoy or the (to them) wild and crazy electrons they read about in the Sunday papers with awe or their child's teacher's way of teaching him reading or the politicians debating taxes on TV. Cultural works are the proselytizers of philosophy. If the works are accepted by a society not necessarily in theory, but in practice—in the form of purchases, enrollments, votes, applause, and the like, reflecting widespread approval—then the ideas they embody reveal a society's actual, functioning philosophy, whether generally acknowledged or not.

The above conclusion can be hypothesized on the basis of the Objectivist philosophy, but it cannot be validated by that means. To validate a generalization one requires a wide range of observational evidence that supports and concretizes it. This is what chapters five through eleven have indicated. So my first inductive generalization, which I now regard as objectively proved, is no longer a mere hypothesis. This first generalization is: Cultural works are the transmitters to a society of philosophic fundamentals.

Some Problems of Non-DIM Analysis

To embody a philosophy, a cultural work as we have seen need not—and most do not—explicitly advocate fundamental ideas. Even for those that do so, the mere advocacy in a product of an idea does not indicate that it is necessary to or even consistent with the work. To discover a work's philosophy, we must ferret out not abstract ideas as such, but rather their role in real-world cultural action—that is, in guiding the minds of cultural creators. And for man the integrator, the thing that determines mental action, and thus its products, is mode of integration.

Our analyses so far have considered only the positive results of the DIM approach. Let us now look at the results of a non-DIM approach—that is, one that attempts to define the essence of a cultural product without reference to modal factors. Here are a few examples of the kinds of problems such analyses face.

a) Consider first the case of Newton. In high-school science courses today, the standard presentation summarizes five or six of Newton's achievements—regarding motion, light, the calculus, etc.—which are treated as more or less unrelated discoveries without wider meaning. This makes it impossible for a student to grasp what Newton represents culturally (or as a physicist) or why his work changed the West.

Even in the best and rarest classes today, in which the teacher *is* concerned with philosophic issues, the class will likely hear an analysis on the following order: Newton invented calculus, thus showing his enthusiasm for quantification and logical deduction as a means of scientific understanding. He acknowledged the influence on him of Kepler and Galileo, showing his understanding of the hierarchical development of knowledge. He discovered important laws, including three of motion and one of gravity, showing his belief in immutable cause and effect. He believed that absolute space and time are the sensorium of God, showing his conviction that there is no conflict between science and religion. He believed that the laws he had discovered apply to the entire universe, showing his conviction that science can generalize validly. He admitted that there were many important questions in physics he could not answer, showing that he saw no conflict between certainty on some issues and ignorance on others. He rejected "hypotheses," showing his disdain for theories not based on data. He made startling predictions, showing his belief in the practical power of physical theory. He invented many scientific instruments, showing the importance he ascribed to sense perception. He performed ingenious experiments, showing his belief that science presupposes not only sensory experience, but also its manipulation.

Each of the above statements about Newton is correct, and most are even important, but how from this list is one to discover the essence or cultural power of Newton's work? Is one to connect all these items, and if so, by what means? Are there perhaps crucial Newtonian elements omitted from the list or insignificant ones included, and by what standard of selectivity is one to decide? Or is there perhaps really no Newtonian essence at all, but merely a conglomeration of discoveries and theories coming under no single "neat label," as today's perceptual-level mentalities would have it?

An enumeration of ideas selected without any objective standard of selection is arbitrary; at best, it is merely a preliminary laundry list. As such, no item on the list—and no combination of or addition to or subtraction from them—makes intelligible Newton's cultural distinctiveness. Experimentation, higher mathematics, natural laws, induction—all these are (or used to be) embraced by physicists of many different persuasions; such agreement is no basis for equating all these men, either in physics or in epistemology.

Modal analysis does provide the requisite standard. It selects from a product its <u>structural</u> features—that is, those that <u>are</u> necessary to the creation of a work as a whole because, put together, they <u>are</u> that whole. Without such features, the product would collapse into a rubble of the juxtaposed. As to non-structural features, they are identified in relation to the structural—either as derivatives, as irrelevant, or as contradictory to the work's essence.

b) Now consider a case where different attributes of a work, taken separately, so far from seeming to be unrelated, actually point to the same essence. Which one then is the key we seek? French classicist plays are a good example. Typically, the playwrights offer some sort of Platonic theme, such as duty versus desire; and they also accept as their aesthetic guide a system of *a priori* rules validated rationalistically. Both these aspects—the content of the theme and the primacy of form—reflect the same philosophic influence. If cultural understanding is our goal, does it make any difference which one is chosen as essential?

Without reference to mode of integration, the choice makes no difference; from a modal perspective, however, it does. Although theme is certainly the integrator of content in many plays, it does not perform this function in a classicist play, where content by the play's nature is secondary. So interrelationships deriving from content are not structural elements of the classicist whole, whose content may not even be connected to the play's formal rules. The conflict between duty and desire, for example, does not necessarily imply such essential features of the classicists as the relative lack of action in their plays, their stress on the unities, or the primacy of decorous poetry over passion. In other words, the thematic conflict does not necessarily reveal what is distinctive to classicism. Undoubtedly, given the school's mode of integration, some sort of Platonic theme is to be expected, and grasping such a theme may indeed point us in the right direction. But we can know that it is the right direction only when we discover the real (integrating) essence. Otherwise, we would have to regard as essentially the same the works of countless writers who present a similar Platonic theme, even though their period and approach are vastly different—writers ranging from the medieval Dante to the modern Somerset Maugham.

c) Now consider a product that seems to many historians to have no essence—no philosophical meaning—not because they see in it too many significant factors, but because they cannot find in it even one. A good example here is the later Roman teachers' obsession with detached linguistic technicalities. This practice, we are regularly told in the textbooks, is unintelligible; it must simply be written off as astonishing for such a practically oriented people; or perhaps it is no more than an overreaction to the overabundance of recently available, lengthy Hellenistic grammar books. Many of these scholars know that the Romans were immersing their students in a world of what I call "floating abstractions," but then shrug off this fact as a mere oddity.

Considered as isolated courses, to be sure, the existence of such abstract training in grammar would prove nothing about a school's essence. But how different is our understanding when, knowing what to look for, we grasp that the approach was not isolated, not restricted to grammar or rhetoric, but rather that it exemplified a deliberately chosen method, implemented throughout the curriculum, of shaping a child's mind for life?

Modal analysis finds no oddity in the Romans' fixation on grammar, but rather a necessary feature of their educational system. And once we grasp this fact, we can relate the Romans' education not only to their products in other fields, but also to non-Roman products in other centuries. For example, from the modal perspective, floating abstractions at the base of these pagan schools foreshadow what is already in the wings: the medievals' outright rejection of matter.

d) In the quest to identify cultural essence, the first, direct objects of study are concretes—that is, single cultural products. These studies in turn make possible the next, higher level of analysis: the discovery of *relationships* among these essences—that is, of the various products' similarities to and differences from one another. We can identify such similarities and differences among the products within any of our four areas in any of the six eras we have surveyed. The discovery of such relationships enables us to gain a broader perspective: to grasp the essence not merely of a single work or field, but of an entire culture—which we have already done several times.

This level of integration also depends on a modal analysis of concretes. It is not otherwise possible.

To concretize this point, consider an attempt to define a whole culture without reference to mode. Let us take as an example the first period of modern culture, during the last half of the nineteenth century, and assume again a philosophical but non-modal observer. Judging by my experience, we could expect to hear from our teacher something along these lines: Naturalists in literature drop values on principle in order to emulate scientists and record objective facts. The advocates of a mixed economy drop principles as extreme, favoring instead compromise, in part because no one can claim for his position objective truth. Pluralists in education enthusiastically promote modern science while continuing to revere the ancient classics. Meanwhile positivists, who dominate science, are declaring that science cannot explain what we observe, so we must restrict ourselves to modest and uncertain generalizations.

Each of the above summaries is true, and each names important facts about its subject. But what does all this information add up to? The period, according to the conventional approach, is one of principle and anti-principle, of objectivity and anti-objectivity, of values and anti-values, of science triumphant and science shrinking toward impotence. Only modal analysis can lay bare the unity of all these seemingly contradictory products, and thus the period's essence, because only modal analysis can discover the D_1 everywhere at work—and by this means the period's underlying philosophy.

The inability of today's cultural commentators to detect similarities short-circuits their capacity to understand the facts they observe. With no inkling of the essence of Romanticism or of capitalism, for example, the consensus holds that the first is escapist emotionalism, while the second is brutal commercialism, the exact opposite. What then is the essence of the cultural period they share? The usual answer is that this question presupposes an arbitrary monism resting on an invalid metaphysical term ("essence"). What then about all the kinds of connections we have found—such as those between Roman schools and Louis XIV, medieval teleology and the theory of everything, Gertrude Stein and John Rawls, Stoic physics and Stalinist literature, Demosthenes and Hugo, Virgil and Einstein, FDR and quantum mechanics, to give a few examples? Today, relationships such as these are not only unknown, but viewed as inconceivable.

Although our D intellectuals are primarily concerned to grasp not similarities but differences, even in this effort analysis without reference to mode continually leads them astray. Sometimes it causes them to elevate insignificant differences into major cultural dichotomies when the movements involved are in fact no more than concretes under the same abstraction (for example, the view that Fascism and Communism are fundamental opposites). And sometimes, even worse, these non-modal thinkers, with no concept of "essential," see so many similarities in a given case that they cannot find a difference that matters to them, as in the view that Aristotle is the philosopher of the Church.

From the foregoing, my second inductive generalization, relating culture and mode, is: Only modal analysis can lead us safely through a jungle of fallacies and objectively lay bare cultural essences.

Since I claim so much for the modal approach, I want to acknowledge the fact that many cultural essences have long been well-known without benefit of the DIM theory. My view is not that other approaches always fail, but rather that modal analysis, being the only objective methodology, is the only one that makes it possible for an analyst to identify correctly *all* cultural cases, and to know that he has done so. Other approaches often yield valuable insights and sometimes profound truth, but in the end even the best discussions to date must be described as flares of brilliance dimmed by insolvable errors, unbridgeable lacunae, and/or the blackness of contradictions.

Now let us combine our two generalizations. Here is the interrelationship we have found among philosophy, culture, and mode: Philosophy leads to mode of integration, which leads to culture. Mode, therefore, is the link, the intermediary, connecting the other two.

Modes can serve as such a link precisely because their level of abstraction is intermediate. Philosophic fundamentals involve the broadest abstractions; they deal with existence and consciousness as such. Modes are less abstract; though they presuppose philosophy, they are its application to a specific cognitive process, offering as guidelines to integrators a series of how-tos (or don'ts). Modes thus express philosophy in terms of narrower abstractions—narrower, but still broad enough to apply to cultural products in any field or era. The products themselves, however, though dependent on philosophy and structured by modes, are no longer abstractions, broad or narrow; they are the observable concretes with and by which men actually live.[251]

Since modes, pure and mixed alike, are abstractions, each of the five, as I have often pointed out, subsumes many different concretes, concretes that may differ widely in specifics—in programs, tactics, mass base, enemies, etc. Although such differences may be important in other contexts, they are not so from the perspective of modal theory, because we are seeking essence, not detail.

The modal approach, precisely because it works through the intermediate in breadth, is what tells us on which level of abstraction to function in our cultural quest. If one's standard of analysis is too abstract, it risks making cultural connections vague, floating, difficult or impossible to identify. If one's standard is too narrow, it risks blinding the analyst to connections that can be grasped only on a higher level of concepts. The first of these errors—too abstract, but once popular—is illustrated by such theorists as Hegel, Toynbee, and Spengler, who regarded history as the self-development of the Absolute, or as successive social responses to challenge, or as a predestined cycle (all are M mentalities). The second approach—too narrow, now popular—regards such floating theories as the mysticism believed to be inherent in any attempt to seek out broad similarities (the D mentality). The alternative to too broad and too narrow is: mode.

The Two Philosophic Issues Underlying Mode

Although a mode presupposes philosophy, that philosophy necessarily deals with many other issues as well. Ultimately, all these issues are interrelated. Despite this, however, a mode, being an application of philosophy to a specific task, is defined by reference to its philosophy's stand on only two questions. The answer to either of these implies the other.

Metaphysically, the issue is the status of this world. Epistemologically, it is the status of concepts. A philosophy's answer to the first tells a man <u>what</u> to integrate—that is, which kinds of connections to look for and which, however they may be sought after by others, are to be dismissed as non-existent or unknowable. The answer to the second tells a man <u>how</u> to integrate—where to start, through what kinds of steps or stages to proceed, how far he should try to go (and, of course, whether he should start at all). This knowledge of the what and the how, I hold, is necessary and sufficient as a guide to integration. An analyst seeking to identify a work's mode, therefore, should be concerned only with evidence pertaining to these two fundamentals. No other issues, however philosophically important, reveal the method of a creator's mind, or therefore the essence of his product.[252]

I do not mean that other philosophic principles evident in a cultural work should be ignored. On the contrary, since all of a philosophy's principles are interconnected, virtually any of them in the right context can be helpful, sometimes almost indispensable in a mode hunt—by narrowing or expanding possibilities, suggesting further angles to explore, lending significance to what might otherwise be obscure. My point is not that these non-modal principles, as we may call them, are irrelevant in the search for essence, but that their relevance does not lie in the mere fact of their presence. They are relevant if and only insofar as they advance the search for the two fundamentals. In other words, though non-modal principles can help point us in the direction of a work's essence, they themselves cannot define it.

A simple example of this fact is afforded by the principle of causality, which is of profound importance in philosophy. By itself, the principle does not offer cognitive guidance; it tells us that objects act in a certain manner, but not what our minds should do about this fact; by itself it pertains to content of thought, not method. There is indeed an obvious relationship between causality and integration; a man's view of causality is certainly not irrelevant to his mode of thought. But what is relevant here is not simply his belief in that content, but rather his interpretation and validation of it—which derive from the basic principles guiding his thought. A creator may consider causality as a principle of Nature learned through observation, and look for causes accordingly; or as a product of God's will learned *a priori*; or as a product of human consciousness learned subjectively; or as a baseless but convenient hypothesis. All of these men may sincerely affirm causality and repudiate chance events. But only when we know the interpretation can we know the role of the principle of causality in a man's thinking. And only his stand on the two fundamental issues can give us this interpretation. The causal principle out of context, in short, does not reveal a mode, or therefore the essence of a product or society. The same is true of all non-modal philosophic principles.

If the union of only two fundamental issues defines mode, we can understand why the number of modes is so limited. In combining these fundamentals, there are not many alternatives. Setting aside the unstable mixtures, in all our history only three internally consistent sets of basic principles have been offered. This trinity or trichotomy has given rise in philosophy to many derivative trichotomies, each identifying, from a specific perspective, some aspect of the fundamental issues. Thus: supernaturalism (Plato), secularism (Aristotle), nihilism (Kant)—these pertain to the nature of reality. Mysticism, sense-based reason, sense perception alone (these pertain to man's means of knowledge). Rationalism, Greek empiricism, modern empiricism (relation of abstractions to observation). Intrinsicism, objectivism, subjectivism (relation of subject to object). And there are many others, including DIM itself, which pertains to the method of integration. Trichotomies such as these define in relation to fundamentals the possible types of philosophy, and thus are indispensable in identifying the essence of a philosophy.

These trichotomies are indispensable to the classification of cultures, too, but for this particular task they are not enough. Faced with three possibilities, a culture can accept, reject, or try to combine, the latter effort creating a viewpoint that I have been calling mixed. Since such mixtures do not advocate new fundamental principles in addition to those of the Big Three, they must be regarded within philosophy as mere variants of the approach of the philosopher at their base. Despite this, however, the mixtures can become very influential and give birth to distinctive and long-lived types of culture.

The mixtures seem to have been unavoidable historical mediators, necessary to bridge the gulf separating one pure culture from another.

It seems unimaginable, for instance, to project a cultural leap from classical Athens directly to the Middle Ages without the Hellenistic-Roman intermediary, or from the Middle Ages to the Enlightenment, or from the Enlightenment to James Joyce and quantum mechanics. I do not mean that a "one" is always necessary to bridge two pure modes, but merely that in the past it has always been so.

In the DIM view, the history of the West has been a progression not of degrees, but of <u>kinds</u> of society, each defined by its method of thinking. As a rule, there is an unsettled, often indefinable period of social upheaval as one mode yields to another. This kind of relatively short-lived process may properly be described as change in degree—but the degrees are comparable to the turning of a steering wheel, after which a new stable direction, the new ruling ideas, mixed or pure, take over and stay, often for a lengthy period. Mixed modes to date, I might add, have far outlasted the pure ones.

As we will see in the next chapter, there is also a form of change by degree within the mixed modes. But it is the sort of change exemplified by ice turning into water. In other words, it is a change of degree within one kind of entity leading at a critical point to another kind.

We may now state a third generalization, hypothesized in chapter four and now inductively established—in this case, a generalization relating culture to modes from a quantitative perspective: There are only five possible kinds of cultures deriving from five possible modes. This generalization will prove to be a valuable tool in cultural prediction. If, in a particular case, we are able to eliminate as a future possibility four of the modes, we will know by that fact alone which one is the only one able to come next.

I do not validate the DIM approach rationalistically. Objectivism is its precondition, but the theory cannot be deduced from Objectivism. The proof does not consist of any kind of syllogism, such as: Mode of integration is essential to thought; thought determines culture and history; therefore, mode of integration determines culture and history. Apart from an extensive observational base, the propositions of this syllogism, though I regard them as true, are arbitrary. For example, even if we agree that integration is essential to thought—chapter one gave an inductive base for this view—it does not follow that modes of integration are the decisive determinant of culture, or that, even assuming their importance, modes are visible objectively in cultural products. What about other possible aspects of creative thought or of human psychology, what about political or economic factors, and what about all the different kinds of products? A rationalist, even if he were to agree with the DIM conclusions, would have no way to validate or even apply them. He does not observe fields and eras, but merely manipulates floating abstractions.

Now, I believe, we have the basis to make history intelligible. And once history is intelligible, prediction becomes possible.

In regard to prediction, I want to point out here in advance that DIM theory applies only to cultures based on Western philosophy. I offer no opinion in regard to Eastern or other cultures, about which I have nothing worthwhile to say. Similarly, DIM does not apply to the countless societies ignorant of and/or indifferent to philosophy that were the rule throughout the pre-Greek era and are still so in much of the world.

If, through educational degeneration, natural catastrophe, social cataclysm, and/or military conquest, the West should lose its tie to philosophy, then modal classifications would lose their foundation in facts. I know of no way to define the possible kinds or sequence of human gangs and tribes—or of their cultural products, if any—once men have abandoned guidance by abstract thought. One cannot predict the forms of barbarism, but only the forms, however debased, of civilization.

Since the time of Greece, however, the West has always clung to its

Greek origin, no matter how seductive the provocation to drop it or how twisted its ideas had become. Men who have discovered philosophy, it seems, find it hard to let it go.

For the reader's future reference, I restate here in compressed terms the key generalizations in this chapter.

Cultural works are shaped by and transmit philosophy through their mode.

Identifying mode is the only means of grasping cultural essence.

Only two philosophic issues—the nature of this world and of concepts—are necessary to the grasp of modes.

There are five, and only five, modes.

CHAPTER THIRTEEN

THE WEST'S MODAL PROGRESSION

THE CHART AT the back of the book summarizes what we have learned so far about the successive cultures of the Western world. In other words, it summarizes the West's modal progression.

As I observed in chapter five, the life span of a culture can be dated only in approximate terms, and even these can be open to legitimate disputes. There is a range of options, because of the gradual nature of much social change, the difficulty in classifying contradictory transition periods, and the possibility of uneven modal development within a period. What I have done is to take a rough average of generally recognized estimates of longevity, and then rounded the figures. So my dates could be off by as many as fifty years or, in regard to long-lived cultures, even by multiples of that. But such errors are not of concern here, because they do not affect the information we are seeking from dates: temporal ratios— that is, the order of magnitude by which certain modes outlive others.[253]

––––––––

The progression of modes is not a march of reified abstractions propelled independently of worldly events by the dictates of some preordained logic beyond human control. On the contrary, a mode is a method of thinking, and method entails content; thinking, if it is non-Platonic, is about particulars. The rise and fall of any mode, therefore, can be understood only in conjunction with a specific triggering event or events—that is, event(s) which, in the context of the period, lead people to question and to conclude that the established mode is unsafe, backward, invalid, and/or evil. The result, other things being equal, will be a modal changeover.

But if a mode by itself is not the cause of change, neither is the triggering event(s) by itself. The cause is the two in concert. No matter what the situation, change from any given mode is possible only when a different mode is known and used as a guide in interpreting the situation—known and used either by influential intellectuals and/or by an aroused even if non-intellectual public.

The triggering event(s) may flow from the mode itself or occur independently. The triggers can (and actually have) run the gamut of the imaginable, ranging from the purely intellectual, such as the appearance of a new philosophy, to socioeconomic developments, to moral revulsion against a society's leadership, to the use of physical force, such as military conquest, and many other factors.

Triggers, accordingly, are sometimes datable events; more commonly they are conditions that have developed and intensified across time. Whatever its form and duration, however, a trigger, as I use the term, is a particular occurrence that prompts a society or its leaders to decide that it is time for modal change. There is no correlation, let me add, between the historical prominence of an event and its ability to serve as a modal trigger. The Lutheran revolt, for example, had a resounding effect on the Catholic Church, but none on its M_2 mode, which the Lutherans shared and perpetuated, many of them all the way to Nazi Germany.[254]

The DIM theory has no distinctive means to predict the rise of disaffection in an era; nor can it identify in advance the concretes that will trigger a changeover. The basic question that modal theory does attempt to answer is this: Given a society's established mode, along with the eruption of such concretes if and when they come, which new mode will people choose to embrace and why?

The DIM Hypothesis rejects determinism. Since men have free will, they are not puppets of the prevailing mode, any more than of the dominant philosophy. When men face critical events and know of a different modal possibility, they are able to decide consciously to evaluate the new developments, whether rationally or irrationally, and in either case go on to work for change. Or they can simply accept passively establishment policy. In Ayn Rand's words, man has the choice "to think or not to think." No method of mental functioning and no crisis of action can necessitate a man's or a country's decision in regard to this choice. In general, therefore, modal changes, like all human behavior, are not inevitable.

Volitional, however, does not mean acausal or inexplicable. Free will is not omnipotent. Men cannot change philosophies or modes by whim. In some eras, they do not know of any other possibility acceptable to them. In others, even in the face of occurrences that are hugely unpopular with the public, dissenters are unable to arouse enough opposition to shake the establishment. On the other hand, there are cases in which modal changeover *is* inevitable, regardless of free will, because a point of no return has been reached. People are free to jump from the roof of a skyscraper, but not to escape the result.

How high up are we on that skyscraper? To find the answer, we must understand the modal rises and falls of our predecessors. Before we can assess rival modes in our own society and their implications, we must discover, again inductively, each mode's strength and weakness—that is, its ability to thrive, and its vulnerability to inner decay or outer assault. Since each of the (non-Kantian) modes appears twice in our history, in a pre-modern and then a modern version, it is best to study the two versions together. We can thus identify any common causes of that mode's rise and fall, along with any relevant differences.

ANCIENT I (Classical Greece)

Since virtually nothing is known about the cause of the I mode's first rise, we can say only that Greece *was* an I culture, and the most philosophical one in Western history.

The fundamental ideas of the Greeks were most fully expressed by Aristotle. But the people who gave birth to philosophy could hardly solve all its problems; hence the many gaps and errors in Greek thought. The greatest philosophical gaps pertained to concepts and to values; even

Aristotle could not define the nature of concepts in purely naturalistic terms; nor, as he himself said, could he ground values objectively in perceivable fact. These deficiencies do not change the Greeks' mode of thought, but they do leave Greek ideas vulnerable to an intellectual attack launched by a knowledgeable anti-Aristotelian philosopher, should one appear. In the ancient world, this was merely a theoretical vulnerability. Aside from Plato—whose system, far ahead of its time, could not have been accepted by Homer-loving Athenians—no modal enemy appeared. For this reason, the failure of the Greek thinkers to validate their fundamentals objectively was not historically decisive; it was, in fact, irrelevant to the fall of the ancient I. Since the Greeks were the West's first and, in their great centuries, the only thinkers, the cause of their fall could not have been thinkers with a different viewpoint.

To my knowledge, the standard account of the fall of Greece is reasonable. Athens was destroyed by wars—first by the Peloponnesian Wars with the Spartans, then by the permanent subjugation of Athens by the Macedonians. With the resulting loss of their self-confidence and the ruin of their city, the Athenians, most historians report, felt overwhelmed and desperate. They concluded that their way of life and of thought had been shown to be unjustified and dangerous, a phenomenon universally described now as their failure of nerve. Here we see a modal fall triggered not by thinkers embracing a new viewpoint, but by a populace incited by military defeat to turn against the epistemological status quo.

Modal change due to war is rare; in the case of Athens, however, the fact is not difficult to understand. Doubtless the Athenians made many serious mistakes in their two hundred years of glory, including their often unwise military strategies, unjust expansionism, political demagoguery, and even democratically approved murder. But even without their mistakes, it is hard to imagine any other ending for a small intellectual city emerging, without technology, into a world that was ignorant of ideas and/or hostile to them, and in the end militarily more powerful. If the enemies of the Athenians had not been the Persians, the Spartans, and the Macedonians, there would soon enough have been equivalent hordes from the camps of anti- or pre-philosophy. As I see it, the astonishing fact in this context—almost as astonishing as the Athenians' ability to create

Western thought—is not their fall, but their ability to survive as epochal creators for as long as they did.

When the Athenians rejected the I mode, they knew only of the two Ms as alternatives. Despite the often popular Oriental cults quickly swarming into it, the city as a whole did not accept a philosophy of Orientalism, which was regarded as alien and barbaric; the Greeks were still too pagan to consider M_2. What they chose was a turn toward the divine regarded as the source and protector of man's happiness in this world— that is, a turn to what I call the M_1 mode. Nor did they experience this change as revolutionary (though it was), but rather as a mere change in emphasis. The reason is that, as we know, M_1 can vary greatly in degree: It can award more importance to this world or less. In this case, having been interpreted by pagans, it started out with the more.

The pagan change to M_1 was possible only because a non-I tradition (religion), though it had been relegated to the back burner, had never been renounced, either by the Athenian public or even, in some terms, by most of the advanced thinkers. A rival mode-in-waiting, whenever there is such, is always a potential threat to the ruling mode; often, as here, its advocates need merely wait for events to move it to the front.

A child creates a painting of unsurpassed beauty. In judging it, his age is irrelevant. But he is a child. So one expects him sooner or later to lapse into childishness.

MODERN I (Enlightenment)

Although the rise of Greece is not yet understood, the cause of the Enlightenment is well-known. Its modern father was Isaac Newton, whose work was a thunderous blow to the remnants of M_1 medievalism. In some respects, the West after Newton came to grasp—more consistently than the Greeks—that men live in a lawful universe knowable by men using their unaided reason based on the data of sense.

Newton's cultural power was his demonstration, unprecedented in the modern world, of the power of Aristotle—that is, of the secular, thinking mind. Newton's discoveries about gravity, Halley's comet, and the rest could not have transformed the West; by themselves, they would have been no more than culturally ineffectual additions to technical physics and mathematics. What Newton's contemporaries had to grasp was the revolutionary mind-set underlying his discoveries. When they did, a newfound sense of man's power and glory propelled Europe into a new age, summed up in Pope's famous couplet: "Nature and Nature's laws lay hid in night; God said, Let Newton be! and all was light."[255]

In its secularism, the Enlightenment inherited the Greeks' fundamental ideas, along with their gaps and errors. But the modern Is were much less concerned with philosophy. As an example, the most historically influential men of the period, America's founding fathers, believed that the important philosophical discoveries had already been made, and that their own task was only to apply these discoveries to practical life.

As a rival mode-in-waiting, religion during the Enlightenment was both weaker and stronger than it had been in Greece. It was weaker in that the traditional religion, Christianity, was not merely given a backseat, but was reviled and ridiculed. Religion was stronger, however, in that most of the modern Is, in contrast to the Greeks, accepted, as a rule unwittingly, religion's philosophic fundamentals. The deists, for example, held that God had now retired, but that, contrary to the ancients' view, he is an omnipotent who had formerly created this world and its laws and could still annul both, though we can be sure he wouldn't do so. The Greeks would have regarded this view as the destruction of secularism and of reason. How long, they would have asked among many other questions, before He returns to work? In ethics, the Enlightenment upheld the pursuit of happiness, but regarded the Christian practice of selfless service as superior to it.

Religion did not define the Enlightenment. It was not men's guide in cultural creation. But God was still far from dead.

The Greeks, of course, did not have instilled into their brain seventeen centuries of Hebraic and Oriental dogma to try to expunge; and, being philosophical, they understood the illogic of combining such dogma with secularism. The Enlightenment Is, by contrast, left their rival-in-waiting with the potential for a much stronger comeback. As it turned out, however, the potential in this case took quite a while to be actualized, because the intellectuals after the Enlightenment rejected the M approach in both versions. Religion nevertheless remained in the background, where it enjoyed substantial albeit culturally quiet public support.

The modern I mode ruled for only a century and then, suddenly, was repudiated on all sides. In no time at all, it seemed, the embrace of Aristotle was no longer a vital presence in the West, but a fading memory.

There were no existential events—no war, no economic crisis, no popular disenchantment—sufficient to bring down the modern I mode, which was confined to no one city, but spanned continents and was unaffected by local eruptions. The trigger this time was a purely intellectual event: the appearance of Kant's Critical philosophy, soon widely accepted by thinkers as the definitive solution to the intellectual problems of the ages, especially those pertaining to concepts and to values. To this bombshell, the relatively unphilosophical Enlightenment figures had no answers. Indeed, so far from offering intellectual opposition, many did not even see Kant's ideas as a threat and had no hesitation in classifying him as a spokesman of the Enlightenment.

In the battle between thinkers adept in dealing with broad abstractions and thinkers ignorant of the battle, there could have been only one outcome. The Athenians did not have to pay for their philosophic defects because there was no one like Kant to cash in on them. But now there was and he did.

The cause of the I downfall in the ancient world was a panic of the populace independent of the intellectuals; in the modern world, it was a passion of the intellectuals independent of the public. In both cases, the fall was rapid. And in the modern case also, the new (D_1) mode in its early stages was seen not as a revolution, but merely as a relatively small change in emphasis.

ANCIENT M$_1$ (Hellenistic-Roman)

Within the I period we see no change across time in regard to the mode's fundamentals or its implications for proper integration. Despite their individual differences, the line of cultural creators—from Thales to

Aristotle, and from Newton to Hugo—is ruled by the same secularism. The reason, discussed in chapter three, is that pure modes by their nature are either/or. But the case is different with a mixed mode, such as M_1. As we have seen, such a mode subsumes a variety of incompatible interpretations, which vary according to tilt: toward the unvarying Plato or the unvarying Aristotle.

A glance at some of our examples from Rome, early and late, reveals the extremes of the ancient M_1 tilts. In literature, we may take as a start Aeneas's reverent but hesitant visit to the next world, within an epic that glorifies Rome now and physical pleasures to continue after death—and centuries later, Apuleius's ecstatic embrace of the Oriental cult of Isis. In science, we see the early Stoic fire-worshiping pantheism, often criticized at the time as materialism, transformed by the time of slave and emperor alike into praise for a God transcending matter. In education, we see grammar taught as a means to political success evolve into language taught as abstractions unrelated to fact and to be studied as an end in itself. In politics, we see the republic's appeal to God's approval as the proof of the practicality of Rome's political system—and later, the deification of the emperors regardless of the practical results of their actions. In regard to mode, there was no revolution in any of these areas. But there was an evolution, a gradual change of emphasis.

It is evident from the above that the different interpretations of M_1 did not arise by caprice, but rather developed in a definite order. Each field moves in the same direction. The era of early M_1, close to the classical secularism, turns slowly into the era of late M_1, verging on anti-secularism, M_2.

Everyone knows that the pagans became increasingly religious across the centuries, a process of change that ended only when an uncompromising religion achieved supremacy. Whatever else underlies this process, there is a modal explanation of it. The pagans' evolution is inherent in the M_1 mode. The M_1 integration, as we know, depends on the hierarchy of its two elements: the divine as the revered base; the worldly as the real but imperfect derivative. If so, wherever the two elements, taken separately, give incompatible guidance to thought or action, as they do by their nature, the base by definition is the one that tends to be favored, and thus the one that increasingly sets the terms and context of future thought, while the derivative is correspondingly minimized, marginalized, and then derogated. In the end, there is no more mixture; the base, assuming it is unchallenged by an anti-M philosophy, wins out.

The ancient M_1s would have experienced this modal progression in concrete terms. The Greeks had initially adopted M_1 as a practical necessity; smitten by self-doubt, they turned to the divine as their protector in a world they could not always cope with. Given this premise, each new inability to cope—a crucial but insolvable domestic problem, an outburst of anxiety over a foreign threat, a time of traumatic loss and grief, a feeling of outrage, frustration, helplessness—and there were always plenty of such traumas as these—all of it led the M_1 communities, given their religious base, naturally to turn ever less to man for answers and ever more to God. Eventually the impossibility of combining eudaemonia as man's goal with obedience to God became obvious to all, and the choice between the two was made.

In and of itself—that is, leaving aside external factors such as philosophic enemies and existential triggers—a pure mode such as I has the potential to exist unchanged indefinitely. By contrast, although M_1 under certain conditions can drag on for centuries, it has always in historical fact been an intermediary that is in process of disappearing. In Marx's terms, it carries within itself the seeds of its own destruction.

The basic cause of M_1's collapse in the ancient world was not existential convulsion (as in Athens), nor the sudden eruption of challenging new thinkers (as in the Enlightenment). The era of pagan M_1 was not killed off by a mob, a war, or a philosophical bombshell. The era moved to its conclusion by a unique route: by the logic of being a modal mixture.

But inner modal logic alone, as we know, is not a full explanation. The changeover from M_1, like that of all modes, requires a trigger or triggers, which in this instance was a variety of existential conditions. In the case of mighty, world-spanning Rome, there was no single datable cause, as there had been in tiny Athens or in the publication of the *Critique*. Provincial revolts, military anarchy, barbarian invasions, debauched emperors, class warfare, spreading cults, the infantilizing of the public—the conventional list goes on.

But by themselves, all these problems, however potent, could not bring about modal change. The only thing that could do so was men's *interpretation* of these problems, reached by some specific type of thought process. To deal with such problems, for example, I thinkers (long vanished) might have counseled the Romans to adopt a more rational philosophy, including a principled secularism to combat the cults and the deified tyrants, a proud morality of eudaemonia to combat the dutiful, the despairing, and the debauched, and also (unknown at the time) the politics of liberty to combat the class warfare flowing from the imperial welfare state. No one of any influence at the time, of course, could have advocated any part of such an interpretation, nor, even if anyone had, would such ideas have been regarded as anything but foolish or worse. To an advanced M_1, the I approach is not only mistaken, but ungodly and outlandish. And once the I mode had been discarded, the era's triggering events could be assessed by the public only in the terms set by M_1's final operative modal base, Platonism, which thus defined the era to come.

The conventionally listed triggers, either alone or together, were not by themselves the cause of Rome's fall. They were the fuel feeding the fire. The fire was the Romans' interpretive framework—the final result of the inexorable drive of M_1.[256]

MODERN M_1 (Renaissance, Age of Reason)

Like the ancients, the modern M_1 movement, from the Renaissance (in germ) through the seventeenth century, subsumed a variety of incompatible interpretations. In this case also, the variants moved in a definite direction toward a definite terminus. This time, however, the cause of the process was the reintroduction of Aristotle by Aquinas in the thirteenth century (see next section). The modern M_1s' source, direction and terminus, therefore, were the opposite of the ancient M_1s'.

Here are some examples of the modern progression: from Marlowe's incredulous approval but heartfelt condemnation of the satanic rebel to Milton's admiring love and muted criticism of him; from the early champions of science whose real discoveries were combined with random streaks of medieval mysticism to the systematic, anti-mystic albeit rationalistic physics of Descartes; from the more God-centered schools of the sixteenth century to the religious but more classics-centered ones of the seventeenth; from the Renaissance kings, who regarded themselves as successors of the popes with powers not restricted to practical matters, to the next century's less powerful (and misnamed) absolute monarchs.

This time the force moving the development was not Plato, the base of the M_1 mode, but Aristotle, that base's opposite. Aristotle's ideas had come to be regarded by medieval scholars as indispensable to proper thinking. Even though theology remained sacred and of more fundamental importance, they argued, the subject by itself is intellectually insufficient. In DIM terms, they were thinking of adding some I features to M_2, and thereby dropping M_2 for M_1. In this context, it was an M_1 on the defensive against a resurgent I. This new M_1 then ran the usual mixed-mode course; this time the terminus was not the triumph of the M_1 base, but its cultural extinction. The explosive beginning of the end was Copernicus's heliocentric theory, which in due course made Newton possible, at which point M_1 was shrugged off by the West as outdated.

M_1, ancient or modern, occurs whenever men seek to integrate supernaturalism and secularism. Then, despite their desire to keep the mixture, they end by moving up to heaven or down to earth. M_1 describes a transition from one of these pure modes to the other: It defines the mindset of a society in which Plato is either coming or going—or, the same thing, in which Aristotle is going or coming.

Here again, as in the fall of the modern I, we see changeover deriving from a new mode competing with and defeating the establishment. In this type of case, the triumphant competitor is not a traditional mode-in-waiting or a future one long known and seen to be gradually approaching, but a new one—a bombshell mode, unprecedented and unpredictable in the era—a mode that gives a culture no intellectual warning, yet is able relatively fast to gain a hearing and admirers. Under these conditions, no popular uprising and no non-intellectual triggers are necessary.

MEDIEVAL M$_2$

In essence, the medieval M$_2$ was Platonism without compromise. There are no ideas inherent in M$_2$ that lead it necessarily to self-destruction. As with the I mode, the longevity of M$_2$ is potentially unlimited. In this instance, M$_2$ ruled the West intellectually for a thousand years. When the Church finally gained complete power, there were no obstacles left to precipitate a modal change: no military force capable of crushing the whole of Christendom, no recalcitrant temporal leaders, not even a well of popular outrage over Church governance or morality. Although there were some heretics in regard to details, as we have seen, they did not disagree with the Church's fundamentals. So the heretics could have no effect on the Church's power or the culture's essence.

Nor was there a popular rebellion against Europe's extreme and universal poverty. In part, this was because the concept of better living conditions was mostly unknown and even unimaginable. More important, it was a result of the religion all treasured. So far from promising rewards in this life, the leadership warned its flock against enjoying even the little they did have. Everything worth having, they all knew, could be attained only after death. If reality was a perfect spiritual realm and thus the opposite of this world, then man's spiritual fulfillment and eternal joy were possible only within that realm; in our present debased life, only continuous suffering was possible. The pursuit of happiness on earth, in sum, was a metaphysical perversion.

On any issue pertaining to earthly well-being, the medieval M$_2$s were invulnerable. Since they promised nothing here, the nothing their system produced did not disillusion the devout. On the contrary, people agreed that the more one "hateth this life," the better off his soul. When suffering is expected and even sought out, evils of all kinds (including flagellation and torture) are viewed as normal and to be accepted. For centuries these Christians obediently lived what we would call the unlivable.

Essential to the M$_1$ mentality had been a kind of moderation—an attempt to achieve the right ratio between the two balls being juggled. The M_2 mentality rejected moderation, requiring principled commitment. In the eyes of such a man, the fact that he himself may have breached his ideals was no reason to question them or the Church, since "all men are imperfect," by the nature of the setup.

Here is a new kind of case, where none of the Greek or Roman triggers are applicable. Instead, we see the first modal change in Western history generated purely by means of intellectual innovation*—the only kind of trigger that under the circumstances could have been effective. When Albertus Magnus and Aquinas (unknowingly) hurled a lethal either/or at a flabbergasted Church, it faced an apparently impossible choice: Its scholars could not live with Aristotle or, it gradually began to seem, without him. Some of the more perceptive authorities tried to strangle the alien influence in its cradle, or to consign it to the status of mere novelty irrelevant to Christian thought; but they did not have the power to seal Christianity off from it. Others decided to follow the Church's longtime method of thought, the one discovered by the pagans and even in that era irresistible to the Western mind: integration. Christian thinkers had long been using this method to systematize the insights of theology; so, they asked, why not articulate an even greater One, a system climaxed by God but including within its Many the new insights of Aristotle?

This acceptance by the Church of Aristotle's ideas is what led to its downfall. Unwittingly, the leadership was allowing, then blessing, a contradiction in fundamentals. In effect, as I earlier noted, they were trying to save M_2 by turning it into M_1. Within the short span of about 150 years, short for the pace of that period, the medieval era gave way to the Renaissance.

Here we see a new cause of modal change. The modern I movement was defeated by the invasion of enemy (Kantian) fundamentals beyond its ability to understand or defend against. The medieval M_2s, by contrast, did understand and try in philosophical terms to defeat the invasion of enemy fundamentals—but they did it by accepting, albeit partially, those same fundamentals. This is the self-defeating attempt to protect a mode by methodically contradicting its essence.

In the medieval case, this fatal policy after the rediscovery of Aristotle

---

* Kant's was the second.

might well have been inevitable. There had been several precursors of Aquinas dissatisfied with Platonism and groping in an Aristotelian direction, men who risked death, but who to an extent could not resist the secular pagan remnants long buried in the West, but never fully destroyed. And there were the many honest Christian scholars, trained in the use of logic, who could not abide an unsolved contradiction or a solution gained by suppressing ideas they regarded as true and important.

As the Christians of the period came to see the situation, it was join with the pagans up to a point or lose. So they joined—and lost.

Pagan culture was no obstacle to the Church at the beginning; rather, it fed the Church's growth by serving up the decadent later Romans as secularism's product, and as the only alternative to Christianity. But a millennium later, pagan thought took its revenge.

MODERN M_2

The advocates of Marxism moved rapidly from theoretical polemics to totalitarian power. Unlike the medieval case, these modern M_2s' final step to success in Russia depended on (civil) war; in their view, the success was independent of ideas, which they thought of as nothing but an impotent superstructure. Despite this, however, and like the medievals, the Marxists, as we have seen, regarded philosophy—that is, their own ideology—as the base and even the essence of reality.

It took the medievals centuries to imbue the West with the Christian fundamentals—to eradicate the pagans' righteous joy in thought and life. But the Communists found their own fundamentals long entrenched, especially in Eastern Europe, in the form of an authoritarian and highly mystical variant of medieval Christianity, to which they added a modern enticement.

Objecting to religion's promise of pie in the sky, these M_2s promised to bring the pie down to earth but in a new kind of society which would provide material abundance, the reward of science, to all. A worldly utopia, which the medievals would have rejected as sin and as impossible, was precisely the stated goal of these moderns. In regard to modal character, this is the greatest difference between the two versions of M_2. Both made fundamental concessions to the philosophic enemy, secularism. But the medievals adopted this policy late, as a seemingly unavoidable means of self-defense against an unforeseen destroyer, whereas the moderns flaunted secularism from the outset as essential to their mass appeal.

It is now widely conceded that the modern M_2s in the West achieved the opposite of utopia. Many valid and important reasons—moral, political, economic, psychological—have been given to explain this failure, but they are outside the confines of my book. The DIM theory, however, considered apart from the above reasons, does suggest another possible explanation: that the Communists' failure is a necessary consequence of their modal conflict. Their supernaturalist dismissal of the world could not deliver on the worldly promise they held out to the world. A body of rulers validated in their own eyes by their immersion in a realm of M_2 ideology—that is, of floating abstractions—could give only lip service and ineffective imitation, not mind or motivation, to the demanding task of discovering and implementing the policies required to create concretes—the concretes that were to make up the material wealth they heralded. A Platonist, it would seem, cannot travel up the divided line to bask in the *a priori* light and then, filled with truth, return to the cave with a passion to establish for the benighted prisoners a society of heavy industry, material riches, and consumer satiation.

The Soviet leadership was concerned with industrial development, but primarily as a means of impressing and intimidating foreigners. When the astonishing poverty they had created was finally revealed to the West, it became clear that the industrialization was only a facade. In essence, Russia under the Communists was a giant Potemkin village.

That material wealth was not the totalitarians' passion is eloquently illustrated by the practices in their concentration camps, Communist and Nazi alike, as Hannah Arendt—perhaps our most profound student of totalitarianism—observes:

> Any work that has been performed [in them] could have been done much better and more cheaply under different

conditions. . . . The incredibility of the horrors is closely bound up with their economic uselessness. The Nazis carried this uselessness to the point of open anti-utility when in the midst of the war, despite the shortage of building material and rolling stock, they set up enormous, costly extermination factories and transported millions of people back and forth. In the eyes of a strictly utilitarian world the obvious contradiction between these acts and military expediency gave the whole enterprise an air of mad unreality.[257]

No Western regime before Communism had promised millions of men so perfect an earthly paradise at the price merely of a short delay, and then failed so spectacularly to achieve it. The contradiction was made worse by the fact that it was the despised capitalist nations who were enjoying everything the Communists had promised. To use a medieval analogy, it would be as though the pope's flock had somehow learned that God was hurling thunderbolts of hellfire at the saints while showering love and salvation on Satan. Of course, the medieval leadership was safe in this regard; its flock could not have been confronted by such a spectacle. But the Communist masses saw it and lived it.

Hitler was defeated militarily by the West, but Soviet Russia was not; on the contrary, it was widely admired by our intellectuals and regularly supported economically by the West, which poured vast amounts of money into the country to rescue its dictators during their frequent crises. Communism collapsed because of internal factors. Intellectuals, the public, even the dictators themselves had come to see that the dogma had failed.

The cause of the Communist fall was not an active popular rebellion, which was virtually impossible given the modern totalitarians' use of technology; not the gradual evolution of a mixed mode; not a new philosophy taking a culture by storm; and not any of the standard nonintellectual triggers, such as political corruption or starvation, both of which were present in the USSR from the outset. The cause—or at least an essential part of the cause, I believe—was a modal deficiency: Though M_2 in itself is stable, it cannot survive if its own champions explicitly misidentify and thereby contradict its fundamentals.

Here again we see the fatal effect on a mode's longevity of philosophic deficiency—in this case, of its defenders' self-contradiction. Whereas the medieval M_2s, when insulated from enemy philosophy, were able to enjoy a lengthy and at the time seemingly endless tenure, the modern M_2s, however tightly they sealed their borders, crashed in a matter of decades. These crashes have led to an almost unanimous dismissal in the West of both Communism and Fascism as viable possibilities for the future—unanimous except for the hard-core holdouts in our universities.

If there are to be successful totalitarians in our time, it would seem, they will have to eschew worldly promises. Neither economics nor biology nor any other science has been able to do the job for them. Promising heaven on earth has not worked. But promising heaven—that is a different story.

———

Now let us survey not individual modes, but their progression across the centuries.

If we take a temporal overview, the most obvious fact is the great difference in pace—in the rate of modal change—between the pre-modern and the modern worlds. For the most part, the pre-modern world was characterized by prolonged modal tenure and leisurely changeover; the modern, by rapid and dramatic swings. The pre-moderns, across a span of nineteen hundred years, adopted three of the modes, whereas the post-Renaissance moderns, across only four hundred, have adopted all five. In the pre-modern world, the average modal life span was something over six hundred years; if we omit Greece's brief I period, the average was about eight hundred. By contrast, in the modern world (including here the Renaissance), the average modal life span—roughly the same for the Ds, the Is, and the Ms—has been about two hundred years.

The standard explanation of the moderns' rapid ideological turnabouts is the development of science, technology, and mass education, which gives a new movement the ability rapidly to reach and be understood by a mass audience. A messenger carrying a scroll in a trireme or on horseback can hardly compete with the printing press, let alone the Internet. On the other hand, I would argue, when opposing ideologies enjoy comparable access to the same modern aids, as they often do, they have—other things being equal—essentially the same chance of reaching potential converts, and thus of achieving if not victory, then at least a prolonged stalemate. The medium is not the message and does not necessarily hasten its acceptance.

The time necessary for a movement to succeed depends, above all, not on the availability of TV, iPads, and social networking, but on the content the rival parties broadcast through these instruments. Technology, it is true, is a necessary condition of the moderns' rapid changes, but it is not sufficient.

To my mind, there is another, more important factor explaining the two different rates of modal change. That factor is the different view of philosophy held by pagans and by moderns. I refer here not to content, not to their different answers to the questions of philosophy, but to their different reasons for regarding the subject itself as of value.

The pagan thinkers, Aristotle included, treasured philosophic contemplation as the highest form of intellectual fulfillment, which they regarded as an end in itself. When a Greek philosopher considered broad abstractions, the question he pursued was their truth, their relation to reality, but not their practical implications for men's actions and future. (This of course is to be expected; the pioneers in defining fundamentals could hardly have grasped the enormity of their practical effects before these had become visible on a large enough scale; they would have had to see the role played by their ideas in the rise and fall of cultures still to come.) Thus although the pagans created philosophy, they were not suitable material to be reshaped by a sudden philosophic revolution. And in fact, as we have seen, there was no such revolution in the whole post-Athenian era, no century or two when Plato suddenly turned a secular civilization upside down; there was only an incrementally growing affinity to his spirit across seven centuries.

The Christians changed everything. They were the first Westerners to grasp that philosophy is not only abstractions of theoretical interest but is also a power in the world—indeed a power on which their own rise and continued rule depended. So a false philosophy, in their view, was not only blasphemous; it was also a practical menace. Later, the emerging moderns saw the feared menace in action. They saw the fading of the Church's power as a result of the unexpected battle between religion and science. And they saw that it was a sudden, philosophically instigated, culture-changing battle, a phenomenon without precedent in the pagan centuries. It taught moderns the worldly importance of philosophy in a form not available to the ancients or even imaginable by them. "Knowledge is power," said Bacon, defining the modern mind—and philosophy, too, is knowledge.

The above, in my understanding, is why the triggers of ancient modal change, though they pre-suppose a philosophic context, are not themselves new ideas, but rather specific evils perceived by the public: military conquest, political corruption, class warfare, and so forth. In contrast, the post-pagan triggers have always been the embrace by intellectuals of abstract ideas unknown at first by the public: the ideas of Aristotle, of Newton, of Kant.

Paradoxically, the moderns (in every mode) have not been nearly as philosophical as their predecessors, and with the rise of the Ds most have lost the earlier respect for abstractions. But for about six hundred years, through the late nineteenth century, the moderns did grasp the practical power of philosophy, and some still do. The result was the modern urgency—the urgency of a new movement to spread its ideas and topple the establishment, and often the urgency of the public not to be left behind. This distinctively modern outlook highlights the unique vulnerability of any Western establishment today that eschews ideas.

There is a second important fact suggested by the overall modal progression. This one pertains not to rate of change, but to relative popularity.

Though I and D have appeared in Western history, they are almost in the nature of interruptions to the rule of M, which in its two forms has been the West's guide for two thousand–plus years. Is and Ds together, by contrast, have totaled about four hundred fifty years, on the order of one-quarter the time.

It is instructive to note here that four of the modes were, and could only have been, developed in or after Greece; there was nothing earlier to parallel or anticipate them. Before the mind and the proper rules of conceptual thought had been identified, there could have been no science, no attempt to integrate it with religion, no rebellion against it. The case of M_2, however, is different. Prior to Greece, of course, there is no M_2 mentality, because M_2 is a philosophical category. But one can say this much: There is a primitive anticipation of M_2 going back to pre-history. Supernaturalism and the demand for faith could not, of course, have been held as ideas in these aeons, since there were no defined concepts yet of "Nature" or "reason." But a concrete-bound form of such an outlook was widespread, expressed as wordless imagery, prayers to the unseen, semi-articulate feelings, obedience to rites not understood—all of it inconsistent perhaps, unintegrated, unconceptualized, but nevertheless in its own way a real factor in men's lives. All these centuries are certainly not representative of Platonism or even of religion in any Western sense, but they are even more certainly not representative of Aristotle or science.

The roots of the primitives' mentality are sometimes ascribed to their unavoidable ignorance. They must struggle to live somehow as men, by using their conceptual faculty, but with no idea that such exists or how to use it. When they dealt with words broader than early-level concepts, as was unavoidable—for example, "life," "luck," "spirit," "power," "destiny," etc.—they had little idea how to relate these to percepts. They could use this level of language largely as floating abstractions—which, as Plato showed, are in fact man's only way to enter another world. But whatever the true causes of the primitive mentality, we can say this much: That the choice of reason and science would have been impossible to them. In primitive eras, the default setting of the mind was non-reason and non-science—until the Greeks reset it.

The above suggests that not all modes are created equal. The overwhelming dominance of M—anticipatory or explicitly philosophical—would mean that its fundamentals have been so entrenched in the mind of our species that we have never truly escaped them. Men, it seems, have remained in some form god-oriented, in part or in whole, almost without exception since the origin of the species. Even the I periods maintained a background belief in the supernatural. Mankind, even its best Western representatives, is still frighteningly close to its primitive roots.

Given the above and even without further evidence, if one were inclined to venture a preliminary opinion, merely an educated guess, about the future of the United States, two points at once spring to mind. If there is to be modal change, it will be a change to the rule of M. And, given the modern pace, if it happens, it will happen soon.

———

For future reference, here are the factors that, alone or in different combinations, we have found to play an essential role in one or more modal changeovers:

1. Instability of a mixed mode.
2. Inability of an establishment, through philosophic deficiency, to defend its mode.
3. Modal rebellion by the intellectuals.
4. Modal rebellion by the public.
5. Knowledge of an acceptable alternative mode.
6. Trigger(s).

CHAPTER FOURTEEN

SECULAR MODES IN THE UNITED STATES TODAY

TO PREDICT THE future, we must know not only the past but also the present. We cannot know what modal condition we are moving toward until we know from what condition we are starting.

Speaking in general terms, Western culture, after modern science overthrew medievalism, turned secular. Religion, of course, remained alive, but mostly as an element of the past relegated to the back burner, no longer as a force shaping the minds of cultural creators.

There are several kinds of secularism, which differ from one another in their strengths, weaknesses, and potential life span. What is the status of each of these varieties now in the United States, and what do the answers imply for our future?

The secular modes, in the broadest sense, are those that deny, at minimum, the exclusive reality of the supernatural—the two Ds, I, and M_1. Since I have already identified the contemporary West as Kantian, I shall begin with the Ds.

D_1 in the United States

As we have seen, D_1 placed an unprecedented limitation on the cognitive role of concepts, an approach that made possible a number of mutually exclusive integrative variants. If so, we must ask whether this fact is relevant to the D_1 movement today, one hundred fifty years after its start. Has D_1 followed the pattern of the ancient mixed mode, M_1? Have the variants of D_1 formed a definite progression since the mid-nineteenth century, continually expanding the scope of their (Kantian) base while cutting back on their (Aristotelian) derivative, producing thereby a culture moving ever farther away from the pro-conceptual orientation?

In literature, Naturalism—which ruled serious art from the mid-nineteenth century—began by rejecting the concern with universal themes, aiming to present not "man," but rather "these men." Early writers like Balzac and Tolstoy, as we've seen, regarded their work as descriptions if not of human nature everywhere, then at least of whole societies or timeless clashes, often featuring protagonists presented as embodying a near universal perspective—for example, France from social top to bottom, or the universal plight of an adulterous wife. Within a few generations, however, Naturalists like Sinclair Lewis and Upton Sinclair rejected such portraits as artificial, concerned with too ambitious and generalized a message, with too little detail; instead, an artwork should be concerned with specifics, depicting, say, the problems of middle-class life in a Midwestern small town, or the working conditions in the meatpacking industry in 1906. Today, even themes of this scope are commonly disdained by critics as didactic and above all as too abstract; now we read about the sex-and-drug escapades of the serial killer next door or, for higher-brows, an ironic account of a Jewish boy's masturbatory practices. (At this point, Naturalism gives way to an artistic movement that upholds non-plot, non-character, non-theme.)

In physics, positivism—the modern influence from the mid-nineteenth century—began by rejecting as non-empirical Newton's universal concepts, such as force and mass, and thus his broad conceptualization of his experimental results. Then came the progression from the still somewhat traditional positivism of Gustav Kirchhoff, going on to a further diminished conceptual apparatus, to the all but militantly anti-conceptual viewpoint of Ernst Mach. In chemistry, at the time an independent science and a stronghold of positivism, there was the progression from Charles Gerhardt's mere ignoring of the atomic theory to the explicit crusade against atoms by scientists such as Marcellin Berthelot. The terminus of these positivist progressions was Rudolf Carnap's tenet that "universal laws appear to be senseless" and so should be "ousted" as "the last remnants of metaphysics in science." (At this point, D_1 in physics had given way to a consistently percept-only physics.)[258]

In nineteenth-century education, the welcome given by pluralists to unrelated subjects and purposes was evident mostly not in a derogation of concepts, but in their schools' relative indifference to integrating classical studies with modern science. An intellectually demanding content was still taught in the early D_1 schools, as indicated by the 1879 *McGuffey's Reader*, a collection of difficult, abstract pieces designed to improve the thinking of primary-level students. But McGuffey himself, aware that there was no connection among the pieces, included in his book's title the word "eclectic." Then, as classical studies and history in general waned in the schools, there was the gradual expansion and splintering of the curriculum, accompanied by the increasing movement in most subject areas toward perceptual-level learning, as we have already discussed in chapter seven. As to the attitude toward concepts of today's teachers, we may note what is happening to the teaching of the most conceptual art: Literature. It is frequently being replaced by media classes teaching "television, newspapers, car repair magazines, and movies." (At this point, the door is open to an undiluted anti-conceptual approach.)[259]

In politics, most nineteenth-century D_1s upheld (though as non-absolute) many broadly defined tenets of capitalism, such as private property and freedom of trade, pricing, hiring, interest setting, and more. Having discarded systems as such, however, they regarded these tenets as isolated guidelines, which did not necessarily imply one another. Gradually, one or two concretes at a time, D_1s came to regard their earlier attitude as rigid because too broad. No generalized abstraction, they started to believe, could tell us how to solve all our diverse political problems, such as those involving tariffs, railroads, or competition, but pluralism *could* point the way. Since it gives us a choice not of either/or but of degrees, we can legislate conditions that justify *some* protectionism, some control of railroads, some requirement for competition, and we can be flexible in doing so.

Today, D_1s regard even such relatively specific focus as naively abstract.

For example, they do not debate the proper conditions or degree of protectionism in general, but ask rather: What size tariff should be imposed this year on LCD television sets from Japan to prevent unemployment above 6 percent in competing domestic industries, and for how long, considering the expected retaliation from abroad and the outcry from consumers and affected industries at home? This is a question no abstract principle(s) can cope with; the political answer, therefore, must be based not on logically proved truth, but on consensus. If the consensus reached angers some important group of voters, an amendment can be made later, and if this in turn antagonizes still other groups, further deals can be made. Who, asks D_1, can legislate in terms of decades? As Lord Keynes observed to wide acclaim, "In the long run, we'll all be dead." In this manner, government controls have grown in concrete-bound steps piecemeal but steadily, and most often without the explicit invocation of ideology. (Action without ideology opens the door to the politicians of anti-ideology.)

All four of our fields offer an abundance of examples of the D_1 progression. What has been its effect on the educated American mind? In answer, I sketch here a hypothetical (but real and even commonplace) discussion, pertaining to the familiar topic of human rights. D_1, say, hears a person claim that man has the right to life, and that this includes the rights to liberty and property.

"Why," an early D_1 would begin, "bother talking about the 'right to life'? All you really want is a government that leaves your person and goods alone; 'life' here is an empty abstraction, which specifies no additional empirical limitation on government." At this point, we have two rights with nothing to connect them. How then do we know what behaviors these two include? If, for example, "liberty" is not defined by reference to the requirements of life, how are we to know why it is a value and what it subsumes? Is one free to do anything? Or is freedom limited to certain concretes, such as, for example, the right to free speech?

"No, not even that," a later D_1 typically replies. "Your error is to try to relate and evaluate a large variety of speech cases by reference to one loose abstraction, 'free.' 'Liberty' means the right to free speech, yes, but not as an all-encompassing generality—not necessarily on TV, especially when children are watching, and not when it is hate speech that offends oppressed minorities, and not when it is obscene as judged by local community standards, and not when it enables corporations to buy an election. The word 'liberty,' you see, gives us no answers; a mere abstraction decides nothing in regard to our day-to-day concerns; concrete challenges require concrete responses."

By the process of clarity through disintegration, our thought is becoming ever more fragmented, ever more non-conceptual. At each stage, new, narrower questions arise, such as in this case: When is conduct "offensive," how do we tell what is "oppressive," and what are the standards by which a judge should determine "hate," or a community discern "obscenity"?

All these terms, later D_1s state, are still too broad—we need more distinctions (that is, more disintegration). In the end, man's rights are mere labels for a juxtaposition of concrete-bound and thus arbitrary decisions detailing various prerogatives of various people chosen to be enforced for a while by the government.[260]

Since concepts are our means of achieving unity, each act of disintegration leaves us with a morass of splintered concretes, and the morass grows with the next such act. In other words, the more one cuts back on the integrating power of concepts, the less cognitive help the remaining concepts provide, and so the more they, too, are cut back. In this way, each set of significant problems that D_1s have encountered has led them to turn ever less to concepts for guidance and ever more to sense data.

What then has been the effect on the educated American's mind? A principle, many students will inform you, is nothing but semantics, theory is true by definition, philosophy is mere speculation, ideology is dogma and an advocate of it is an "ideologue," a self-evident reproach. Anyone who has taught in this milieu knows the eager certainty with which so many students pounce if he is benighted enough to declare as an absolute even so elementary an abstraction as 2 + 2 = 4. The gleeful comeback is: "Only to the base ten—and not if you mix two quarts of water with two quarts of alcohol."

Modern thinkers adopted D_1 because, after Kant, they regarded it as necessary for the success of science. Having thus lost much of the early empiricists' (partial) confidence in the cognitive power of concepts, they seized on sense perception as the essence of scientific method, with thought relegated to the position of mere auxiliary, helpful but not indispensable. Eventually, however, these moderns saw that the mixture essential to their approach could not be sustained; no alternative then was left to them but an unbreached embrace of the Kantian rejection of concepts.

D_1's pluralism started out as a real effort to save science by combining two philosophies widely regarded as opposites. But the very nature of the combination increasingly pushed its advocates to tilt away from and eventually repudiate one element in favor of the other. Here again we see the ancient mixed-mode pattern: two elements that, together, imply incompatible epistemological possibilities, leading in the end to the unbreached rule of the one at the base. Again, in another form, we see that a mixed mode contains the seeds of its own destruction.

In essence, ancient M_1s tried to unite the rejection of this world with its acceptance, in the process turning ever more to a realm of floating abstractions while reducing reliance on the world of experience—which they ended up losing. Modern D_1s have tried to unite the rejection of concepts with their partial acceptance, in the process becoming ever more concrete-bound while reducing reliance on the faculty of thought— which they ended up losing. M_1, we may say, displays <u>perceptual</u> shrinkage; D_1 displays <u>conceptual</u> shrinkage. And if and when the shrinkage runs its course, then there is nothing left but the rejection of the shrinking element: on the M side the rejection of percepts as such (which means M_2)—and on the D side the rejection of concepts as such (D_2).

The two different types of shrinkage entail two different estimates of philosophy's importance. The modern M_1s (in the seventeenth century) championed an integrated philosophy, which they regarded as essential to fight their enemies. By contrast, the D_1s discounted and dropped the subject of fundamental truths and now even disparage it. These moderns go well beyond their two most unphilosophical antecedents. They turn away from philosophy not because, like the Romans, they see it as impractical, nor because, like the founding fathers, they believe its important questions have already been answered; they reject the subject because of the clash between their mode of thought and the very nature of philosophy which is the most abstract of human studies.

Despite this, however, D_1s continue to endorse philosophic <u>negations</u>, the ones basic to the whole Comtean enterprise (although they do not describe these as philosophic). Metaphysically, they believe, the objects we experience are not to be described as reality, in the sense of an independent, external world (such a description to them is nonsense). Epistemologically, they believe, man's mind is not a faculty of gaining knowledge that extends beyond noting the flow of largely unrelated sense appearances.

For obvious reasons, it is impossible to quantify the extent of either type of shrinkage (M_1 or D_1) within a society—that is, to identify in numerical terms when a mixed rule will self-destruct, or how far along the process is at any given point. On the basis of our discussions of D products in part two, I think it is safe to say that no Western society has ever been as anti-conceptual as our own. Kant's takeover has been so thorough and swift that our current culture would have been unimaginable even fifty years ago. What then can we expect fifty years from now?

Given the variety of factors potentially relevant to a modal changeover, the mere number of a mode's adherents at a given time is not a decisive basis for cultural prediction. But size is not necessarily irrelevant in every case either. The D_1 mentality, it would appear, is not formed primarily in the home (though this may prepare children for a D_1 future); ultimately, I think, it is formed in college. If this is so, the size of the D_1 group in the United States is related in some fashion to the size of college enrollments, especially in the humanities, social sciences, and education.

In recent times, some six hundred thousand of these "soft" BAs, as they are called, have been awarded annually by U.S. colleges. Let us assume in favor of the D_1s the most optimistic, albeit unrealistic, interpretation: that all students graduating with a four-year degree support the D_1 modal approach they have been taught, and remain its enthusiastic exponents for a generation, after which, for most people, age and life leach out any college-bred rebelliousness and, probably, much interest in ideas. If these guesses are in the ballpark, then in any given period there are about fifteen million D_1s in the United States (600,000 x 25). Obviously, many factors would move this total up or down markedly, including the many D_1s in the hard sciences, the many D_1s without higher education but influenced by its graduates, the large number of "soft" graduates concerned with socializing as against ideas, and the growing number of students who reject the D orientation in favor of a religious mode. On its face, it seems that the net result of such corrections would be to reduce substantially the size of the D_1 group. But since I am aiming only for a ballpark estimate here, I will simply cancel out such adjustments and stick with the fifteen million figure.[261]

It is from this 5 percent of the U.S. population that the larger and more old-fashioned part of our establishment has been drawn.

D_2 in the United States

As M_1 led to M_2, so D_1 leads to D_2. To the fully anti-conceptual mentality, even the partial integration sought by the D_1s is an unwarranted concession. A coherent story, a causal law, organized school lessons, an even semi-principled government—these and their like in other fields are reactionary nostalgia, conservative verbiage left over from a discredited past.

I do not mean to suggest that D_1 (or M_1) is the only cause of the rise of its subsequent "two." There were ancient mystical sects for centuries, Christianity being one of them, that were independent of the M_1 progression, and there have been avant-garde modernists coming straight from Kant quite apart from the D_1 progression. For the most part, however, these independent phenomena, on the M and D sides alike, did not become a cultural power until the establishment "ones" (M_1 or D_1) had prepared the West to accept or at least tolerate them.

Although the division within the D movement is real, there is not much cultural rivalry between them at this point. D_2s in most areas have found little difficulty in flourishing within a D_1 society, especially in its later stages—and even in being welcomed into the establishment, institutionalized, and federally funded. The ancient M_1s, even late in their development, continued to defend elements of paganism, however inadequately, by reference to their own philosophic principles—and for this very reason were intolerable to the rising M_2s, who methodically stamped them out. The two Ds, by contrast, are more tolerant of each other. The percept-oriented pluralism of the D_1s welcomes the juxtaposition of the traditional and the avant-garde. And since both variants reject ideology, neither encounters intellectual opposition from the other. At times, they do have differences: D_1s may rebel against some especially outrageous D_2 concrete such as a statue of Christ immersed in urine; and D_2s against some especially benighted (to them) D_1 political concession, such as a tax cut for the rich. But these squabbles do not affect their generally cordial relationship.

The result of such modal affinity is a unique type of society: one ruled by a harmonious modal coalition, with the power shifting gradually from one partner to the other. The general public, however, unaware of such distinctions, sees no difference between the conventional side of the establishment and the nihilists, and now views the latter as a normal part of the system. And, as time goes by, there will, in fact, be ever less difference for people to see. In practical terms, this means that if actions by partisans of either D variant antagonize or enrage people to the point of rebellion against forces they see as destructive, both D modes will be brought down together, for the same reason and at the same time.

D_2, like M_2 and like I, is not a modal compromise; there is no mechanism inherent in the mode necessitating its evolution to self-destruction. On the contrary, it is the end of the D_1 road, the final destination of the mode's evolution. As a cultural phenomenon, accordingly, D_2's nature has not changed in tilt, degree, or emphasis since its first appearance, even though, as with most rising modes, some fields were riper for an early takeover than others. Serious literature and theoretical physics—both products of individuals—began turning to D_2 at the end of the nineteenth century, about fifty years into the Kantian era. In education, a public institution, D_2 did not become a major factor until a generation or more later, by the 1930s, say. It came later because parents, who did not yet care much about Joyce or Schrödinger, did care about their children. So the parents themselves first had to be schooled in the virtues of the new trend.

The final invasion by the new mode occurred in politics, which is almost always the last bastion to be taken over, assuming the citizens have some kind of freedom and a say in the process. Among other reasons, virtually the whole country can see that political change of this kind is drastic, affecting every aspect of their lives; so further decades may be necessary to prepare people to accept it. In the United States, the first D_2s in politics were the children of the Progressivized parents of the thirties; these were the children who, in the sixties, became the New Left, which gained national power two generations later. The best evidence of this power to date has been the policies of Obama, the first New Left president.

Conservatives are mistaken in calling Obama a socialist. State ownership of the means of production defines the economics of totalitarianism, a system that, as we have seen, depends on thought control flowing from and producing a fervently held ideology. In DIM terms, socialism is M_2— while Obama's people state indignantly (and to me convincingly) that they have no ideology, no interest in finding a metaphysical base for their policies, and no plan someday to create a utopia. If Obama is reaching for ever greater state power, his followers say, he is doing so piecemeal—that is, merely as a necessary means of addressing urgent concrete problems as they arise.

What kinds of means have been found necessary? Besides working energetically to expand the reach of political correctness and environmentalism—and besides his unprecedentedly militant replay of the standard attacks on business, banks, and Wall Street—Obama has endorsed some new measures and defended them on new grounds. Obamacare, for example, was defended not as compassion for those in medical need, but because equality of health care is a value in itself, quite apart from any special needs of the poor. The attorney general, Eric Holder, wanted American civilians and captured terrorists to be tried in the same courts, not because he sympathized with terrorism, but because all men, Americans and jihadists alike, being equal, have equal rights. Mr. Holder in this instance was applying to a legal situation the president's own approach to foreign policy in general, exemplified by his regular apologies to other countries for America's long and harmful delusion of "exceptionalism"—a delusion because all countries are equal, and should have been so treated by the United States.

To my mind, the most eloquent indication of Obama's mind-set is his demand for confiscatory taxation of what he calls "millionaires and billionaires," not because these individuals are misusing their wealth or obtained it immorally, but simply because they have it, an unacceptable condition, since inequality of income, no matter its source, is unfair. It was once the American dream to climb "from rags to riches," to make it big, to be able to crow proudly about becoming a millionaire. Now the administration tells us that it is unfair to achieve the dream because some people haven't, and that the successes must be shot down until everyone's rags match.

I agree with Obama's critics in regard to the crippling results of his policies. The president, of course, denies these charges. On the whole, however, he seems to be perfunctory when indicating the beneficial future results of his policies—but on fire in fighting for the policies no matter what. For example, asked by ABC whether he would raise the capital gains tax even if he knew that cutting it would bring the government more revenue, he replied that even then raising taxes might be justified as a matter of "fairness."[262]

A political policy taken as an isolated concrete is open to many interpretations, but the integration here is unmistakable. For three years, as I write, we have seen an administration essentially unconcerned with Americans' well-being, and even at times with its own unpopularity—an administration methodically wreaking destruction in the name of "justice as fairness." This is the D_2 mentality.

Not all of Obama's actions are egalitarian. He has also taken some traditional steps, even angering his D_2 admirers by some of his compromises. On balance, perhaps, Obama's presidency should be classified (at minimum) as a late D_1 that has ingested a large dose of D_2.

The fact that Obama is president does not mean that nihilism now rules American politics, or even that it will have the enduring power in government that it has had in other fields. For one thing, its flowering in politics is so recent that one cannot yet reach a comparable clarity about its status. For another, D_2 in American politics has to contend with a unique obstacle: the legacy of the founding fathers, who left no such obstacle in other fields. At the present moment, Obama is unpopular. But the ups and downs of public opinion and political parties are unceasing; one can judge their modal significance only across a span of years, sometimes decades. All one can say now is that the D_2 movement has a strong foot in the Washington door.

As to the size of the D_2 movement—that is, the number of supporters who understand and agree with its essence—these individuals appear mostly within the intellectual avant-garde, including their mind-mates in the government, schools, and media—and also to some extent in the protest and lib movements these intellectuals generate. While the D_2s tend to write off the public as reactionary, the public itself, including most of its educated members, has little or no knowledge of this mode as such—because its fundamental ideas have not been publicized by the D_2s or in many cases even been stated in terms accessible to non-intellectuals. All the other modes define and even flaunt to the world their real beliefs, which people therefore generally understand up to a point, whether they accept them or not, but D_2, aloud, says very little. And even if it did, its nihilism, as we have seen, would be incomprehensible to non-philosophers in America. Americans do support a great many D_2 policies, especially in politics, from affirmative action to garbage recycling. So far, however, they view these policies not as connected expressions of an assault on values, but as unrelated goals pursued case by case in the name of practicality or short-term remedial justice. Such acceptance of D_2 concretes, even though meant as non-ideological, adds tradition and momentum to the D_2 trend. When conditions are right, a country can move rapidly: A policy seen as revolutionary becomes "innovative," then "familiar," then something "we've always done."

Since the general public and the more old-fashioned intellectuals are excluded from this category, one must conclude that the number of D_2 supporters is small. As a sheer guess at a figure that cannot be objectively identified or even approximated, I suggest a number in the high six or low seven figures—in any case a tiny minority, numerically insignificant, but with an influence out of all proportion to its size.*

---

* To include the OWS movement and all the other protesting D_2 spinoffs, one would have to enlarge this number, but by how much I do not know.

I in the United States

Because the dominance of the I mode was only a brief exception in modern history, its status in the United States today is hardly astonishing. Condemned and dismissed by Kantians, the distinctive products of the Enlightenment have either been forgotten or never discovered by most of the country, educated as it has been largely in D schools. In every cultural field the I mode long ago disappeared—at least as a consciously identified and upheld cognitive approach. But as we have seen in regard to Greece, an earlier, antagonistic mode can persist in a later society—not in the form of explicit ideas shaping its cultural products, but as a "sense of life" observable in the background, and potentially influential, capable under certain special circumstances of bringing down the current mode. The special circumstance in Greece was the infancy of the radically new I mode in the face of the whole history of man. The pre-I approach, though it did not shape the classical Greek mind, nevertheless did persist as a sense of life in the society's emotional outlook, and subsequently did make possible the religious reshaping of its course.

There is also a special circumstance in the United States, since it is the first case in history of a nation consciously founded on an I philosophy by men whose acceptance of it was not, as in Europe, a mere transient phase, but a principled commitment—men still revered today by the country they created. If the Greeks presented the spectacle of an I society harboring an anti-I underground, is it possible that the United States presents an anti-I society harboring an I underground? Specifically, is there still among Americans a unique sense-of-life legacy from the Enlightenment, and thus a heightened potential receptivity to the ideas of secularism and reason? In the Greek case, evidence of the pre-I mentality was sometimes explicit, as in the Greek dramas. Our own cultural products today, however, offer little or no trace of the pre-D era. In the present context, therefore, we must look for answers purely to the sense-of-life level. But since a sense of life as such, whether of an individual or a country, is subconscious and unverbalized, there is no direct way to detect its presence or assess its potential influence. All we can do is identify some representative features of American life in various areas, and see what, if anything, they add up to.

On the positive (pro-I) side, the main evidence is the long-term split between the intellectuals and the common-sense-oriented U.S. public. This split is unique. It has no counterpart in Europe, as evidenced by the American public's rejection of so many popular European trends—a rejection indicated by the time lag necessary for their adoption in America—such trends as non-objective art, sex-interpreted man, and class-war-interpreted society. According to our intellectuals, America is always backward—which is a correct evaluation by their standards, and one that reflects a contempt for their own countrymen and history without parallel anywhere else in the world. The public are backward, they say, not only as philistines, but also because they are materialists. This charge is also true in the sense that Americans are more disposed than people elsewhere to regard the pursuit of wealth as moral, to be less envious of the wealth of others, more committed to earning it by their own actions, and more confident of their ability to succeed. The much greater proportion of small business here than anywhere else suggests that Americans put a distinctive premium on initiative, self-reliance, and entrepreneurial spirit.

In regard to politics, the descendants of the founding fathers are notably less eager than others to subordinate the individual to ever bigger government. Where else could the Tea Party, even if it proves ephemeral, have arisen and gained such a following? On almost every issue, from the introduction by FDR of the welfare state to its latest, still controversial expression in socialized medicine, America, though it has followed Europe, has lagged well behind, the intellectuals having to drag a reluctant public into the future.

Jean-Paul Sartre famously complained that Americans did not believe in evil—that is, in human impotence and depravity—a charge that speaks directly to the role of the Enlightenment in shaping the country's subconscious. Some forty years ago Ayn Rand quoted Eve Curie (daughter of Marie), a liberal, on her astonishment at American audiences: " 'They are so happy,' she kept repeating, 'so happy. . . . People are not like that in Europe.' "[263]

Now, so many years later, what is the contrary (the anti-I) evidence? There is still a split between the intellectuals and the American public, but its root, at least when voiced publicly, no longer seems to be the public's common sense, but the opposite: the public's embrace of religion (see next chapter). There is less moral approval today of the pursuers of wealth and even some real antagonism to them. There is greater willingness to accept without protest the continual incremental lowering of the country's standard of living when this is demanded by fashionable environmentalists. And there is less confidence in the ability of an individual to achieve his goals by his own independent actions, leading to more dependence on group membership, ethnic or other, as the means of survival. The melting pot and Horatio Alger are long gone. And sensing the decline of the country at home and its growing inability to cope with enemies abroad, much of the public now does believe in evil, albeit not yet enough to satisfy Sartre.

In regard to politics, while many still avow their opposition to big government, most of the country's active subgroups regularly demand the retention or expansion of the handouts, regulations, and policies they regard as beneficial to themselves. On the one hand, Americans are proud of their nation's long history of upholding individual rights, and they venerate the Constitution that protects these. But the same people approve their country's history of increasingly violating men's rights, and do so with no sense of contradiction, having been taught to reinterpret the Constitution along ever more Christian and/or egalitarian lines. One explanation of this contradiction might be that the Enlightenment ideas in America are now largely rhetoric, and that people actually have no coherent ideas or even feelings on such subjects. If representatives of today's America were to gather in convention in Philadelphia to update the Constitution, some observers think, they would likely turn out a document virtually the opposite of the original, and would do so in the sincere belief that they were modernizing, not destroying, the work of the founding fathers. The spirit of a philosophic document can hardly survive the disappearance of its philosophy.

Whatever the ultimate implications, the public for decades now has continued to move in an anti-I direction. People today accept—happily, passively, or unknowingly—countless developments that their ancestors even just a few generations back would have found intolerable or even inconceivable. Our grandfathers, accustomed to high school graduates with reasonable literacy and knowledge, could not have imagined today's de-conceptualized, inarticulate, rock-blasted teenagers, whose rank in educational standing among twenty-six industrial nations goes from "in the middle" (grade four) to "bottom third" (grade eight) to "near dead last" (grade twelve). Nor, having participated in the nationwide uproar when Truman as an emergency measure attempted to take over the steel mills, could our grandfathers have imagined a time when a good part of the public would cheer Washington's taking emergency control of the banks, the auto industry, and Wall Street. Nor—remembering the urgent nationwide mobilization for war after Pearl Harbor with no less a goal than the enemy's unconditional surrender—could they have imagined the public's uncomplaining acceptance of two successive presidents' deliberately feeble responses to 9/11, and even of these leaders' practice of regularly praising the enemy. Whatever else is true, the American character today in many crucial respects would be unrecognizable and even repugnant to the founding fathers.[264]

The evidence in regard to the American sense of life, in sum, is incoherent, being on its face almost systematically contradictory. What does the typical American today feel about man and life? Is he still at his core a descendant, however confused, of the Enlightenment? *Is* there still a typical American, given the widespread reduction of personal identity to group membership? And even if to some extent the American sense of life does still exist, has it faded to the point of historical irrelevance? As far as I can make out, there is some, but far from conclusive, evidence for and against several incompatible interpretations.

Even the best sense of life in a country, I must add, is not enough; explicit philosophy is necessary to give it historical power. The implicit as such is culturally impotent. Without an identified overall viewpoint— that is, without broad integrations—men can react only to concretes, while being ignorant of their interrelationships and implications. No matter how opposite to the establishment a people's souls may be, they cannot—merely as souls with feelings—redirect a nation's course. Such people can reject many establishment concretes in accordance with their emotions, but since they know of no abstraction uniting these concretes, they have no way to know when other feelings of theirs may be contradictory, or what to do in cases where no feeling presents itself. With this lack of intellectual equipment, much of any public, including one with an I sense of life but no more, is ready much of the time unwittingly to applaud a hostile but articulate establishment even as it subverts ever further the very principles underlying their feelings. Feeling as such cannot prevail over thought, not if one is dealing with intellectual issues. The subconscious cannot defeat the conscious.

If, however, those who hold a sense of life find and accept the requisite philosophic ideas, they can then become a potential, even a potent historical contender—because then they are men united by fundamental emotions expressed in explicit convictions. Such a combination of feeling and thought makes possible the consistent implementation of their sense of life in the issues of daily concern. Men of this kind would have no guarantee of success over their rivals, but they would at least be able to make a fight of it.

What then of the I mode in the United States at this time? It is possible that the Enlightenment outlook on life is widespread and waiting within the American subconscious, and it is possible that it is not. What Ayn Rand wrote about this forty years ago is, I think, still correct: "It is impossible to tell."

The most we can say of the I mode's cultural power here is this. It's not a "yes." But it's not a "no" either. Today, we have to—and still can—say: It's "maybe someday."

M₁ in the United States

Despite its Platonist base, M_1 may be regarded as a form of secularism in that it holds this world to be fully real. Historically, as we have seen, this mode has ruled during eras of philosophic intersection whose clash created a culture with a commitment to both supernaturalism and worldliness, or, in DIM terms, to elements of both M and I. Clearly, the absence from a culture of either of these elements would have eliminated the possibility of their mixture: Without the lingering Aristotelian element, Platonism would have led the pagans directly to M_2—just as, without their Platonism, the medievals' admiration for Aristotle would have led them directly to I. Today, however, the ideas of Aristotle are absent from Western culture and have been so for well over a century. So there is no contemporary movement working to create, or even to define, an M_1 culture adapted to our time and place.

The same applies to the United States in the nineteenth century. Most Americans then regarded as crucially important both Christianity and science, but there was little effort to integrate these two—that is, to fashion a unified M_1 culture resting on identified epistemological principles.* Rather, the popular commitment of the period was largely piecemeal: a sincere affirmation of traditional religion juxtaposed with an enthusiastic admiration of scientific method—in other words, an eclectic, unphilosophic endorsement of incompatible trends reflecting incompatible philosophies. Because of this eclecticism, the nineteenth-century religion-science combination could not answer or defeat any rising mode, and did not outlive the century.

In our time, the descendants of this eclecticism would seem to be concentrated in the establishment churches—that is, the mainline Protestants and the Catholics. In contrast to their nineteenth-century ancestors, however, these groups are commonly described as moderate, staid, liberal, and/or accommodating to the mainstream. To my knowledge, the leadership of these groups makes little attempt to imbue their congregations with an understanding or even awareness of philosophic fundamentals, let alone with religious or biblical passion. Many within these groups do seem to advocate a traditional religion-science outlook on the question, but their distinctively twentieth-century policy has been to adapt this outlook to the mainstream in which they have been educated—that is, to the world of the Ds. As a result, they tend to oscillate between a halfhearted religiosity and a half-skeptic relativism.

Many of this breed—how many I do not know—especially among the

---

* There was more of an effort in ethics—e.g., the idea that worldly success is a proof of God's favor.

Protestants, have effectively abandoned philosophy and to some extent even Christian dogma. Among such people, according to *New York Times* observer David Kirkpatrick, the doctrines of old-time religion are falling by the wayside: "[F]ew . . . [believe] in a literal hell or [talk] much about the Second Coming." In their place we see what is sometimes called a "live-and-let-live" theology—that is, religion all but disappearing into a D mentality. "Scripture is open to interpretation; it means what you want it to mean," says a professor of political science at Clemson, encapsulating this trend. We also see evidence that many churches, having adopted pluralism, are losing confidence in their own superiority—some going so far as to concede that outsiders, too, though filled with doctrinal error, may yet be eligible for heaven.[265]

The Greeks and the Romans in their epistemological naïveté did not see any inherent clash between their (newborn) science and their (tame) polytheism. But Newton, though a pious man himself, unwittingly ended this naïveté when he defined scientific method as I—that is, as contradictory to religion—and then demonstrated the cognitive and practical power of that method. Thereafter, as science, regularly denounced by religion, continued to advance, the clash between the two became almost inescapable. By the twentieth century, the earlier attempts to combine the two largely lost their appeal. Since both sides by then had rejected I, the more religious started moving to M_2, while much of the pro-science group were moving to D_2.

Today's religionists have made no attempt to reinstate the Worldly Supernaturalism of ancient Rome or the seventeenth century. There are no cultural figures like Virgil, Descartes, or would-be Louis XIVs anymore, and if somehow there were, then—aside from a bow to them as classics—they would be laughed off the scene as irrelevant to real-life concerns. There is no way any longer to re-create the seemingly comfortable union of Plato and Aristotle, which was enjoyed for so long in eras with less knowledge.

There are true M_1 representatives among us today, but they are a niche presence, best represented by some of the more old-fashioned Catholic theologians. On the popular level, a good example is the entertaining talk-show host Dr. Laura Schlessinger, although it is impossible to tell how many of her thirteen million listeners tune in primarily for religious reasons; the hostility her show generates among our cultural commentators is another sign of M_1 today. In physics, I should add, there is the M_1 of Einstein, although it has been virtually co-opted by the ruling M_2.

In regard to size, the standard estimate now for the establishment religious congregations is some 40 percent of the nation, about 120 million people, divided about equally between Protestants and Catholics. But these mode-less churches have been shrinking for years, not only in numbers, but also in influence. As of 2010, mainline Protestant churches in the previous thirty years had lost more than a third of their membership. Even the Catholic Church, by far the most stable and philosophical of Western religious institutions, has seen itself pushed almost to the brink of cultural impotence by the cascading signs of its deterioration, including too little money, too few priests, and too many pedophiles. Undoubtedly, the eclecticism of so many of these churches and their resulting lack of conviction, the empty spiritual hand they hold out to potential converts, have been major factors in their loss of national power.

According to a UCLA survey, the United States is now "mov[ing] away from all middle-of-the-road theology." Or, in DIM terms: There is no M_1 in the foreseeable future, not even as a possibility.[266]

———

D_1 and D_2 are now a unit—and that unit, in the American mind, is the philosophy of secularism. Since the I mode is at best an unidentified emotion and M_1 does not exist, people are unable now even to imagine any other way to understand secularism; the other ways are no more or not yet.

To believe in this and only this world, people are taught, you must reject the idea of external objects. To believe in man's ability to gain knowledge beyond sense perception is pretentious self-deception. To seek moral principles based on objective fact is to pine for a discredited fantasy. And if all this makes you unhappy, the lesson concludes, if you feel you cannot survive without a grasp of reality, a faculty of thought, and a code of morality, then you are not facing the fact that life on earth is inimical to man—that it cannot give you the fundamental insights or values you need. In other words, you must admit the ultimate truth: Existence is chaos and leads to doom.

The above, in the D viewpoint, is what it means to champion Nature without super-Nature.

The choice now being offered to the country is: an unreal, unknowing, unmoral, soul-destroying life on earth—or a non-perceivable, otherworldly entity offering you otherwise unattainable knowledge, values, hope, and salvation.

As we have seen, the "one" modes, within M and D alike, have always used their Aristotelian element to escape the extremism (as it would now be called) of the "twos." But today, without Aristotle, there is no such escape. If there is a culture war in America, it can be only a clash of the "twos,"—that is, between D_2 and M_2. This is a break from the whole pattern of Western history, which always presented a substantial transitional period to ease the passage from one pure mode to another—from I to M_2, through M_1; from M_2 to I, through M_1; from I to D_2, through D_1. But now, with epistemological mediation out of the picture and the door to the mixtures closed, the pattern is broken. If a modal change does occur in our country, the change will not be gradual, moderate, or unnoticeable. You will notice it.

The only mode now left to survey is M_2.

CHAPTER FIFTEEN

THE ANTI-SECULAR REBELLION

TO GUIDE US in assessing the implications of the data presented in this chapter, I must make some preliminary remarks about the nature of modal prediction.

The essence of historical prediction, in the DIM approach, is inference to a society's future from its modal character in the present. By definition, such inference can identify only the future mode of the society, not the specifics that express it. As we have often seen, concretes within a given mode may take a variety of forms, differing from one another in regard to a wide range of details. Such variations are especially obvious in the ever-evolving "ones," but they are present in the pure cases as well (e.g., Homer and Hugo, both Is).

If variant subgroups representing the same mode are not sufficiently philosophical, they may not recognize their modal allies and may even regard them as enemies. There is often competition among such subgroups along with frequent ups and downs—the temporary dominance of one, its fading and replacement, the merging of some, the factional splintering of others, etc. Subgroups representing the same mode, in short, may come and go. In the run-up to an era's modal changeover, there is nothing in DIM theory enabling us to predict which particular variant will win out.

By definition, however, struggles among variants do not affect either their modal identity or its cultural-political implications. Different forms of instilling the same fundamentals into people's minds—however dramatic and striking the differences—do not change the essence of the society that will result from those fundamentals. The obvious political examples here are Communism and Nazism, which, though self-described as mortal enemies, represented the same mode and created essentially the same society with the same results. When the two fought each other to take over the Weimar Republic, modal analysis alone, on the basis of the whole modal picture, could have predicted the ultimate triumph of M_2, but only that much. It can predict the essence of the outcome, but not the identity of the winners.

If a non-establishment mode is growing ever more powerful in the mind of a nation, and if it is doing so without intellectual opposition, that is a solid basis from which to hypothesize and even in some cases to predict the ultimate success of that mode *in some form*, though not necessarily in its current form. The new face of the future society can put on different and changing kinds of makeup in the present, but it is still the same face.

Since men have free will, their choices can sometimes invalidate a seemingly unassailable modal extrapolation to the future. A solid prediction in 1200 would have been nullified by the unexpected rediscovery of Aristotle—and one in 1750 by the unexpected arrival of Kant. Such fundamental philosophic eruptions cannot be foreseen, but this does not mean that prediction is futile. The truth rather is that prediction, like all scientific discoveries, is contextual: The facts, one must state, warrant such-and-such a conclusion if, within men's cognitive context at a given time, there is no evidence that a revolution in regard to philosophic fundamentals is in the offing. In other words, prediction is of this kind: The modal nature of a particular society—as identified from cultural observation within the available cognitive context—entails a specific modal future.

In predicting the future, it is necessary to observe any change in philosophic fundamentals accepted by a society's leaders and/or people. In this sense, any prediction must remain up-to-date. But this is needless in regard to modal analysis when no new view of philosophic fundamentals has been introduced. In that circumstance, no matter how the competing

groups rise and fall, their mode and its future march on. To predict a
mode's success, therefore, we need only take a modal snapshot of the
present, including both the establishment and the evidence of disaffection from it, combined with any increasing embrace of an alternative.
Such an alternative can become difficult for the establishment to cope
with—then, if it recasts men's method of thinking, it can even become
virtually impossible to overthrow—since, as we have seen in other cases,
its veterans and converts begin to rely on the new method in judging its
alternatives. As a result, though the modal snapshot at any moment fades,
its message remains steady over long stretches of time. If one specific
group within a mode has a powerful presence, and is then replaced by
another within the same mode, the prediction is unaffected. For example,
the number of Catholic believers who become Baptists—or even the
number who reject Christianity for Ouija boards—makes no difference
to modal analysis.

My own modal snapshot was taken in 2009–2010 and will undoubtedly change in many ways in the next years, to say nothing of the next
generations. But such changes, judged by our present state, will be irrelevant.

Christianity as Today's M_2

Considering our nation as it is today, the most prominent representatives
of the M_2 mentality—the largest, most articulate, and most militant
groups of rebels against the establishment—are to be found among the
fundamentalists, the evangelicals, the Pentecostals, and in general the
born-agains. We may call these overlapping groups New Christians, new
because the consistency of their religious ideology and the scope of their
cultural ambition have not been seen in the West for many centuries.
Whether or not Christianity will remain the major carrier of M_2, its present influence is revealing, because it enables us to gauge the M_2 penetration today in the United States—to find out to what extent the American
public is receptive to an M_2 change in culture, society, and method of
thought. If it is receptive, it will be so indefinitely as long as no modal

opposition confronts it. First, then, what *is* the mode of the New Christians? On what basis is it classified as M_2?

There is not much serious New Christian <u>literature</u> today, nothing to compare even with *Everyman*, let alone Dante. But there are many lesser New Christian stories read by enthusiastic admirers. The direction such works take is indicated by the *Left Behind* series of Tim LaHaye and Jerry Jenkins, which depicts the Second Coming of Christ, including the Rapture, the Tribulation, and Armageddon. From what I can tell (I have not read much of it), action in these stories is the prerogative of Jesus or the devil, who are presented in essence as the abstractions of love, anger, or evil, in relation to which men are pawns. The pawns do not pursue personal goals, because the natural world is to man a chaos of unpredictable acts of God, and also because the better men have no interest in earthly values. So there is not much characterization; the series presents primarily a contest of abstract human collectives—the godly/obedient versus the secular/arrogant. Rather than giving us characters—whether classic, Romantic or Naturalist—who enact a sequence of events, the series offers religious lessons in thriller form. It is a popularization of biblical tales full of bloodthirsty vengeance against unbelievers, providing the reader with "all the gruesome detail of a Hollywood horror movie," in the words of Kirkpatrick. In this type of work, beneath the blood and vengeance lies the message, which here is everything. The modal comparison to the fiction and fury of M_2 literary works in other times and places can hardly be escaped.[267]

The New Christian readers do not want only biblical reenactments. They have no objection to many of the classics or to many current genre novels. But what they want most is spiritual meaning, which to them requires some religion-confirming message. They want this message to animate not only literature, but art in general and especially Hollywood's sex-violence movies, movies being today's popular replacement for books. Moral values—in their eyes the same as religious values—are, they believe, the only protection against the basic cause of the corruption now rampant in American art: secularism. The cause must be secularism, because, as Dostoevsky famously put the point: "[I]f there is no God, then anything is permitted."

When I checked, the *Left Behind* series had sold sixty million copies in print, video, and cassette form, and had been outsold only by the *Harry Potter* series. Observing the wider literary picture, Lynn Garrett, religion editor at *Publishers Weekly*, commented, "They've broken out of the Christian ghetto and into the mainstream." *U.S. News & World Report* called it "one of the most profound changes in American publishing in the past decade." (And there was, of course, the mammoth attendance at Mel Gibson's movie *The Passion of the Christ*.)[268]

Like their otherworldly antecedents, the New Christians propound no distinctive system of <u>physics</u>. Sometimes they attack science as such because it is empirical and secular—in other words, it spurns faith in order to study the unreal. But often the movement uses science as a device to court unbelievers.

As proselytizers, the New Christians accept, reject, or rewrite the findings of science pragmatically, according to the effect on their creed's popular acceptance. They apply this approach comprehensively, far beyond their rejection of evolution. The universe, most hold, is only six thousand years old, "starlight only *seems* as if it has traveled millions of years to reach the Earth," dinosaurs and men lived happily together before original sin, simultaneous orgasms are possible (or at least easier to reach) only to those who have been premaritally abstinent, abortion can cause breast cancer, and so forth.[269]

Following the lead of Kant and Marx, no doubt unknowingly, the movement holds that it is impossible for real facts to contradict the *a priori* (the Bible), because God—in this regard the equivalent of Kant's categories and Marx's dialectic—is in fact the creator of facts; so the alleged scientific evidence against Christianity must be fantasy, error, or lies. These people, sums up Michelle Goldberg, a senior writer at *Salon*, are "undermining the very idea of empirical reality, dismissing inconvenient facts as the product of an oppressive ideology."[270]

The evolution within modern physics has been most helpful to these Christians in the task of undermining empirical reality. For example, late M_1 followers of Einstein, such as Steven Weinberg and Stephen Hawking, giving less importance to matter than he, conclude: "[T]he reality we observe in our laboratories is only an imperfect reflection of a deeper and more beautiful reality, the reality of the equations that display all the symmetries of the theory." When pure Platonism becomes a force in the minds of scientists, science is no longer an enemy of religion, but a form and thus an ally of it.[271]

Further, many believers counter their critics, where has science's empirical observation led us? The dominant view among scientists themselves, the movement points out, is that their own vaunted method leads them to the conclusion that the physical world is unintelligible, that even their surface descriptions are uncertain, and that the very enterprise of science rests on faith, with no more rational basis than that of any other faith. Even if rationality is your concern, some add, which of the competing faiths is worse? The one built on dogma that may seem to be contradictory, such as the Incarnation and the Resurrection, but which holds that these truths will ultimately be understood? Or the one that flaunts the eternal unintelligibility of Schrödinger's cat? You cannot refute Tertullian's *credo*, they point out, by asserting that the universe is absurd.

It is obviously better, they conclude, to have real conviction expressing faith in a value-laden reality, which relatively soon will answer our questions and provide us with eternal happiness. Even some famous scientists, they often add, recognize when they leave the lab that science is not only cognitively inadequate, but also that it cannot satisfy the deepest needs of man, and that their only alternative is to turn to some kind of transcendent dimension, Christian or otherwise. Thus Schrödinger, for example, who jumped from his D_2 cat to this:

> [T]his life of yours which you are living is not merely a piece of this entire existence, but is in a certain sense the "whole. . . ." This, as we know, is what the Brahmins express in that sacred, mystic formula which is yet really so simple. . . . "I am in the east and the west. I am above and below, *I am this entire world*."[272]

Religion was once on the defensive in the face of a proudly self-assertive science. The opposite now seems to be true.

Between one and two million American students now get their

education in home schools. Some 90 percent of these, while offering traditional subject matter, define their fundamental purpose as religious
training. One gathering of such educators indicates the kind of content
they teach. The convention floor was papered with booths selling:

> Christian curricula, videos, and educational games for stu-
> dents of every age. There were great piles of Bible-themed col-
> oring books and creationist science textbooks . . . instruction
> manuals for raising chaste, submissive girls . . . and dense,
> scholarly tomes of history and biblical exegesis.[273]

"[I]f Jesus Christ is Lord of the family"—theologian R. J. Rushdoony's
Chalcedon Foundation explains—"he is also Lord of the laboratory and
the board room. . . ."[274]

In method of teaching as in content, these schools are guided by their
purpose. James Dobson, an admired figure within the movement, advises
parents to read to their children a UPI news story recounting the fate of
a fifteen-year-old girl, Ann Turner, who, disregarding her parents' warn-
ings, stared at a solar eclipse and went blind. He urges fathers to instill in
their young the moral:

> this terrible thing happened to Ann because she didn't
> believe what she was told by her parents and other adults. She
> trusted her own judgment, instead. . . . [You must] *believe* the
> warnings that you've been taught, rather than trust your own
> judgment. . . . You can accept what your eyes tell you, like
> Ann, or you can believe what your mother and I have said, and
> more important, what we read in God's Word.[275]

Independent thought is all well and good, such parents argue, but we
have tried the godless public schools for many decades, and look at the
kind of graduates they turn out: children who are bored with learning,
undisciplined, amoral, ignorant, and, too often, violent, drug-addicted,
or medication-dependent. Isn't it time to try the alternative to this secularist disaster—the anti-godless school?

In <u>politics</u> the fundamental principle of the New Christians is dominionism, a theory—in Michelle Goldberg's words—"hugely influential in the broader evangelical movement. . . ." Dominionism holds that the secular authorities in the United States must be replaced by men of faith who will refashion American life according to God's teachings. U.S. civil law, holds Pat Robertson, one of the movement's originators, must be replaced by biblical law. As to the founding fathers' demand for a wall separating Church and state, dominionists reply that this interpretation of the Constitution is a lie invented by secular humanists. America, they say, was founded as a Christian country. The bill of rights had nothing to do with protecting unbelief. The founding fathers fought to protect men from godless tyrants, not from teachers of holy writ; they cherished freedom <u>of</u> religion, not from it. Under their own religious rule, dominionists add, Americans will still enjoy liberty, if the concept is properly interpreted. "[T]he goal," says Rushdoony, "must be God's law-order in which alone is true liberty. Any other kind . . . is simply an assertion of man's 'right' to be his own god; this means a radical denial of God's law-order. . . . If men have unrestricted free speech and free press, then there is no freedom for truth. . . ."[276]

The New Christianity, Goldberg writes, is a "total ideology"; the goal is the takeover of "every aspect of public and private life," including but not limited to "government, science, history, culture, and relationships. . . ." "Christian politics," writes George Grant—director of Coral Ridge Ministries (Florida)—"has as its primary intent the conquest of the land [America]—of men, families, institutions, bureaucracies, courts, and governments for the Kingdom of Christ." As in all forms of totalitarianism, the fundamental purpose of this theocracy is to spread the ideas regarded as holy, and eliminate opposition to them. Such a purpose requires a thoroughgoing reorientation of the national mind, entailing thought control. The result will be a nation conditioned to forget facts, understanding, and individualism, while remembering Jesus, God, and His earthly representatives in the Church.[277]

Across the board, the New Christianity is M_2. As we have seen, however, politics is usually the last area to yield to modal change, and most New Christians, accordingly, are not at present willing to accept the politics of their philosophy.

Traditionally, conservative Christians have rejected big government, and many still do in emphatic terms, as the Tea Party movement has made clear. Judging by press coverage, however, the Tea Party rightists protest the size of our taxes, deficit, and regulatory burden, but they say little or nothing about the entitlement and welfare programs that necessitate these evils, because Christianity makes these programs a moral duty. The establishment conservatives, which include most of the Republicans, are less extreme (their word) than the Tea Party in opposing big government. For about a century, these moderates, regularly praising capitalism in their speeches, have attacked each new welfare-state measure—then, when in power, amended it insignificantly and helped to institutionalize it.

Against this background of conservative Christians' ineffectuality, many of the New Christians, holding their religion seriously, have begun to shed the traditional conservative perspective. They have started to think that the atrophy of capitalism may not be an evil at all, but rather a moral necessity, since a system built on worldly greed seems clearly to be the opposite of what the Bible recommends. The spokesmen for these New Christians accept big government and actively proselytize for it, recognizing it as a precondition of their own rule.

Christians, many of them now say, should stop denouncing the welfare state; rather, they should aim to take over the job themselves and do it properly—in effect, profit from the state-expanding achievements of the Ds. Ralph Nader, seeing an aspect of this development, writes of "a convergence of liberal-progressives with conservative-libertarians. . . ." The *Wall Street Journal* has described this politics as the "religious left," which is also a good name for the politics of the Middle Ages.[278]

Whatever degree of statism they accept, however, most Christians regard the Constitution as a religiously inspired document and seek God's "return" to the United States. They heartily disapprove of what they see as the only alternative: the directionless, unprincipled, secular politicians in Washington, with their wheeling-dealing, flip-flopping, lavish private earmarking, and empty public rhetoric; their nihilism, sensed in part by people without definition and sarcastically called "political correctness"; and often their anti-religious bias. If, as everyone tells us, this is freedom, some of the New Christians are starting to wonder, then is freedom compatible with God and morality?

In each of our diagnostic areas, the application of the New Christian ideology has been clearly defined, and in most cases widely accepted within the movement, while the establishment products, when not condemned, are ignored. Few pick up Joyce as multitudes once did Homer and Hugo, or acclaim Bohr or even Einstein as they once did Newton, or respect our dumbed-down schoolbooks as they once did the *McGuffey Readers*. And, aside from Obama's short-lived canonization, few admire our leaders in Washington as they once did Washington, Lincoln, and even Ronald Reagan.

The American people—not only Christians—do not understand what is today called art. They do not understand what is called science. Their children do not understand what the schools teach. And the politicians, people think, understand nothing. It adds up to a historic popular feeling: Something fundamental has gone wrong with the United States.

The only possible fix, the New Christians tell them, is authentic religion—meaning religion shorn of secular concessions. Unlike the leaders of the Great Awakenings in our past, our new sounders of the alarm have moved far beyond the old-fashioned theological disputes, short-term bursts of fervor, and quests for scattered reforms. What they seek is revolution across the whole of American culture, in the name of a mode of thought that has not ruled here since the time of the Puritans.

M_2 Power in the United States

Because it is defined in terms of fundamental principles, the New Christianity is not, as some think, inherently provincial—restricted to Southern, uneducated, poor whites, without any possibility of broad national reach. For one thing, the new movement cuts across denominational lines. Its Baptist origin has not prevented its spread across the religious spectrum—from the fringes, such as the Jehovah's Witnesses, to the more respectable Mormons, to the heart of the non-Protestant establishment: the Catholics. About a million Mormons and another million Catholics are now thought to be enthusiastic advocates of this originally Baptist radicalism.

For the same reason, the once-white movement cuts across racial and ethnic lines. "Evangelicalism," states Alan Wolfe, director of the Boisi Center for Religion at Boston College, "dominates African-American religion. . . ." According to a 2006 report by the Baylor Institute for Studies of Religion, if God is defined in "authoritarian" terms—that is, as "highly involved in [men's] daily lives," helps believers in decision making, is "responsible for global events" including tsunamis, and is angry—then 52.8 percent of blacks identify themselves as believers in God. The same trend seems apparent among Latinos. Hispanic Catholics have been turning to evangelicalism at such a rate, says Catholic theologian Andrew Greeley, that it has become for the Catholic Church an "ecclesiastic failure of unprecedented proportions." As to Asian-Americans, Southern Baptists have established branches reaching out successfully to Koreans, Chinese, and Filipinos. Asian-Americans, moreover, according to the Baylor study, "comprise over 25% of evangelical college students at New York City colleges and universities." In agreement with all these ethnics, as modal if not creedal or political allies, are a not inconsiderable segment of Orthodox Jews, and of American Muslims connected to the Middle East, who define themselves as Islamic fundamentalists. Clearly, all these groups do not live in shacks on the Suwanee. Indeed, Southern Baptism has now become "one of the top four denominations in a dozen *northern* states."[279]

Despite the relative severity of its demands, the New Christianity is not restricted to adults. Observe, among many other examples, the secular businesses that promote religion-affirming toys; the big-selling teen magazines that include the New Testament (usually, I am told, uncut), along with advice on dating and acne; the Christian Tattoo Association, with some hundred parlors nationwide; the Jesus-loving youngsters who sense God during the rock concerts held at mega-churches; the soaring sales to teenagers of Christian music; and the structured miniature golf courses with the Creation at the first hole and the Resurrection at the eighteenth. Two journalists sympathetic to the trend—John Micklethwait and Adrian Wooldridge of *The Economist*—sum up the situation this way: "You may start out in a Disney theme park but you end up in the heart of Evangelical America." Further examples of this trend among the young are regularly reported in the press by an incredulous left.[280]

Although it is of value in assessing a nation to observe adults in church and teenagers at play, it is more instructive to observe adults at work. Out of many national institutions essential to our society, I have selected three, each of which not long ago had the reputation of being non- or even anti-religious: the colleges, the military, and the political parties.

The New Christians are no longer ignorant and poor. On the contrary, according to *The New York Times*, they "have made great strides in entering mainstream institutions like academia, government, the media and business." Graduating from academia, clearly, is a precondition of the other strides. Since college professors until recently generally were (or were thought to be) unbelievers, college education was long viewed as a threat to religion. Hence the rise since 1990 of religious colleges, which have grown by 70 percent, as against private schools (up 28 percent) and public schools (13 percent)—and which now enroll one in ten American college students, most of whom study not theology but the standard cultural and professional fields.[281]

Increasingly, however, religious colleges are becoming unnecessary, as students find out that the faithful are no longer a despised minority condescended to by secular professors. "Scholars and administrators are noticing that our students are more religious than previous generations of college students," says professor Darren Sherkat at Southern Illinois U. A 2004 Harvard Institute of Politics poll points in the same direction, reporting that "35% of college students call themselves 'born again,' and 22% identify as evangelical or fundamentalist Christians."[282]

Stanley Fish, currently at Florida International University, is widely recognized as one of the most acute observers of our culture; so his statement about college life after the death of Jacques Derrida is instructive.

I was called by a reporter who wanted to know what would succeed high theory and the triumvirate of race, gender and class as the center of intellectual energy in the academy. I answered like a shot: religion. . . . Announce a course with

"religion" in the title, and you will have an overflow population. Announce a lecture or panel on "religion in our time,"
and you will have to hire a larger hall.[283]

Although religion for some students is merely a fad, it seems to be
more than that for most. According to a UCLA survey, "more than 70
percent of students said they prayed, discussed religion or spirituality
with friends, found religion personally helpful and gained spiritual
strength by trusting in a higher power." "My generation," states the
twenty-eight-year-old founder of Relevant Media, "is discontent with
dead religion. . . . We don't want to show up on Sunday, sing two hymns,
hear a sermon and go home. The Bible says we're supposed to die. . . ." A
girl who writes about Christian music for *Billboard* agrees; quoted in *The
New York Times*, she explained that students need "something more spir-
itually meaty" than the standard fare. Then she offered the best definition
of today's religiosity: "People don't want Christian lite."[284]

Christian lite is God diluted by worldliness, and faith by science; in
effect, it is the outmoded M_1. "Christian real," by contrast, means the
practice of religion undiluted—that is, a life fundamentally connected to
an all-embracing transcendent. Thus the booming business of "praise
and worship" music played in college auditoriums filled with rapt students on their feet singing—in the words of one eighteen-year-old,
"directly connecting to God, one on one." Many of these young people
say that what they most want out of college is to find life's purpose by
developing the non-materialistic side of their nature. The secular courses,
they say, are not enough; these courses offer stacks of assorted facts and
random theories vouched for by a pile of authorities, with the professor
emphasizing that all of it is value-free, that none of it is certain, and that
a lot of it is no more than the expression of race/class/gender prejudice.
What kind of *meaning*, the students complain, do we get from all that?[285]

Now the military. In the World War II era, though the majority of
Christians cheered it as defenders of Christianity, a small minority criticized the institution as inherently anti-Christian, concerned as they saw
it with vengeance, not forgiveness. The military, in turn, though it
remained staunchly Christian, stayed away from religious talk; whatever

the military establishment's own opinions, they thought it essential to be seen by the country as non-ideological professionals. A soldier's religion, in this period, though regarded as crucial to his personal life, was also regarded as irrelevant to his function as a soldier.

Things have changed.

Ranking officers now commonly state publicly that the United States is a Christian nation, and that soldiers are "God's warriors." The official newspaper of the Air Force Academy, the most overtly (but not the only) religious branch of the services until semi-quieted by sympathetic but embarrassed higher-ups, ran ads proclaiming "that Jesus Christ is the only real hope for the world." "The ads," writes David Antoon, a decorated Vietnam War pilot, "were signed by sixteen department heads, nine permanent professors, both the incoming and outgoing deans of faculty, the athletic director and more than two hundred academy senior officers and their spouses." The army seems to be extending a similar embrace: It harbors a movement of Christian dominionists—a movement, the Military Religious Freedom Foundation estimates, that makes up "between 20 and 30 percent of U.S. service members."[286]

The penchant for a new, zealous Christianity runs to varying extents throughout the services, from bottom to top. For example, the Department of Defense at one point prepared "freedom packages" to send to soldiers in Iraq. The packages contained not weapons or food, but "Bibles, proselytizing material in English and Arabic and the apocalyptic computer game" based on the *Left Behind* series. These packages were produced by a "fundamentalist Christian ministry." The program was aborted, it seems, not through fear of discovery by liberals, but because of complaints from Muslims that they were not being given equal time. In a different incident, an adviser to the Joint Chiefs of Staff, Major General Jack Catton, described his position in these words: "a wonderful opportunity to evangelize men and women setting defense policy. My first priority is my faith. I think it's a huge impact."[287]

Without faith, these military men say, we have neither the motive nor the inner strength to go to war. How, they ask, can we risk our lives in defense of our beloved America if we accept the creed that God is irrelevant, and so our thoughts are non-absolute, our actions non-principled, and our patriotism merely a subjective feeling that is no better than that of our enemies?

I do not survey businessmen in this study, but for what it is worth, here is a sentence from a book sympathetic to Christianity: "America's executive class is probably its second most religious elite in the country after the senior military."[288]

As to our political parties, the Republicans, in this context, need little discussion. It is generally understood that the party's values—those backed by real commitment as against mere rhetoric—are no longer those of big business but increasingly of the Christian right, which is now its mass base. A recent column in *The Philly Post* reported that, while 40 percent of Americans believe in creationism, "more than half of registered Republicans" do so. Writer Kevin Phillips, a staunch foe of the New Christians, identifies the political situation in the following terms: Within a few decades the Republicans have transformed themselves into "the first religious party in U.S. history." To my knowledge, the Tea Party, though it has campaigned not for God, but—bravely—for the Constitution, also regards Christianity as its moral and philosophical base. In one poll, for example, 63 percent of them oppose abortion.[289]

More indicative of our cultural state are the Democrats, who, though always nominally religious, traditionally regarded the separation of Church and state as constitutionally mandated, and concerned themselves primarily with secular, economic issues. Today, though their concern with material issues continues to be prominent, many in the party are urging a soft-pedaling of secularism and a new stress on God. In the words of Micklethwait and Wooldridge, "Democrats as well as Republicans are repeatedly evoking religion to justify their actions."[290]

Some of the Democratic leadership are obviously sincere in their faith. But it is doubtful whether one can turn around a party of today's politicians primarily by intellectual or spiritual means. College students and military men may be turning to God in the quest for meaning, but in all likelihood what the Democrats (and most Republicans, too) are looking for is not meaning, but votes.

The Democratic Party is starting to think that the Republicans have an unfair electoral advantage because of their arrogantly claimed monopoly on faith. Amy Sullivan—Baptist, Democrat, and an influential editor at *Time* magazine—attracted attention from many as she stated in her book title the task ahead: *The Party Faithful: How and Why the Democrats Are Closing the God Gap*. Were secular politicians actually to become believers, it would be an eloquent sign of the times, but when politicians eye a religious mantle pragmatically because otherwise they will lose elections, that is a much more eloquent sign. It tells us not just about Washington, but about Main Street.

Describing a nationally broadcast CNN forum on faith and values in June 2007, featuring John Edwards, Hillary Clinton, and Barack Obama, Amy Sullivan writes: "[W]here once Democratic politicians would have worried that God-talk during the primary season would alienate or scare off their base of voters, these leading candidates were unabashedly embracing the subject of religion." At a Compassion Forum on April 13, 2008, Obama—whether sincerely or pragmatically—described his goal in these terms: "[W]hat I try to do is, as best I can, be an instrument of [God's] will. . . . [M]y entire trajectory . . . has been to talk about how Democrats need to get in church, reach out to evangelicals, link faith with the work that we do."[291]

Like the president, many liberal Democrats hold that the party's program is in no way incompatible with religion; on the contrary, the love taught by Jesus is the moral base of the party's priorities. I am a liberal, such people say, because of, not despite religion—a formulation that gives religion primacy over politics. The most striking Democratic example of this new trend that I have seen was offered at one of their official, publicized forums. According to Sullivan, "The young Democrats [in attendance] were beaming. 'Who would have thought?' one of them (Vanderslice) asked, looking up at the bright television lights on the stage and the enormous banners labeled FAITH, VALUES, and POVERTY. 'Three years ago, who would have thought?'" When this semi-Marxist party, whose main economic concern has been the redistribution of wealth, turns to salute the banner of *poverty*, something has happened.[292]

Before we draw a general conclusion about the strength of religion in America, let us note some seemingly contrary evidence that is increasingly publicized these days by alarmed Christians and heartened

secularists alike. Bruce Feiler, bestselling author and conservative com-
mentator on national radio and TV, offers some relevant facts.

> The number of people who claim no religious affiliation,
> meanwhile, has doubled since 1990 to fifteen percent. . . . Non-
> believers now represent the third-highest group of Americans,
> after Catholics and Baptists. . . . The number of Christians has
> declined 12% since 1990, and is now 76%, the lowest percent-
> age in American history.

In the same vein, Eric Gorski, education writer for the Associated
Press, writes that "campus affiliates of the Secular Student Alliance, a sort
of Godless Campus Crusade for Christ, have multiplied from 80 in 2007
to 174 [in 2009]."[293]

Such facts as these, and there are many more, do represent some
degree of popular recoil from religion or at least from organized
religion—a recoil, I believe, mostly because of the emptiness of the old
version and the sometimes scary, even lunatic zealotry of the new. But I
doubt that this recoil involves a change in fundamentals—for example, a
rejection of supernaturalism as such. Less than 5 percent of the American
public describe themselves as atheists or agnostics, a figure that has not
changed much for generations. And even for this 5 percent, the operative
mode is often unclear. An atheist as such need not be a secularist; his
rejection of God leaves open to him all the non-theistic forms of supernaturalism, from magic to Marxism. Agnosticism is even more receptive
in this regard: It affirms the possibility even of the Christian God Himself. As to the religiously unaffiliated, many reject religion only as an
institution, but accept the traditional faith with as little doubt as their
churchgoing kin. Indeed, almost a third of them pray occasionally, while
one in ten still believes Jesus to be the Son of God.

There is also a new breed of quasi-religious non-Christians, especially
on the West Coast and the eastern seaboard. The latter was once the
country's bastion of rational thought. Many of these non-Christians are
turning from belief in the God of old to something else: belief in the
paranormal, the power of the stars, UFOs, or some other phenomenon

commonly taken to be inaccessible to science. For example, 21 percent of Americans state that they believe in witches, and 37 percent in haunted houses.[294]

Most of today's unbelievers, it seems, still believe. They dislike conventional religion, but not the essence of its philosophy. In this regard, Feiler, though he bemoans the shrinking of Christianity, is correct when he observes that a solid basis for religion among Americans still exists; their "relationship with God," he writes, "is still intact." Irreligion in this form—as scattered variants within M_2—is no threat to the M_2 rebels.[295]

Turning now to an overview of the rebels' strength, let us start with numbers, understanding that here as elsewhere they do not tell the whole story, but only part of it. Estimates of the size (in 2010) of the Protestant congregations who embrace the new movement vary widely, depending largely on the researcher's definition of the beliefs required for a group to qualify. But even this dispute is instructive, because it takes place in the numerical stratosphere: 60 million New Christians, say the most restrictive counters; 120 million, say the most inclusive—so an average estimate of 90 million, somewhat less than one-third of the U.S. population. Add to this the Christians among the 120 million U.S. mainline churchgoers who do not like the evangelicals, but do not disagree with their fundamentals. Add to this the self-styled non-Christians, religious or otherwise, who reject the mythology in the Bible, but not its metaphysics or ethics.

According to a study not only of evangelicals, but of Christians in general: 55 percent said that they regard the Bible as literally accurate; 64 percent believe that God parted the Red Sea for Moses; 80 percent believe in the Day of Judgment. Many of these believers, though certainly not all, are inviting candidates for non-lite proselytizers. If we combine those who believe in an "authoritarian"* God (highly involved in daily life, causes global events, angry, 31.4 percent)—with those who uphold a "critical" God ("does not interact with the world, but views today with displeasure which will be felt in the next life," 16 percent), we reach the conclusion that 47.4 percent of Christian Americans, or at least a large

---

* Mentioned above on page 318.

part of them, now hold a pre-Enlightenment, and even a pre-modern, view of the world. However one calculates, the total of such people substantially exceeds the highest projected number of evangelicals. One cannot, of course, include within this total the millions of Christians who are indifferent to ideas and follow no method of thought. But I do count most of the Christian millions, because, as we have seen, a tradition going back to pre-history has made easily accessible to the non-intellectual and even to the most uneducated the fundamental ideas of God, faith, and sacrifice. From the behavior of the New Christian masses, it seems apparent that they do understand this much.

My figures may be off by tens of millions, and Christianity itself may become outdated in a few generations, although I doubt both of these. Nevertheless, judging by present evidence, one solid conclusion emerges: The M_2 penetration of the American mind and culture is real. It is broad and deep—and growing.

M_2 and Environmentalism

It is possible for a society, following its intellectual leaders, to accept the fundamentals of a new mode, and yet in some issues unknowingly contradict it. For the leaders of a growing mode, this can be a major problem.

The lure of worldly possessions is just such an obstacle facing the M_2s. Even though millions have become convinced that Nature is unreal, unintelligible, and irrelevant to values, most of these millions, especially in America, are still enamored of material goods. Houses, cars, jet planes, computers—the believers strongly desire them, with no idea that such desire involves ideological issues. But a reliable flock of the faithful, as the medievals saw, must give up such desires. M_2 has no future in a nation where men, even though they disparage material wealth on Sunday, gorge on it the rest of the week. Otherworldliness cannot take over if men are in love with worldly things. An American flock may sincerely agree that we are living in Plato's cave, but so long as we are, they think, the cave should be furnished with every comfort and luxury—it's only a cave, yes, but make it a first-class one with all the perks.

Destruction is disintegration, a principle we have already seen applied by the Ds in the fields of metaphysics and epistemology, who thereby leave these fields open for an M_2 takeover. The same principle applies in regard to values; so in this issue, too, we can expect the Ds—and particularly the specialists in destruction, the D_2s—to become helpful albeit unintentional allies of the M_2s.

The two transformational events of our world, the existential sources of modern "materialism," are two revolutions: the American and the Industrial. The first, by recognizing the rights of the individual, enshrined men's earthly life and their creation of material property. The second, by applying science to life, showed men that an unprecedented abundance was possible. The result of this combination is today's "materialist" outlook, which would have been impossible and even unimaginable in any earlier era. It is these two pillars of secularism that the aspiring New Christians have to bring down.

In regard to government, there is not much left for the New Christians to do. The dismantling of the political system of the founding fathers is now the norm and the expected in the country. Nor is there any political group able to stop the statist march, or even slow it down much. As the D_1 intellectuals tell us regularly, the age of individual rights and limited government was the nineteenth century, and has no relevance today. The nation's whole progression, from the Sherman Act to Obamacare, has been continual lurches away from capitalism.

At this point in history, the supreme practical obstacle to M_2 rule is no longer the spirit of the founding fathers but the lifestyle that has been generated by the Industrial Revolution. The medievals faced an earlier version of the problem: how to kill or subdue the pagans' desire for worldly goods. But because there was comparatively little wealth in existence at the time, this obstacle was far less formidable, and gradually succumbed to the new culture of religious admonition (or went underground).

In our time, however, to kill men's love of material goods requires a powerful force. It is not enough any longer simply to demand a life of poverty. Instead, the leadership has found a much more powerful weapon in its arsenal: a new proof of anti-materialism believed to be unanswerable because of its source. The new proof, we are told, derives not from the Bible, but from its onetime nemesis, science—which shows irrefutably the evils wrought by man's production and consumption of goods, and thus the necessity of sharply curtailing these activities and the desires underlying them. The M_2s, although antagonistic to the scientific enterprise, are prepared to use it when it is helpful. The science they have discovered is the anti–Industrial Revolution version of D_2 nihilism called environmentalism. The religious trend it has spawned is "green Christianity."

In 2004 during an Earth Day service, the National Council of Churches, said to represent fifty million Americans, addressed a prayer to the heavens: "God of mercy, we confess that we are damaging the earth, the home that you have given us. We buy and use products that pollute. . . ." Speaking from England, the archbishop of Canterbury was a bit more explicit, explaining that mankind faces a real challenge: "to let go of their security and some of their prosperity . . . sacrifice is necessary and important. . . ." It's all in Deuteronomy, say enthusiasts: "Do not cut down trees even to prevent ambush or to build siege engines, do not bottle waters or burn crops even to cause an enemy's submission." Not so long ago, under the so-called Protestant ethics, the earth damagers and tree cutters were praised, told by their religious leaders that these activities would earn them heavenly reward. Not anymore.[296]

In the earlier years of the environmentalist movement, the Christian right opposed it as left-wing subversion, and there are still some rightists of this kind. But gradually, it seems, this criticism has been marginalized as the original rightist veterans give way to new and younger leaders. Andrew Walsh, who studies religion in public life at Trinity (Connecticut), gives us an example of this development. He reports that there has been "a generational change among evangelicals"; two-thirds of them "want immediate action on global warming," an issue, he adds, that is especially important to the "younger lot."[297]

Many religious leaders now accept environmentalist doctrines genuinely, not merely as strategy; they view it as a derivative of faith, not merely of science. Nature as God's creation, material sacrifice as man's duty, purely spiritual fulfillment as his ultimate goal—what else, they wonder, is religion? And if so, asks a professor of philosophy at Worcester Polytechnic (MA), what man could call himself a believer in "God the Designer if His design was being clear-cut, paved over, or rendered extinct by the fur trade?"[298]

The medievals held that human initiative and material innovation are in essence a rebellion against God's plan, which will lead the culprits to disaster, in the form of the unendurable heat of hell. Their D_2 counterparts today ask that we "let it be" because otherwise we will end in catastrophe, in the form of the unendurable heat of global warming. God won't tolerate worldly achievement, said the medievals; Nature won't, say these moderns. If and when "climate change" or some such term replaces global warming, it will not affect the essential similarity of the two movements.

The above is another reason why the traditional dichotomy between the right and the left is disappearing. The religious right now also tends to believe in the need for more government to support not only traditional religious causes, but also the ever-more-inclusive programs of the greens.

Does the American public buy the environmentalist gospel? When asked to identify issues that are important to them, according to a recent poll, voters evaluated environmentalism as the last out of twenty choices offered. This result, however, hardly means that the movement has no influence. Undoubtedly, people are skeptical of, and many rightists even ridicule, some environmentalist claims—but not others. Some of these issues, the public believes, are important, but not their concern (especially in a recession), because the government is taking care of things. Whatever the polling data, however, two facts are clear: To my knowledge, no one, among the public or the rightist critics, voices opposition to environmentalism in terms of philosophic fundamentals or can even identify it as an ideology with an essence and allies. As in politics and economics, the opponents are able to fight only concretes—and for each one they have put to rest, five new ones spring up.

As a result, the greens are mostly viewed favorably by the public; at worst, some are regarded as "extremist" but in a worthy cause. The best evidence of the public sentiment is the widespread national compliance with (or tolerance of) specific environmentalist demands and policies—demands that continually remove physical enjoyment from people's lives, policies that just fifty years ago would have provoked in America howls of incredulity. For example, in regard to daily standard of living, leaving aside here more profound economic issues, we see everywhere the growth of shrinkage: deliberately inflated gas prices, the elimination of popular car models, the mandating of lightbulbs that emit dimness and of toilets that do not flush, the weekly sorting of garbage, the advocacy of clothes-lines over dryers and of cutting down air-conditioning by official setting of thermostats, the fight to ban the expansion of highways and the building of dams, the condemnation of fur coats and of any other object or practice defined as harmful to animals. In regard to the latter, a recent poll shows "that only about half of Americans support the use of animals in health-related research, down from near-universal support 40 years ago."[299]

Since the schools laud all this "anti-materialism" and people do not complain much, the term "green" has taken on a positive connotation and has been enthusiastically adopted nationwide. Business and professional groups, for example, now hurry to boast that they are "going green for God," and make at least token contributions to demonstrate it.

Do they all really believe it? In the long run, it does not matter to the M_2s; they hardly expect their mass base to turn into saints. What matters to them is the ideology of material wealth as evil. Once people accept this as the *moral* viewpoint, they are no longer an obstacle to the unworldly; such people can transgress without threat to the system because, self-defined as guilty, they go underground and stay quiet.

Like any concrete under a broad political abstraction, the whole environmentalist movement could prove ephemeral. This would be no problem for the M_2s, as long as it was replaced by another form of nihilism working—under the guise of some secular justification—to equate production with evil. In today's fertile context, there is little doubt that such helpful D_2 groups would be found.

The philosophic relationship between environmentalists and Christians is increasingly being recognized not only by Christians, but by many environmentalists themselves who are trying to work the alliance in the opposite direction—that is, to use religion to foster their own goals. In particular, the D_2 avant-garde proposes to gain converts from M_2 by building on its ideas. People, some D_2s explain, can be convinced of the need to give up specific material goods only if given specific practical reasons; they will not give their goods up as an end in itself or as a sacrifice to Nature seen only as Nature. Experience, these D_2s conclude, has shown that environmentalism cannot be successfully marketed merely on the grounds of practical considerations. But people will accept it, they think, if they see Nature not as secular and prosaic, but as the sacred handiwork of God, and their own sacrifice as a requirement of its preservation. Thus the new "religious environmentalists" who, in the words of Worcester philosopher Gottlieb, have discovered

> the unique gifts religion offers to help us respond to the environmental crisis . . . why and how religious participation in public life, a participation that religious environmentalism requires, can be a positive force for . . . a sustainable global society . . . and why the unique features of secular environmentalism make it a natural ally of religion.[300]

Tom Hayden, California's hippie turned legislator, says it more succinctly: "[W]e need to see nature as having a sacred quality, so we revere it and are in awe of it. That forms a barrier to greed and exploitation and overuse."[301]

Since environmentalism has always presented itself in America as scientific, its appeal to religion would seem to be merely a pragmatic strategy. But we must remember the real identity in this context of the M_2 and D_2 schools: their common denunciation of worldly values. It is also possible that some of these D_2s are incipient religionists without a religion yet, and in that sense are sincerely embracing the fundamentals of the Bible as the base of their cause. The conversion of a D_2 to an M_2 must, in my theory, be difficult, although antithetic modes are possible within a compartmentalized mind. I have already cited as an example Schrödinger at work and at home. In any event, whatever the motive of these media-acclaimed religious D_2s, and whatever their size within the broader movement, what a great boost that movement is giving to the M_2 cause. Because now there can be no question of rejecting Christian abstinence as weird right-wing extremism.

The M_2/D_2—and more broadly the M_2/D alliance—is now a cultural reality. This alliance does not rest on a modal kinship, as in the D_1/D_2 partnership; it does not diminish the clash between the two modes. The D_2 effort to destroy a cherished value is welcomed by modern M_2s only when it is a value that is an obstacle to their own transcendent cause. The D_2s' work, by contrast, is all-embracing: to destroy all values. The M_2s destroy only selectively, as a means to man's ultimate reward; they seek to annihilate not man, but only his wicked passions. In essence, the D_2s want to kill human desires because they <u>are</u> desires; the M_2s only because they are the wrong desires (which in time are to be replaced by much better ones). Once M_2s have come to power, accordingly, they have no further use for the D_2s they earlier embraced, as both Stalin and Hitler demonstrated.

Each side of the M_2/D alliance believes that it is working to defeat the other and achieve its own ends. But as strength drains from one group to the other, the outcome of the battle is increasingly visible.

The haters of God are a godsend to His lovers.

CHAPTER SIXTEEN

WHAT'S NEXT

RELIGIOUS TOTALITARIANISM IN America—that is my prediction.

"God is dead," said Nietzsche in the nineteenth century. To which a recent book title gives the twenty-first-century reply: *God Is Back.*

There Is Nothing to Stop M_2

In surveying Western history, we have found six factors, one or more of which is necessary and sufficient to produce modal downfall and replacement. These are: the instability of a mixed mode; the inability of the establishment philosophically to defend its mode; modal rebellion by the intellectuals; modal rebellion by the public; knowledge of an acceptable alternative mode; trigger(s). As applied to the United States today: The compromise of the mixed D_1 mode, falling apart, is reaching the end of its road. The Ds of both kinds, through their disdain for philosophy, have turned it into their own greatest liability. No new philosophy has emerged to inspire rebellion by the intellectuals, who are committed to the status quo. But there are many signs of public rebellion, led by men who know and approve only one alternative mode.

As to the sixth factor, one cannot, as we know, predict or even delimit the trigger(s) that could be decisive once the groundwork has been laid.

The final straw could come from anywhere. It might be moral outrage over some establishment-blessed anathema, such as a ban on teaching creationism in public schools. Or a decree that in the name of equality hotel rooms must stock not only the Bible, but also, next to it, the Torah and the Koran. Or a close presidential election generally considered to be rigged against a religious candidate by secular media widely thought to be a mere arm of a secular government. Or a packing of the Supreme Court with secular humanists in the majority and including, say, a partner in a gay marriage or an outspoken atheist.

Or the trigger might be economic in nature, such as runaway inflation, a 1929-scale depression, skyrocketing unemployment, taxes that cannot be borne, a middle class wiped out financially, or national bankruptcy. Or the trigger might be the result of foreign and security policy, such as escalating Muslim attacks on American soil met by U.S. appeasement, or Western oil starvation met by U.S. appeasement, or foreign missiles launched against Israel or Taiwan met by U.S. appeasement, or U.S. silence in the face of domestic outbreaks of lawless protesters, all of it observed with growing anger by the American police and military.

Is the trigger one of the above or all of them? Some combination? Something else? The only relevant observation at this point is that in one form or another the basis for each of the above has already been laid in the United States and is now visible. When every failure of the secular government becomes a boost to the champions of the anti-secular, the specific nature and sequence of these failures are irrelevant to the ultimate outcome.

The decline of America has often been compared to that of ancient Rome. From the DIM viewpoint, this comparison has substantial but not complete validity. Rome was the first Western culture to push a dissatisfied populace into the arms of an M_2 religion sneered at but unanswered by an establishment disdainful of philosophy. This comparison is true as far as it goes, but it omits an important modal difference between the two. The Romans had long been guided by an evolving M_1 orientation, so their fall into otherworldliness might be seen as more thoroughly prepared than ours, being a move merely from one version of M to another. A more exact parallel to the U.S. situation would have to be a takeover by M_2 of a country run by the Ds. Many people today still remember this very type of modal transition.

The Weimar Republic had its own background tradition of M_2 Christians—Lutherans, Junkers, et al—who in the 1920s were out of power. The new Republic, which replaced them, was "the first modern culture," according to historian Peter Gay; regarded as the opposite of Christianity, it was a hotbed of pioneering D_2s in every intellectual field, including art and science, flourishing under the benevolent gaze of the new political establishment. The government was a coalition of three democratic parties, each a variant of D_1 and thus concerned primarily to secure concrete-bound compromises among pressure groups. Both types of D were against Hitler, but neither offered philosophic opposition, mostly because of their disdain for ideology, but partly also because of the continuous demands on the D_1s to cope with successive emergencies and pay their bills. In addition, it was difficult to argue with Hitler when both they and he agreed on the same conventional and uncontroversial code of ethics—namely, the ethics of duty, of sacrifice to (German) society. Seeing all this and the economic disasters to which it led, the German people despised the Weimar Republic, ridiculed the politicians as unprincipled non-entities, and cursed the nihilists as "cultural Bolsheviks" (a term that mistakenly equates nihilism with Communism). Meanwhile, the German youth—roving bands of seemingly ungovernable, guitar-strumming hippies (as they were called in the sixties)—were disenchanted with everything adult. All these rebels, fanned by the public and nearing a boil, knew of only one alternative mode. With the triple trigger of the Versailles Treaty, the runaway inflation of 1923, and the depression of 1929, the nation voted that alternative into power. Like the rest of the country, the ungovernable youth at once fell into line. Hitler told them their duty, and they dropped their guitars. What they picked up instead we know.

In a highly educated nation governed by civilized, law-abiding democrats within a culture whose respectable political voices, dominating such media as then existed, were almost always on the left, a "blood-and-soil"-spewing maniac identified as a rightist rose from the gutter to the throne, and then, virtually unopposed, annihilated the entire D enterprise. It seemed inconceivable before it happened, and still so when it did happen—and to many it still seems so. But it happened.

There are limits to the German parallel. The government here is not (yet) the fragile reed of Weimar. More broadly, Americans, even leaving aside the question of their sense of life, are far more rational and individualistic than the Germans ever were, and are to that extent less susceptible to a totalitarian takeover. But such differences do not by themselves invalidate the German parallel, either. The pagans were far more rational and individualistic than the Christians. But virtue without consistency or defense is historically impotent.

Form of an American M_2

Although the DIM Hypothesis can predict only the mode to come, it is possible, within the context of a given DIM prediction, to glean from independent observation something of the specific form an American M_2 will take.

First, the M_2 movement in America, in my judgment, will be religious; it will not present itself as secular nor as the means to worldly success; nor will it appeal to science for its validation. I infer this not only from the positions of the M_2 leadership, whose favorite target is secular humanism, but also—after the horrors of Russia and Germany—from the culture-wide disillusion with modern-style totalitarianism. Social planners now seem to understand that omnipotent government and an industrial standard of living are mutually exclusive, and we have seen which alternative our intellectuals are choosing. Also relevant here are the strong anti-Communism of Americans in particular—and the declining prestige almost everywhere of science.

Because religion is not restricted to one particular church or dogma, we cannot rule out several possibilities (not yet probabilities) in this context, such as schisms within today's M_2 movement, the fading of a current favorite due to scandal, the rise of a newly created religion, or even invasion by a foreign religion able to popularize itself. Given the present state of the country new contenders would have to offer at least some appearance of allegiance to or at least compatibility with Christianity. But the result might no longer look much like the Christianity familiar to us today. A country ready for takeover cannot limit the invitation to only one candidate.

Besides its religious commitment, it is highly probable that an M_2 movement here (especially if not foreign-based) will appeal to the nation's strongly patriotic citizenry by stressing its own admiration of America and of American exceptionalism. The M_2s will declare, as they now do, that America is the greatest nation in history, and that this greatness is a blessing from God. Of course, by its nature, the M_2 mind will reinterpret Americanism: Patriotism would likely become nationalism; individualism, collectivism; and liberty, pious obedience.

As to the capitalist advocacy of private property, it is highly likely, in the light of American anti-Communism, that private property would be retained in name, but used and disposed of in fact according to the decisions of the totalitarian state (which would be merely an extension of our present D_1 view of private property). If the new regime, once consolidated, then follows the course taken by all its predecessors—this one is likely, but less certain—it would adopt some version of group warfare, pitting the poor against the rich and/or, more likely, its own people against the rest of the world: God-fearing Americans versus godless foreigners. The next step would be to give God's word its due world dominance, which would require control by the regime of the world's thought, to be gained by some form of crusade against the infidels.[302]

Private property as the official but merely rhetorical policy at home, along with nationalist aggression to spread the truth abroad—these policies are not broad abstractions but a specific program. It would have been impossible in the medieval era, before the breakup of Christendom into nations and before the Industrial Revolution. Nor could this program have been adopted in a Communist state, with its demand for public ownership of the means of production and its elevation of economic class above nation as the locus of value. The program impossible to both these groups was accepted as essential by one and only one totalitarian movement so far. The program was the distinctive form of M_2 upheld and carried out by Hitler.

Not just a religious totalitarianism, but a religious-fascist totalitarianism—that is my prediction of the American future.

When It Will Happen

The Christians needed centuries after Jesus to take over the West. Not only did they lack technology, but they had the daunting task of turning pagans into ascetics or at least respecters of ascetics. Although the later pagans were intellectually and increasingly vulnerable, it took the Christians a long stretch of time to defeat the ideas (and derivative institutions) inherent in the worldly element of M_1. The modern M_2s, by contrast, have been able to move fast. The Communists—counting from Marx to the Soviet Union—took about seventy years; it took Hitler, emerging at the end of World War I, only about fifteen. The moderns had technology and the modern era's relative speed on their side in effecting modal change. Most important, however, they encountered no meaningful philosophic opposition. The Soviets faced a long-supernaturalist, faith-embracing (Russian Orthodox) country—in other words, one steeped in a variant of their own M_2 ideology. The Nazis faced Germany's powerful traditional M_2 groups (supplemented by the Communists) with the Weimar coalition preaching in essence a vacuum.

Our own M_2s, clearly, have a much easier task than that of the ancient Christians. Like their modern European ancestors, the New American Christians are making full use of the available technology; they too are on the fast track of modern change; they too face no philosophical opposition. And when the triggering crises strike, they too, like the Nazis, stand to be the only beneficiaries—the only ones able to speak up—to offer connected answers, not piecemeal trial balloons, and for this reason to be listened to by the country.

If we date the rise of the New Christians from their start in the Reagan years with the emergence of groups like the Moral Majority, the M_2s here have taken about thirty years to reach their current prominence. They have made this progress—in recruitment, training, and cultural placement—with remarkable speed, gaining a following of which, at the time of Reagan, no one dreamed.

What the M_2 forces still need to produce are more intellectuals to disseminate their ideas more widely, along with a variety of cultural creators in all the key areas, especially literature and education—in order to reach and help shape the public, and thereby to create an ever-growing Christian base. Such a development would bring forth the kind of charismatic leader who knows how to use these assets.

If the speed of M_2 progress here so far is maintained—what is there to slow it down?—it is not undue pessimism to estimate the time of takeover as being relatively close. As the bromide puts it, "It's later than you think."

To succeed, we must remember, the M_2s need not convert or even appease the establishment, but must merely create and channel the social pressure necessary to unseat it. Nor need they win over a majority of the country, but merely an active, sizable minority who know how to stride to a goal through the philosophical vacuum surrounding them. And there is another factor relevant to time here: momentum. Typically, a movement without opposition accelerates as it develops, growing ever faster as its strength opens more doors to money and power, and as nonconverts begin to see where their authorities and friends are going.

So: when? Leaving aside for now the issue of the American sense of life and the possible emergence of a new and competing mode, we must factor in the following: the time frame of the modern antecedents of the M_2s in modally similar conditions, while abstracting away from inapplicable differences; the speed of the M_2s' progress here so far, and the amount of preparation they must still complete; the time frame within which a decisive trigger can be expected to occur; and the speed of the D_1 atrophy.

No exact figure can emerge from these factors, but all in all, it could not take anything like the time required by the early Christians—nor, I think, could it happen nearly as rapidly as in Germany. Other things being equal, I would project a time span for the M_2 takeover here neither of centuries nor of mere years, but of decades. A public disenchantment with the Christians for some reason might slow them (or their replacement) down; and a public disaffection from the establishment more intense than presently known might speed the movement up.

Given all these factors and being as specific as one can be, I estimate the M_2 triumph to be complete within another forty to fifty years at the latest—say, two generations. On current evidence, though, it might very well be a generation earlier.

This estimate rests on two factors: my theory of DIM categories, and my application of the theory to current America. That is, it rests on the validity of the DIM Hypothesis, and of my reading of the current American scene. This last may be mistaken even if the DIM theory is sound. But I do not think it is mistaken, and I stand by my conclusion.

If my prediction does not come true within this time frame, that fact, in my eyes, would refute it, no matter what happens thereafter. Anyone can predict a bad future "ultimately," but that is Nostradamus, not reason. If the M_2s, given my reading of the current state of the United States, cannot consolidate their power in another fifty years, then I do not see how they could do so later. If—with no new philosophic invasion—they prove to be that weak and/or some non-DIM opponent proves to be that strong, I would have to say either that we are not living in an era of modal transition, or at least not one involving a D/M_2 changeover; or that the DIM theory as such does not apply. In which case, I am at a loss, unable to make any prediction, or even to identify in DIM terms where we are now.

As I write, however, the evidence supports the DIM analysis. It seems fantastic to believe that America—the land of the free and the home of the riches they created—is now moving toward an age of poverty, obedience, and secret police. But given the facts, where else can we be headed?

As I have often said, a mode of integration, once established in a society, is a difficult thing to change, because it governs the people's process of thinking about and evaluating a proposed change. Historically, with a few exceptions inapplicable here, the life span of any kind of mode, once in power, has ranged from about one hundred fifty years to about a thousand years.

If M_2 does happen here, the likelihood is that it will not be a mere phase. It will not go away soon.

Can the DIM Prediction Be Certain?

No prediction of the success even of a growing mode is *certain*—not if there is some evidence pointing to the triumph of a different mode. In epistemology, "certain" denotes a case in which all available evidence points to one conclusion and none to any other. If, however, there is evidence, objective albeit slender, suggesting a different conclusion, then neither of them is certain. In such a case, the one supported by the preponderance of the evidence is described as "probable"; the other, because it has some basis in fact, even though not much, is called "possible." These assessments subsume a large range of measurements, such as barely possible, a real possibility, a good bet, highly probable, all but conclusive, and beyond all doubt.

In these terms, the takeover of America by the M_2s is not certain. In my judgment, it is only probable. But it is so highly probable as to border on certainty.

Besides the evidence provided by the present state of America, there is the evidence provided by the past—not merely the American past, but reaching back into the mists of pre-history. M_2, as we have seen, is unique: Subservience to something beyond the things we see, something accepted on faith has in pre-philosophical form been the orientation of the species from the start. From this perspective, America's trend today is not a mere fad; it has deeper roots. The nation is moving to regress to the mind of primitivism, which, it seems, despite all the values produced by modern civilization, remains ineradicable in the species. Twice, for a brief span, the West has escaped from the pull of the non-rational, and twice it succumbed. "It is earlier," Ayn Rand once remarked, "than you think."

This is why an M_2 future is so probable. Given America's present condition and the historical factors, it is almost impossible to overestimate the likelihood of its occurrence.

America, it has often been said correctly, is the most religious of the industrial nations, and at the same time it has built the strongest wall separating state and religion. This is the combination that will have defeated it. Metaphysics trumps politics, especially when the metaphysics resonates with the whole of human history.

Is There Still Hope?

The DIM perspective gives us a distinctive, <u>epistemological</u> means by which to understand the American dilemma and the force pushing the country to its fatal destiny. The basic premise of DIM theory is the fundamental role of integration in human thought. If this is true, we would expect to discover that the basic conflicts among men ultimately have to do with integration. Today, this conflict takes a post-Kantian and thus unprecedented cultural form: floating abstractions versus concrete-boundedness. Even though, as a purely philosophical judgment, these are equally great errors, the present state of our country is evidence that men can tolerate the rule of one of these errors, but not of the other. They have lived for millennia, however poorly, when guided by concepts detached from percepts, and now when in trouble they yearn to do so again. Men, it seems, cannot cope for long with life in a world of percepts detached from concepts.

Floating abstractions give men a sense of integration, of the whole, and thus at least the illusion of understanding the world and knowing what to do in it. Concrete-boundedness gives men nothing but the sky above and the cave under their feet.

The only way to uproot a philosophy is to replace it with another—in the present case, to replace both errors, M and D, with some form of Aristotle. Just as the Aristotelian approach defeated the medieval M_2s, so it alone can defeat their descendants. My claim that an M_2 success is not yet certain depends on my view that a resurgence of Aristotle is still possible. There is some evidence now pointing to the germ of an I revolution in the United States—that is, to an I philosophy with cultural potential here.

The only current philosophy of this kind known to me is the one I myself accept and on which the DIM Hypothesis rests: Ayn Rand's philosophy of Objectivism. Since I have presented her system elsewhere,

I will not attempt to summarize it here. In the context of this discussion, I can merely observe that she rejects both M and D, both Plato and Kant. She defines an Aristotelian approach purified for the first time of all Platonic accretions, a system that makes no concessions to philosophic antagonists. As an Aristotelian, she repudiates the supernatural, but not as the Ds do, through their Kantian negation of all reality. She repudiates it as an arbitrary projection that contradicts everything we know about reality through the exercise of perception and reason. With the full consistency Aristotle lacked, she gives us a view of the world made not of floating abstractions or unrelated concretes, but of a fully naturalistic "One in the Many." In this way, she is the historic nemesis of all forms of M. She goes far beyond a short-run intimidation of the otherworldly mentality, which is all that her predecessors—whether polytheists, deists, or positivists—could do. In regard to the phenomenon of religion in all its forms, her work leaves behind not a temporarily cowering body, but a corpse with a stake in its heart.

Is it possible for such a radical philosophy to take root and spread in the United States within the time still left to us?

As of 2010, Ayn Rand's books had sold over twenty-seven million copies; fifty years after the publication of *Atlas Shrugged*, to the astonishment of the publishing world, its sales skyrocketed, more than tripling. These are huge figures for non-genre backlist titles condemned by academia. A small but growing movement of her admirers, mainly in the United States, is visible, mostly among college students in the soft fields and professionals in the hard. Yaron Brook, the executive director of the Ayn Rand Institute, has estimated that those who accept and to some extent can articulate Ayn Rand's fundamental principles probably number somewhere in the five-figure range—at most, perhaps, a hundred thousand. Compared to the millions of Ms and Ds, this makes Is by a vast margin the smallest group today. Although many of them are active in cultural areas, there is as yet no appreciable Ayn Rand presence in the four fields we have been studying. There is a slowly increasing Objectivist presence in college philosophy departments, though Ayn Rand's ideas are not yet a significant academic factor; indeed, as I have indicated, most academics are either ignorant of or hostile to them.

Although this movement is now real and has begun to grow, it is evidently still in its infancy. Can it, in the time remaining, produce a generation of what Ayn Rand calls "new intellectuals" capable of establishing a dominant presence in academia and thence in the culture, and thereby reach and liberate the Nature-and-science-loving character of the American public, assuming that such is indeed what at bottom the public really loves? Clearly, success in such a daunting task is not probable, given the preponderance of counter-evidence. But is it still possible? Is there some evidence to support at least the minimal claim that it is barely possible?

My answer is yes. Though such success is highly unlikely, it is still barely possible. I do not base this answer simply on the fact of man's free will, which cannot achieve miracles and could not save a country that was already past the point of no return. Rather, I base my optimism, if it can be called that, on two specifically American assets already indicated, each of which is historically unique.

The philosophy we need has now been formulated in its pure, and therefore most powerful form. And it is addressed to the only nation ever to have been founded explicitly on ideas—and not only on ideas, but on the ideas of the Enlightenment, the most rational period since the Greeks. We have already concluded that the Enlightenment legacy *may* still be alive here as a sense of life.

A philosophy largely unknown in the country and the possibility of a receptive though now merely implicit national subconscious are certainly not a juggernaut. But they are not nothing, either. In Germany and Russia a century ago, there was no such evidence on either count, nothing to suggest that *maybe* an M_2 takeover could be stopped. There was no sign of an I philosophy or movement, however small, and no sign in the national past or observed character to suggest that, if such a new philosophy had been presented to the country, it would have received a positive response, either from the intellectuals or the general public. On the contrary, it is a certainty that in both countries an I philosophy would have been viewed not only as false, but as evil.

Cases such as Germany and Russia define *impossible* in the present context. And we are not yet one of them.

So, again: when? If a modal changeover to I is possible, how long would it take, assuming for a moment the best from the I viewpoint: a growing movement of Objectivist intellectuals spreading rational ideas to the academy, thence to the culture, and thence to a receptive American subconscious? To assume the best, we must posit that the I spokesmen remain free to write and speak—that is, that they are not forcibly silenced by a new theocracy.

Judging by the I cases in the past, it would take a long time to happen. It took the Greeks centuries—how many we do not know—to emerge from primitivism and develop into rational men intoxicated by thought. It took more than three centuries after the rediscovery of Aristotle for the West to emerge from the M era and enter the Enlightenment. How long then would it take a new form of I philosophy to win a similar kind of battle? On the one hand, the new philosophy is stronger than its predecessors. On the other hand, this very strength makes it an unprecedented threat to the other modes.

Taking everything into account, it turns out that the most optimistic timetable I can reach matches closely the independently reached projection of an Objectivist banker-philosopher for whom I have long had the greatest respect: John Allison, not an unworldly academic like me, but the highly successful and nationally known longtime CEO of BB&T.

It would take twenty-five years from now, we think, for Objectivism to reach the point when one could see that in another twenty-five years it would dominate the intellectual world, and then about two generations more to move from intellectual to cultural and finally political dominance. In short, it would take something on the order of a century to win out.

Even Kant, who could count on all the entrenched Christian premises along with the whole progression of modern philosophy before him, required several decades to take over the mind of the West, and fifty years more to overthrow the Enlightenment politics. By contrast, Objectivism, far from relying on entrenched ideas, declares war on them. In this context, the projection of an Objectivist victory as requiring a century cannot be regarded as unrealistic or defeatist. The Kantians had the additional advantage of proselytizing in a free and stable I or early D_1 era, whereas today the probability of M_2 success means the improbability that even the partial freedom we still enjoy can be sustained for another whole century.

If there is to be a race between M_2 and I, it seems, one side will have an almost insuperable advantage: A religion of some kind in all likelihood would come to power fifty years earlier and then remove the possibility of public opposition. There can always be unexpected gains or setbacks on either side. If the Is do make major strides, that might slow down the other side. But on present evidence, to the extent that it can be identified and weighed objectively, I cannot see that such ups and downs will affect the modal outcome.

The evidence of another, better outcome, however, even though the Enlightenment's legacy is visibly shrinking, is still there. "Almost insuperable" entails "can still be defeated," and no one so far can validly remove the "almost." At this point no one can prove that America has passed the point of no return. To be sure, I cannot project in much detail the steps of the scenario by which the possible I victory becomes an actuality; I cannot concretize the passage from now to then. But the possible, by definition, is that which by some means, even though not yet fully known, *can* become the actual. And, in an issue where a given outcome is possible to men, free will *can* achieve "miracles."

I do not write my final book as Cassandra preaching resignation before the Apocalypse.

The high probability of a monstrous evil should not induce paralysis in those who see it coming. It should lead not to the end of action, but to the beginning. It is a paradox, but still a truth: The worse the coming future, the *more* it should motivate its opponents—the more it should strengthen their passion to defend themselves and their values against the approaching onslaught, even when the odds of their failure are high, so long as there is still a chance of success.

If your beloved is strolling unwittingly toward the edge of a cliff and you are so far away that even if you run at top speed and scream at top volume you very probably will not be heard, even then you do not give up, shrug, and ponder the tragedy of existence, not if you really do love her. For every moment she is still alive, you keep on running and screaming, however much your lungs and your throat have turned to fire. You do it because rescue is possible—barely possible, but still really possible.

In most cases in life, the probable outcome, by definition, is the one that occurs. But not always. Across the ages, men have on occasion been able to achieve a cherished goal even when facing seemingly insuperable odds. The greatest Western example of this took place, fittingly, in ancient Greece.

In 480 B.C., in the Battle of Thermopylae, three hundred Spartans (with modest assistance) led by King Leonidas repulsed for three days hundreds of thousands of barbaric Persian invaders led by Xerxes I (Herodotus says there were over a million of them). During the three days, the Spartans were killed to the last man, but their indomitable character won out: The Athenians had been given enough time to prepare for and later defeat the enemy in a historic naval battle. Against incalculable odds, the Oriental mystics had lost, and Western civilization, which would otherwise have been strangled in its cradle, had been saved.

Now, in more modern dress, the mystics are invading again, this time from within. To repulse them, we, too, must be Spartans (in regard to courage, not philosophy). The odds we face are about as lopsided. But at least our weapons are stronger: We can repulse the enemy not merely with spears, but with that which ultimately moves the world—ideas. "History is philosophy teaching by examples," Dionysius of Halicarnassus told us in 30 B.C. We have the philosophy now. What remains is to make history with it.[303]

To win the battle for America will not be possible much longer.

Irvine, CA
2004–2011

ENDNOTES

CHAPTER ONE

1   Ayn Rand, *Introduction to Objectivist Epistemology*, 2nd ed. (New York: Meridian, 1990), p. 13.
2   Ibid., p. 63. In this book, Ayn Rand presents her theory of concepts in full.
3   Integration is not man's only cognitive ability. Indeed, there would be nothing to "put together" if we could not differentiate; we can grasp the One in the Many only if we have the ability to grasp the Many. My point is that the role of differentiation (and other processes) in human cognition is as a precondition necessary to create and use man's new faculty of mental compression. Animals can differentiate, in many situations better than men, but they cannot use their differentiations as data for integration. So they remain on the perceptual level. The uniquely human problem in cognition is not to grasp differences among objects, but to learn how and when to ignore them, in the sense of abstracting from the objects their similarities. Differentiation is essential to thought, but as such it is not thought. Integration is.
4   See Rand, *Introduction*, pp. 88–89.

CHAPTER TWO

5   Walter Burkert, *Greek Religion* (Oxford: Blackwell, 1985), p. 322. *Plato: The Collected Dialogues*, ed. Edith Hamilton & Huntington Cairns (New York: Bollingen, 1961), p. 49, *Phaedo* 66e.
6   *Sophist*, p. 259d-e, trans. Robert Mayhew in personal communication. For the conventional translation, see ibid., p. 1006.
7   Aristotle, *Posterior Analytics*, *Works*, ed. W. D. Ross, trans. G. R. G. Mure (Oxford: Clarendon Press, 1925), 100a10.
8   The term "One in the Many," which, following tradition, I employ throughout, suggests what Ayn Rand rejects as the "intrinsicist" approach. I am using the phrase in a broader sense, however, to subsume the advocacy of any secular factor, intrinsic or otherwise, taken as uniting the Many while preserving the reality of the individual constituents.

9   For an eloquent defense of the Kantian view of logic, see *Prolegomena Logica* by Henry Mansel.

10   For a fuller discussion of Kant's nihilism, see Rand's *Introduction*.

11   This interpretation of Kant's ethics is presented in my book *The Ominous Parallels* (New York: Meridian, 1993), see chapter four, esp. pp. 74–84.

12   The negativity of modern culturati does not derive from their experience of twentieth-century wars, concentration camps, and mass slaughter. Their attitude is philosophical, as their own spokesmen make clear. The schools of education do not offer the World Wars as a root of Progressive education; nor do Joyce's followers invoke Auschwitz to explain *Ulysses*. Indeed, Modernism in every key cultural area appeared first in the last two decades of the nineteenth century, when peace and freedom were still the rule in the West.

13   Don Tompson, personal communication, August 11, 1998.

14   It is interesting to note here that the Big Three often reinterpret a contradictory idea in ways that minimize the clash. Plato's paganism is Spartan, not Athenian; Aristotle's "pure form" is miles from Plato's ineffable Good; Kant's demand for sacrifice as an end in itself is a break with the age-old Christian bargain offering heaven later for virtue now. In these cases, it seems, the essential integration works to subvert and thereby marginalize a clashing non-essential.

15   In the words of his contemporary Moses Mendelssohn, Kant is "the all-destroyer."

CHAPTER THREE

16   For a discussion of this overview, see Ayn Rand, *For the New Intellectual* (New York: New American Library, 1961), title essay, and my *Objectivism: The Philosophy of Ayn Rand* (New York: Meridian, 1993), pp. 451–59.

17   *The Essential Comte*, ed. Stanislav Andreski, trans. Margaret Clarke (London: Croom Helm, 1974), p. 34.

18   Comte believed that he himself had discovered important universal generalizations, although his followers soon dropped such ambitious claims.

19   Within this Kantian context, Mill himself was a champion of causality, renowned for identifying five methods of discovering cause and effect.

20   John Stuart Mill, *An Examination of Sir William Hamilton's Philosophy*, vol. 1, 3rd ed. (London: Longmans, Green, 1865), p. 331.

CHAPTER FOUR

21   There is a level much lower than that of the unphilosophical producer: the mindless copier. Though outside of any modal category, such a person may within limits produce a work that does have a DIM identity, by virtue of its similarity to the products of the creators being copied.

22   For a similar reason, I do not apply DIM to such scientific areas as oceanography, meteorology, anatomy, and the like. These pursuits, limited as they are to a relatively lower level of abstraction, are too closely connected to specific observations to allow their practitioners much freedom to depart from fact.

23   When a cultural creator knows enough to apply a mode consistently to his own work, then both he and his product share the same DIM classification; this is by far the commonest case. There are, however, other possibilities, including creators

who—not through error, but through choice—apply a given mode only in part, and thus inconsistently. These individuals may believe that conflicting modes properly apply to different attributes of their products, or even to different features within the same attribute. Or, a different case, an individual may regard a certain attribute as unimportant and not worth much effort and so present a product that is modally guided in some attributes, but accidental in others. Or he may grant the importance of modal consistency, but violate its requirements through fear of offending his contemporaries. In all such cases, modal analysis can do no more than identify the inconsistencies. As a rule, the latter diminishes a product's influence. But if one of the modes is dominant in the work, that is the one the work will help to prevail.

CHAPTER FIVE

24 *Encyclopædia Britannica*, "Architecture, The History of Western Classicism, 1750–1830."
Classicism was not the first literary rebellion against the medievals. Renaissance innovators such as Shakespeare and Cervantes illustrate the non-medievalism of the period. The Renaissance, however, is a transitional, not a fully modern culture; as such I treat it at the end of chapter eleven.

25 Victor Hugo, "Preface to *Cromwell* (1827)," *Harvard Classics* (New York: Collier, 1909), vol. 39, see pp. 354–408. Paul Landis, *Six Plays by Corneille and Racine* (New York: Modern Library, 1931), pp. viii–ix.

26 *A Guide to the Study of Literature: A Companion Text for Core Studies 6*, "Introduction to Neoclassicism," academic.brooklyn.cuny.edu, October 7, 2010.

27 Will & Ariel Durant, *The Story of Civilization: Part IX* (New York: Simon & Schuster, 1965), *The Age of Voltaire*, p. 165. Ibid.

28 John Milton, *Paradise Lost and Paradise Regained*, ed. Christopher Ricks (New York: Signet, 1968), p. 68, p. 59.

29 Ibid., p. 59.

30 Ibid., p. 35.

31 Ibid., p. 299.

32 Ibid., p. 125.

33 See Ayn Rand, *The Romantic Manifesto*, 2nd rev. ed. (New York: Signet, 1975), especially chapter six.

34 Hugo, op. cit., p. 408.

35 Rand, *Romantic Manifesto*, p. 99.

36 Ibid., p. 82. Aristotle, *Poetics*, *Works*, vol. XI, ed. W. D. Ross, trans. Ingram Bywater (Oxford: Clarendon Press, 1924), 1459a20.

37 Rand, *Romantic Manifesto*, p. 168. Aristotle, *Poetics*, 1451b.

38 Presenting a theme is not the same as didacticism or proselytizing. If a work not only offers a number of speeches, but presents a perceptually re-created reality, then that reality is the essence of the work, which offers the reader a unique kind of experience, not a series of lessons. By observing concrete events and characters, however, the reader *can* grasp an abstract meaning, but the meaning as such is not art, but theory. *Anna Karenina*, *Gone With the Wind*, *Atlas Shrugged* have themes, but none of these are didactic, even though the reader does learn from them. A theme without characters or story is a very different case; such a work offers only lessons, which are usually political propaganda. A Romanticist theme may or may not be stated

explicitly; in this issue, length is irrelevant to classification. The point is not quantity of words, but their connection to the events and characters presented in the work.

39   Hugo, op. cit., p. 392.

40   Ibid., p. 26.

41   "Realism and Naturalism," *Columbus State Community College*, global.cscc.edu, March 26, 2007.

42   Ayn Rand, *The Art of Fiction* (New York: Plume, 2000), p. 139.

43   John Barth, "The Literature of Replenishment (1979)," *The Electronic Labyrinth*, elab.eserver.org, March 26, 2007. Christopher Keep, Tim McLaughlin, & Robin Parmar, "Postmodernism and the Postmodern Novel (2000)," *Labyrinth* above.

44   Gertrude Stein, *What Are Masterpieces?* (New York: Pitman Publishing, 1970), p. 88.

45   Donald Heiney & Lenthiel H. Downs, *Recent American Literature after 1930* (Woodbury, NY: Barron's, 1973), p. 271.

46   Thomas Mann and similar figures are not full Modernists, but eclectics—so inconsistent as to be unclassifiable.

47   Rand, *Romantic Manifesto*, pp. 76–77.

48   Barth, op. cit.

49   Socialist Realism should not be confused with social realism. The latter is a form of Naturalism that emphasizes the depiction of social injustices.

50   James Muckle, *A Guide to the Soviet Curriculum* (London: Croom Helm, 1988), p. 107.

51   Jeffrey Brooks, "Socialist Realism in *Pravda*: Read All About It!" *Slavic Review*, vol. 53, no. 4, Winter, 1994. Kendall E. Bailes, *Technology and Society under Lenin and Stalin, 1917–41* (Princeton: Princeton University Press, 1978), pp. 386–89.

52   Jeffrey Brooks, "Revolutionary Lives: Public Identities in *Pravda* During the 1920s," *New Directions in Soviet History*, ed. Stephen White (New York: Cambridge University Press, 1992), pp. 27–40. "Predannost'" means "devotion . . . with all its religious connotations. . . ." (*Pravda* 8/24/34)

53   Aleksandr Fadeev, "Young Guard (1947)," *SovLit.com*, sovlit.com/youngguard, April 25, 2007.

CHAPTER SIX

54   *Philosophical Writings of Descartes*, trans. John Cottingham, Robert Stoothoff, & Dugald Murdoch (Cambridge, England: Cambridge University Press, 1985), vol. 1, p. 288.

55   Ibid., p. 266.

56   Isaac Newton, *Opticks*, based on the 4th ed., London 1730 (New York: Dover, 1952), p. 404.

57   Newton, *Principia*, trans. Andrew Motte, rev. Florian Cajori (Berkeley: University of California Press, 1934), *Vol. 2: The System of the World*, p. 545. Ibid., *Rules of Reasoning*, no. 3, p. 398. Newton, *Opticks*, p. 404. He is aware that scientists may encounter new phenomena that require previous conclusions to be reformulated. He covers this by saying that inductive conclusions in science are "accurately or very nearly true"; this does not, however, significantly affect his claim that what he has established is true.

58   *Principia*, pp. 43–44.

59 Benjamin Brodie, *The Atomic Debates*, ed. W. H. Brock, quoted in *The Logical Leap*, David Harriman (New York: Penguin, 2010), p. 217.

60 Harriman, ibid., p. 216. Immanuel Kant, *Kant's Philosophy of Material Nature*, trans. James W. Ellington (Indianapolis: Hackett, 1985), p. 93. John Stuart Mill, *A System of Logic* (London: Longmans, 1959), p. 310.

61 Igor Naletov, *Alternatives to Positivism*, trans. Vladimir Stankevich (Moscow: Progress Publishers, 1984).

62 Friedrich Kekulé, quoted in Mary Jo Nye, *Molecular Reality* (New York: American Elsevier, 1972), pp. 4–5. Marcellin Berthelot, quoted in Harriman, op. cit., p. 220.

63 Ernst Mach, *History and Root of the Principle of the Conservation of Energy*, trans. Philip E. B. Jourdain (Chicago: Open Court, 1911), p. 74. Mach, *The Analysis of Sensations* (1897), trans. M. C. Williams and Sydney Waterlow (New York: Dover, 1959), p. 30.

64 Naletov, op. cit.

65 Max Jammer, *Einstein and Religion: Physics and Theology* (Princeton: Princeton University Press, 1999), p. 57.

66 Einstein, "Autobiographical Notes," in *Albert Einstein: Philosopher-Scientist*, ed. Paul Schilpp (New York: MJF Books, 1949), p. 81. Einstein, *Essays in Physics* (New York: Philosophical Library, 1950), p. 34.

67 Descartes, op. cit., p. 245. "Reminiscences of Einstein," *Some Strangeness in the Proportion*, ed. H. Woolf (Reading, MA: Addison-Wesley, 1980), p. 523.

68 Einstein, *Out of My Later Years* (New York: Citadel Press, 1956), pp. 96, 72.

69 Jammer, *Einstein and Religion*, p. 131.

70 Einstein, *Out of My Later Years*, p. 61.

71 Einstein, *Relativity: The Special and General Theory*, trans. Robert W. Lawson (New York: Crown, 1961), p. 162.

72 Max Jammer, *Concepts of Space*, 3rd ed. (New York: Dover, 1993), p. 163.

73 Sometimes, in a religious mood, Einstein seems to conceive the One as being more akin to a mystic's wholeness than to the equations of science. When he is in this frame of mind, "Individual existence impresses him as a sort of prison, and he wants to experience the universe as a single significant whole." (Einstein quoted in Jammer, *Einstein and Religion*, p. 78). This kind of mysticism, however, was never offered by Einstein as his view qua physicist.

74 Werner Heisenberg, *Physics and Philosophy* (New York: Harper & Row, 1958), p. 48.

75 Dugald Murdoch, *Niels Bohr's Philosophy of Physics* (New York: Cambridge University Press, 1990), p. 31.

76 Heisenberg, op. cit., p. 41.

77 Harriman, *The Philosophic Corruption of Physics* (Los Angeles: Ayn Rand Institute, 1997).

78 John Gribbin, *In Search of Schrödinger's Cat* (New York: Bantam Books, 1984), p. 205. Heisenberg, op. cit., p. 201. David Finkelstein quoted in *Quantum Reality*, Nick Herbert (New York: Anchor Books, 1987), p. 21.

79 P. C. W. Davies, *The Ghost in the Atom* (Cambridge, England: Cambridge University Press, 1986), p. 31.

80 Murdoch, op. cit., pp. 106, 221.

81 Ibid., p. 218.

82 *Quantum Questions: Mystical Writings of the World's Great Physicists*, ed. Ken Wilber (Boston: New Science Library, 1985), p. 181, p. 9.

83 Bohr quoted in Murdoch, op. cit., p. 55. Quoted in *Einstein: His Life and Universe*, Walter Isaacson (New York: Simon & Schuster, 2007), p. 324.

84 George Johnson, "Challenging Particle Physics as Path to Truth," *The New York Times*, December 4, 2001.

85 Lederman, public television, *Closer to Truth*, "When and How Did this Universe Begin?" Show 105. George Johnson, *The New York Times*, July 14, 1998.

86 Lawrence M. Krauss, "Science and Religion Share Fascination in Things Unseen," *The New York Times*, November 8, 2005. David Gross, quoted in Ed Regis, *Who Got Einstein's Office?* (Princeton: Perseus, 1987), p. 273.

87 Paul Ginsberg & Sheldon L. Glashow, "Desperately Seeking Superstrings," *Physics Today*, May 1986.

88 The M_2 category is usually associated with a totalitarian state, which mandates a mode of integration for all human endeavors which it regards as significant to its purpose. But the M_2 mentality, as the only mode that sweeps aside the Many without restriction, does not regard science as significant. There is no distinctive Communist approach to motion, electromagnetism, particle theory, and the rest. The Communists' only concern with science has been its practical results: its support of or threat to the ideology, and its ability to produce military weapons. So no theory of physics or of the proper mode of integration in science has been offered by the movement. In art and education, totalitarian purpose dictates a specific modal treatment; in physics, by contrast, it mostly leads to picking at random the pockets of scientists. Insofar as totalitarians do make reference to laws of the physical world, I cover this in the movement's metaphysics.

CHAPTER SEVEN

89 William Boyd & Edmund J. King, *The History of Western Education*, 12th ed. (Lanham, MD: Barnes & Noble, 1995), pp. 174–75.

90 Benjamin Franklin, *The Writings of Benjamin Franklin*, ed. Albert Henry Smyth (New York: Macmillan, 1905), vol. 2, p. 394.

91 *Encyclopædia Britannica*, "Development of Western Education: The Renaissance."

92 Ibid.

93 *Encyclopædia Britannica*, "Development of Western Education: The 17th Century." Johann Amos Comenius, *The Great Didactic of John Amos Comenius*, ed. M. W. Keatinge (London: Adam & Charles Black, 1896), p. 337. John Locke, *Some Thoughts Concerning Education*, 7th ed. (London: A. & F. Churchill, 1712), p. 245.

94 David V. Hicks, *Norms & Nobility* (Lanham, MD: University Press of America, 1999), pp. 19, 144.

95 *Encyclopædia Britannica*, "Modern Changes in U.S. Education."

96 Robert R. Rusk, *Doctrines of the Great Educators*, 4th ed. (London: Macmillan, 1969), p. 312.

97 Charles Vandegriffe, Sr., *A Living Legacy* (Longwood, FL: Xulon Press, 2004), p. 74.

98 Jim Stingley, review of *Escape from Childhood* (New York: E. P. Dutton, 1974) by John Holt, *Los Angeles Times*, July 28, 1974.

99 A. S. Neill, "Myths and Realities (2000)," *Summerhill* first-ask.de/summerhill2000, May 18, 2000. Aristotle, *Politics*, 1339a.

100 Alpine Valley School, users.aol.com/alpineval, May 18, 2000.

101 Boyd & King, op. cit., p. 405.

102 F. James Rutherford quoted in *The New York Times*, January 31, 1984.

103 Anemona Hartocollis, "The New, Flexible Math Meets Parental Rebellion," *The New York Times*, April 27, 2000. Wilfried Schmid quoted in Hartocollis, ibid.

104 Quoted in "Socializing Students for Anarchy," Glenn Woiceshyn, *Los Angeles Times*, February 18, 1997. John Dewey, *The School and Society* (Chicago: University of Chicago Press, 1956), p. 15.

105 Catherine S. Manegold, *The New York Times*, May 5, 1994. In his collectivist aspect, Dewey may be said to endorse a One of sorts, a Heraclitean One, so to speak: a flux of peer groups that absorb the individual. But collectivism is not distinctive to, or even consistently carried out in, Progressive education; those who are consistent about it, the M_2s, advocate a different approach to schooling.

106 John Taylor Gatto, *Dumbing Us Down* (Canada: New Society Publishers, 2002), p. 2.

107 Jacques Barzun, *Teacher in America* (Indianapolis: Liberty Press, 1981), p. 287.

108 Ayn Rand, *The Voice of Reason* (New York: Meridian, 1990), p. 214.

109 Barzun, op. cit., p. 148.

110 Debbie Stone, "This Teacher Commands Attention," *Wisconsin State Journal*, May 1, 1994.

111 V. I. Lenin, *Lenin on Literature and Art* (Rockville, MD: Wildside Press, 2008), p. 133.

112 Nadezhda Krupskaya, *On Labour-Oriented Education and Instruction* (Moscow: Progress Publishers, 1982), p. 116, emphasis in original.

113 Chris Trueman, "Nazi Germany and Education (2000)," *History Learning Site*, historylearningsite.co.uk, March 23, 2006.

114 For the Objectivist view of Montessori, see "The Objectivist," June 1984, p. 9.

115 As an example, David Harriman has worked out a curriculum for pre–high school physics. Across two years, he presents the history of physics from Greece to the present, showing the step-by-step derivation of each important law and theory; every principle, in essence, is learned by the method by which it was actually discovered. At each point, therefore, the class can understand with relative ease how and why the conclusions they hear were reached. Physics thus becomes to them not a collection of theories and laws, but an integrated whole derived from observation.

CHAPTER EIGHT

116 England was not an example of absolute monarchy, because of the supremacy of Parliament and the country's stronger tradition of liberty. Some English kings did endorse the divine-right theory, but without enjoying the corresponding power.

117 King James I quoted in Durant, vol. 7, p. 138. George H. Sabine, *A History of Political Theory*, 3rd ed. (New York: Holt, Rinehart & Winston, 1961), p. 396. Jean Domat, *Le droit public, suite des lois civiles dans leur ordre naturel*, *Works*, ed. Joseph Remy, *Oeuvres completes, nouvelle edition revue corrigée*, trans. Ruth Kleinman (Paris: Firmin-Didot, 1829), vol. 3.

118 Robert Filmer, *Patriarcha or the Natural Power of Kings*, EEBO Editions (reproduced from the London, 1680, original), p. 99. Edward McNall Burns, *Western Civilizations*, 7th ed. (New York: W. W. Norton, 1969), p. 560.

119 Domat, op. cit.

120 Filmer, op. cit. Sabine, op. cit., p. 393.

121 Sabine, ibid.

122 Alexander Hamilton, James Madison, and John Jay, *The Federalist* (Cambridge, MA: Glazier, Masters & Smith, 1842), p. 64. Individualism is a broader, moral-political term, which I do not use as a synonym for capitalism.

123 Peikoff, *Ominous Parallels*, p. 110.

124 Original provisional constitution (1766) of the State of New Hampshire. Samuel Adams, "Report of the Committee of Correspondence" (Nov. 20, 1772), in *Ideas in America*, ed. G. N. Grob & R. N. Beck (New York: Free Press, 1970), p. 107.

125 Ibid., p. 108.

126 *The Second Treatise of Government*, ed. T. P. Peardon (Indianapolis: Bobbs-Merrill, 1952), p. 15. This passage and others from Locke are quoted by Samuel Adams in *Report of the Committee*.

127 Some founding fathers—not the majority—did hold a negative view of human nature, and argued for limitations on government in order to prevent man's sinful-ness from leading to the rise of a dictator who would rape the country.

128 Charles Backus, *A Sermon Preached in Long-Meadow at the Publick Fast* (Spring-field, 1788), repr. Grob & Beck, op. cit., pp. 133–34. Isaac Kramnick & R. Laurence Moore, *The Godless Constitution* (New York: W. W. Norton, 1996), p. 17.

129 *The Godless Constitution*, ibid., p. 37. The 1797 Treaty of Tripoli mentioned in George F. Will, book review of *The Moral Minority* in *The New York Times*, October 22, 2006.

130 Ibid. J. M. Kelly, *A Short History of Western Legal Theory* (Oxford: Clarendon Press, 1999), p. 259.

131 John Locke, *An Essay Concerning Human Understanding*, ed. Alexander Campbell Fraser (New York: Dover, 1959), vol. 1, p. 137. Thomas Jefferson, *The Life and Writ-ings*, ed. S. E. Forman (Indianapolis: Bowen-Merrill, 1900), p. 242. Paragraph two of the Declaration of Independence. *The Federalist*, p. 92. Several word choices in the Declaration have been taken as evidence of the founders' inconsistency on this issue. The claim that "these truths are self-evident," for example, has been held to be rationalistic, since rights, the critics say, cannot be established on the basis of observation (a view with which many of the founders would disagree). But, it seems, the founders had no common view on meta-ethical questions, nor even much inter-est in them. It is more likely that they regarded "self-evident" not as a technical term denoting an epistemological category, but rather as a rhetorical synonym without deeper meaning for "obvious," "uncontroversial," and the like.

132 William James, "The Moral Philosopher and the Moral Life," *The Will to Believe and Other Essays in Popular Philosophy* (New York: Longmans, Green, 1896), p. 190, emphasis in original. The D_1 approach to law was defined by John Austin's legal positivism, which denies the possibility of objective law and therefore of law, any law, as being open to moral evaluation. So, he says, we must leave aside the meta-physical notion of proper law in the abstract; all we can know is the multiplicity of observable and not necessarily related laws of a specific state at a specific time. On this view, a citizen is obliged to obey the law because of "pain," in Austin's words—that is, because of the punishment the sovereign will inflict on the disobedient. Cf. Robert N. Beck, *Perspectives in Social Philosophy* (New York: Holt, Rinehart & Winston, 1967), p. 204. And since in a democracy the people are the sovereign, their subjective desires, whatever they be, are the ultimate authority.

133 Walter Lippmann, *The Essential Lippmann*, ed. Clinton Rossiter & James Lare (Cambridge: Harvard University Press, 1963), p. 190.

134 Washington Gladden, quoted in *Laissez Faire and the General-Welfare State*, "The Gospel of the Kingdom," Sermon, January 27, 1889, Gladden Papers. Ibid., emphases added.

135 Ibid. Ann Marlowe, "Strategy vs. Tactics in Afghanistan," *Wall Street Journal*, June 2, 2010.

136 John Dewey quoted in *Perspectives in Social Philosophy*, Beck, op. cit., p. 336. This viewpoint does not prevent Dewey or any of the pluralists from stating goal(s) in terms of broad abstractions, such as the common good or the public welfare. To pluralists, however, such terms are shorthand for the solutions of innumerable unrelated problems that have been dealt with piecemeal.

137 Edwin R. A. Seligman, "Continuity of Economic Thought," in Richard Theodore Ely et al, *Science Economic Discussion*, pp. 1–2.

138 Robert Ley quoted in E. Kohn-Bramstedt, *Dictatorship and Political Police* (London, 1945), p. 178. Marx quoted in *Marx's Concept of Man*, Erich Fromm (New York: Frederick Ungar, 1969), p. 78. Marx, *Economic and Philosophical Manuscripts*, trans. and ed. T. B. Bottomore, repr. Fromm, op. cit., p. 130, emphases in original.

139 From Karl Marx, *A Contribution to the Critique of Political Economy*, trans. N. I. Stone (Chicago: Charles H. Kerr, 1904).

140 V. I. Lenin, *Philosophical Notebooks*, Russian ed.

141 Lenin quoted in Beck, op. cit., p. 309.

142 From the *Manifesto of the Communist Party* by Karl Marx and Friedrich Engels, ed. Engels (Chicago: Charles H. Kerr, 1888). Cf. Beck, op. cit., p. 290. Ibid.

143 Nikita Khrushchev quoted in *Contemporary Radical Ideologies*, Anthony James Gregor (New York: Random House, 1968).

144 Louis Dupré, *The Philosophical Foundations of Marxism* (New York: Harcourt, Brace & World, 1966), p. 215.

145 Sabine, op. cit., p. 775.

146 The Nazis are too blatantly opposed to thought to be called rationalists. They are irrationalists. But they nevertheless resemble rationalists in their fundamental approach to the ideas they broadcast: the manipulation of floating abstractions apart from or in conflict with observed facts.

147 Sabine, op. cit., p. 763. Karl Popper, *The Open Society and Its Enemies: Hegel and Marx*, 4th ed. (New York: Harper & Row, 1963), vol. 2, pp. 61–62. On this point, Fascism was often explicit. "The world seen through Fascism," states Mussolini, "is not this material world which appears on the surface, in which man is an individual separated from all others and standing by himself . . . [but rather a man whose mission is] to restore within duty a higher life free from the limits of time and space. . . ." "The Doctrine of Fascism," trans. M. Oakeshott, repr. William Ebenstein, *Great Political Thinkers* (New York: Rinehart, 1951), p. 590. Popper, op. cit.

148 Sabine, op. cit., pp. 762, 779–80.

149 Peter Singer, *Practical Ethics*, 2nd ed. (New York: Cambridge University Press, 2005), p. 12. Equal treatment for this school is not identical treatment. Usually, in fact, it entails opposite treatment, as in the redistribution of wealth.

150 Quoted by Seneca, *On Anger*, 14.1.

151 Eugene Kennedy, " 'Do-gooders' don't when they eradicate competition from life," *Chicago Tribune*, July 12, 1993.

152 John Rawls, *A Theory of Justice*, rev. ed. (Cambridge, MA: Harvard University Press, 1999), p. xviii.

153 Kai Nielson, *Equality and Liberty*, repr. *Equality: Selected Readings*, ed. Louis P. Pojman & Robert Westmoreland (New York: Oxford University Press, 1997), pp. 206, 217.

154 Even when the value to be equalized is stated in abstract terms, such as equal concern, the abstraction is not taken as a unifying principle but, in standard pluralist fashion, as the name of a multiplicity of unrelated issues and behaviors addressed piecemeal, and distinguished from other issues largely in perceptual-level terms.

155 For Stanford, see Samantha Harris, "The Feds' Mad Assault on Campus Sex," *New York Post*, July 20, 2011.

156 Marshall Cohen, review of *A Theory of Justice* by John Rawls, *The New York Times*, July 16, 1972.

157 William Grimes review of *Anatomy of a Nightmare* by Philip Short, *The New York Times*, February 18, 2005.

158 Roger S. Gottlieb, *A Greener Faith* (New York: Oxford University Press, 2006), pp. 83, 5.

159 Paul R. Ehrlich, "An Ecologist's Perspective on Nuclear Power," *Federation of American Scientists Public Interest Report*, nos. 5–6 (May–June, 1975), p. 5. Bret Stephens, "The Totalities of Copenhagen," *Wall Street Journal*, December 7, 2009.

160 Anthony Watts, "TV Network Tells Kids How Long Their Carbon Footprint Should Allow Them to Live (2008)," wattsupwiththat.com.

161 Gottlieb, op. cit., p. 42. *Newsweek*, January 26, 1970. David Graber, *Los Angeles Times Book Review*, October 22, 1989, quoted in Ayn Rand, *Return of the Primitive*, ed. Peter Schwartz (New York: Meridian, 1999), in Schwartz, "The Philosophy of Privation," p. 221. Keith Lockitch, "Environmental Angst," *The Washington Times*, January 9, 2009.

CHAPTER NINE

162 Aristotle, *Poetics*, op. cit., 1450a20.

163 Richard Jenkyns, *Classical Epic: Homer and Virgil* (London: Bristol Classical Press, 2001), p. 18. Durant, op. cit., vol. 2, p. 211.

164 Some of the most famous works are atypical in this regard. The *Odyssey*, even though it offers overall a logically structured story, is in large part a "pre-Homeric" recounting of episodic adventures driven by the whim of the gods. *Oedipus Rex*, for another example, would seem to have little meaning if taken simply as the story of a man with the bad luck not to recognize his family. But these are exceptions to the rule. Aristotle, *Poetics*, 1459a20. Jenkyns, op. cit., p. 18.

165 Ibid., p. 9. Homer, *The Odyssey*, trans. W. H. D. Rouse (New York: Mentor, 1937), p. 134.

166 Durant, p. 211.

167 Sophocles, *Antigone* trans. Francis Storr (London: William Heinemann, 1912), p. 341.

168 Aristotle, *Poetics*, Ch. 15: 1454b, pp. 11–14. "I draw men," says Sophocles, "as they ought to be drawn." "I draw them," answers Euripides, "as they are." Perhaps, but even if true, this does not affect the connection of events, nor the larger-than-life characters built on fundamentals. Medea is hardly women "as they are."

169 H. D. F. Kitto, *The Greeks* (Baltimore: Penguin, 1951), p. 51. Cf. Robert Graves, *The Greek Myths* (Baltimore: Penguin, 1960).

170 *Sacred Disease*, Loeb Classical Library, trans. W. H. S. Jones (London: Harvard U. P., 1923) chapter one. Hippocrates, *Precepts*, trans. W. H. S. Jones (London: Harvard U. P., 1923), vol. 1.
171 Abraham Edel, *Aristotle and His Philosophy* (New Brunswick, NJ: Transaction Publishers, 1996), p. 64.
172 Ibid.
173 John Herman Randall Jr., *Aristotle* (New York: Columbia University Press, 1963), p. 170. That the attempt is not fully successful is evident from Aristotle's frequent description—to him, a plainly observed fact—of many laws as obtaining "always or for the most part." Only Newton and his heirs could subsume the "mosts" under the "alls."
174 Empedocles quoted in Randall, op. cit., p. 208.
175 Frederick J. E. Woodbridge, *Aristotle's Vision of Nature* (New York: Columbia University Press, 1965). This reference is from memory and I am unable to verify it. Aristotle is so committed to observation that he is prepared, if necessary, to modify even a cherished principle of his own, such as his teleology. W. D. Ross gives an example (his words): "[M]any natural phenomena are due to simple or absolute necessity. They flow inevitably from the nature of the matter . . . there are cases in which mechanism alone is at work. We must not always look for a final cause; some things are to be explained only by material and efficient causes." *Aristotle*, 6th ed. (New York: Psychology Press, 2004), p. 82. (Whether in his lost works Aristotle reconciled this contradiction, we do not know.)
176 Kitto, op. cit., p. 172.
177 Ibid., p. 173.
178 Durant, p. 298.
179 Hamilton and Cairns, op. cit., p. 322, *Protagoras*, 326b.
180 Kitto, op. cit., pp. 44–45.
181 Boyd & King, op. cit., p. 25. John Lewis, personal communication.
182 Kitto, op. cit., p. 169.
183 Ibid., p. 127.
184 Ibid., p. 75.
185 Sabine, op. cit., p. 18.
186 C. M. Bowra, *The Greek Experience* (New York: Mentor, 1959), p. 88.
187 Durant, p. 259.
188 Sabine, op. cit., p. 28. Durant, p. 258.
189 H. I. Marrou, *A History of Education in Antiquity,* trans. George Lamb (New York: Mentor, 1964), p. 139. Burns, op. cit., p. 188.
190 Marrou, op. cit., p. 138.

CHAPTER TEN

191 Philip R. Hardie (1986) quoted in Richard Rutherford, *Classical Literature: A Concise History* (Malden, MA: Blackwell, 2005), p. 37.
192 Virgil, *The Aeneid*, trans. and rev. ed. David West (London: Penguin, 1991), p. 174.
193 Ibid., p. 135.
194 Jenkyns, op. cit., pp. 63, 63–64, 65.
195 Ibid., p. 61.
196 Rutherford, op. cit., p. 38.

197 Cecil John Herington, "Senecan Tragedy," *Arion* 5 (1966). Carl Deroux, *Studies in Latin Literature and Roman History,* vol. 301 (Latomus, 2006), vol. 30, pp. 422–71.

198 Durant, vol. 3, p. 468.

199 David C. Lindberg, *The Beginnings of Western Science*, 2nd ed. (Chicago: University Press of Chicago, 1992), p. 140.

200 *The Meditations of Marcus Aurelius*, book XII, 26, *The Stoic and Epicurean Philosophers*, ed. Whitney J. Oates (New York: Random House, 1940), p. 583.

201 "Discourses of Epictetus," Oates, ibid., p. 290.

202 Oates, op. cit., p. xx.

203 Stewart C. Easton, *The Heritage of the Past*, 3rd ed. (New York: Holt, Rinehart & Winston, 1970), p. 369.

204 *Meditations*, book IV, 45, Oates, p. 514.

205 Lindberg, op. cit., p. 140.

206 *Encyclopædia Britannica* (1993), vol. 18. Marrou, op. cit., pp. 317, 319–20.

207 Robert R. Rusk, *Doctrines of the Great Educators*, 4th ed. (New York: St. Martin's Press, 1969), p. 46.

208 Marrou, op. cit., p. 364.

209 Ibid., p. 371.

210 Ibid., p. 376.

211 I. L. Kandel, *History of Secondary Education: A Study in the Development of Liberal Education* (Cambridge, MA: Riverside Press, 1930), pp. 35, 36. Tacitus quoted in Kandel, ibid., p. 36. Henry Nettleship, *Lectures and Essays*, 2nd series (Oxford: Clarendon Press, 1895), p. 58ff.

212 Polybius, *The Rise of the Roman Empire*, trans. Ian Scott-Kilvert (London: Penguin, 1979), p. 311.

213 Ebenstein, op. cit., p. 133. Ibid.

214 Polybius, op. cit., p. 349. Polybius ascribes this religiosity to a wise hypocrisy on the part of the aristocracy, who realize that religion is necessary to tame the irrational masses. This is irrelevant even if true. See chapter four.

215 Marcus Aurelius, *Meditations*, trans. George Long, 1862, in Ebenstein, op. cit., p. 159.

216 Ibid., p. 160. "Epictetus" in Oates, op. cit., p. 300.

217 Easton, op. cit., p. 303.

218 Durant, pp. 30, 31.

219 Ibid., pp. 213, 223.

220 Easton, op. cit., p. 360.

221 Ibid., p. 348. Sabine, op. cit., p. 173.

222 Sabine, op. cit., p. 147.

223 Steve Jolivette, personal communication.

CHAPTER ELEVEN

224 *The Divine Comedy*, trans. Carlyle-Wicksteed (New York: Modern Library, 1950), p. 469, p. 416.

225 Ibid., p. 485.

226 Ibid., pp. 489, 551.

227 Dante, though orthodox in his beliefs, was no papist. He fought attempts to expand the temporal power of the Church, and did not hesitate, when he thought it necessary, to criticize its personnel.

228 Ecclesiastes 12:8.

229 J. Huizinga, *The Waning of the Middle Ages* (New York: Anchor Books, 1954), p. 151. Easton, op. cit., p. 642.

230 Carl Stephenson, *Mediaeval History*, 3rd ed. (New York: Harper & Brothers, 1951), p. 259. As an explicit epistemology, medieval rationalism developed gradually and even gingerly, faced as it was by the objection that reliance on reason, however conceived, engenders in man pride and the illusion of self-sufficiency. Bernard of Clairvaux may be taken as symbolic of such hostility to reason. (Easton, op. cit., p. 628.) Despite this, the need for integration could not forever be ignored, and thus thinkers increasingly held, especially after the rediscovery of pagan thought, that so far as man is able to understand Christian dogma, he has no alternative but to make use of his conceptual faculty, and that such use can be consistent with Christianity so long as the axioms of one's thought are based on an authoritative text.

231 Stephenson, op. cit., pp. 266, 358. Easton, op. cit., p. 644.

232 Meister Eckhart quoted in Richard E. Rubenstein, *Aristotle's Children* (Boston: Houghton Mifflin Harcourt, 2004), p. 265, brought to my attention by Tore Boeckmann.

233 A. F. Leach quoted in Kandel, op. cit., p. 45.

234 Luke 22:42.

235 Quoted in Kandel, op. cit., p. 43. Ibid.

236 Kandel, op. cit., p. 54.

237 A. F. Leach, *Educational Charters*, in Kandel, op. cit., p. 48.

238 "Quadrivium," Wikipedia. Although scholars disdain this source, I must agree that its definition in this instance is excellent.

239 Easton, op. cit., p. 632.

240 *Encyclopædia Britannica*, "Development of Western Education: The Middle Ages."

241 Durant, op. cit., vol. 4, p. 762. Pope Boniface VIII, "The Superiority of the Spiritual Authority," *The Portable Medieval Reader*, ed. James Bruce Ross and Mary Martin McLaughlin (New York: Penguin, 1978), p. 234.

242 Stephenson, op. cit., p. 221.

243 J. B. Trapp, Douglas Gray, and Julia Boffey, *Medieval English Literature*, 2nd ed. (New York: Oxford University Press, 2002), p. 513. Sabine, op. cit., p. 234.

244 Sabine, op. cit., p. 272. An element of utopian anarchism was sometimes added. "And without evil," Stephenson summarizes the views of Augustine, "there would be no need of governors, armies, police, courts, and penal laws. The state, therefore, was an ephemeral thing. . . ." (Stephenson, op. cit., p. 221). Or, as a modern might put it, after (or if) the dictatorship of the pope accomplished its soul molding, the state would wither away.

245 Saint John in Durant, vol. 4, p. 776.

246 "Compared with the persecution of heresy in Europe from 1227 to 1492," Durant remarks, "the persecution of Christians by Romans in the first three centuries after Christ was a mild and humane procedure." (vol. 4, p. 784.) The so-called Papal Inquisition, though less cruel than the Spanish, paved the way for it.

247 Thought control could not be a goal of rulers before thought had been defined and understood to be a factor in human life.

248 Pope Boniface VIII in Ross and McLaughlin, op. cit., p. 233.

249 Bradley cites examples of chance incidents from *Romeo and Juliet*, *King Lear*, *Othello*, and *Hamlet*. A. C. Bradley, *Shakespearean Tragedy: Lectures on Hamlet, Othello, King Lear & Macbeth* (Middlesex: Echo Library, 2007), p. 8. He amends this

later to say that there is no "large admission of chance" in the plays. It is difficult in this context to define the distinction between appreciable and large.

250 Bacon quoted in Burns, op. cit., p. 442.

CHAPTER TWELVE

251 Physics qualifies as a concrete in regard to its social influence. A theory in physics, qua theory, is of cultural importance insofar as it impacts the concrete mental process of a society (and not merely of intellectuals). Specific scientific discoveries sometimes do this, and may even instigate a new mode or threaten an old. For example, predicting Halley's comet or creating the atom bomb has helped move a society (to I in one case, or some version of non-I in the other). It is not the abstract physical theory that has influence here, not $F = ma$ or $E = mc^2$, but the acclaimed public concretes; these are what promote in a society a certain view of the universe and of thought.

252 According to Objectivism, these two issues do not occupy the same hierarchical position in philosophy. Existence (this world) is the primary self-evident axiom, grasped implicitly by a newborn in his first act of awareness; this axiom is fundamental because all other knowledge rests on it. The fact and nature of concepts, however, are not fundamental, but must be learned by a complex adult process of observation, differentiation, and induction. Despite this, however, the issue of concepts is fundamental in the present inquiry—in the sense that cultural creation is guided by some view of concepts. In short, the place of an issue in the hierarchy of philosophy does not necessarily indicate its relative importance in a narrower study, pertaining to applied philosophy.

CHAPTER THIRTEEN

253 The individualism of Protestantism was a factor in the rise of worldliness, but not a primary cause. In reference to some of the dates on the chart: Classical Greece ended abruptly; by 307 B.C., there was already a highly popular religious cult in Athens. As to the Christian period, it is reasonable to argue that it should begin with the late third century, rather than the fourth, on the grounds that by that time Rome was already very much weakened and that intellectually the atmosphere was already Christian. I have chosen A.D. 400 as the start simply by selecting two significant dates: Constantine's official adoption of Christianity in 315, and by 476 the Church's rise to ultimate political power. So halfway between these dates is a reasonable approximation of the start of Christian cultural influence. The Dark Ages I regard as Christian, to the extent they were anything; I date this period roughly A.D. 600 to 950. I owe the content of this paragraph to Dr. Steve Jolivette.

Newton's cultural dominance obviously preceded the Enlightenment by at least sixty years, as would be expected, since he was the modern cause of the Enlightenment.

It is difficult for a society to change its fundamental method of thinking, because most men during such transitions must rely on the established method, while at the same time gradually learning to criticize and replace it. So transitions take time—a decade, a generation, or even longer. As a rule, people tend to sympathize for a longer time with the old ideas during transitions, though in diminishing degrees. So I place these years within the time frame of the older mode—changing the classification only when the new is clearly in power.

254 I recognize the Lutherans' contribution to modern individualism, but regard it only as an auxiliary factor, not a primary cause of the modern mind.

255 Newton, of course, did not write in a vacuum, and his cultural influence depended in part on trends in other areas. One example here is the Reformation. But no amendment to Catholicism could by itself bring about an anti-Christian age.

256 I am here discussing only the influence of mode on the interpretation of problems. Obviously, the Roman problems in many cases were also caused by the mode.

257 Hannah Arendt, *The Origins of Totalitarianism* (New York: Harcourt, Brace & World, 1966), pp. 444–45.

CHAPTER FOURTEEN

258 Rudolf Carnap, quoted in Naletov, op. cit.

259 Arn and Charlene Tibbetts, *What's Happening to American English?* (New York: Scribner's, 1978), pp. 80, 76.

260 In this work I can offer only a brief overview of the D_1 progression. But this important type of historical development deserves thorough specialized study by itself, identifying within each area the figures involved and their differences in degree of tilt across the century. The same applies to M_1, though with less immediate relevance.

261 Figures obtained from the U.S. Department of Education, Digest of Education Statistics: 2006, Table 257. Steve Jolivette alerted me to this source.

262 Jonah Goldberg, "The Debt Fight and O the Ideologue," *New York Post*, July 20, 2011.

263 See *The Ayn Rand Letter* (Palo Alto, CA: Palo Alto Books, 1979), November 22, 1971, p. 18.

264 "American Education Not World Class," 4brevard.com, November 8, 2011.

265 David D. Kirkpatrick, "The Return of the Warrior Jesus," *The New York Times*, April 4, 2004. Laura Olson, "Religion and the 2004 Election," *Religion in the News* (Fall 2003), "Mainline Protestants," trincoll.edu.

266 John Leland, "Christian Cool and the New Generation Gap," *The New York Times*, May 16, 2004. Of the five modes, only an I sense of life, because of its connection to the country's founders, is worth checking out in this context. Three of the other modes are explicit and their significance already known. As to M_1, there is no basis to suspect a subconscious public attachment. The United States was founded not on the principles of M_1, but on the founders' revolution against them. Nor has there been any intellectual revolution since to implant M_1 in a modern's subconscious.

CHAPTER FIFTEEN

267 Kirkpatrick, *The New York Times*, op. cit.

268 For latest sales, contact Tyndale House Publishers. Jeffery L. Sheler, "Nearer My God to Thee," *U.S. News & World Report*, May 3, 2004. Ibid.

269 Michelle Goldberg, *Kingdom Coming: The Rise of Christian Nationalism* (New York: W. W. Norton, 2006), p. 5.

270 Ibid., p. 102.

271 Steven Weinberg, *Dreams of a Final Theory* (New York: Pantheon Books, 1992), p. 195.

272 Schrödinger quoted in Ken Wilber, "The Mystic Vision," *Quantum Questions: Mystical Writings of the World's Great Physicists*, ed. Ken Wilber, rev. ed. (Boston: Shambhala, 2001), p. 98.

273 Michelle Goldberg, op. cit., pp. 4–5.

274 Ibid., p. 84.

275 James Dobson, *The Strong-Willed Child: Birth through Adolescence* (Wheaton, IL: Living Books, 1985), pp. 77–78.

276 Michelle Goldberg, op. cit., p. 13. Rousas John Rushdoony, *The Institutes of Biblical Law* (Nutley, NJ: Craig Press, 1973), issue 1, pp. 581–82. Ibid.

277 Michelle Goldberg, op. cit., pp. 5–6. George Grant, *The Changing of the Guard* (Ft. Worth: Dominion Press, 1987), pp. 50–51.

278 Ralph Nader, "Where Left and Right Converge," *Wall Street Journal*, August 18, 2010.

279 Alan Wolfe, "Evangelicals Everywhere," *The New York Times Book Review*, November 25, 2007. "American Piety in the 21st Century," Baylor Institute for Studies of Religion, September 2006. Andrew Greeley quoted in Kevin Phillips, *American Theocracy* (New York: Viking, 2006). C. Calhoun, M. Aronczyk, D. Mayrl, and J. VanAntwerpen, *The Religious Engagements of American Undergraduates*, Social Science Research Council, religion.ssrc.org, May 2007. Phillips, op. cit., p. 133.

280 John Micklethwait and Adrian Wooldridge, *God Is Back* (New York: Penguin, 2009), p. 191.

281 Wolfe, op. cit.

282 Darren Sherkat quoted in Calhoun, et al, op. cit. Harvard poll ibid.

283 Stanley Fish, "One University Under God," quoted in Micklethwait and Wooldridge, op. cit., pp. 195–96.

284 John Leland, "Christian Cool and the New Generation Gap," *The New York Times*, May 16, 2004. Leland, "Christian Music's New Wave Caters to Audience of One," *The New York Times*, April 17, 2004.

285 Ibid.

286 David Antoon, "U.S. Air Force Academy's New 'Rocky Mountain Bible College,'" Daily Kos (Albuquerque, NM: Military Religious Freedom Foundation, 2007).

287 Michael L. Weinstein and Reza Aslan, "Not So Fast, Christian Soldiers," *Los Angeles Times*, August 22, 2007. Jeff Sharlet, "Ten Things I Learned from the Pentagon's Prayer Team," alternet.org, 2007.

288 Micklethwait and Wooldridge, op. cit., p. 156.

289 Christopher Moraff, "The Christian Hijacking of America," *The Philly Post*, September 29, 2011. Kevin Phillips, "How the GOP Became God's Own Party," *The Washington Post*, April 2, 2006.

290 Micklethwait and Wooldridge, op. cit., p. 130.

291 Amy Sullivan, *The Party Faithful: How and Why Democrats are Closing the God Gap* (New York: Scribner, 2008), p. 205. Obama on CNN "Compassion Forum," April 13, 2008.

292 Sullivan, op. cit., p. 210.

293 Bruce Feiler, "Where Have All the Christians Gone?" FoxNews.com, September 25, 2009. Eric Gorski, "Atheist Student Groups Flower on College Campuses," *USA Today*, November 24, 2009.

294 Figures from Gallup USA, June 2005.

295 A recent spate of atheist books will not in my view threaten the M_2s, because these books are written by Ds who profess uncertainty as a conviction, and offer only the

negation of religion, as against any positive philosophy. Whether a devout public can be persuaded by this means to drop what they see as their salvation is doubtful. The atheist cause is not helped by the fact that these books also endorse the Sermon on the Mount or its equivalent as the definition of morality.

296 Gottlieb, op. cit., p. 10. Rowan Williams, "Climate Change Action a Moral Imperative for Justice," Anglican Communion News Service, January 1, 2008. Deuteronomy 20:19–20.

297 Andrew Walsh quoted in "Many Religious Leaders Back Climate-Change Action," Brad Knickerbocker, *The Christian Science Monitor*, December 20, 2007.

298 Gottlieb, op. cit., p. 33.

299 Foundation for Biomedical Research in Washington, DC, quoted in "America's Other Most Wanted," P. Michael Conn and James Parker, *Wall Street Journal*, May 18, 2011.

300 Gottlieb, op. cit., p. vii.

301 Tom Hayden, "Chronicle," *The New York Times*, August 3, 1991, quoted in Peter Schwartz, op. cit., p. 230.

CHAPTER SIXTEEN

302 In my view, Europe, too, is at a D dead end with nothing ahead of it but an M_2 future. Without any influential religion of its own, however, it will be subsumed under religious totalitarianism through some foreign crusade, waged, if not by American Christians, then probably by Muslims. For some facts suggesting the latter outcome see "Who Lost Europe?" the widely publicized speech of the Netherlands' Geert Wilders, chairman of the Party for Freedom, given at the Four Seasons Hotel in New York City on September 25, 2008.

As to China, as of this writing it reflects no coherent approach to integration, seeming to combine a Western M_2 in politics, with something resembling D_1 in economics. I do not regard this as an integrated or, therefore, stable society, but I cannot guess where it will end up, largely because that would require a knowledge of Eastern philosophy, which I do not have.

303 From Dionysius of Halicarnassus's *Roman Antiquities*. This gem came from Michael Brown.

(After the General Index there is an Index of DIM Terms. In either index, cross-reference terms marked with an asterisk link to headings in the other index. An overview chart follows the indexes.)

GENERAL INDEX

INDEX OF DIM TERMS

Western History in DIM Terms

(one or two word reminders of key topics covered)

Culture	Dates	Literature	Physics	Education	Politics	Mode
Greece	500–300 B.C.	Homer	Scientific Method	Rational Self-Fulfillment	Democracy	I
Rome	300 B.C.–400 A.D. (including Hellenistic)	Virgil	Stoicism	Grammar School	Republic, Empire	M_1
Middle Ages	400–1400 (including Dark Ages)	Dante	Divine Teleology	Instilling Christianity	Totalitarianism	M_2
Renaissance	1400–1600	Transitional				$?/M_1$
Age of Reason	1600–1750	Classicism	Rationalism (until Newton)	Classical	Absolute Monarchy	M_1
Enlightenment	1750–1850	Romanticism	Newton	Classical	Capitalism	I
Modern	1850–present (first phase)	Naturalism	Positivism (until early 1900s)	Pluralist Schools	Mixed Economy	D_1
Modern	1900–present (contemporary)	Non-Objectivity	QM (plus AE M_1 and String M_2)	Progressivism	Egalitarianism	D_2
Modern (Eastern/ Central Europe)	1900–2000	Socialist Realism	Dialectic Teleology	Instilling Communism	Totalitarianism	M_2